Smoking in
British popular culture
1800–2000

MANCHESTER
UNIVERSITY PRESS

STUDIES IN POPULAR CULTURE

General editor: Professor Jeffrey Richards

Already published

Films and British national identity: from Dickens to *Dad's Army*
Jeffrey Richards

The car in British society: class, gender and motoring 1896–1939
Sean O'Connell

Forthcoming titles

Cultures of drinking in Britain since 1750
David Gutzke

Spiritualism and British society 1918–39
Jenny Hazelgrove

Capital entertainment: the transformation of popular culture in London 1890–1960
Andrew Horrall

Women's leisure in England 1920–60
Claire Langhamer

Music for the middle classes: a cultural history of amateur operatics
John Lowerson

Science and technology in popular culture
Simon Nightingale

Coming together: sex and popular culture in Britain 1800–1999
Tim O'Neill

The North in the national imagination: England 1850–2000
David Russell

The British seaside holiday
John K. Walton

Smoking in British popular culture 1800–2000

Perfect pleasures

MATTHEW HILTON

Manchester University Press
Manchester and New York
distributed exclusively in the USA by St. Martin's Press

Published by Manchester University Press
Oxford Road, Manchester M13 9NR, UK
and Room 400, 175 Fifth Avenue, New York, NY 10010, USA
http://www.man.ac.uk/mup

Distributed exclusively in the USA by
St. Martin's Press, Inc., 175 Fifth Avenue, New York,
NY 10010, USA

Distributed exclusively in Canada by
UBC Press, University of British Columbia, 6344 Memorial Road,
Vancouver, BC, Canada V6T 1Z2

British Library Cataloguing-in-Publication Data
A catalogue record for this book is available from the British Library

Library of Congress Cataloging-in-Publication Data applied for

ISBN 0 7190 5256 4 hardback
     0 7190 5257 2 paperback

First published 2000

06 05 04 03 02 01 00   10 9 8 7 6 5 4 3 2 1

Typeset in Hong Kong
by Graphicraft Limited
Printed in Great Britain
by Biddles Ltd, www.biddles.co.uk

STUDIES IN
POPULAR
CULTURE

General editor's introduction

There has in recent years been an explosion of interest in culture and cultural studies. The impetus has come from two directions and out of two different traditions. On the one hand, cultural history has grown out of social history to become a distinct and identifiable school of historical investigation. On the other hand, cultural studies has grown out of English literature and has concerned itself to a large extent with contemporary issues. Nevertheless, there is a shared project, its aim, to elucidate the meanings and values implicit and explicit in the art, literature, learning, institutions and everyday behaviour within a given society. Both the cultural historian and the cultural studies scholar seek to explore the ways in which a culture is imagined, represented and received, how it interacts with social processes, how it contributes to individual and collective identities and world views, to stability and change, to social, political and economic activities and programmes. This series aims to provide an arena for the cross-fertilisation of the discipline, so that the work of the cultural historian can take advantage of the most useful and illuminating of the theoretical developments and the cultural studies scholars can extend the purely historical underpinnings of their investigations. The ultimate objective of the series is to provide a range of books which will explain in a readable and accessible way where we are now socially and culturally and how we got to where we are. This should enable people to be better informed, promote an interdisciplinary approach to cultural issues and encourage deeper thought about the issues, attitudes and institutions of popular culture.

Jeffrey Richards

To my mother

Contents

Illustrations

Tables and figures

Tables

Figure

Acknowledgements

There are a number of people without whom this book could not have been written. In particular I would like to thank Jeffrey Richards for the opportunity to write this book and for his constant support over the last few years. At Lancaster University, where the research for this book began, I am grateful to Stephen Constantine for initially putting me in the right direction, to Mike Winstanley for his support and direction as my PhD supervisor, to John Walton for his much valued encouragement in the early stages of my research, and to Paolo Palladino and Rhodri Hayward for early comments and stimulating ideas. Friends and colleagues at Birmingham and elsewhere have also been invaluable in more recent years, commenting on various chapters and providing encouragement. I would like to thank Kate Davies, Martin Daunton, James Chapman, Frank Trentmann, Alison Clarke, Maria Balshaw and especially Johanna Liddle, who read through and commented on the penultimate draft of this book. Simon Nightingale's exciting comments, conversations and ideas can be found throughout. Finally, I have enjoyed and appreciated the opinions and ideas of literally hundreds of smokers, from chance associates, people in pubs, near and distant relatives, close friends, strangers in all sorts of queues and waiting rooms, and even Cuban tobacco farmers, all of whom became unwitting research respondents and who came to shape the central arguments of what follows.

The research for this book has been conducted at several archives and libraries around the country. I am grateful to Maureen Watry of the University of Liverpool Library, Suella Postles of the Brewhouse Yard Museum, Nottingham, and the staff at the Public Record Office at Kew, Nottingham Record Office, Bristol Record Office, Colindale National Newspaper Library, the British Library, ASH, Quit, FOREST, the Mass-Observation Collection at Sussex, the BBC Written Archives Centre at Caversham and the libraries of Lancaster University, Birmingham University, the London School of Economics, Cambridge University, the Bodleian, Oxford and the Wellcome Institute for the History of Medicine.

I wish also to thank the Economic and Social Research Council for funding my research for three years and the Nuffield Foundation for a small research grant which allowed me to extend substantially the scope of the study. I am grateful for permission to reproduce illustrations 2, 3, 4, 6 and 7 by courtesy of the University of Liverpool Library, the Fraser Collection, Special Collections and Archives, and to the National Portrait Gallery for the portrait of Frederick Burnaby. Illustrations 10–13, 16–17 and 20–22 are reproduced with kind permission of the Imperial Tobacco Company. Faber and Faber allowed me to reprint sections of Tony Harrison's *Prometheus*.

Abbreviations

ASH	Action on Smoking and Health
ATJ	*Anti-Tobacco Journal*
BAAS	British Association for the Advancement of Science
BECC	British Empire Cancer Campaign
BMA	British Medical Association
CCHE	Central Council for Health Education
CCSH	Co-ordinating Committee on Smoking and Health
FOREST	Freedom Organisation for the Right to Enjoy Smoking Tobacco
Fraser	Fraser Collection, University of Liverpool Special Collections
HEC	Health Education Council
IACL	International Anti-Cigarette League
M.-O.	Mass-Observation
MRC	Medical Research Council
NSNS	National Society of Non-Smokers
Player's	Player's Archive, Nottingham Record Office
P.P.	Parliamentary Papers
PRO	Public Record Office, Kew
RCP	Royal College of Physicians
SMA	Socialist Medical Association
TMSC	Tobacco Manufacturers' Standing Committee
TTR	*Tobacco Trade Review*
TWJ	*Tobacco Weekly Journal*
Wills	Wills Archive, Bristol Record Office

General editor's foreword

'A woman is only a woman but a good cigar is a smoke', wrote Rudyard Kipling. What a wealth of class, gender and leisure assumptions is encapsulated in that one, much quoted aphorism. In his extensively researched, thoughtful and groundbreaking study of the role of tobacco in British culture and society, Matthew Hilton explores all these aspects and many more. He is analysing a habit which was engaged in by four-fifths of adult men and two-fifths of adult women by the middle of the twentieth century and which carried with it a variety of connotations relating to masculinity, femininity, maturity, sexiness and sophistication. Hilton assesses all these connotations in depth.

Dividing his account into three sections covering the nineteenth, early twentieth and late twentieth centuries, Hilton examines the history and nature of the tobacco industry, the relative popularity and cultural significance of pipe, cigar and cigarette, the language of the literature of smoking, the imagery of tobacco advertising, the literary and cinematic iconicity of smoking, and the role of the mass media in both promoting and discouraging smoking. He concludes with an account of the politics and science of smoking and health from the 1950 report in which Doll and Hill first securely linked smoking and cancer to the present when court cases are being fought to establish the responsibility of the tobacco companies for the illnesses of cigarette smokers.

In each period of his study, Hilton locates smoking securely in the culture of individualism, a culture which changes and evolves but which remains rooted in notions of the self and selfhood. At once scholarly and readable, authoritative and engaging, this is cultural history at its best – revealing, stimulating and timely.

Jeffrey Richards

A cigarette is the perfect type of a perfect pleasure. It is exquisite, and it leaves one unsatisfied. What more can one want?

Oscar Wilde, *The Picture of Dorian Gray*

By the cigars they smoke and the composers they love, ye shall know the texture of men's souls.

John Galsworthy, *Indian Summer of a Forsyte*

Sometimes a cigar is just a cigar.

(Attributed to) Sigmund Freud

Introduction

There are many great smokers in this book, both real and fictional. In each of the ten chapters an icon of British smoking culture from over the last two hundred years makes an appearance to illustrate or exemplify a defining moment in the history of the pipe, the cigar and the cigarette. Charles Lamb, Lord Byron and Rudyard Kipling, authors of the now classic eulogies to the 'sublime' weed, provide the initial context for a plant so 'divine' and 'superexcellent' that it could only be smoked with true appreciation by such superhuman characters as Sir Arthur Conan Doyle's Sherlock Holmes and Ouida's nonchalant 'Beau Lion' of the *Chasseurs d'Afrique*, Bertie Cecil. Their real-life equivalents can be found in J. M. Barrie, who devoted an entire book to his 'Lady Nicotine', and in Colonel Fred Burnaby, the 'true blue' hero of the Royal Horse Guards who famously rode to Khiva in 1875–76 before being gloriously killed in action in the Sudan in 1885. Oscar Wilde maintained the dandified and bohemian associations of the cigarette in the 1890s, while Holmes' literary successors – Sapper's Bulldog Drummond, Buchan's Richard Hannay and Fleming's James Bond – would emphasise the centrality of different forms of smoking to masculine identity in the twentieth century. At the same time, the briar pipe became quintessentially British, it being firmly gripped between the teeth of J. B. Priestley, Stanley Baldwin and Harold Wilson, although Churchill's cigar served as a reminder of a flamboyant aristocratic manhood that only a figure of his historical presence could pull off without irony. At the other end of the social spectrum, Humphrey Bogart perfectly encapsulated the egalitarian and romantic elements of the cigarette, his smoke mingling with that of his most celebrated opposite number, Lauren Bacall. Her glamorisation of the cigarette followed on from the smouldering images of Marlene Dietrich, Bette Davis and Jean Harlow which had appeared throughout the 1930s. The centrality of smoking to their assertive femininity mirrored the earlier efforts of 'new women' such as Dorothy Richardson who had smoked to liberate themselves symbolically from political and social suppression. Rather differently, in the post-war period, the everyday cigarette of the burgeoning smoking democracy perennially drooped from the mouth of Andy Capp, a prime target for lung cancer and other smoking-related diseases which have come to mark the latest period in the history of tobacco.

All of these icons are the subject of this book. They are all cultural representations of a society and economy which has placed the pipe, the cigar and the cigarette at the heart of British popular culture. They are all selected from a period in which smoking, to borrow A. J. P. Taylor's description of the cinema, became 'the essential social habit of the age'.[1] Just as going to the movies, the music hall and the dance hall, drinking in the public house, gambling from an illegal betting shop, supporting a local football team and annually visiting the seaside resort have all been shown to have occupied the larger part of the working man and woman's normal leisure activities, so too did the cigarette form a part of this mass commercial culture. The difference was, of course, that smoking could be enjoyed during participation in all these other forms of entertainment. By the mid twentieth century, four-fifths of adult men and two-fifths of adult women were smoking, a figure which works out at 7 lb of tobacco per adult (aged over fifteen, smoking and non-smoking) per year. Quite how much smoking's popularity is a twentieth-century phenomenon is illustrated by the fact that prior to the mid nineteenth century, the annual consumption of tobacco per adult had remained stable at approximately 2 lb from the late seventeenth century.[2]

The explanation offered here to account for this mass phenomenon is that smoking has remained central to individual and group identity. However, this identity is firmly rooted in a specific liberal notion of the self, which was especially promoted by bourgeois gentlemanly smokers of the pipe and the cigar in the mid to late nineteenth century. How they thought about their smoking habit provided the dominant meaning of tobacco which has subsequently come to be shared by other social groups in later periods. They provide the most insightful means of understanding the role of smoking in the supposedly homogenised world of the mass market of the early twentieth century and in the post-Second World War period when the medical dangers of the cigarette ought, according to a particular type of scientific rationality, to have convinced everybody to quit. The book is therefore split into three sections, each dealing with three historical, though overlapping, periods: the nineteenth century; the early twentieth century; and the late twentieth century. These three periods

...ating to the culture, the economy and the science (and poi...   and are almost symbolised by the pipe and the cigar in the firs...   ..., the cigarette in the second, and the diseases associated with smoking ... the third. If the periodisation appears too clinical or neat, it is essential to understand that the characteristics which marked the most significant development in the understanding of smoking in any one period always persisted into the next and have subsequently never lost their significance. The central thesis which links the three sections of the book and which will be summarised below is that the culture of individuality which marked what has been identified as the bourgeois-liberal context of smoking in the nineteenth century gave way to a technological rationality which sought to create a mass of standardised individuals in the early twentieth century. In the late twentieth century, the rise of epidemiology and the statistical correlations of the dangers of smoking saw a new scientific understanding of smoking which provoked a politics of individualism as smokers sought compensation for the harm they had suffered as a direct consequence of their personal habit.

What is meant by the bourgeois-liberal context of smoking is outlined in chapter 1. It is bourgeois because the culture of smoking was promoted by a specific cohort of the male population which had sufficient economic and cultural capital to buy expensive pipes, cigars and tobacco mixtures. They discussed, read and learnt about their favourite habit or hobby in the pages of periodicals such as *Chambers' Journal*, *Macmillan's Magazine*, *All the Year Round* and *Once a Week* and in numerous books and 'odes' devoted to smoking. The price and literary style of these publications would have precluded any truly mass consumption but they were well within the reach of an expanding middle class at whom the burgeoning periodical press was targeted. The context is liberal because the understanding of smoking put forward in the periodical press stressed the central tenets of this national political, economic and cultural creed: individuality and independence.[3] These two principles formed the core of how men talked about their participation in parliamentary politics, of how they supposedly examined each issue detached from specific interests or the corrupting influences of external institutions. Independence and individuality of character also lay behind notions of 'self help', an ethic which dictated many Victorian attitudes to social reform and the belief that man could rise above his social and economic situation through the application of effort. In economic thought, man was held to behave as an independent, rational agent, free to make his own choices and decisions. The economic, cultural, political and social all came together in that classic liberal cause, Free

Trade, which emphasised the necessity of minimal state interference and protection in all forms of trade, from the local to the global. In history, industry, science and even evangelical religious thought, individuality was stressed through celebrations of 'great men' who could overcome adversity through strength of will and character, freeing themselves of the shackles of unnecessary luxury and vice to triumph through single-minded dedication and purposeful commitment. But liberal notions of independence and individuality were also applied to masculine consumption as men sought to demonstrate how their use of tobacco was not dictated by habit or enslavement but through the laboured appreciation of the 'majestic leaf'. Smokers such as Holmes and Barrie emphasised the idiosyncrasies in their smoking habit, carefully constructing a personal relationship with a divine weed reified, feminised or anthropomorphised into a trusty companion, but which was always sufficiently subjugated to the smoker's masculine control as he maintained his strong-minded grasp on the material world.

The first chapter of each Part of the book serves to outline the promotion of the dominant trend in the history of smoking, while the other chapters examine the pervasiveness of this understanding. Consequently, in the first Part, chapter 2 tests the applicability of the bourgeois-liberal culture to other smokers, noting the survival of an aristocratic version of masculinity promoted through representations of the cavalry officer's dandified, swaggering pleasure in the arrogant cigar and the effeminate, hand-rolled cigarette. A more communal pleasure and use of smoking can be discerned in the public houses frequented by the labouring classes in which the free issue of clay pipes (through which the far greater proportion of all tobacco was smoked in Britain) suggested a certain traditional ritual of hospitality but which has received, in comparison, little artistic, literary or popular cultural illustration. The omnipresence of the liberal ideology is no better illustrated, however, than in chapter 3, which traces the small but belligerent anti-tobacco movement created by Thomas Reynolds in 1853. Although positioned in direct opposition to the pro-smoking culture, its vociferous attack was based on exactly the same liberal principles. Individuality and independence were translated into the need to maintain the physical body's freedom from enslavement to a luxurious pleasure since anything that damaged what had been created from God's own vision was inherently sinful and a distraction from the higher purposes of the evangelical's mission.

The culture of liberalism came to be overshadowed by the technological revolution of the late nineteenth century which 'rationalised' the economy through mass production. This led to an attempt to homogenise the individual-ity of each smoker within the mass market. The crucial date in the history of tobacco is 1883, when W. D. & H. O. Wills of Bristol began producing cigarettes with the Bonsack machine. This transformed the industry as previ-ously cigarettes had been hand rolled at a cost which could only attract an elite and limited sale. With the potential to manufacture 300 cigarettes each minute, Wills was able to sell packets of five Woodbines and Cinderellas for just one penny, providing sales could be maintained at a level sufficient to make profitable the economies of scale involved in production. What this involved was an attempt to translate the rationality of production into a rationality of consumption, as Wills and later other tobacco manufacturers re-organised their selling and marketing organisations to try to create a national market for their goods. The principal medium used in such a venture, as chapter 4 demonstrates, was the advertisement, the product of an industry itself revolutionised by recent developments in printing and copying. Adver-tising in this period can be read as an endeavour to create order amid the myriad desires of the consuming public, to create rationally a market where consumers acted in accordance with the interests of the manufacturers which required, if not only in this period, the establishment of a stable mass market to make profitable their production of cheap commodities. Tobacco, but especially cigarette, advertisements thus presented images which referred to the lowest common denominators in society, appealing to the attractions of patriotism, the nation's past, the universal virtues of health and beauty, and the optimism of the consumer-oriented future. How far the manufacturers succeeded in overriding the segmented economy of the liberal Victorian period forms the basis for the next three chapters, as separate case studies of men, women and children in the early twentieth century are examined in detail to demonstrate the actual practices and influences on different types of smoker. What these three chapters show is the widespread promotion of smoking by a much broader popular culture than that provided by the advertising image. The cinema and the Hollywood film here provided a particularly strong incentive to smoking as screen 'gods' and 'goddesses', from Dietrich to Bogart, were transformed into sophisticated icons of the culture of the cigarette. In practice, though, there was a continued diversity of beliefs about the rituals of smoking which existed among consumers who were able to inscribe similar discursive representations of individuality into their machine-made cigarettes as their bourgeois counterparts had in the nineteenth century with their personalised tobacco mixtures.

While such rationalist attempts to control consumption are seen as having separated the older culture of liberalism from the new economic principles of the mass market, there is also evidence to suggest that manufacturers' interests were becoming more closely aligned with those of successive governments.[4] In the increasingly corporatist state, manufacturers had a greater involvement in the government decision-making process, to the extent that their rationalist economic assumptions overtook liberal notions about the individual and his or her ability to take control of his or her life and situation, notions which had characterised government activity throughout the nineteenth century. From the beginning of the twentieth century, the ever expanding state has intervened in an increasing number of spheres, from production and the workplace to, health education, social welfare and the economy. In doing so, governments have mirrored the attempts of manufacturers to control rationally the market of consumers, as they have directed individual lives according to their own ideas as to what is best for them. Such intervention stands in marked contrast to Victorian governments, when ideas of liberal citizenship dictated that the individual must be entirely responsible for his social and economic situation. By the time of the development of the welfare state after the Second World War, the state was well accustomed to investigating its workers and consumers according to statistical investigations which provided the basis for interventionist policy.

It is against such a background that the relationship between smoking and lung cancer was accepted and contested from as early as 1950, when Richard Doll and Austin Bradford Hill first published their preliminary findings in the *British Medical Journal*.[5] If the statistical correlations uncovered by their epidemiological research were to be accepted by a wider public, the demands it made on government health policy were not the cure of the patient once smoking-induced cancer had set in, but the rational re-direction of consumption patterns in order to prevent people from ever starting to smoke. Previously, government activity had been in the sphere of production, in issues related to the workplace and employment; only rarely had governments attempted to direct individuals' consumption decisions, which surviving liberal principles held as being independent of, or existing beyond, the authority of the state. The debate over the extent to which the state can legitimately intervene in an individual's smoking decisions still continues and has proved to have been influenced by powerful economic and political interests,[6] but it is this tension between the liberal independent individual and the interventionist state which accounts for the immediate reception of Doll and Hill's findings in the 1950s and 1960s.

In the final Part, then, on the politics and science of smoking and health, chapter 8 uncovers not quite so much what was known by a far from monolithic medical profession, but what was presented through what are referred to as 'official' channels: government ministries and professional medical bodies which advised state representatives. Although the official message soon accepted that the association between smoking and lung cancer was real and was the product of a direct causal relationship, this did not translate into a determined campaign to make people stop smoking. Instead, liberal principles about the freedom of the individual in regard to his or her health mediated the message so that policy was always influenced by the desire to inform smokers of the dangers so that they could make up their own minds, independently of state directives. This attitude served to limit the evidence presented to the public and it worked on a principle of utilitarian rationality which did not correspond with the ways in which most smokers came to their decision to smoke in the first place, never mind the consequences of physical addiction. The diversity of attitudes to smoking and health was no better represented than in the popular media, and chapter 9 focuses on four newspapers and the BBC to show how the smokers' understanding of the official anti-smoking message was highly dependent on the newspaper they read or the broadcaster to whom they listened. Finally, chapter 10 examines the attitudes of smokers themselves, demonstrating that the vast majority of smokers were aware of the dangers of smoking throughout the 1960s but that this knowledge was located in a cultural context which also included the denials and refutations of the tobacco industry, the promotion of smoking by the continued heavy expenditure on advertising, the scepticism of the popular cultural channels through which medical knowledge was disseminated, and the ability of the mass of individual smokers to refute the medical evidence, sometimes quite ingeniously, or to argue that the dangers of smoking did not apply to themselves. The manufacturers had an obvious financial interest in refuting or challenging the medical evidence, but the key to understanding the history of post-war smoking is the survival of the liberal notions of the smoking individual within a broad popular culture which contested the ability of the state to intervene in lifestyle decisions. It is this culture which encouraged smokers to deny the validity of the medical evidence and to argue, most crudely, that it 'never did [them] any harm'. Indeed, such arguments were highly necessary since by this time the pipe and the cigarette were crucial to both self and group identity, factors which have helped to maintain the reified and celebrated role of tobacco in contemporary society.

Primarily, *Smoking in British popular culture* is a history of one aspect of mass, commercially based, leisure. It is an attempt to understand why the cigarette has replaced the pipe and become so widely consumed even when, during the last fifty years, the dangers inherent in its consumption have been increasingly understood and accepted. This general project bears many similarities with other histories of particular forms of leisure and popular culture and follows the familiar desire of many social historians to understand the motivations of ordinary men and women when their behaviour does not correspond to the apparently rational expectations of the late twentieth-century analyst. But it is also an economic history, or at least an exploration of the relationship between the marketplace and popular culture in a period in which commerce has decisively come to shape what has been elusively termed 'modernity'.[7] And, in attempting to uncover the relationship smoking has had with science, society and the economy, it is a work of cultural history, particularly in its emphasis on liberalism as the dominant ideological paradigm through which to understand modern consumption. Throughout, literary evidence is relied upon to represent, illustrate and add colour to certain trends in society. However, the relationship between the 'real' and the 'fictional' in the history of smoking could never be so straightforward. Many literary representations of the pipe, the cigar and the cigarette have come to have an iconic status to the extent that figures such as Sherlock Holmes, Humphrey Bogart and Lauren Bacall have in themselves become constitutive of the culture they were ostensibly portraying. If in what follows there appears to be too easy an interchange between fictional and non-fictional evidence, it is in recognition of the extent to which the social history of smoking has been intertwined with the history of popular literary culture.

Smoking in British popular culture should be read as a contribution to the expanding field of material cultural studies. It is about the role of an object in society, of how it gave visual representation to social relations, and how those concerned with the object understood its meaning and articulated their relationship with it.[8] Here, as a case study, it is in an incredibly privileged position, since few other products have had so much written about them. Instead, scholars have had to extrapolate the meaning of a commercial object according to theories about the transfer of its meaning from one sphere to another, from the manufacturer to the retailer, from the retailer to the consumer, mediated at each point by a visual or rhetorical communicator of the object's value.[9] Because of the bourgeois-liberal culture (if not cult) of smoking in the late nineteenth century, however, there is an opportunity here to uncover the meaning of an object constructed entirely by the consumers themselves and which, in that period at least, would dominate all other representations of smoking offered in part by a highly segmented manufacturing interest. In this sense, there exists a minutely articulated, deliberately expressed and at times sophisticated analysis of consumption which other studies have instead had to discern and uncover from the actual practices of object use. Chapter 1 should therefore be recognised for its peculiarities in the history of material culture, and it perhaps provides a discursive model for the role of consumption in identity formation that one cannot fully investigate for other products. For this reason, too, the fluency given to the role of tobacco by this and other groups makes this history a contribution to the study of the construction of femininity and masculinity, a field which is increasingly realising the importance of consumption to any understanding of gender.[10] Such a rich vocabulary describing the act of smoking has marked its history over several centuries. This language persisted throughout the initial smoking and health 'controversy' of the 1950s and 1960s, and provides the historian with many examples of how medical knowledge was understood by a pre-existing culture. Consequently, tobacco's special position as a highly contested object enables this book to be also a case study of the dissemination of scientific knowledge. The three chapters of Part III provide a history of how science was interpreted, understood and even constructed by various publics which had an interest in establishing the meaning of tobacco in relationship to health.

Many other historians have admirably covered the history of tobacco from either its role in Amerindian culture or its introduction into Britain and Europe in the late sixteenth century.[11] This story will not be reworked here as the focus will move on to a more detailed analysis of smoking over the last two hundred years. The aim of this study is to provide a convincing account of the rise of the cigarette in British popular culture, though this necessarily involves an examination of the culture which immediately preceded its phenomenal popularity. Likewise, much has been written on the history of smoking in the United States, a country whose promotion of the cigarette has had such an impact on Britain and whose own smoking history so closely mirrors the United Kingdom's. The two countries' relationship with tobacco has been especially similar when the two cultures have come together, principally during the tobacco war at the turn of the century when James Buchanan Duke's American Tobacco Company transformed the marketing practices of British firms when it tried to take away their customers and during the post-war period when there has been much international collaboration in the medical investigations into smoking and health. Several excellent works have already been written on US smoking culture, as well as on Australia, which also shares many similarities with Britain, but this book provides a separate study of Britain for two particular reasons.[12] First, the assumptions made about the history of tobacco, especially that advertising deliberately promoted a healthy lifestyle and that smokers were unaware of the dangers of cigarettes in the 1950s and 1960s, could only be tested by a comprehensive focus on a single country. Second, although liberal assumptions can partially explain attitudes to smoking across the western world, the forceful articulation of these values in the nineteenth century and on throughout the smoking and health controversy in the late twentieth century suggests that British culture might contain certain peculiarities in its understanding of tobacco. Perhaps this is indicated in the liberal assumptions found in Britain's legal system, which have ensured that the prosecution of tobacco companies for selling products that allegedly they themselves knew to be harmful has remained years, if not decades, behind the more pro-active American social and legal system. In Britain, the assumed independence of the liberal individual may have provided a greater check against the interventions of the state in smoking and health policy beyond the more obvious practical fiscal, financial and economic considerations.

However, this is not a legal, political or social policy history of the attempts to control or promote tobacco. Again, this has been covered by others and this book instead attempts to demonstrate how these debates have, to a degree, been shaped by popular culture.[13] Also, it cannot be a comprehensive medical history. The 50,000 books and articles produced since the first reports on smoking and health appeared in the 1950s preclude any detailed consideration of the evidence. The only medical knowledge presented here is that which entered discussions of popular culture, though medical arguments are analysed when they have very much constituted that culture, such as with the pamphlets of the anti-tobacconists in the nineteenth century. More specifically, there is little discussion of the scientific explanations offered for smoking behaviour.[14] The psychoanalytical interpretations offered in the inter-war period have long since given way to more nuanced accounts of smoking personality and psychopathology. These include nervous habit models, psychodynamic theories, sensory gratification explanations, pure physical addiction and the categorisation of smoking styles into positive and negative effects; that is, the idea that certain people smoke for the love of smoking, while others do so to compensate for that which they consciously or otherwise feel they are lacking in their lives.[15] All of these models may be particularly adept at untangling the various reasons for smoking continuation and for helping health workers with information on how to encourage smokers to quit, but they do little to explain why smokers take to the habit in the first place or why they continue to that stage when they are recognised as 'confirmed' smokers. Physical addiction is not generally assumed to override social and psychological factors until the smoker reaches the rate of twenty a day, and while this has been an important factor in ensuring that smoking rates in the UK are still approximately one-third of the adult population, there is a whole history behind each successive generation's adoption and persistence with the cigarette before physical addiction sets in.[16]

What this book does offer, then, is a cultural history of a society which still witnesses 120,000 people dying each year from smoking-related illnesses. This figure may well be reduced as the next cohort of the population reaching mid to later life has not smoked to quite the same extent as those who are now suffering from lung cancer and heart disease. But since smoking rates have levelled off at just over 30 per cent of the population and are beginning to rise again among secondary school children, the problems are likely to remain substantial for several decades to come. However, given what is presented in the following pages, that likelihood must be taken as a probability. The emphasis in popular culture on the importance of smoking to self identity has remained constant throughout the post-war period and has benefited, within the last decade, from an almost subcultural celebration of smoking as a ritual of resistance against the perceived 'health fascism' of contemporary society. In the renewed celebration of smoking taking place in film and magazine culture, the cigarette's protagonists are essentially modernising that bourgeois-liberal tradition which characterises the history of smoking in British popular culture. In the nineteenth century it raised smoking from an act of consumption to an art of connoisseurship; in the early twentieth century it resisted the perceived homogenising tendencies of the mass market; and from the 1950s it belligerently stood in defiance of the health promotion campaigns that were held as infringements of the independence of the smoker who ought to have been free to make up his or her own mind about the medical dangers of smoking. If the health campaigns had achieved some success by the 1980s, especially over the issue of passive smoking which seemed to legitimate the extension of restrictions on cigarette promotion, they would later come up against a small but increasingly pro-smoking backlash that has ensured the act of smoking has maintained its romantic status in popular culture.

Notes

1 A. J. P. Taylor, *English History, 1914–1945* (Harmondsworth, Penguin, 1976), p. 392.

2 Figures taken and derived from J. W. Hobson and H. Henry, *The Patterns of Smoking Habits* (London, Hulton Research Studies, 1948), p. 2; B. R. Mitchell and P. Deane, *Abstract of British Historical Statistics* (Cambridge, Cambridge University Press, 1971), pp. 355–8; P. N. Lee, *Statistics of Smoking in the United Kingdom* (7th edn; London, Tobacco Research Council, 1976), pp. 21–3.

3 F. Trentmann, 'Wealth versus welfare: the British Left between Free Trade and national political economy before the First World War', *Historical Research*, 70:171 (1997), 70–98; E. F. Biagini, *Liberty, Retrenchment and Reform: Popular Liberalism in the Age of Gladstone, 1860–80* (Cambridge, Cambridge University Press, 1992).

4 F. Trentmann, 'The transformation of fiscal reform: reciprocity, modernisation, and the fiscal debate within the business community in early twentieth-century Britain', *The Historical Journal*, 39:4 (1996), 1005–48; H. Mercer, *Constructing a Competitive Order: The Hidden History of British Anti-Trust Policy* (Cambridge, Cambridge University Press, 1995).

5 R. Doll and A. B. Hill, 'Smoking and carcinoma of the lung: preliminary report', *British Medical Journal*, ii (1950), 739–48.

6 M. D. Read, *The Politics of Tobacco: Policy Networks and the Cigarette Industry* (Aldershot, Avebury, 1996); P. Taylor, *Smoke Ring: The Politics of Tobacco* (London, Bodley Head, 1984).

7 J. Naremore and P. Brantlinger (eds), *Modernity and Mass Culture* (Bloomington, Indiana University Press, 1991); J. Jervis, *Exploring the Modern: Patterns of Western Culture and Civilisation* (Oxford, Blackwell, 1998).

8 M. Douglas and B. Isherwood, *The World of Goods: Towards an Anthropology of Consumption* (London, Allen Lane, 1978); A. Appadurai (ed.), *The Social Life of Things: Commodities in Cultural Perspective* (Cambridge, Cambridge University Press, 1986).

9 G. McCracken, *Culture and Consumption: New Approaches to the Symbolic Character of Consumer Goods and Activities* (Bloomington, Indiana University Press, 1988); D. Miller, *Material Culture and Mass Consumption* (Oxford, Basil Blackwell, 1987); B. Fine and E. Leopold, *The World of Consumption* (London, Routledge, 1993). For a thorough bibliography see D. Miller (ed.), *Acknowledging Consumption: A Review of New Studies* (London, Routledge, 1995).

10 For example, a recent study of masculinity and consumption can be found in F. Mort, *Cultures of Consumption: Masculinities and Social Space in Late Twentieth-Century Britain* (London, Routledge, 1996). A comprehensive bibliography, as well as a series of excellent essays, is contained in V. de Grazia and E. Furlough (eds), *The Sex of Things: Gender and Consumption in Historical Perspective* (London, University of California Press, 1996).

11 J. Goodman, *Tobacco in History: The Cultures of Dependence* (London, Routledge, 1993); V. G. Kiernan, *Tobacco: A History* (London, Hutchinson, 1991).

12 R. Sobel, *They Satisfy: The Cigarette in American Life* (New York, Anchor Books, 1978); L. White, *Merchants of Death: The American Tobacco Industry* (New York, William Morrow, 1988); A. Brandt, 'The cigarette, risk, and American culture', *Daedalus*, 119 (1990), 155–76; R. B. Walker, *Under Fire: A History of Smoking in Australia* (Melbourne, Melbourne University Press, 1984).

13 Read, *Politics of Tobacco*; Taylor, *Smoke Ring*; On America see P. Pringle, *Dirty Business: Big Tobacco at the Bar of Justice* (London, Aurum, 1998).

14 In 1922, the *International Journal of Psychoanalysis* published a special issue on psychoanalysis and smoking.

15 For a recent overview of the scientific understanding of smoking types and personalities, see D. G. Gilbert, *Smoking: Individual Differences, Psychopathology, and Emotion* (Washington, DC, Taylor and Francis, 1995). On the history of addiction, see V. Berridge, 'Morality and medical science: concepts of narcotic addiction in Britain, 1820–1926', *Annals of Science*, 36 (1979), 67–75; V. Berridge, 'Morbid cravings: the emergence of addiction', *British Journal of Addiction*, 80 (1985), 233–43.

16 Department of Health, *Report of the Scientific Committee on Smoking and Health* (London, HMSO, 1998).

Part I

Culture:
the cigar and the pipe
in Victorian Britain

Good companions: bourgeois man and the divine Lady Nicotine

At the beginning of *The Adventure of the Yellow Face*, Sherlock Holmes and Dr Watson return to 221B Baker Street where they find lying on the table a 'nice old briar' pipe with a long amber stem. With a typical display of his renowned logical-deductive reasoning, Holmes is able to create a vivid impression of the pipe owner's physical appearance, personality and social situation. From the expensive silver bands which have been used to repair the pipe, Holmes can tell that the owner values his smoking materials highly. The charring on the right-hand side of the bowl of the pipe, the teeth marks on the amber and the remains of the eightpence-an-ounce Grosvenor mixture all make it possible for the most singular detective to observe that 'the owner is obviously a muscular man, left-handed, with an excellent set of teeth, careless in his habits, and with no need to practise economy'. Although Watson is left astounded at his friend's unerring ability, he was mistaken to have been so, since Holmes had already stated that 'pipes are of extraordinary interest . . . Nothing has more individuality save, perhaps, watches and boot-laces.'[1] Because every man smokes his pipe in his own distinctive manner, it is possible to deduce something of the individual character of the smoker.

The use of tobacco, and the paraphernalia necessary for its consumption, is a classic narrative device of Conan Doyle. In numerous adventures the crucial key to the successful solution of a mystery is found in clues left by smokers: in *The Adventure of the Red Circle*, Holmes can tell that whoever discarded a cigarette at the scene of the crime was a clean-shaven man; in *The Adventure of the Golden Pince-Nez*, the footprints in the ash deliberately left on the carpet by Holmes reveal the presence of someone in the room other than the bed-ridden professor; and in *A Study in Scarlet*, Holmes is able to deduce from the ash left on the floor that the murderer smokes Trichinopoly cigars, a skill he later uses in *The Boscombe Valley Mystery* when he famously tells

Watson about his 'little monograph on the ashes of 140 different varieties of pipe, cigar, and cigarette tobacco'.[2]

The reason why Conan Doyle finds tobacco such a useful tool in the unwinding of his plots is because he shares a belief common among his smoking contemporaries that each man smokes in his own individual way. Indeed, Conan Doyle makes his hero one of the most idiosyncratic smokers of all time. From *The Hound of the Baskervilles* we know that Holmes buys his 'strongest shag tobacco' from a tobacconist named Bradley. From the adventures of *The Mazarin Stone*, *The Musgrave Ritual* and *The Naval Treaty* we know that he keeps his cigars and pipes in the coal scuttle and his tobacco 'in the toe-end of a Persian slipper'. And, from *A Case of Identity*, we know that as well as his 'everyday' briar pipe, he smokes an 'old and oily clay pipe' and sometimes a 'long cherrywood' when in a 'disputatious rather than a meditative mood'. His smoking habits include the use of a glowing cinder held by a pair of tongs with which to light his pipes (*The Copper Beeches*, see figure 1) and the smoking of 'all the plugs and dottles left from his smokes of

'TAKING UP A GLOWING CINDER WITH THE TONGS.'

1   *Taking up a glowing cinder with the tongs*, Sherlock Holmes in *The Adventure of the Copper Beeches*, *Strand Magazine*, 1893

the day before' for his before-breakfast pipe (*The Engineer's Thumb*). Occasionally, he prefers to smoke cigarettes, such as when in his 'old nonchalant
mood' in *The Adventure of the Empty House*, or when there is a certain
rapidity in his conversation, as in *A Scandal in Bohemia*. While he never took
snuff, he was occasionally inclined to produce a cigar for moments of con-
viviality or hospitality (*The Adventure of the Cardboard Box*).[3]

Of the sixty cases in the Holmes canon, there are only eleven adventures in
which no smoking appears, the other forty-nine illustrating in their various
ways the complicated character of the consulting detective.[4] In no way should
it be thought that Holmes' smoking was simply a habit, a trivial aspect of
consumption possibly only important to his private identity. For, although
Holmes has subsequently come under much criticism for not being a connoisseur of tobacco, his smoking served a public purpose. Frequently, the
lighting of a pipe by Holmes marks the point at which he listens to the initial
facts of a case before setting out among 'the teeming millions of this great city'
to make sense of that 'dense swarm of humanity' which makes up London,
'that great cesspool into which all the loungers and idlers of the Empire are
irresistibly drained'.[5] Only Holmes had the strength of mind and powers of
rational reasoning to uncover the mysteries of the criminal underworld and it
was only through his pipe that he could achieve this. The difficulty of the
case would determine his mode of smoking. In a most celebrated passage,
Holmes declared that the *Red-Headed League* presented a 'three-pipe problem',
but in *The Man with the Twisted Lip* Holmes sits cross-legged all night on an
Eastern divan, smoking an entire ounce of strong shag tobacco.

Out of so many references to smoking, what emerges is a man who engages
in the consumption of tobacco for two quite distinct reasons, yet which
together constitute a paradoxical aspect to his personality. On the one hand,
he smokes to present a private image of himself which is completed only
when placed alongside his violin, his index books and his stooge Watson,
who accepts his role as a similar sort of object through which Holmes can
channel his more self-indulgent desires for romance, acclaim and inebriation,
the latter highlighted through occasional references to a long-held cocaine
habit. Such indicators of his individuality would, perhaps, remain unimportant or ephemeral were it not for the fact that his ostensibly private acts of
consumption also serve an important public purpose. Pipes, tobacco, cigars
and cigarettes are not mere indulgences, but are the actual tools of his trade.
Smoking is an act which enables his great mind to work at its best, focusing
his attention and stimulating the creation of a logical narrative of criminal

intent, method, identity and means of capture. So while his smoking says much about the man, what is of more lasting consequence is the benefit it brings to the public good, here defined narrowly as the solving of numerous frauds committed from within the underworld by Holmes' seeming antithesis, Professor Moriarty.

The image of Holmes has become iconic, but at the time he was more a representation of a particular masculine culture that was essentially bourgeois in social background and vaguely liberal in outlook. In numerous books devoted to the subject of tobacco and smoking, and in literally countless articles appearing in Victorian periodicals consumed by an expanding middle and lower-middle class, a culture of smoking became increasingly prominent. This culture followed closely that embodied by Holmes and which proved to be of sufficient resilience that it has come to influence both the developments in the emergence of the mass market economy in the early twentieth century and the presentation of scientific findings about the harmful effects of smoking in the post-Second World War period.

It is this bourgeois-liberal culture of smoking that this chapter seeks to explore. What becomes apparent in reading through the articles of *Chambers' Journal, Once a Week, All the Year Round, Fraser's Magazine, Cornhill Magazine, London Society* and *Gentleman's Magazine* is both a celebration of what has come to be called the 'Lady Nicotine' and the 'divine weed', and also a rationalisation of an act of masculine consumption. Recent historical works have demonstrated that throughout the nineteenth and twentieth centuries, although both men and women were often consumers in practice, there was a particular and possibly class-specific male rhetoric which posited the marketplace and consumption as feminine. In contrast, production and the workplace were deemed masculine, and sober-minded men were held to be blind to the sparkling allure of the ephemeral fripperies of commerce.[6] A few commodities, however, such as fine wine, original paintings, athletic race-horses, expensive jewellery and precious stones, tailored clothing, good tobacco and mechanical gadgets could be consumed by men with passion, though that appreciation had to be set in a language which demarcated it from the supposedly passive consumption that women and the masses were said to experience when they consumed. In a sense, then, the periodical article became the site through which men could learn about objects in a language suitable to their own masculine identity. Writers of smoking eulogies transformed their very private, self-indulgent form of consumption into an activity in accord with the perceived male role in life. Pro-smoking writers and journalists engaged in a very public discussion of all aspects of tobacco, from its history, cultivation, production, manufacture, anthropology, statistical economic relevance and literary background, to its scientific and medical properties. This provided a body of knowledge about tobacco, presented as a worthwhile area for general public readership and interest, which could form the basis of men's numerous eulogies to their favourite indulgence. So while, just as with Holmes, their celebration of their favourite smoking anecdotes, their favourite items in the paraphernalia of tobacco and their poetical odes to the weed, might seem ephemeral, immoderate and even irrational, rooting such devotion to an object within the masculine spheres of production, science, medicine and history would legitimate its use. Furthermore, just as knowledge and learning served to de-feminise their consumption, so too did their focus on the individualised nature of their smoking experience, as this made the smoker independent of the market forces that could manipulate and make passive the effeminised body of everyday consumers. The independent train of thought said to be induced by the cigar and the pipe, and which took the relaxed smoker away from the pressures of the world and into the hazy environs of 'smokiania', was posited as an essential ingredient in the make-up of the bourgeois gentleman, since it enabled him to re-enter the public sphere outside his smoking room while at the same time cultivating those aspects of independence and individuality so crucial to the liberal outlook on life.

Much of this literary output was derivative in style, J. M. Barrie's *My Lady Nicotine* perhaps best exemplifying many of the light-hearted themes of the genre.[7] Many of the periodical articles borrowed heavily from the works of such tobacco 'worshippers' as Byron, Kingsley, Johnson, Lamb and Thackeray, but none were able to add substantially to this literary praise. The many articles that focused on the more 'rational' aspects of tobacco eventually adopted a narrative formula that generally began with the antiquity and botany of the tobacco plant, moved on to the history of smoking post-1492, quickly whirled through cultivation, curing and manufacture, before finishing with a few statistics demonstrating the centrality of smoking to modern economies. It is a style of writing parodied in Gissing's *New Grub Street* when the brash, young and arrogant journalist, Jasper Milvain espouses his ideas on how to write a successful column for a periodical: 'The kind of thing in which ones makes a column out of what would fill six lines of respectable prose. You call a cigar a "convoluted weed", and so on, you know; that passes for facetiousness.'[8] Clearly, many borrowed so much from one another that accusations of plagiarism would not be out of place and the style became so hackneyed that even a self-confessed non-smoking woman was able to join in the desultory eulogy.[9]

Such criticism is, however, to miss the point, and more can be learnt about the social context of the articles from their length and even their titles. The number of times 'whiff' appears is demonstrative of how they were supposed to be read. Along with individual chapters of Barrie's work or a poem or essay found in the literary collections of Machen or Walter Hamilton,[10] these works were meant to be read in brief 'pipefuls', to be 'laughed at over a cigar and forgotten with its ashes' in 'the drawing rooms of South Kensington and the smoking dens of Hampstead'.[11] Traditions of such literature stretched back to the eighteenth century, particularly in the pages of *Gentleman's Magazine*,[12] but it was not until the mid to late Victorian period that this genre truly flourished, a time when an expanding middle and lower-middle class sought justification for their outward displays of social status. The style of many of these articles almost deliberately aided the aspiring bourgeois gentleman in confirming the legitimacy of his consumption, as authors would pass through every stage of the production process of a cigar before finally joining the reader and lighting one up themselves in the closing paragraph. The reader would at this point have shared the author's knowledge that what he smoked was the authentic article, personally checked and verified at every stage of production by a fellow smoker, and not some adulterated fraud cast upon him by a market which had identified him as an easy, ill-informed dupe.[13] The smoker was then at liberty to rest easy in his arm-chair, alone in his drawing room or safe among the fraternity of smokers at his club, knowing that he was not a 'consumer' but instead an 'ardent votary', a worshipper, disciple and true friend of 'the divine lady nicotine'.[14]

Such is the background to what was, numerically, a minority smoking culture. But the articles are important because as an imprecisely bound corpus, united principally through the emphasis on the pleasure to be gained from smoking, they also presented a coherent body of ideas about tobacco which became the dominant public discourse concerning smoking. As we shall see in the next chapter, other images of smoking existed within the popular culture of the time, but these have not had quite the same continued or lasting grip on the consciousness of smokers. What follows, then, is a detailed outline of the 'ideology' of smoking and a loose conceptual framework for understanding how a particular literate section of the male population legitimated their activity in the perceived feminine world of consumption. How they did so was, first, to emphasise the rational, pointing to the intellectual, the skilful and the purposeful aspects of smoking. They then used this as a solid base from which to explore the second, more irrational or ephemeral, aspects of their individuality. Here, they tended to reify, anthropomorphise and feminise tobacco, emphasising spatial and temporal escape and the personalisation of the habit which, in turn, could be further rationalised within a broader bourgeois-liberal outlook.

The first means by which smoking was made into a rational activity in the periodical literature was the creation of a substantial knowledge base, a wealth of data being provided on the cultivation, biology, manufacture, production, pharmacology, anthropology and literature of tobacco. Informed of all these specialist areas of study, the reader would be taken away from the passive sphere of consumption and rooted instead in the more masculine spheres of data collection and production. The most frequently referred to area of public knowledge within which tobacco was located was history. Just about every popular discussion of smoking, both then and now, would mention Sir Walter Raleigh, the *Counterblaste* of James I and the prevalence of snuff taking in the eighteenth century. What follows is a summary version of all of these histories, which by the end of the nineteenth century had become extremely formulaic and predictable. They condensed into a few pages the perceived important dates and facts, with emphasis on the peculiar an spectacular which could then presumably be repeated by the reader to his friends once he had quickly read the history during the course of his cigar or pipe.

  Occasionally, an article might refer to the 'antiquity' of tobacco smoking in the Americas and, apparently, East Asia, but most would begin in 1492 when Columbus first stepped off his boat and noted the natives clasping 'lighted brands' in their mouths. The habit was soon imitated by sailors who travelled to the New World and the plant itself was later brought to Spain by Hernando de Oviedo. In 1559, Jean Nicot introduced it to Catherine de Medici and his name lives on in the botanical classification of *Nicotiana*. By 1560, tobacco had reached Italy and in 1565 Sir John Hawkins brought it to England, though most writers preferred to make more of its other Elizabethan proselytiser, Sir Walter Raleigh, who, in 1585, was famously drenched with water when his servant thought he was aflame about the mouth. The narrative then usually moved on to the varied reception that tobacco received across Europe, from its hailing as a medical panacea (the prophylactic virtues of tobacco being especially praised during the Great Plague of 1665), to the more lurid stories of Pope Urban VIII and Pope Innocent IX issuing Bulls in 1624 and 1690 excommunicating anyone caught snuffing in church. Sultan Amurath IV made smoking a capital offence, and in Russia smokers were placed under the threat of having their noses cut off if caught in the act. In England, in 1616, James I published his *Counterblaste to Tobacco*, the most famous passage of which was repeated in Victorian print surely as often as it must have been read in the early seventeenth century: 'a custom loathsome to the eye, hateful to the nose, harmful to the brain, dangerous to the lungs, and in the black, stinking fume thereof resembling the horrible Stygian smoke of the pit that is bottomless'.[15]

After overcoming these initial obstacles tobacco was held to have triumphed before being repackaged in the late seventeenth and eighteenth centuries in the form of snuff, its popularity being spread through the courts of Europe (Frederick the Great had special large pockets made for his excessive consumption), as well as becoming the staple fare of England's coffee-house literary circles of Pope, Swift, Addison, Bolingbroke and Congreve during and after the reign of Queen Anne. In the early nineteenth century, the cigar became popular among the dandies of London and, after the Crimean War, the cigarette among Britain's officer class. These potted histories would then culminate with a discussion of the breakdown of the early Victorian social stigma attached to public smoking brought about by the increased popularity of the pipe, the cigar and the cigarette.[16]

As each historical anecdote was read by the humorous 'pipeful' so too did such yarns perform the more serious task of transforming the ignorant consumer of tobacco into a knowledgeable smoker or connoisseur, who could then expound at length on the more 'solid' and 'real' aspects of his favourite indulgence. History served the same function as a number of other disciplines: exegeses appeared on forms of knowledge regarded as central to active rather than passive consumption. Scientific data were a particular favourite and readers would be told of the many different classifications of the tobacco plant, the pharmacological properties of the finished product, findings in the experimental development of new crop varieties, the chemical composition of the smoke produced upon ignition, and the beneficial and harmful properties of tobacco smoke – though, as will be seen, many of these latter discussions took place as a direct form of counter-propaganda to the anti-tobacco movement.[17] In addition, anthropological accounts would discuss the ceremonial use of tobacco in Amerindian cultures, and the many different types of pipe and smoking method from around the world would be collected to form a brief compendium of tobacco facts.[18] No article would then be complete without a few references to tobacco's literary heritage and a final blast of statistical data, twisted and contorted to arrive at figures of a more colourful nature:

> The tobacco contained in this number of cigarettes would weigh over nine thousand three hundred tons, and if it were stowed in carts, each carrying a ton, and the carts were marshalled in a line with twenty feet for each horse and vehicle, a procession would be formed over thirty-five miles long . . . Reckoning each cigarette to be three inches long, . . . it would make a line from here to the moon and nearly half the way back again.[19]

But if consumption was held to be the sphere of women, then production and manufacture were seen as masculine domains and it was to the factory and the field that numerous articles took their readers. Many were the writers who recounted their experiences of venturing to Cuba to sample the best tobacco in the world. They wrote authoritatively on the various regions for cultivating tobacco, debating the relative merits of the soils and climates of the Vuelta Abajo and the Vuelta Arriba growing regions. Detailed descriptions were given of how these leaves were then collected, hung out to dry and cured in large tobacco barns before being taken to one of the two hundred cigar *Fabricas* of Havana. Here, the writers would appear at their white imperialist best, waxing lyrical on the various skills of the native workers as they stripped the leaves of their stems, selected the appropriate cigar wrappers and fillings, and, expertly rolled the Partagas', Cabañas', Larrañaga's and Muria's, before having them packaged ready for export to Europe and the United States.[20] While such detailed knowledge was necessary for the cultivation of an image as connoisseur, there existed also a certain eroticism as writers dreamed of the 'beautiful white hands with taper fingers' of 'sylph-like', 'sweet-sixteen'-year-old female cigar rollers touching every part of an object that now lay between their lips. One writer for *All the Year Round* became particularly obsessed with the 'hundreds upon hundreds of fair faces' who made up the factory workforce:

> There was not a male worker to be seen. They were all girls, the majority of them very young, and every one of them held at that moment a handful of tobacco leaf, which she was rolling into a cigar . . . It was a busy scene. Girls, girls everywhere, all neat and tidy and cheerful, many of them exceedingly pretty. The effect of these four thousand white fingers nimbly plying their task was that of a dancing light – like the sunlight glistening through rustling leaves.[21]

The writer then diverges but ultimately comes back to these 'happy cigar girls' to discuss at considerable length how well they were cared for in the factory, how fond they were of singing and how paternalistic their employer was with regard to their education. Popular twentieth-century marketing-led mythology has subsequently transformed the race of these young women into 'dusky maidens' who roll the cigars in their own highly improbable manner, but the crucial image that such writing connotes is essentially the same: that of beautiful native women working to serve the luxurious desires of western man.

This emphasis on service is crucial to understanding how the British imperialist male regarded subjugated colonies in terms of his consumption of the products made there. But coupled with a clear divide between who laboured and who was to enjoy the fruits of such labour was a desire to know everything about each stage of production to ensure the authenticity and the quality of the finished article. Smokers were told that in the cigar factories of Havana, the most highly skilled minds were employed to perfect a particular process. Yet at the same time emphasis was also placed on describing how the tobacco still had to be carefully rolled in the palm of a hand. Here, then, the benefits of scientific manufacture were entwined with the human touch, ensuring the perfection and personalisation of production.[22] The western male consumer literally colonised the 'authentic' labour of the native worker.

Although descriptions of the manufacture of tobacco were usually confined to pipe tobaccos and cigars, towards the end of the nineteenth century a fascination became apparent with the new machine processes involved in cigarette manufacture. From within this particular masculine culture cigarettes were frequently regarded as inferior and effeminate, yet a knowledge of their production still added to the general expertise of the tobacco connoisseur. And, it seems, the perfectibility of cigarettes was judged by a set of criteria which assumed that they could never reach the degrees of taste expected of the authentically hand-made cigars and pipe tobaccos. Instead, the production process was enjoyed because the cigarettes produced were 'perfect in form and wonderfully even in their filling', suggesting here that fascination with the power of the machine so prevalent in early twentieth century life and art.[23] But, whatever the process of manufacture described, articles would then be able to end having completed the education of the smoker, so that he could sit back and enjoy what he then knew to be the authentic article.

Much has been made here of the necessity of a knowledge of production to produce the image of a connoisseur, but the second aspect of the bourgeois rationality of consumption – that of skill – required a far more developed system of education before the consumer could become a true 'aficionado' of tobacco. Once one had learnt one's cigars, where they were made, how to store them and how to recognise 'quality', then one had served one's apprenticeship and become a gentleman, a social being clearly encircled by just a few commodities of explicitly graduated taste:

> Only to unwary people who happen to be young and wealthy I will say this: whenever you have anything to do with cigars, or with sherry, or with pictures, or with horses look out. Some advisers would include women and diamonds in their caveat; but I halt at horses. They may have a flaw in them, but a woman is a woman, and a diamond a diamond, and you can tell paste at once.[24]

Within such a framework, it was important to learn the hierarchies of taste, though with cigars price was often a useful indicator: 'A cigar that sells at threepence, is made of Havana inside and out; one of twopence, of Cuban inside, and German out; one at a penny, of German inside and out; or, as some assert, of straw inside, and cabbage out; but that has nothing to with *us*.'[25] That passage was written in 1858, and such hierarchies would continue, though in ever changing form. At the top were the cigars of Cuba, followed by others from around the Caribbean, and from there were a number of fine gradations working down to top quality British cigars (made with Cuban leaf in British factories) and then to cheap penny cigars such as Pickwicks. Similar hierarchies existed for pipe tobaccos, though here there was much more room for personal preference, and many writers formed their own system of classification, Kenneth Grahame preferring his pipe to the 'vainglorious cigar' although, unfortunately, 'a false social system' had allowed the unappreciative 'capitalist' to become 'its temporary guardian and trustee'.[26]

Whether cigars or pipe tobaccos were preferred, however, two positions in the hierarchy of smoking were clear. At the very bottom were adulterated products and, particularly in the 1850s and 1860s, there was a perhaps understandable obsession with fraudulent commodities. Given what is known about the smoker's desire for authenticity at this time, it becomes clear why many writers were especially vigilant in searching for the 'ingenious swindles', 'impudent deceptions' and 'detestable "dodges" '.[27] The second grade of tobacco which united lovers of the pipe and cigar was the cigarette, an item largely condemned by true connoisseurs for its effeminacy and lack of taste. There emerged a fascination with all things oriental in the nineteenth century and the world of smoking was no exception. Hierarchies of cigarette appreciation were thus created as Turkish and Egyptian blends were praised above the cheaper Virginian. However, the more general attitude within the periodical literature was that the tobacco used in cigarette manufacture was of an inferior quality to that found in cigars or pipe mixtures and that it had been loaded with all forms of adulterants which gave the clear impression that the 'flavour and odour are of tobacco *plus* something'. Indeed, 'the finicking toy of the foreigner' – the cigarette – was 'a miserable apology for a manly pleasure', perhaps appropriate to the 'effeminate races of the Continent and the East'. Even when the writer wrote in a more charitable mood, referring to the cigarette as 'a stepping stone to the art of smoking', it still remained 'unworthy' for British 'manhood'.[28] The increased prevalence of the cigarette, available in mass-produced form in the 1880s, was incomprehensible to the more 'manly' smokers of the pipe and cigar, and provoked all manner of insinuations, the inhalation of the smoke being seen as 'dirty' and 'shameful', reducing men to the 'slavery' of addiction to a false pleasure. The cigarette smoker, extracting the smoke from the tobacco and taking it 'down his bronchial tubes and into his lungs' was immediately weakened, his nerves were destroyed and 'cigarette-smoker's throat' was induced.[29] As will be shown below, cigars and pipes formed retreats from the reality of the world, but the problem of the cigarette was that it was very much tied to the problems of the speed and pressure of late nineteenth-century modern city life:

> Thus the big muscular man who is full of animal spirits, and whose mind is never more seriously exercised than upon questions of sport, suffers infinitely less than he who lives in a great city, is of a somewhat nervous temperament, and spends laborious days in thought and study. It is the latter who is by far the most addicted to the [cigarette] habit and who falls to the lowest depths.[30]

The article from which the above passage is taken follows a trend of the time in making a sharp distinction between the manly, knowing and discriminating pipe and cigar smoker and the passive user of the cigarette, who is referred to not as a smoker but as a 'consumer', this word serving to connote all the corrupting feminising influences of the marketplace that prevent real appreciation of a product. Not all writers were so condemnatory, as cigarettes of quality (almost always the hand-rolled variety) were occasionally allowed into the world of the connoisseur,[31] but what most articles shared was this concept of distinction between 'real' and 'false' smoking. Dichotomies were created between those who smoked Havanas because they knew they were good and those who smoked them because they were told to do so;

between those individuals who cultivated their habit as an art form and the common 'mass' of smokers; and, according to the idiosyncratic whim of Kenneth Grahame, between those who could blow smoke rings (which could only be made by the 'exceptionally gifted smoker') and those social status-seeking capitalists who could not.[32] Grahame's peculiarities here hit upon a crucial aspect of the ideology of the smoking literature, for, just as thousands of public-school-educated sportsmen opposed the professionalisation of sport, the essence of the 'gentleman' was that one engaged in one's vocation or recreation as an amateur.[33] One article even makes the identity of connoisseurs synonymous with those of the 'real amateur', and holds up the skills of the professional native cigar tasters of the Havana *Fabricas* as the ideals to which the British amateur smoker should aspire: 'These men arrive at such a delicacy of taste that they can not only distinguish the soil on which each [cigar] is grown, the place of its fabrication, but also if the leaf has been gathered at the beginning or end of harvest.'[34] The assumed amateur 'ardent votary' reading this article is taken on a journey through the spheres of knowledge outlined above, cutting a swath through the corrupting aspects of capitalism and arriving at the real product that only the non-professional can truly appreciate, influenced by neither financial nor social considerations.

Crucially, the connoisseur did not obtain his knowledge from the market, and it is here that the periodical article serves as both the source of the distinction between smokers and consumers of tobacco, and the means by which readers had the potential to move from the passive to the discerning, 'true' type of smoker. While books of etiquette might serve the more deliberate purpose of educating people (and particularly women) about the socially correct forms of consumption, these articles could indirectly educate the male reader as to how to smoke, store, select, purchase and talk about tobacco in a manner appropriate to his assumed social position. Through descriptions of the anthropology, cultivation, history and culture of smoking, the reader could also take from them a knowledge of how to smoke himself, not in an obvious way that would seem to allow people rapidly to attain a false position of connoisseurship, but surreptitiously, not directly challenging the privileged status of tobacco's gentlemanly amateurs.

A third, final area of the rationality of smoking emerges out of the skilful and the intellectual as tobacco was mobilised to serve a purpose either for private need or public good. The purposeful element of smoking is best encapsulated by a much quoted passage of Charles Kingsley's *Westward Ho!*, written in 1855 and found on every Westward Ho tobacco packet: 'A lone man's companion, a bachelor's friend, a hungry man's food, a sad man's cordial, a wakeful man's sleep, and a chilly man's fire.' Tobacco thus served a variety of important functions to a range of states of day-to-day existence. Other eulogies would go into much further detail of the basic human needs which tobacco either supported or temporarily staved in order that the smoker might perform some necessary task. Smoking was thus enrolled as a patriotic act since it helped the soldier to perform his duty to his country and, perhaps more crucially to a British sense of national identity, it comforted the sailor on his long voyages at sea to the far outposts of the Empire. For the ordinary smoker back at home, a patriotic purpose always remained through the huge contribution to the public purse made by the brotherhood of excise duty-paying smokers: 'The Chancellor of the Exchequer – the entire working of the machinery of government in this great country – the existence and efficiency of our army and fleet – largely depend upon the financial results of the consumption of tobacco by our truly patriotic smokers.'[35]

Tobacco was promoted as necessary for the mobilisation of the intellectual and creative talents. Particularly in the debates with the anti-tobacco movement, various figures from the past such as Newton and Hobbes would be transformed into exemplars of the effectiveness of smoking to inspire a scientific discovery, work of art, a poem or piece of literature, a military strategy or an act of ingenious diplomacy. In the creative sphere, Byron was a particular favourite, his 'sublime tobacco' regarded as both a hymn to, but very much the product of, tobacco smoking:

> Sublime tobacco! Which from east to west
> Cheers the tar's labour or the Turkman's rest;
> Which on the Moslem's ottoman divides
> His hours, and rivals opium and his brides;
> Magnificent in Stamboul, but less grand,
> Though not less loved, in Wapping or the Strand;
> Divine in hookahs, glorious in a pipe,
> When tipp'd with amber, mellow, rich, and ripe;
> Like other charmers, wooing the caress,
> More dazzlingly when daring in full dress.
> Yet thy true lovers more admire by far
> Thy naked beauties – Give me a cigar![36]

J. M. Barrie took the argument still further, delineating the types of smoking necessary for different artistic forms: in Thackeray's *Vanity Fair*, Becky Sharp had clearly been created through the smoking of manilas, but Cabañas', Barrie surmised, had to be smoked to produce Lord Steyne.[37]

Literary anecdotes such as these were collected to serve the same purpose as compendiums of other forms of knowledge. For the writer at least, the collection of any information or objects associated with smoking took the use of tobacco away from a private act of personal pleasure and towards a public act of knowledge creation. It has been argued that men created collections in order to rationalise their consumption; by depositing such collections in museums and exhibitions for public utility, they served to express the interests of the state.[38] While collections of tobacco ephemera could not be said to have been on the same scale as exhibitions of antiquities in the British Museum, the motivation was the same: by making a collection of one's items of consumption – of literary anecdotes, of pipes, tobacco boxes, cigars, ornamental snuff boxes and later cigarette cards – one transformed consumption into a purposeful act. Better still, if one could then write about one's collection or exhibit it as with, for example, a collection of tobacco storage jars, one could see oneself as offering a contribution to the encyclopaedia of public knowledge.[39] Books on tobacco themselves became collector's items and were in turn written about, the most famous English collection being that of William Bragge of Sheffield, who sold his 'Bibliotheca Nicotiana' at Sotheby's in 1882; another large collection belonging to Alderman William Ormerod was made available in Todmorden Free Library.[40] The largest and most well known has, however, become the George Arents collection, deposited at the New York Public Library, the bibliography for which itself extends to six large volumes.[41] What all such acts of consumption did was to transform a personal hobby into a repository of public knowledge, easily rationalised in serving the interests of the state through public education. The bourgeois male smoker, then, not only collected a detailed knowledge about his minor vice, but structured that knowledge into a hierarchy appropriate to the identity of a connoisseur, and finally presented this ideology of consumption to a public audience as a gift for the nation's benefit. Who could suggest, therefore, that his smoking habit was a purely self-indulgent act, designed solely to gratify his own desires?

The answer to the above question came from the smoking writer himself. Having built such a solid base from which to justify his habit, he was then at liberty to explore and expound upon the more transient aspects of his consumption. This he did at much length and in ways similar to those that tobacco has been praised ever since its introduction to western culture. As such, much of what follows is part of a longer and continuing history that has focused principally on tobacco's paradoxical virtues and vices, conjuring up such elusive phrases as Byron's use of the 'sublime' but which has remained largely true to Robert Burton's description from the early seventeenth century:

> Tobacco, divine, rare, superexcellent tobacco, which goes far beyond all their panaceas, potable gold, and philosopher's stones, a sovereign remedy to all diseases . . . But, as it is commonly abused by most men, which take it as tinkers do ale, 'tis a plague, a mischief, a violent purger of goods, lands, health, hellish, devillish, and damned tobacco, the ruin and overthrow of body and soul.[42]

What was perhaps specific to the late nineteenth-century praise of smoking was the degree to which tobacco was anthropomorphised into a trusty companion, feminised into a wife or lover, and even deified into a God itself. By drawing upon all the existing literature of tobacco, the resulting praise became greater than the sum of its parts. Again, the titles of the eulogies provide the initial clue: 'My cigar: memoir and an appreciation' immediately places the object as an equal, worthy of the respect and attention that one might give to any long-time friend or colleague. J. M. Barrie's *My Lady Nicotine* perhaps provides the most interesting case study. If the gender of his title was not sufficient to invoke his thoughts about his tobacco, the individual chapters of his book drive the message home. The first chapter, 'Matrimony and Smoking Compared', is an ironic, bitter-sweet justification for his decision to follow his fiancée's wishes that he must give up smoking in order to marry. That woman and tobacco be considered as alternatives is sufficiently telling of the attitudes of a culture which produced many works along the lines of Kipling's 'a woman is only a woman, but a good cigar is a smoke'.[43] But it is a culture that made the analogy all too often:

> Nay, lady, never knit thy brow,
>   This harmless weed to see;
> Nay, scorn it not – for, lady, know,
>   'Tis but a type of thee.
>
> Woman, of Nature's works the best,
>   And thou the fairest far,
> Can soothe at will my troubled breast;
>   But so can my cigar.
>
> In its form, so ladylike and slim,
>   No waist but thine can vie;
> The lustre of its glow might dim
>   All but my Mary's eye.[44]

The comparison was frequently found in he popular literature of the day, too. In Wilkie Collins' *The Moonstone*, Franklin Blake is moved to reflection when he realises he is unlikely to win the love of Miss Rachel:

Is it conceivable that a man can have smoked as long as I have without discovering that there is a complete system for the treatment of women at the bottom of his cigar-case? Follow me carefully, and I will prove it in two words. You choose a cigar, you try it, and it disappoints you. What do you do upon that? You throw it away and try another. Now observe the application! You choose a woman, you try her, and she breaks your heart. Fool! Take a lesson from your cigar-case. Throw her away and try another![45]

Kenneth Grahame's romance with tobacco provided an outlet for his more misogynist tendencies as he expressed contempt at those illogical women whom he held to be unable to appreciate the taste and smell of a cigar and consequently restricted smoking in their homes.[46]

Not only were tobacco and cigars given feminine attributes, but they were then placed on a pedestal and worshipped varyingly as gods and goddesses. In a legend attributed to Amerindian mythology, a stag was said to have descended from the clouds with the gift of tobacco. From then, its virtues became limitless and it was hailed as a panacea as it spread throughout the western world. From the historical narratives described above, readers learnt that it was only through tobacco's superhuman qualities that it was able to circumvent the obstacles of opposition placed in its path through the centuries. Such was the 'Goddess in the clouds' to whom those in pursuit of 'Diva Nicotina' should sings hymns and eulogise in prose and verse.[47]

Not all writers took smoking to such exalted heights, but they did seek to ascribe a personality to their tobacco in order to place the act of smoking beyond the ordinary level of consumption to one in which there was real appreciation for what was being burnt. Individual to individual, then, the smoker had to recognise the vagaries of his cigar, pipe or tobacco's distinct personality and coerce, court and dally with 'him' or 'her' until 'she', 'he' or it became a true companion to be enjoyed for its particular speciality. Such a process of anthropomorphism was taken to an extreme in a *Chambers' Journal* article of 1858 when the cigar actually took over the narration. From there, the cigar was able to bring to light the various characters of tobacco from around the world: the 'head of the family' resided in Havana; Yara tobacco was of a 'dry, independent, sarcastic disposition'; Brazil was 'scrappy-looking'; Latakia was 'aristocratic', 'enervated' and 'listless'; Turkey was bright and light but without much strength; Holland was 'respectable'; Java 'volcanic'; and German tobacco was 'a poor relation whom we are loath to own, with a most prolific growth – which poor relations always have'.[48] The style might have been pompous, light-hearted and seemingly trivial, but it was also capable of raising consumption to an act of playful, yet sophisticated appreciation, very much on a higher level than the supposedly thoughtless use of objects by women and the mass of the population.

Hand in hand with their tobacco, these readers of the periodical press were led into a smoking utopia, of either a spatial or temporal kind. That is, they were encouraged to retreat with their tobacco to their favourite smoking den, or else let their mind drift away to an idealised existence for just a few, brief moments as they rested from the stresses and strains of the real world. Many writers described their ideal smoking environment. For one *All the Year Round* writer it was his 'lawn at Chalkerton, under a beech-tree, whose clear bark is mottled with sunshine, and whose half transparent leaves are like fragmentary Venetian blinds between me and the shafts of Phœbus'.[49] For another, it was a smoking room, a masculine hideaway for himself and his friends, 'situated in a remote corner of the house' and filled with the clutter and junk of an active life, 'each eloquent with the recollection of happy nights and days, such as can only be happy to one in the full strength and hardihood of young manhood'.[50] But the smoking room at the club always maintained a special position in the mythology of tobacco, an idealised smoking utopia of rest, meditation, loungeful conversation and, most of all, sheer dedicated concentration on the joys of one's cigar.[51] As Ouida put it in 1867: 'that chamber of liberty, that sanctuary of the persecuted, that temple of refuge, thrice blessed in all its forms throughout the land, that consecrated Mecca of every true believer in the divinity of the meerschaum, and the paradise of the narghilé – the smoking-room'.[52]

Perhaps, however, in recognition that not all smoking readers would have access to a club or special room to retreat from the world, the eulogy writers also emphasised that the time it took to enjoy a pipe or cigar could offer a temporal release, aided with the 'whiffs' of tobacco presented in the periodicals. The mind was held to wander, to meander across the consciousness of one's reminiscences, just as the clouds of one's smoke circled and floated around the room, before gently disappearing into nothing:

> Leaning back leisurely upon his sofa, if he have one, and puffing his amber mouth-piece, ideas, thoughts, feelings, rush in rapid succession upon the mind prepared for kindly and soothing emotions. In the curling wreathes of vapour, which ambiently play around him, he discovers lovely and exquisite images . . . The aromatic leaf is the material of his incantations. Yes, there is magic in the cigar.[53]

The series of anecdotes provided the perfect literary form for a man in such a mood, unwilling to focus too long on any particular topic. The style often matched the mood suggested, many articles reading as a stream of conscious-ness or an idealised hyper-present in which the mind floated away of its own accord through a series of anecdotes only tenuously related to the one that came before. Whether through space or imagination, then, the smoker reached his own paradise, an idealised smoke-filled world at once both removed from the pressures of ordinary existence and yet filled with the reminiscences of an idealised past. The concept is embodied in Barrie's celebration as he describes the 'Arcadia' smoking mixture of the halcyon days of his smoking youth, the invented brand connoting images of a perhaps ungraspable time and place of peaceful smoking perfection.[54]

The smoker's Arcadia was a place for the exploration of one's individuality, for cherishing the experience of one's own tobacco-induced thoughts and emotions. It was such individuality which provides the final, though central, aspect to the construction of the smoking culture in the periodical literature. Writers surrounded themselves with the paraphernalia of smoking consump-tion, from the tools of their habit (clay pipes, briar pipes, meerschaums, churchwardens, pipe cleaners, matches, cigar holders, cigar cases, ash trays, pipe-lights, spills, spittoons, tobacco pouches, storage jars, snuff boxes, pipe racks, etc.) to the more general objects that completed the smoking experi-ence (favourite smoking armchairs, tables, slippers, jackets, hats, plus all the other trinkets of manhood stored in that vast monument to bourgeois mascu-line consumption, the smoking room).[55] In *My Lady Nicotine*, Barrie devotes separate chapters to his favourite blend of tobacco, his favourite pipes, his tobacco pouch, his smoking-table and even his favourite smoking compan-ions. On a surface level, such commodity fetishism might seem irrational and unimportant to the smoker's identity, but together they built up a distinctive picture of the smoker as different from everybody else.[56] Such an emphasis on individuality, or independence from the moods and fashions that gripped, say, the passive cigarette smoker, were crucial to locating consumption within a wider liberal outlook on life. This stressed the virtues of individuality and independence as central to the freedom necessary for trade and enterprise to take place between equal partners, on either the local or multinational level. Thus to build up a distinctive collection of smoking paraphernalia, to reminisce about one's own smoking experiences or to stress the personal relationship one might have with either one's local tobacconist or international cigar manufacturer was, in essence, a patriotic act: it celebrated the stoical inde-pendence of the British character (though mixed with a certain recreational light-hearted whimsical smoking flourish) in juxtaposition to the supposedly effete, cigarette-smoking foreigners.[57] Smokers became real smokers, then, when they became known for their distinctive individualistic smoking habits and mannerisms.

Finally, it should be remembered that this individuality was rooted in an empathetic fraternity of smoking companionship. There existed in the rhetoric of Victorian periodical literature a community of consumption, a 'freemasonry of smokers' and a camaraderie based on a shared knowledge of the tobacco experience.[58] Within this community, just as with any other, there existed a hierarchy of smokers, at the top of which existed the greatest eulogists and proselytisers of the past, followed by those individuals renowned for breaking down the barriers of convention that barred smoking in certain times.[59] Next came the gradations brought about by the skills of the connoisseur, and so on to the bottom of the pyramid where resided that potential great number of men who knew how to appreciate a good cigar or a pipe. Although let in at times, cigarette smokers were generally excluded from this freemasonry and, of course, so too were the anti-tobacconists. Indeed, the effect of the anti-smoking organisations – a relatively small radical arm of the temperance movement with little real influence – was to unite the pro-smoking writers against a common enemy. The debates which took place between the two groups will be analysed in greater detail in chapter 3, but it is sufficient here to comment that the 'tobacco-stoppers' came in for much ridicule in the periodical press. In reporting on the 'Great Tobacco Controversy' of 1857, which raged in the correspondence columns of the *Lancet*, *Chambers' Journal* hailed an emphatic victory for the smokers, who were said to have easily destroyed the pedantic arguments of the pleasure-hating philanthropists. Other articles, however, took a more moderate line, condemning only those anti-tobacconists who took their accusations against the weed to the extreme: that is, that smoking led to paralysis, insanity and death.[60] Further articles recounted the longer history of anti-tobaccoism to demonstrate the tendency towards foolish extremes taken by anti-smoking campaigners. But perhaps the main objection of these bourgeois-liberal smokers was the threat that such 'anti-tobacco' interference brought to the sanctity of the individual and his ability to make up his own mind and decide for himself what to put in his own free body. Even when an article proved sympathetic to some of the medical claims of the anti-tobacconists, they would still conclude with the argument of the independent man: 'A man must judge for himself as to whether smoking is good for him or not.'[61] As we shall see, this was an attitude which, on the one hand, was not wholly divorced from the ideology of the anti-tobacconists themselves and yet which, on the other, has proved so crucial to any understanding of the reception of new scientific evidence linking smoking to lung cancer in the 1950s. The extent to which this attitude formed the basis of all smoking cultures of the nineteenth century, however, is the subject of the next chapter.

Notes

1 A. Conan Doyle, *The Adventure of the Yellow Face*, in A. Conan Doyle, *The Original Illustrated Sherlock Holmes* (Edison, NJ, Castle, 1997), pp. 214–15.

2 A. Conan Doyle, *The Boscombe Valley Mystery*, in A. Conan Doyle, *The Adventures of Sherlock Holmes* (Harmondsworth, Penguin, 1994), p. 97.

3 The adventures of Holmes cited in the text can be found in *The Original Illustrated Sherlock Holmes*.

4 J. L. Hicks, 'No fire without smoke', *Sherlock Holmes Journal*, 1955, reprinted in P. A. Shreffler, *Sherlock Holmes by Gas Lamp: Highlights from the First Four Decades of 'The Baker Street Journal'* (New York, Fordham University Press, 1989). There are at least forty articles devoted to Sherlock Holmes' smoking habits in the various journals set up by appreciation societies around the world: see E. Umberger, *Tobacco and Its Use* (New York, Rochester, 1996), pp. 219–20.

5 A. Conan Doyle, *The Valley of Fear* (1914–15), in *The Case-Book of Sherlock Holmes* (Ware, Wordsworth, 1993), p. 894; *The Blue Carbuncle* (1892), in *The Adventures of Sherlock Holmes* (Harmondsworth, Penguin, 1994), p. 151; *A Study in Scarlet* (1888; Oxford, Oxford University Press, 1993), p. 6.

6 For the best entry (and bibliography) into the debates about the creation of gendered notions of consumption, see V. de Grazia and E. Furlough (eds), *The Sex of Things: Gender and Consumption in Historical Perspective* (London, University of California Press, 1996).

7 J. M. Barrie, *My Lady Nicotine* (1890; London, Hodder & Stoughton, 1902).

8 G. Gissing, *New Grub Street* (1891; Ware, Wordsworth, 1996), p. 147.

9 Anon., 'More about tobacco' (parts I & II), *Once a Week*, 4:103 (18 December 1869), 424–7; 4:104 (25 December 1869), 455–8.

10 A. Machen, *The Anatomy of Tobacco* (London, Redway, 1884); G. Redway, *Tobacco Talk and Smoker's Gossip* (London, Redway, 1886); W. Hamilton, *Poems and Parodies in Praise of Tobacco* (London, Reeves & Turner, n.d.). However, it has been argued that Redway's publication was also the work of Arthur Machen: N. Van Patten, 'An unacknowledged work of Arthur Machen?', *Papers of the Bibliographic Society of America*, 20 (1926), 95–7.

11 Reviews of Barrie's *My Lady Nicotine*: *Spectator*, 64 (7 June 1890), 800–1; *Athenaeum*, 3 (3 May 1890), 564; William Wallace in *Academy*, 951 (26 July 1890), 64–5; Anon., 'Notes on tobacco books', *Bookworm*, 3 (1889–90), 193–5.

12 'Occasional Correspondent', *Gentleman's Magazine* (June 1792), 500.

13 Anon., 'Havana cigars', *All the Year Round*, 17 (26 January 1867), 108–13.

14 Anon., 'The weed', *Chambers' Journal*, 9:449 (3 August 1872), 484–8.

15 James I, 'A counterblaste to tobacco', in R. S. Rait, *A Royal Rhetorician* (London, Constable, 1900), p. 54.

16 A full list of references to articles which referred to the history of smoking would be too large to list here, though the following pieces were used to draw up the summary, almost all of which followed a similar narrative pattern: Anon., 'Snuff-taking in England', *All the Year Round*, 17:409 (30 September 1876), 62–7; Anon., 'A whiff from the pipe', *All the Year Round*, 1:7 (16 February 1889), 160–5; Anon., 'Tobacco', *Penny Magazine*, 1 (14 July 1832), 148–9; Anon., 'Illustrations of tobacco-smoking', *Penny Magazine*, 4 (5 September 1835), 349–51; Anon., 'The most popular plant in the world', *Chambers' Journal*, 22:50 (16 December 1854), 393–5; Anon., 'A bird's-eye view of tobacco', *Chambers' Journal*, 7:176 (16 May 1857), 317–20; Anon., 'Snuff-taking', *Chambers' Journal*, 4:172 (13 April 1867), 238–40; Anon., 'Nicotiana', *Chambers' Journal*, 72 (2 March 1895), 143–4; Anon., 'On the antiquity of tobacco-smoking', *Macmillan's Magazine*, 74 (1896), 289–99; J. Bowie, 'My Lady Nicotine', *Good Words*, 45 (1904), 51–4; Anon., 'More about tobacco'; 4:104 (25 December 1869), 455–8; Anon., 'All smoke', *London Society*, 10 (1866), 306–15; Anon., 'The divine weed: in two parts', *All the Year Round*, 69 (19 and 26 September 1891), 271–8, 296–301; P. Kent, 'A whiff of tobacco', *Gentleman's Magazine*, 45 (1890), 575–82; Anon., 'All smoke', *Every Saturday*, 2 (1866), 495–500.

17 Anon., 'The most popular plant in the world'; Anon., 'The weed'; Anon., 'Nicotiana'; Anon., 'To smoke or not to smoke?', *All the Year Round*, 13 (1865), 413–18; Anon., 'More about tobacco'; Anon., 'A cigar scientifically dissected', *Practical Magazine*, 6 (1876), 334; M. Jules Rochard, 'Tobacco and the tobacco habit', *Popular Science Monthly*, 41 (1892), 670–82.

18 Anon., 'Concerning pipes', *All the Year Round*, 10:245 (9 September 1893), 245–8; A. Vambery, 'A paper of tobacco', *Every Saturday*, 3 (1867), 621–5; J. Hawkins, 'The ceremonial use of tobacco', *Popular Science Monthly*, 43 (1894), 173–83.

19 Anon., 'Cigarettes and cigarette-making', *Chambers' Journal*, 2:56 (24 December 1898), 56.

20 Anon.,'A bird's-eye view of tobacco'; Anon., 'The weed'; N. Amarga, 'My cigar: a memoir and an appreciation', *Temple Bar*, 114 (1897), 589–97.

21 Anon., 'Cigars', *All the Year Round*, 13 (4 February 1865), 35–8.

22 Anon., 'The weed', p. 486.

23 Anon., 'Cigarettes and cigarette-making', p. 57; 'The weed', *ibid*.

24 Anon., 'Havana cigars' p. 112.

25 Anon., 'A screw of tobacco', *Chambers' Journal*, 10:239 (31 July 1858), 72.

26 K. Grahame, 'Of smoking', in *Pagan Papers* (London, Elkin Matthews & John Lane, 1893), p. 62.

27 Anon., 'Havana cigars', p. 111.

28 Anon., 'Cigarettes', *Saturday Review*, 67 (4 May 1889), 528–9; Anon., 'Cigarettes', *Chambers' Journal*, 5:248 (26 September 1868), 617–18.

29 Anon., 'Cigarettes'; Anon., 'Confessions of a cigarette-smoker', *Chambers' Journal*, 80:6 (1902), 4–8.

30 *Ibid.*, p. 6.

31 W. C. Flood, 'How to make a cigarette: a lesson for smokers', *Harmsworth Magazine*, 6 (1901), 351–3; Anon., 'Havana cigarettes', *London Society*, 21 (1872), 505–10.

32 Anon., 'Cigars'; Anon., 'The costs, joys and woes of smoking', *London Society*, 15 (1869), 553; Grahame, *Pagan Papers*, p. 58.

33 J. A. Mangan and J. Walvin (eds), *Manliness and Morality: Middle-Class Masculinity in Britain and America, 1800–1940* (Manchester, Manchester University Press, 1987).

34 Anon., 'The weed', p. 487.

35 Anon., 'The costs, joys and woes of smoking', p. 559.

36 Lord Byron, 'The island' (1823), canto II, verse xix: *The Poetical Works of Lord Byron* (London, John Murray, 1857), p. 268.

37 J. M. Barrie, 'Wicked cigar', *Illustrated London News*, 98 (21 February 1891), 255; Anon., 'Literature and tobacco', *Academy*, 61 (14 September 1901), 225–6.

38 L. Auslander, 'The gendering of consumer practices in nineteenth-century France', in De Grazia and Furlough, *The Sex of Things*, pp. 79–112.

39 H. How, 'The biggest tobacco-box in the world', *Strand Magazine*, 8 (1894), 465–76.

40 Anon., 'Notes on sales: books on tobacco', *Times Literary Supplement* (14 September 1922), 588; Anon., 'Notes on tobacco books', p. 25.

41 J. E. Brooks, *Tobacco: Its History Illustrated by the Books, Manuscripts and Engravings in the Library of George Arents*, 4 vols (New York, Rosenbach, 1943).

42 Robert Burton, 'Democritus to the reader', second partition, section 4, member 2, subsection 1, in *The Anatomy of Melancholy* (New York, Tudor Publishing, 1948), p. 577.

43 R. Kipling, 'The betrothed', in *Rudyard Kiplings Verse: Definitive Edition* (London, Hodder & Stoughton, 1940), p. 49.

44 Anon., 'Defence of my cigar', *Fraser's Magazine*, 17 (1837), 155.

45 W. Collins, *The Moonstone* (1868; Ware, Wordsworth, 1993), p. 164.

46 Grahame, *Pagan Papers*, p. 59.

47 Anon., 'All in the clouds', *All the Year Round*, 15:369 (19 May 1866), 448–50; Anon., 'A whiff from the pipe'; 'An old smoker', 'Apropos of tobacco', *Bentley's Miscellany*, 15 (1844), 264–6; Anon., 'The weed'.

48 Anon., 'A screw of tobacco', 71–3.

49 Anon., 'All in the clouds', p. 448.

50 Anon., 'In a traveller's smoking room', *All the Year Round*, 71:8 (26 November 1892), 517–22.

51 Anon., 'The smoking-room at the club', *Cornhill Magazine*, 6 (1862), 512.

52 M. L. de la Ramée [Ouida], *Under Two Flags* (1867; Oxford, Oxford University Press, 1995), p. 18.

53 'An old smoker' 'Apropos of tobacco', p. 264.

54 Barrie, *My Lady Nicotine*, ch. 3.
55 Anon., 'The costs, joys and woes of smoking', pp. 553–4; Anon., 'In a traveller's smoking room'.
56 And, as we have seen, such paraphernalia could be brought together into the more rational form of collection or written about as a worthwhile area of study: for example, R. Quick, 'The antiquity of the tobacco pipe', *Antiquary*, 42 (1906), 20–3.
57 R. Lynd, 'Farewell to tobacco', in *Essays on Life and Literature* (London, Dent, 1951), pp. 246–50; Anon., 'Cigars'.
58 Anon., 'Havana cigars', p. 109.
59 Anon., 'Smoking and snuffing in church', *Chambers' Journal*, 63:3 (3 July 1896), 429–31.
60 Anon., 'A bird's-eye view of tobacco', p. 317; Anon., 'The weed', p. 487.
61 Anon., 'Are our pipes to be put out?', *Once a Week*, 8:187 (29 July 1871), 93.

2

Vanity Fair: a panoply of Victorian smokers

Smoking is ubiquitous in the Victorian novel. In Thackeray's *Vanity Fair* it is used to signify a variety of heroes and protagonists. Written between 1847 and 1848, but set in the period 1810–30, the book opens with a 'great quantity of eating and drinking, making love and jilting, laughing and the contrary, smoking, cheating, fighting, dancing, and fiddling'.[1] The bawdiness is soon contrasted with the refined images of the smoking cavalry officers of Waterloo (who mirror Thackeray's own devotion to the cigar), who in turn are positioned in juxtaposition to the 'horrid pipe' of the 'old, stumpy, short, and very dirty' Sir Pitt Crawley, whose tobacco was seemingly indiscriminately purchased for him by his charwoman.[2] Sir Pitt cared little for respectable society, preferring instead the company of his butler and his servants, who were of a class that gossiped in pubs 'over their pipes and pewter pots'.[3] His pipe smoking was a means by which he could demonstrate his affinity with their simple way of life, rather than the pretentious habits of his own social peers who, like Lady Jane, his daughter-in-law, were shocked at the stink of tobacco which emanated from his clothes and his library, and which contrasted with the grace of the cigars and the moustachios of her more refined brother, Southdown.[4]

Pipes also appear in the form of the oriental hookah, as smoked by Jos Sedley, the vain, lazy and rather pompous civil servant recently returned from Utter Pradesh with his 'hookahbadar' (a servant whose sole purpose was to fill the pipe); as a rather elaborate meerschaum as smoked by Lord Varinas; and in the form of a short clay as smoked by the nineteen-year-old Jim Crawley who, as a university student, smoked pipes to demonstrate a certain bohemianism shared with 'poor artists with screws of tobacco in their pockets'.[5] Snuff, too, makes an appearance in *Vanity Fair*, as it was taken by Cuff, the school bully, as Thackeray's hero Dobbin reminisces. But this is recalling an earlier period, which must have been around the turn of the nineteenth century, and snuff makes something of a literary exit at the beginning of the novel, to be replaced, at least in the society of young cavalry officers, by the cigar, which was first introduced into Britain by such men during the Peninsular Wars of 1804–13.

Dobbin, George Osborne, Rawdon Crawley and their comrades at the club and in the mess-room all smoke cigars and sometimes a smaller version, the cheroot, to demonstrate a very different form of masculinity from that outlined in chapter 1. They were effete dandies, flippant and whimsical, addicted to good company and yet devoted to their military calling. They could be serious and purposeful when called into battle, but at other times irresponsible and indifferent to the point of callousness, Osborne even lighting his cigar with a love note from his fiancée, Amelia. They often shared that culture of smoking of the bourgeois gentleman, but they were more willing to adopt a less rigid approach to the meaning of their cigar, just as when Rawdon Crawley falls victim to the gloriously manipulative charms of Rebecca Sharp:

> 'You don't mind my cigar, do you, Miss Sharp?' Miss Sharp loved the smell of cigars out of doors beyond everything in the world – and she just tasted one too, in the prettiest way possible, and gave a little puff, and a little scream, and a little giggle, and restored the delicacy to the captain [Crawley]; who twirled his moustache, and straightaway puffed it into a blaze that glowed quite red in the dark plantation, and swore – ''Jove – aw – Gad – aw – it's the finest segaw I ever smoked in the world – aw,' – for his intellect and conversation were alike brilliant and becoming to a heavy young dragoon.[6]

Thackeray, then, offers a range of smoking types and images which allow a first step to be made towards understanding the diversity of smoking practices in the Victorian period. Other authors provide similar clues. We have already seen how Conan Doyle placed smoking at the centre of his adventures, and smoking references litter the works of Dickens and Trollope, if not quite to the same extent as with Thackeray. Although many of Dickens' heroes were non-smokers, including Nicholas Nickleby, Martin Chuzzlewit, Charles Darnay, Barnaby Rudge, Pickwick and Pip, many of the associates of these characters made much use of tobacco to situate their social position and personality: Mr Quilp of *The Old Curiosity Shop* smoked smuggled cigars and chewed tobacco with watercress at breakfast; Perker, the attorney employed by Pickwick, was a snuff taker, as was Sally Brass in *The Old Curiosity Shop*; all the members of the Pickwick Club, apart from their illustrious leader, liked to smoke cigars after dinner; and David Copperfield was one hero who did at least attempt to smoke, as well as drink, on one evening with his young friends, though the experience was not a pleasurable one. The smoking habits of the author were perhaps significant in the representation of tobacco: Dickens' moderate cigar smoking enabling both favourable and unfavourable representations of smokers, whereas Hardy's abstinence accounts for the paucity of smoking in his novels.[7]

The extent to which the smoking culture of chapter 1 dominates the smoking practices of this range of characters forms the substance of what follows. It begins with a description of the smoking culture of manufacturers and retailers, demonstrating that they shared, if not followed, the representations of tobacco found in the periodical literature. It then moves on to examine the smoking practices of those who consumed the greatest part of the nation's tobacco in clay pipes. Despite the difficulties of uncovering the rituals of a cohort of the population which lacked the cultural and economic capital to leave its own smoking testament, there is sufficient evidence to realise that a more communal, if regionally diverse, masculine world of consumption existed in the public houses and work environments of the labouring classes. Other cultures were also promoted among the initial smokers of cigars and cigarettes, the smoking of the military officers presenting a far more self assured yet seemingly effeminate notion of masculinity which contrasted sharply with the sober rationality of the solid briar, the badge of the British bourgeoisie.

Tobacconists were more than happy to share in the eulogies to the 'weed'. From the financial point of view, a diversity of smoking practices where individually prepared smoking mixtures and expensive cigars had to be provided to discerning customers meant higher profit margins. But, culturally, specialist 'respectable' traders held much in common with the culture of smoking outlined in numerous journal articles. Just as the latter stressed individuality and independence as the benchmarks of distinguishing the connoisseur from the 'consumer', so too did tobacco dealers emphasise the virtues of individuality and independence in marking out the tradesman of quality from the mass of 'fly-by-night' 'illegitimate' multiple stores, co-operatives and general traders which specialised in branded, proprietary articles and which proliferated towards the turn of the century. Perhaps as a genuine expression of a trading philosophy, but also in part as a reaction to the standardising influences of the mass market economy, specialist tobacco traders expounded a broadly 'laissez-faire' liberal ideology based around, in practical terms, forging personal relationships with one's customers, being able to sell a range of products distinctive to one's establishment, not being controlled by a large creditor, and maintaining control over one's prices, mixtures and stocks. For the specialist tobacco traders at least, therefore, the politics of tobacco consumption matched the politics of tobacco supply.[8] In their emphasis on connoisseurship, the authenticity of the product and the smoker, the effeminacy of the cigarette, and the superiority of the individualised, heterogeneous 'mixture', retailers exactly paralleled the smoking culture of the drawing room and the club.[9] Indeed, their periodicals, *Tobacco Trade Review*, *Tobacco* and *Tobacco Weekly Journal*, often carried articles reprinted from the pages of *All the Year Round*, *Chambers' Journal* and *Saturday Review*.[10]

Manufacturers, too, were keen to spread the culture of smoking. At a time when advertising had not developed into its 'mass' stage, Cope Brothers, a Liverpool firm as famous in the 1870s as Wills of Bristol and Players of Nottingham would become in the twentieth century, consciously strove to promote a committed devotion to tobacco. Making rapid advances in commercial lithography, Cope's employed the services of the artist George Wallace (known as 'George Pipeshank', in homage to the political caricaturist and illustrator for Dickens, George Cruickshank) to produce a series of cards throughout the 1870s which featured illustrations of famous literary, cultural and political figures of the day.[11] Selling for 6d or 1s each, these cards and calendars served as both advertisements for Cope's and as publicity material for smoking in general, receiving much favourable comment in the press for introducing art into the world of commerce.[12] They were produced with the leisured gentleman very much in mind, as they assumed he had the time available to examine the caricatures closely and to work out who they were, and they all played directly on the feminisation and reification of tobacco and smoking outlined in chapter 1. One such poster, released in 1878, was entitled, 'The peerless pilgrimage to Saint Nicotine of the Holy Herb' and featured '65 Victorian celebrities travelling, like Chaucer's pilgrims, to worship at the shrine of tobacco' (figure 2).[13] Another was entitled, 'In pursuit of Diva Nicotina' and featured thirty characters in a style copied from Sir Noel Paton's painting, 'The pursuit of pleasure' (figure 3). An accompanying key plate was published along with the poster so that smokers could verify that the worshippers included William Morris, Canon Farrar, Lord Lytton, Lily Langtry, Sir Stafford Northcote, Bismarck and the Emperor of Austria. Trampled underfoot were the anti-tobacco figures of the Rev. John Kirk, Dr Charles Drysdale and Professor F. W. Newman. Above, in the clouds, flew

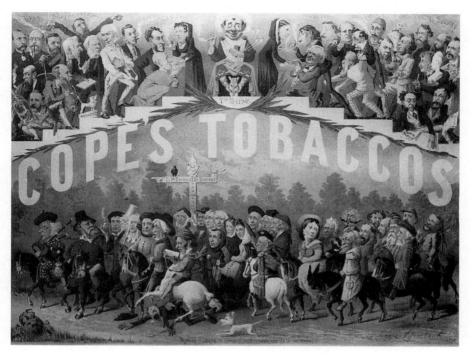

Peerless pilgrimage to Saint Nicotine of the Holy Herb, Cope Brothers'
advertisement, 1878   **2**

the 'denouncer of doom' with his 'umbrella of cant', 'livid with impotent
spite and envy, utterly unheeded by the ardent votaries in ecstatic pursuit of
our most gracious and glorious DIVA NICOTINA'.[14] Other posters distributed
featured a similar range of real and fictional characters collected together 'for
the seaside', 'for the holidays' and 'for the tourists' and, in the 1890s, Wallace
painted a series of golfing pictures which comically represented political
situations of the day. Cope's had a very clear idea as to the sort of man who
could share in this smoking culture, representing him in one image smoking
away the cares of the world, which included the horrifying spectre of the anti-
tobacco movement (figure 4).

The promotion of smoking by Cope's, however, extended much further
and was a product of Thomas Cope's own literary ambitions which had seen
him court and fraternise with the sort of journalist who wrote the eulogies to
tobacco. In March 1870, Cope's launched its own literary periodical, *Cope's
Tobacco Plant*, published monthly until January 1881. Edited and printed by
John Fraser, the well-known and well-respected Liverpool figure connected

3   *In pursuit of Diva Nicotina,* Cope Brothers' advertisement, 1879

4   *How to Cope with care,* Cope Brothers' advertisement, 1870s

with Cope's for over forty years, the journal became what Richard Altick has described as a distinctive and peculiar example of Victorian journalism, since it was both a part of the trade press and a 'very respectable literary journal'.[15] It devoted itself to 'Tobacco; all about Tobacco, and nothing but Tobacco' and, priced at only two pence, obtained a wide readership and favourable reception in the press.[16] From 1889 to 1894 many of the articles were reworked and published in fourteen issues of *Cope's Smoke Room Booklets*,[17] which concentrated on such topics as the contribution of James Thomson to the original *Cope's Tobacco Plant*, extracts from the works of literary figures including Lamb, Carlyle and Ruskin, and various collections of poetry which eulogised tobacco and smoking.[18] What the publications of Cope's attempted to instil was a collective identity for smokers as a group apart from the rest of society with its own interests and agendas. The language and tone of the journal avoided the snobbery and hierarchical attitudes of the connoisseur, while it was, at the same time, far more explicit about the purpose, beauty and role of tobacco than its non-commercial counterparts in the more general periodical press. Cope's deliberately sought to define smokers in their opposition to the 'humbug philanthropists' of the anti-tobacco movement, and their eulogies to the weed equalled and surpassed in hyperbole anything that was conjured up by the anonymous writers described in chapter 1. Cope's was a commercial organisation and was obviously interested in promoting smoking, yet it did so not by competitively extolling the virtues of its own brands, but by sharing and heightening a culture of smoking which already existed. To this extent, Cope's followed the lead taken by the periodical writers, but helped to ensure the dominance of the smoking ideal in the written culture of the time.

The extent to which this culture pervaded all forms of tobacco consumption is open to speculation. What is clear is that the vast majority of tobacco consumed in Britain in the nineteenth century was done so through the clay pipe, a method almost wholly absent from the smoking cultures so far described. Meerschaum pipes were too expensive for the ordinary smoker and briars were not popularised until the 1880s.[19] Before the rise of the cigarette, then, the clay was a staple part of working-class masculine consumption, belonging to a culture which was regionally diverse and which, in its spoken form, may have been as sophisticated as the written culture of the periodical press. Yet the local tastes and customs associated with the clay pipe received only one-dimensional representations in the Victorian novel. When a working-class smoker appeared there was little exploration of what smoking meant to him, just a simple assumption that the clay pipe was part of the everyday life of the common man, whether at work or at leisure. To mention just one example, the pipe appears as a badge of class in Dickens' *The Pickwick Papers*, Tony Weller being a prolific smoker once ensconced in the public house.[20] In many ways, authors were not concerned with exploring the smoking culture of the ordinary man, but in using his smoking as a deliberate juxtaposition with the smoking cultures of the bourgeois and aristocratic characters. Thus in Ouida's *Under Two Flags*, the malignant 'Welsher', Ben Davis, smokes with a pipe 'between his teeth', suggesting a rather crude appreciation of tobacco that stands in contrast to the refined cheroot and cigar-smoking sensibilities of his officers.[21] In Wilkie Collins' *The Moonstone*, the loyal, straight-talking servant, Gabriel Betteridge, is defined by just two objects – his pipe and his copy of *Robinson Crusoe* – to both of which he turns for solace and reflection in a manner in which the bourgeois male might reflect through the haze and dreams of his own smoke. But Betteridge is never allowed the degree of sophisticated smoke-induced reasoning which allows his young master, Franklin Blake, to espouse at length on the similarities between a woman and a cigar, as seen in chapter 1.[22] Anne Charlton, writing about smoking in Galsworthy's novels, has perhaps provided a useful generalisation for all Victorian fiction when she says of his book, *The Man of Property* (written in 1906 but set in 1886–92), 'smoking is shown mainly as a pleasure to those "above the property line" and as a prop to those below'.[23]

Smoking is therefore seen as an essential part of working-class culture, ubiquitous but unworthy of deeper analysis other than accepting it as a given. This literary attitude reflected many general assumptions about smoking. Even retailers, who had first-hand experience of the diversity of smoking patterns, regarded consumption by the greater number of ordinary people as a habit necessary for the performance of their everyday tasks at work. A writer for *London Society*, supposedly examining in detail the smoking of 'the mass of the community – those who may be said to smoke as workers' (as distinct from those who smoke as an 'art'), simply noted that 'some of our mechanics in England literally smoke all day'.[24] Despite such cursory treatment of working-class smoking cultures by middle-class commentators, anecdotal and statistical evidence begins to build a more nuanced image of clay-pipe smoking. What is known is that clays were given a variety of names, from the 'alderman' and the longer 'churchwarden' of rural England, to the 'cutty' of Scotland and the 'dudeen' (or 'dudheen') of Ireland, all of which originated in a seventeenth-century, pre-industrial culture.[25] These were the basic, most common forms of pipe, but because there were small clay-pipe manufacturers all over the country, there were a great number of names and shapes. Some of the more intricately moulded pipes cost around one penny, but most people were able to obtain their short clays free of charge from the public house, *Tobacco Trade Review* estimating that each publican gave away 'eighty to one hundred gross of pipes per annum [11,520–14,400]'.[26] This association of drink with tobacco is keenly reflected in the literature of the period, but it suggests also that smoking played a strong communal role in the life of ordinary working men. The fact that pipes were given away free further suggests the importance of hospitality in the smoking ritual, the publican now more formally taking the place of the private citizen of an older custom in which pipes would be given out ready to enjoy a shared smoking experience. It is a phenomenon noted in *The Moonstone*: on both occasions that Gabriel Betteridge takes visitors to Cobb Hole, a small country cottage, 'good Mrs Yolland performed a social ceremony strictly reserved for strangers of distinction. She put a bottle of Dutch gin and a couple of clean pipes on the table, and opened the conversation by saying, "What news from London, Sir?" '[27]

What the working man put in his pipe depended very much on where he lived. Prior to the introduction of branding, begun in 1847 by W. D. & H. O. Wills of Bristol with their Best Bird's Eye and Bishops Blaze brands, tobaccos were sold loose, each ounce being weighed out by the local trades-man. Even with the increased popularity of pre-packaged mixtures, retailing at anything from 5*d* upwards per ounce, loose tobaccos still dominated the market, and with prices of 3*d* per ounce not being altered until the 1909 budget (a price 'not to be tampered with'), the trade remained remarkably consistent throughout the mid to late nineteenth century.[28] Tobaccos were generally split into three types, though there was much diversity within each category. First, there were cut tobaccos of the type which have now come to dominate the trade and which included a large range of 'shags' (the best was said to be finely cut Virginian), flakes (more coarsely cut than shag but ready for smoking) and birdseye (so called because it contained a small quantity of finely cut stem which bore a resemblance to actual birds' eyes). Because they were loose, they tended to have a high water content, and it is to these types that most accusations of adulteration were made as it was said that unscrupu-lous traders increased the moisture level in order to increase the weight. Second, there were cakes and plugs which consisted of tightly packed leaves pressed together to give a hard tobacco which had to be broken off when required and moistened in the palm of the hand. Cavendish came in the form of a cake, and flake tobacco was made up of fine slices cut from this. More commonly, tobacco leaves were rolled into a type of rope (variously called twist, roll or pigtail depending on the thickness) and then coiled up, ready to be sold in bulk to dealers who would then serve such plugs in one ounce amounts. Third, tobacco was sold in mixtures, in which tobacconists would put together various different flavours of tobacco (usually milder leaves such as Virginian were mixed with the stronger flavours of Latakia, Perique or Turkish). These were often expensive but gained in popularity over the period and would come to be popular with briar-pipe smokers from the 1880s, who were more inclined to turn to branded items where some consistency in the quality of the mixture could be guaranteed.[29]

There is little information on the popularity of these different types of tobacco around the country but some generalisations have been made. An article in *Tobacco Trade Review* in 1891 claimed that there had been a substantial decline in the popularity of shags and birdseyes, though shags were still popular in the eastern counties, South Wales and Monmouthshire, and birdseye was enjoyed in Yorkshire. Rolls and flakes were said to be becoming more popular, the success of roll in particular provoking much competition, driving many smaller manufacturers out of business. Roll was convenient and cheap for the working man, in comparison to cake tobacco it did not require much manipulation before it was ready for the pipe, and it had a certain versatility in that it could be simply bitten off and chewed if that method of tobacco consumption was preferred. Flake, the slices of cake cavendish, began to take over from cavendish itself, also because it was ready to smoke and, through being roughly cut, provided a cooler smoke. Its popularity was due to the high quality fine gold Virginia leaf of which it often consisted, though this increased its price and explains why it was mainly popular among the better paid clerks and tradesmen. Of the many types of roll, thick twist (previously called 'Limerick') and the variations on it, such as 'nailrod' and 'sticks' (more expensive and made of good quality Virginian leaf), were extremely popular in Ireland and the North of England, where several companies were said to be devoted entirely to its manufacture. Brown roll, manufactured solely of light-coloured American tobacco, was popular in the Tyne district and in Scotland. Given the ease of consumption of flakes and rolls, the demand for cake cavendish did not increase, nor did it for the more pungent shags and twists, there being a discernible trend towards comparatively lighter tobaccos over the nineteenth century, particularly in London. Differences in taste also seemed to be the product of one's work. Scottish miners were renowned for high levels of consumption when on strike, Welsh miners were noted for their preferences for strong shags and rolls, dock labourers for their taste for thick twists, cabmen for Irish roll, and the better paid for their ability to afford high quality Virginian tobaccos. In jobs where smoking was not allowed, especially in the cotton and textile mills of Lancashire and Yorkshire, snuff continued to be commonly used, by women as well as men, as were varieties of chewing tobaccos, which were also commonly used by miners when at the coal surface.[30]

What all this diversity of consumption patterns and tastes demonstrates is that there existed a far richer culture of smoking among working-class smokers than the monolithic explanations offered in literary representation. With so many different tastes being catered for by a flexible market, it is probable that there existed just as many explanations for these tastes, so it is likely that those who preferred strong shags spoke of their tobacco consumption in ways different from those who preferred lighter flake. Many of these explanations would lie with local customs and cultures of masculinity operating within a particular workplace, but within all of these there existed also the survival of pre-industrial patterns of smoking which owed more to collective experiences of sharing tobacco than to an individual's independent regard for an object. Such traditions would account for the ability of working people to continue smoking at similar rates even when unemployed, as others would readily allow them to fill their pipes from their pouches.[31] It is entirely possible that working-class smokers spoke of their tobacco in a language similar to that presented in the periodical literature, but without access to an authentic voice no firm conclusions can be drawn. But what is more probable is that just as the pleasure of smoking a cigar was expressed through means which made sense to others who shared a similar cultural background, then so too would the smoker of thick twists and strong flakes locate his consumption within the culture of the work environment, the gender and the region of which he was a part.

A similar divergence from the dominant ideal of the periodical press can also be read into the early history of the cigar and the cigarette. Following the introduction of the cigar by military officers during the Peninsular Wars, it quickly became associated with the rather aristocratic 'dandy' and his middle-class imitator, the 'swell', in the early years of Victoria's reign. Smoking had fallen out of fashion in the polite society of the late eighteenth century as snuff became the main form of tobacco consumption, so it is not difficult to imagine how the odorous smoke of the cigar offended those not accustomed to its finer qualities. Purely as an item of fashion, and in reaction to the customs of the time, the cigar caught on among young 'gents' as a rather bohemian gesture. Exotic and decadent cigar divans were set up in London in the 1830s for these young men, who had also arrogantly taken to smoking in public, defiantly contravening the label of 'boor' that was usually attached to such behaviour. As the habit spread, so too did the number of spaces deemed acceptable for gentlemanly smoking, it becoming common from the 1820s and 1830s for women to leave the table after dinner while the men remained behind to smoke their cigars.[32]

Such a trend towards the acceptance of smoking did not go unchallenged. One writer has suggested that smoking was not tolerated on the street, in the railway carriage or after dinner at any time before the Crimean War in the 1850s, and there is certainly evidence to confirm such an opinion as notices were put up in public parks asking smokers to take heed of ladies' complaints against the cigar.[33] The cigar also helped to divide domestic space as women's complaints against the smell that lingered on the upholstered furniture and heavy drapery of Victorian drawing rooms provoked many men to set aside a special room in their house for their smoking habit. Indeed, in many ways women could use their assumed prejudice against tobacco as a means of empowerment, to avoid social situations in which they did not want to be involved. In Trollope's *The Way We Live Now*, Sir Felix Carbury aptly summarises his exasperation with women's ability to use cigar smoking to their own advantage: 'Some women swear they like smoke, others say they hate it like the devil. It depends on whether they wish to flatter or snub a fellow.'[34]

The prejudice against the aristocratic cigar smoker seems to have given way to a prejudice against middle-class 'swells' who, even more commonly, smoked in the street. By the mid century, cheaper cigars were more readily available, Dickens commenting that they were sold at Greenwich Fair for just two pence. In the 1880s, Cope's deliberately segmented the market, distributing Court cigars at 1*d* for the lower middle class, Burgomaster at 3*d* for the middle class and St George, at 4*d*, for the 'aristocracy', though this latter price suggests that the cigar was aimed at a more emulatively minded middle class.[35] In 1869, *Tobacco Trade Review* railed against the 'swells' who were said to smoke such cheap cigars, yet it is inconceivable to imagine that these smokers would not also have legitimated their habit in ways which brought them into that same smoking hierarchy from which others sought to exclude them. Aside from such prejudices, however, the nineteenth century saw the gradual social acceptance of cigar smoking, helped at the highest level by Prince Albert, an enthusiastic cigar smoker who installed a 'smoking haven' at Osborne, 'the only room with a solitary "A" instead of an entwined "V & A", over the door'.[36] The increasing visibility of the cigar in the novels of Dickens, Thackeray and Trollope further normalised its presence, and the eulogies which began to predominate increasingly throughout the period eventually placed the cigar at a level largely beyond social censure. By the mid to late Victorian period, the battle over the cultural significance of tobacco use had shifted away from the cigar and towards the cigarette.

The effeminate, foreign and somehow inferior connotations of the cigarette were mirrored in literary representations, though there was also an acceptance that these objects too could be appropriated into symbols of masculinity. In Wilkie Collins' *The Woman in White*, Count Fosco is a typically flamboyant, sartorially elegant Italian, his cigarette smoking standing in contrast to his down-to-earth cigar-smoking British host, Sir Percival. However, it is Fosco who is clearly the more resourceful, the more cunning and the domineering presence. All his cigarettes are hand rolled for him by his submissive wife, Madame Fosco, a woman who had always been regarded as forceful, opinion-ated and independent until she had been 'tamed' by her masterful husband. Collins created a character who would all too easily have been dismissed by the bourgeois smoker as lacking in manhood, yet in many ways he is pre-sented as the ideal type in the novel; even the immensely capable spinster, Marion Halcombe, is forced to admit, 'If he had married me, I should have made his cigarettes, as his wife does – I should have held my tongue when he looked at me, as she holds hers.'[37]

Even tobacco retailers, the most frequent upholders of the smoking ideal, were willing to accept the diversity of masculine types played out through the use of the cigarette. An article of 1874 celebrated the aesthetic beauty of the well-groomed swell:

> A real English 'swell' well dressed, as he invariably is, smoking his cigarette, with that quiet imperturbable air which is his chief characteristic, artistically exhaling the smoke from between his lips, or titillating the mucous membrane as he passes it through his aristocratic nostrils, delicately holding the while the fragile instrument of his pleasure between the first and second fingers of his well-gloved hand, is a pleasant picture of a smoker, and one likely to disarm the prejudices of the Anti-Tobacco Society, and all lady objectors to the habit of smoking.[38]

The cigarette had become a 'favourite accessory of luxury, indulged in by *flâneur* and statesman, epicure and aesthete alike'.[39] Rather than the cigarette representing effeminacy, then, it could also be the symbol of a very different form of masculinity.

This is no better outlined than in the character of Bertie Cecil in Ouida's *Under Two Flags*. Selling over 700,000 copies by the time of the author's death in 1908, the book is the classic Victorian romance, establishing the genre of the flight from respectability to the French Foreign Legion, and celebrating a cult of masculine military *indifférence* established in Mrs Gore's *Cecil* (1841) and G. A. Lawrence's *Guy Livingstone* (1857). Bertie Cecil – 'Beauty of the Brigades' – was an officer of the First Life Guards, forced to flee the country to join the *Chasseurs d'Afrique* in order to shield his less honourable brother and protect the name of Lady Guenevere. While the girl-soldier of the deserts of North Africa, Cigarette, would provide other connotations for her namesake, it is the beginning of the book which sees Bertie Cecil and his fellow officers make the cigarette the symbol of a seemingly paradoxical masculinity. Cecil forms part of the elite of the British military service. When called into battle he is fearless, devoted to the cause of his country and without any regard for his personal well-being. His skills are those of the supreme amateur; he wins horse races not through training or apparent effort but through an innate ability that just *is* Bertie Cecil; his physical appearance includes 'long lithe limbs, light enough and skilled enough to disdain "all training for the weights"'.[40] Yet when he is not engaged in any activity his character becomes nonchalant, his personality effete and his demeanour bored. A deep sense of languid ennui surrounds Bertie between the calls to arms, which is only filled through the pursuit of his Zu-Zus (mistresses), his sports (gaming and hunting), the card table, the careful attention to his dress and the smoking of Turkish cigarettes, though he is also known to smoke papelitos, cheroots and cigars.

The image is decidedly feminine, if not what might now be termed 'camp'. And it appears to have been a literary type which had much influence on the performance of masculinity at the time. In many ways Frederick Gustavus ('Colonel Fred') Burnaby was the living embodiment of the Ouidan ideal. His portrait by Tissot hangs in the National Portrait Gallery and shows a rather effete, pale-faced officer, languidly stretched out at one end of a sofa (figure 5). He delicately holds a cigarette away from his body while his 'long lithe' legs stretch out across the entire painting. As with Bertie, he is immaculately dressed, he stares out across the canvas with an air of disinterested boredom, and his mind seems to wander to a reality of adventure and travel away from the ephemerality of the whimsical pleasures with which he surrounds

Frederick Gustavus Burnaby (1842–85), by James (Jacques-Joseph) Tissot, 1870, National Portrait Gallery

5

himself. One cannot but help concluding that this is very much a feminine image, yet Colonel Fred Burnaby was one of the most celebrated military adventurers of his day, his famous 'Ride to Khiva' establishing him as one of the country's leading popular heroes, a man to be immortalised in song and prose. To many, he was the epitome of British masculinity, fearlessly finding his way through to Central Asia, leading the battle in Turkey and Russia, before meeting a glorious death at Abu Klea in the Sudan. As one inscription beneath a cartoon in the periodical, *Vanity Fair*, ran upon his return from Khiva: 'he may be said to possess all those qualities which in an idle and self-sufficient age go to the making of its best kind of man'.[41]

The real and fictional manliness of Burnaby and Cecil was both militaristic, powerful and resourceful and yet also rather effete and feminine. They provide the context for the flippant wit of Oscar Wilde, who penned the immortal question, 'A cigarette is the perfect type of a perfect pleasure. It is exquisite and it leaves one unsatisfied. What more can one want?', as well as Lady

Bracknell's comment in *The Importance of Being Earnest*, upon hearing that Jack is a smoker: 'I am glad to hear of it. A man should always have an occupation of some kind. There are far too many idle men in London as it is.'[42] Wilde both celebrates the cigarette in a manner similar to that found in the periodical literature, yet also imbues the cigarette with a wistful, dandy-esque quality that should be seen not so much as a form of proto-camp behaviour but as a typical example of the bored nonchalance so central to Victorian youthful masculinity.

However, by the end of the century a far more popular meaning was being ascribed to the cigarette. As it came to be smoked at all times rather than at certain moments reserved for the appreciation of a cigar, the cigarette was seen not so much as an escape from everyday life than as tool for getting through it. In Galsworthy's novels, one can detect this change in smoking patterns as there is a move away from smoking as a form of pleasure and relaxation, as in the earlier *The Man of Property*, to smoking as a form of stress relief, as seen with the use of cigarettes by Val Dartie in *In Chancery*.[43] Similarly, in Gissing's *New Grub Street*, when nervous and troubled, Jasper Milvain gives up his usual pipe and swaps it for a dozen cigarettes.[44] Significantly, Gissing sees these as adding to Milvain's nervousness: the cigarette does not bring escape from the pressures of the world, but, because of the very nature of its manufacture (the machine), it is both a part and a symbol of the modern world. As the periodical literature would have it, the smoking of a cigarette brought one in rhythm with the speed and nerves of the modern city; it did not bring relief from it. Whether cigarette smokers themselves regarded their tobacco in such a manner will be the focus of the second part of this book. But, if cigarette consumption of the twentieth century was to follow a pattern similar to that outlined for the pipe, the cigar and the cigarette in this chapter, then it is clear that smokers would have attached a diverse range of styles and meanings to their smoking practices.

Notes

1 W. Thackeray, *Vanity Fair* (1847–48; Oxford, Oxford University Press, 1983), p. 1.
2 *Ibid.*, p. 82.
3 *Ibid.*, p. 562.
4 *Ibid.*, p. 500.
5 *Ibid.*, p. 533.
6 *Ibid.*, p. 130.

7 For reviews of smoking in the literature of Conan Doyle, Dickens, Trollope and Thackeray, see U. Walsh, 'Nicotine in Dickensland', *Dickensian*, 30 (1934), 217–21; H. Cockerell, 'Tobacco in Victorian literature', in S. Lock, L. Reynolds and E. M. Tansey (eds), *Ashes to Ashes: The History of Smoking and Health* (Amsterdam, Rodopi, 1998), pp. 89–99; A. Charlton, 'Galsworthy's images of smoking in the Forsyte chronicles', *Social Science and Medicine*, 15 (1981), 633–8; R. Altick, *The Presence of the Present: Topics of the Day in the Victorian Novel* (Columbus, Ohio State University Press, 1991), pp. 240–74.

8 M. Hilton, 'Retailing history as economic and cultural history: strategies of survival by specialist tobacconists in the mass market', *Business History*, 40 (1998), 115–37. On the liberalism of retailers and the petite bourgeoisie more generally, see G. Crossick, 'Shopkeepers and the state in Britain, 1870–1914', in G. Crossick and H. G. Haupt (eds), *Shopkeepers and Master Artisans in Nineteenth-Century Europe* (London, Methuen, 1984), pp. 239–69; M. Winstanley, *The Shopkeeper's World, 1830–1914* (Manchester, Manchester University Press, 1983); F. Bechhofer and B. Elliot (eds), *The Petite Bourgeoisie: Comparative Studies of an Uneasy Stratum* (Basingstoke, Macmillan, 1981).

9 *Tobacco Trade Review* (hereafter *TTR*), various issues, 1868–1900.

10 *TTR*, 'Cheap cigarettes', 22:256 (April 1889), 96–7; *TTR*, 'Cheap cigarettes', 22:257 (May 1889), 124; *TTR*, 'A critic of cigarettes', 22:258 (June 1889), 156.

11 H. Mallalieu, 'Of pipes, puffs and politics', *Country Life* (12 August 1993), 48–9; A. V. Seaton, 'Cope's and the promotion of tobacco in Victorian England', *Journal of Advertising History*, 9:2 (1986), 5–26.

12 The Papers of John Fraser, University of Liverpool Special Collections (hereafter Fraser), 680.

13 Seaton, 'Cope's', p. 12.

14 Fraser, 1105. See also the unpublished MA dissertation held at the Fraser Collection: S. F. E. Scott, 'A good joke and a good smoke: tobacco advertising ephemera in the Fraser papers', May 1995.

15 Obituary in *Cigar and Tobacco World*, 14:3 (March 1902), 129, held in Fraser 682 (5); R. D. Altick, '*Cope's Tobacco Plant*: an episode in Victorian journalism', *Papers of the Bibliographic Society of America*, 45 (1951), 333–50.

16 *Cope's Tobacco Plant*, 1:1 (March 1870), 12, in Fraser 665. From 1870 to 1880 John Fraser collected press cuttings that commented on tobacco and Cope's publications: Fraser 680.

17 In 1885 there was a similar promotional event with the publication of a collection of *Cope's Tobacco Plant* articles as *Cope's Tobacco Leaves for the Smoking Room* (Fraser 626).

18 *Cope's Smoke Room Booklets*: 3. *Selections from Original Contributions by James Thomson to Cope's Tobacco Plant* (1889: Fraser 632); 4. *Charles Lamb in Pipefuls* (1890: Fraser 633); 5. *Thomas Carlyle, Table Talk* (1890: Fraser 634); 13. *John Ruskin on Himself and Things in General* (1893: Fraser 642) (the Ruskin publication was withdrawn after a few days following legal proceedings by Ruskin's publisher); 2., 6. and 10. *The Smoker's Garland* (1889–90: Fraser 631, 635, 639).

19 *TTR*, 'Cheap pipes', 19:217 (January 1886), 1; *TTR*, 'Clay pipes', 19:225 (September 1886), 215; Anon., 'The divine weed: in two parts', *All the Year Round*, 69 (19 and 26 September 1891), 271–8, 296–301.

20 C. Dickens, *The Pickwick Papers* (1836–37; Ware, Wordsworth, 1993), pp. 188, 241.

21 M. L. de la Ramée [Ouida], *Under Two Flags* (1867; Oxford, Oxford University Press, 1995), p. 116.

22 W. Collins, *The Moonstone* (1868; Ware, Wordsworth, 1993, p. 164).

23 Charlton, 'Galsworthy's images', p. 634.

24 Anon., 'The costs, joys and woes of smoking', *London Society*, 15 (1869), 555; *TTR*, 'On smoking', 2:22 (October 1869), 158.

25 Anon., 'All in the clouds', *All the Year Round*, 15:369 (19 May 1866), 448; Anon., 'Old English tobacco pipes', *Chambers' Journal*, 73 (1 August 1896), 495–6; *TTR*, 'Clay pipes', 6:70 (October 1873), 123; R. Quick, 'The antiquity of the tobacco pipe', *Antiquary*, 42 (1906), 20–3. An extensive literature can be found in E. Umberger, *Tobacco and Its Use* (New York, Rochester, 1996), pp. 146–69.

26 *TTR*, 'On smoking', 2:22 (October 1896), 158; *TTR*, 'Novelties', 8:85 (January 1875), 6; Anon., 'Concerning pipes', *All the Year Round*, 10:245 (9 September 1893), 247.

27 Collins, *The Moonstone*, p. 282.

28 B. W. E. Alford, *W. D. & H. O. Wills and the Development of the UK Tobacco Industry* (London, Methuen, 1973), p. 97; *TTR*, 'Changes in the loose tobacco trade', 32:373 (January 1899), 4.

29 *TTR*, 'What to smoke?', 4:41 (May 1871), 59; *TTR*, 'On the tobacco trade', 10:115 (July 1877), 79–80.

30 Alford, *W. D. & H. O. Wills*, p. 109; *TTR*, 'Increase of the Irish roll trade', 2:13 (January 1869), 8–9; *TTR*, 'Decline of the snuff trade', 2:16 (April 1869), 56; *TTR*, 'On the tobacco trade', 10:115 (July 1877), 79; *TTR*, 'The tobacco trade of Scotland', 19:218 (February 1886), 42; *TTR*, 'The tobacco trade of Scotland', 20:231 (March 1887), 78; *TTR*, 'Irish roll', 23:270 (June 1890), 158; *TTR*, 'Trade topics', 24:277 (January 1890), 24; *TTR*, 'Trade topics', 24:279 (March 1890), 68; *TTR*, 'Chewing tobacco: points for the retailer', 27:323 (November 1894), 337–8.

31 *TTR*, 'The tobacco trade of Scotland', p. 42.

32 Seaton, 'Cope's', p. 17; Altick, *Presence of the Present*, p. 242.

33 W. Beatty-Kingston, *A Journalist's Jottings* (London, Chapman and Hall, 1890), 'The triumphs of smoke', pp. 136–42; Altick, *Presence of the Present*, p. 244.

34 A. Trollope, *The Way We Live Now* (1874–75; London, The Trollope Society, 1992), p. 19.

35 Walsh, 'Nicotine in Dickensland', p. 220; Seaton, 'Cope's', p. 7.

36 Altick, *Presence of the Present*, p. 249.

37 W. Collins, *The Woman in White* (1859–60; Harmondsworth, Penguin, 1994), p. 192.

38 *TTR*, 'The manufacture of cigarettes', 7:77 (May 1874), 54.

39 *TTR*, 'Notes of novelties', 14:161 (May 1881), 81.
40 Ouida, *Under Two Flags*, p. 23.
41 M. Alexander, *The True Blue: The Life and Adventures of Colonel Fred Burnaby 1842–1885* (London, Rupert Hart-Davis, 1957), p. 82.
42 O. Wilde, *The Picture of Dorian Gray* and *The Importance of Being Earnest*, in *The Works of Oscar Wilde* (London, Collins, n. d.), pp. 96, 293.
43 Charlton, 'Galsworthy's images', p. 635.
44 G. Gissing, *New Grub Street* (1891; Ware, Wordsworth, 1996), p. 248.

3

The 'evils of smoking' in the Victorian anti-tobacco movement

In 1855, Thomas Reynolds, leading campaigner and Secretary of the British Anti-Tobacco Society, visited Cambridge to lecture to the students and local residents on the dangers and evils of smoking. He had already toured fifteen counties and was aiming to cover the whole of Britain. He was used to speaking in sparsely attended town halls and Mechanics' Institutes, but at Cambridge he found the room packed to the rafters with boisterous under-graduates who had come brandishing their pipes and cigars ready to protest at what they felt to be a ridiculous movement. Reynolds was not a man to be intimidated by such a presence and it seems they provoked him into levels of hyperbole extreme even for his colourful denunciations of 'the devil's weed'. When the students began to puff at their pipes and cigars Reynolds lost 'his presence of mind, expressed himself somewhat warmly, and a general distur-bance ensued; forms were overthrown, women screamed . . . and assaults were committed'. Eventually there was a 'general *melee*', the Mayor and police were sent for, several students were arrested and Reynolds had to be escorted to a side room 'to escape the fury of his assailants'.[1]

That one is able to learn of this 'disgraceful incident' is indicative of Reynolds' personality. Not content with provoking what might normally have been regarded as an embarrassing fiasco to be quickly forgotten, he went on to publish a pamphlet entitled, *A Memento of the Cambridge Tobacco Riot*, complete with press cuttings and commentaries. Reynolds thrived on such adversity, taking a perverse pleasure in the difficulties he came up against in what he clearly saw as his 'crusade' against smoking. When he launched the *Anti-Tobacco Journal* in 1858, he claimed to have suffered degrees of torment similar to John Bunyan's hesitations over *Pilgrim's Progress*.[2] By the time of his death in 1875 he had lectured to numerous public meetings, boys' clubs, temperance organisations, schools and chapels, as well as the British Association for the Advancement of Science (BAAS), where the President of the physiological section demonstrated an affinity with the Cambridge undergraduates as he 'condemned' Reynolds' whole lecture as 'unworthy of a scientific society'.[3]

In this sense, it is easy to locate Reynolds as a typical public-spirited Victorian evangelical philanthropist, imbued with a missionary zeal against what he saw as the source of all vice. But the tone of his arguments ensured that both he and his movement did not enjoy quite the same popular appeal as, say, the temperance societies. While the moral and medical arguments employed against tobacco might have won many sympathisers, some of the more vivid examples of his own wild imaginations brought sustenance only to his detractors. For instance, he confidently but groundlessly told of how all but one of a ship's crew was murdered by a group of cannibals, the exception being the smoker who did not appeal to the barbarians' palate for he tasted too much of tobacco.[4] Reynolds claimed that if 5 per cent of the £26,000 spent on expanding Manchester's gaol facilities had been used instead in a campaign against smoking, then 'there would have been no need of additional prison accommodation', and that both Napoleon and Guy Fawkes were under the narcotic influence of tobacco when they made their fateful decisions.[5] All such inventions were secondary to the evangelicalism of Reynolds' anti-tobaccoism: 'Not only is the use of Tobacco an infringement to the laws of nature, but it defeats the designs of our God, our Maker; and that which defeats His designs for purposes of mere sensuous gratification, must obviously be an affront to his Divine and excellent Majesty.'[6]

Such was the man whom Cope's represented as a spectre in the clouds, a 'denouncer of doom . . . livid with impotent spite'.[7] Reynolds may have been his own worst enemy in the attention he occasionally attracted to his Anti-Tobacco Society but the movement as a whole should not be dismissed. Beginning in 1853, the Society attracted sympathetic responses from a whole range of concerned medical, religious and philanthropic figures, and was able to continue throughout the rest of the century as another society was set up in Manchester in 1867, established along similar radical evangelical principles. By the turn of the century, the movement had received renewed impetus in the campaigns against juvenile smoking led by other figures and organisations which had some bearing on the form of the 1908 Children's Act, which prohibited the sale of tobacco and cigarettes to persons under sixteen years of age.[8]

Throughout, the movement employed a variety of religious and scientific arguments which together provided a particular yet coherent critique of smoking. That anti-tobaccoism was only ever something of an extremist fringe of the temperance movement is demonstrated by the reactions to Reynolds and the ability of the pro-smoking forces (which were considerable at the time as they included most of mainstream printed culture) to caricature its proponents to the point of derision. However, there was much shared in the ways in which different groups spoke about tobacco. On one level, those who sought to celebrate the 'divine weed' were diametrically opposed to those who saw it as the work of the Devil, but on another, there was much held in common in the debates as to the meaning of this object. Both pro-smokers and anti-smokers could be said to have shared a broadly liberal outlook on life, as both placed particular emphasis on individuality and independence. Male smokers wrote of the need for independence in the cultivation of highly individualistic tastes and consumption mannerisms. Anti-smokers thought one lost one's physical and moral independence through the 'enslavement' to a 'habit' that detracted from one's true devotional duty, which could only be to God. For one group, individuality came through the freedom to choose how and what to smoke; for another, individuality was only realised in the freedom gained in not smoking.

There were many other strands to anti-tobaccoism that ran alongside radical nonconformity, but what will be made evident is that the culture of individuality and independence is the most appropriate means to understand both smoking and the reactions to it in the mid to late nineteenth century. The chapter will begin with a brief overview of the developments in the history of organised anti-tobaccoism, before moving on to a discussion of the reception of the movement in the periodical and popular press. A detailed analysis will then take place of the constituent elements of anti-tobacco propaganda, and a final section will study the specific attitudes to juvenile smoking and why other groups were ready to generate their own agendas against this aspect of tobacco use. That the government was able to introduce legislation against a specific act of consumption – that is, to interfere in the liberal individual's right to determine what to put in his own body – was due to an increasingly accepted attitude that children and adolescents did not enjoy the full discerning powers of the rational adult.

Anti-smoking ideas have a history stretching back to the introduction of tobacco into European culture. Smoking was negatively portrayed and represented in sources as diverse as early seventeenth-century Dutch art and the notorious *Counterblaste* of James I.[9] Although fiscal necessities would moderate

James' attitude to tobacco, he famously complained of the dirt, waste and self indulgence of the habit, thereby setting the terms of reference for the debates about tobacco over the next 250 years,[10] when the rise of the cigar-smoking dandy in the 1840s brought about renewed controversy.[11] In this decade, Thomas Cook, the travel industry entrepreneur, attempted to start an anti-smoking movement with his journal, the *Anti-Smoker and Progressive Temperance Reformer*, but it was not until the 1850s that the organised movement took off to any noticeable extent.[12]

In April 1853, Thomas Reynolds instituted the Anti-Tobacco Society. Of the initial 146 promoters of the Society, 38 were active scientists, the remainder being moralists, evangelicals and social critics.[13] In this sense, the Society was part of that broadly nonconformist tradition which influenced so much of Victorian public life, and it is best to understand the anti-smokers as a minority fringe element of those other medico-moral campaigns against the perceived vices of drinking, opium taking and gambling.[14] In its initial four years of existence its activities were minimal, and the degree of support it received is best reflected in the fact that Reynolds was able to raise only £267 over two years to set up his *Anti-Tobacco Journal*. However, the movement was able to take advantage of the 'Great Tobacco Controversy' which raged in the pages of the *Lancet* in 1857. The Edinburgh surgeon and member of the anti-tobacco society, Professor John Lizars, had earlier published his *Practical Observations on the Use and Abuse of Tobacco* (1854), but it was not until Samuel Solly's 'Clinical lectures on paralysis' appeared in the *Lancet* in December 1856 that the medical profession turned its attention to tobacco.[15] Solly provoked a heated debate when he linked the recent upsurge in tobacco consumption with the cases of 'general paralysis' that were being more frequently cited. With letters from self-proclaimed authorities on the issue pouring in every week, the *Lancet* eventually devoted two editorials to the issue, in the hope of ending the controversy until an extensive investigation had been made. The arguments expanded outwards to other journals, ranging from medical publications such as the *British Medical Journal*, to the *Athanaeum*, to more general interest monthlies, and on to *The Times* and the popular press. The evidence cited in the debates ranged from reviews of other investigations to single cases of tobacco poisoning. In the early letters, readers of the *Lancet* were provided with the useful hint that one should not smoke when suffering from typhoid because it led to peritonitis and consequently death.[16] Apparently, teetotallers who broke their pledges were always smokers,[17] and 'all our greatest men . . . intellectually, statesmen, lawyers, warriors, physicians and surgeons, have either not been smokers, or, if smokers, . . . have died prematurely'.[18] On the other side, pro-smoking medics argued their position by reference to more general opinions such as, 'the fact of smoking being almost universal appears alone sufficient to indicate that there can be no very great harm resulting from it'.[19] At times, the arguments approached the slanderous, with the anti-tobacconists accusing those in favour of smoking and who had left their letters unsigned of being infiltrators in the debate from the tobacco trade;[20] the pro-smokers referred to the 'excited imaginations' of those against.[21] Medical and moral arguments were, therefore, inextricably linked during the *Lancet's* 'Great Tobacco Controversy'.

After 1857 and the initial flurry of pamphlets by Reynolds and his Anti-Tobacco Society, which sought to capitalise on this great media event, anti-smoking activity again became minimal to the point of obscurity. After Reynolds' death, his daughter edited the *Anti-Tobacco Journal* until the turn of the century, but it was continued with no great enthusiasm. Instead, activity shifted northwards with the formation of the Manchester and Salford Anti-Tobacco Society in 1867, later known as the North of England Anti-Tobacco Society, then in 1872 as the English Anti-Tobacco Society and, by the time of the publication of its official organ, the *Beacon Light*, in the 1890s, the British Anti-Tobacco and Anti-Narcotic League. The membership was similar to the earlier Society in that there existed a strong nonconformist religious element but, perhaps because it was a Northern-based institution, there were far fewer prominent medical figures and many nonconformist Liberal manufacturers already associated with the temperance cause.[22]

The movement appears to have been slightly larger than the earlier one, though its finances again amounted to only a few hundred pounds per annum.[23] Membership figures fluctuated around the six hundred mark, but often about half of these had to be reminded that their subscriptions were due, perhaps hinting at a certain lack of enthusiasm among the contributors to Society funds. The Society refrained from the use of public lectures, quickly realising the difficulty in attracting smokers, and instead chose to concentrate on the distribution and sale of books, tracts and pamphlets, though total annual distribution rates of all materials only ever amounted to a few tens of thousands and the movement faced difficulties in getting its material published.[24] By 1878 its *Monthly Letter* had a circulation, if not a readership, figure of over twenty thousand. This developed into the *Beacon Light* in 1896, the official organ of the movement, which sold at $\frac{1}{2}d$ every month and which claimed that the Anti-Narcotic League was the 'most thorough-going

Temperance Society in existence', since it pledged total abstinence from drink, tobacco, chlorodyne, opium and laudanum.[25]

Despite such a broad set of objectives, however, the movement was increasingly focusing its efforts on juvenile smoking, a late Victorian and Edwardian social problem identified by a whole range of organisations within and without the existing anti-smoking movement. As will be seen in chapter 7, neither reformers from outside the Manchester organisation nor Reynolds' older Anti-Tobacco Society provided the impetus for the new bodies set up to oppose specifically juvenile smoking and to provide the evidence in the government committees which examined the perceived problem. After the smoking clauses of the Children's Act effectively met the legislative calls of the anti-juvenile smoking organisations, many rapidly withered away, ceasing to exist. The *Beacon Light* continued to be published until December 1928, but it showed an ever declining membership of the Anti-Narcotic League, and eventually the movement was replaced by the National Society of Non-Smokers, an organisation set up not to oppose tobacco but to defend the interests of those who preferred not to consume it. The final publication reprinted the tobacco catechism, written by Thomas Reynolds many decades earlier, and reported on the £10 million legacy left by Sir George Alfred Wills of the Imperial Tobacco Company. Taken together, the former seemed to represent the inapplicability of Reynolds' mid Victorian evangelicalism to early twentieth-century society, and the latter the final triumph of the anti-smokers' main enemy, the tobacco manufacturer.[26]

The anti-tobacco movement, then, was never as successful in Britain as the campaigns against the other 'minor vices', nor as prominent as a similar movement had been in the United States at around the same time. Yet there were periods when its message did stretch outside of the chapel and beyond the occasional lecture at the Mechanics' Institute. The 'Great Tobacco Controversy' received much comment and the arguments of the anti-tobacconists were intermittently pitted against those in favour of smoking in the periodical press.[27] Part of the problem for the anti-tobacconists, however, was that much of the medical evidence they presented was highly contentious and seriously disputed by many other scientific professionals, the *British Medical Journal* being particularly keen to rise above a debate 'not very creditable to the members of a learned profession'.[28] Its scepticism came not so much from claims that smoking caused dyspepsia and lip and throat cancer, but from the more apocalyptic illnesses few medics or smokers would have witnessed: deafness, blindness, and physical, mental and moral paralysis. Often, pro-smoking medics

summarily dismissed many of the arguments of the anti-tobacconists, com-
paring them with the equally meddlesome vegetarians who 'would reduce
mankind to live upon sky-blue and an apple'.[29]

More significant were the attacks on the anti-tobacconists made in the trade
press, periodicals, books in praise of tobacco and national daily newspapers.
By satirising and ridiculing the anti-smokers, the chances of anti-smoking
ideas capturing a wider audience were severely restricted. For instance,
although *Punch* could in no way be said to represent the whole spectrum of
Victorian public attitudes, its persistent attacks do testify to the problems
that the anti-tobacco movement was facing. On hearing of the existence of a
group of anti-smokers, in addition to vegetarians and drink prohibitionists,
Punch suggested organisations should be set up by 'restless and officious
noodles' against, among other things, coffee, butter, music, dancing, whist,
cricket, fishing, and soap and water: 'And, if that should not be enough to
make all rational people sick of Anti Societies, an Anti-*Punch* society to consist
of all the quacks, and humbugs, and blackguards, and asses, and curmudgeons
on the face of the earth'.[30]

As was seen in chapter 1, Cope's of Liverpool incorporated a satire of the
anti-tobacconists as part of its marketing strategy. As well as the ghostly
spectre and the trampling of the leading lights of the anti-tobacco movement
in 'In Pursuit of Diva Nicotina' (figure 3), the anti-tobacconist was further
portrayed pointlessly lecturing to a group of pipe-smoking storks, herons,
penguins and flamingos, and falling over roller skating while others were
clearly enjoying themselves (figures 6 and 7). In *Cope's Tobacco Plant*, a long-
running campaign mocked the dire financial situation of the movement, the
manufacturers cheekily offering Reynolds a £1,000 testimonial if he would
stop publishing the *Anti-Tobacco Journal*. Later, so confident were they of
the strength of their own position over the supposedly hysterical rantings of
the anti-tobacconists, they offered to devote a page of each issue of *Cope's
Tobacco Plant* to the anti-smoking cause.[31] They suggested that Reynolds was
his own worst enemy, they parodied his *Anti-Tobacco Journal* articles, and
even proposed the setting up of an 'Anti-Teapot Society' to suggest the
pointlessness of his task.[32] Reynolds never rose to the bait, but had he done so
he would at least have found himself communicating to a larger number of
people than he had ever done before.

At the same time, the anti-tobacconists received no support from *The
Times*. Whereas this newspaper had reported on the 'Great Tobacco Controversy' with a degree of impartiality, listening in earnest to the anti-smoking

The anti-tobacco lecture, Cope Brothers' advertisement, 1870s **6**

Rinking, Cope Brothers' advertisement, 1877 **7**

arguments of qualified medics, by the 1870s its patience with the wilder accusations against tobacco had run out. Reprinting an article from the *Pall Mall Gazette*, readers were told that although a meeting of the British Anti-Tobacco Society had been small, 'this deficiency was compensated by the remarkable magnitude of the conclusions at which the meeting arrived'. In response to the claims that smoking led to cancer, insanity, paralysis and 'a number of terrible and incurable diseases', the article claimed that non-smoking led to the 'pedantry, arrogance and bigotry' of James I, the immorality of the Restoration and, having 'the evidence of the chairman himself to its fatal effects upon business habits and upon the qualities which lead to commercial success', to the society's own annual balance of account of '£42 9s 6d on the wrong side'.[33] Thus when the business of the Anti-Tobacco Society finally made national news for the first time, it was definitively presented as a hopeless lost cause.

Given this background of limited success – the huge increase in tobacco consumption in the late nineteenth century being a particularly illustrative guide to the impact of the anti-smoking movement – there is still much to be learnt from the content of anti-tobacco thought. Naturally, it shared much with ideas utilised against other psychoactive substances, and the movement could be regarded as the radical wing of the campaign against drink. What made the politicisation of tobacco distinctive, though, is the extent to which medical arguments played a prominent role in the critique of the substance. This is no better shown than in the initial impetus given to Reynolds' organisation from the 1857 *Lancet* debates. The medics writing in the *Lancet*, however, should not be seen as existing outside of the moral temperance tradition, as many of their arguments were closely aligned to classic examples from the canon of anti-drink propaganda. While research into the scientific properties and physiological effects of tobacco was most prominent, the letters written in the first half of 1857 were permeated with moral and religious concerns. Many did point to aspects of tobacco and smoking which were both then and now held to be true (e.c. poison, nausea, tobacco amblyopia, dyspepsia, epithelomenia), but they also referred to other illnesses which would become the mainstays of anti-tobacco propaganda in subsequent decades (paralysis, insanity, idleness, hysteria, rickets, impotence, loss of memory), showing how interwoven were medical and moral concerns. The 'eminent' Samuel Solly, at founder member of the Anti-Tobacco Society in 1853, first called for more research and argued that tobacco smoking could lead to irritability, nervousness, and intermittent pulse, as well as the paralysis to which he had already referred. By the time he penned his second letter he had moved beyond the medical and scientific evidence to complain about the high expenditure made on tobacco by male youths of the middle class: 'But how many a lad spends such money when his father can little spare it out of his hard-earned income?'[34] Solly believed it was more manly and Christian to face one's problems than to use tobacco to soothe them and, eventually, he positioned himself well within the rhetoric of mid nineteenth-century temperance: 'Are not all troubles sent by an all-wise Providence to improve the character, and, by self-control, raise the soul above the influence of the carnal nature?'[35]

In contrast, some writers from outside the medical profession used an overtly religious message also found in the campaign against the 'demon' drink and which made little use of any medical evidence. Several authors would refer to scripture extensively in their condemnation of the smoking vice to demonstrate that enslavement to a habit prevented devotion to the Lord.[36] And others still, of a more imaginative nature, vividly recalled their demonic dreams:

> I thought I was smoking a cigar and it broke in the centre, and out of it came a fearful looking bug which swelled to a large size, and had the head of *Satan* on it, and after grinning horribly at me, it reduced its size, and while I was wondering at it, suddenly it leaped down my throat, and the gnawing pain woke me up.[37]

Beyond the extremities of such anti-tobacco hallucinations were ideas more in tune with general attitudes in Victorian society. There was much debate on the nature of moderation and excess (alternatively termed 'use' and 'abuse'), the *Lancet's* attitude being particularly illustrative of the spirit of compromise many periodicals occasionally made with the anti-tobacconists. The editors openly professed their philosophy of life to be moderation and they attempted to define what this and 'excess' were.[38] Smoking before breakfast was excess, as was 'slavery to the habit', 'premeditated sensuality' and more than two pipes or cigars a day. Also, any smoking by children and youths was deemed to be inherently excessive: 'The influence of immoral associations, and the solicitations to, and opportunities of, vice, which surround the youthful devotee to tobacco, are hardly to be resisted by the feeble will, the plastic temper, and the warm passions of juvenescence.'[39] Finally, a language of rational expenditure permeated a number of anti-tobacco statements in a manner similar to that found in temperance thought and which might have betrayed what many historians of popular culture have described as class-based 'social control'. For instance, Professor Frank Newman of the Manchester anti-tobacco organisation clearly believed it to be more important to attack working-class consumption than that of the middle or upper classes:

> Rich men may with impunity squander the shillings and pounds which smoking costs; but in working men, the expense of smoking, as of drinking, is a grave deduction from the slender funds which are to support a wife and rear children; a mere sensual and pernicious indulgence of the 'head' of the family at the expense of the 'rest'.[40]

But the main thrust of anti-tobacco rhetoric in the late nineteenth century was the continued combination of religion and science first found in the debates of 1857. A common device adopted in the pamphlets of the organised movement was to make extensive use of such figures as Samuel Solly, the physician Sir Benjamin Brodie, Charles Drysdale and Benjamin Ward Richardson, intertwining their medical evidence within a moral and religious context. With little further research into the effects of tobacco in the late nineteenth century, much of this cited medical evidence remained remarkably consistent: nausea, dyspepsia, blindness, lip and throat cancer, hysteria, paralysis, insanity, plus a variety of other illnesses rarely supported by the results of specific research. But just as the *Lancet* contributors explicitly demonstrated their moral and religious concerns, so too did those pamphleteers from outside the formal medical profession draw on scientific claims to express a commonality of shared medico-moral assumptions. For instance, the pseudonymous tract of 'Scrutator' drew on the work of Brodie, asking his readers to 'duly consider the delicate, but intelligent and faithful intimation of the illustrious Baronet. *It is as though he had said* – Smoking has a tendency to diminish that capacity which God has given you for transmitting the nature you have received.'[41] Five years later, in 1865, another famous physician, Benjamin Ward Richardson, noted how blood cells lost their round shape and became oval due to smoking.[42] Because he refused to ally himself to the anti-tobacconists, a 'Medicus' was called upon to amplify the moral elements of these medical statements in the same way that 'Scrutator' drew on Brodie's work; the implication here being that the oval cells acted on the brain in an irregular manner, thus promoting immorality as the brain became dysfunctional.[43] Other evangelical anti-tobacconists were able to use the scientific evidence more generally and attempted to provide a coherent and authoritative support to their moralistic arguments. Francis Close, Dean of Carlisle and President of the Anti-Tobacco Society, spoke at the Athenaeum in Carlisle in 1859:

Had no moral evils been traceable to the immoderate use of this powerful weed I might have left the discussion of its properties to the chemist, the physician or the natural philosopher . . . [B]ut inasmuch as every person who is in the last degree acquainted with the subject knows that it does, and must, exercise a powerful influence over the moral man through his nervous system and by the brain, I conceive that this is a matter of debate which not only lies within the proper province of the divine, but loudly demands his serious attention. If tobacco be a moral agent, its use must either impede or promote our direct religious labours – it must be our handmaid, assisting us in our spiritual and pastoral duties, or it must be a hindrance.[44]

Here, Close separates the physician and the chemist from the divine, in order to ensure the authority of clerics, if not in medical debate *per se*, then at least in its broader implications. Just as medics have been held to have discursively distinguished between science and religion in order to increase their own authority in the mid nineteenth century,[45] then so too did Close similarly establish clerical authority in what was a social debate about correct conduct in one's body and mind. By such means Close was then able to present himself as an indispensable authority who commanded the expertise to translate from the medical to the moral.

Other pamphleteers were less sophisticated and there was a tendency for a number of articles to cite the medical evidence in varying degrees of detail before they were able to give voice to their moral and religious objections to smoking.[46] But a number of medics sought to translate from the moral to the scientific, actively strengthening their medical evidence with religious references. Charles Drysdale, in the interests of 'the mission of the Science of Hygiene', claimed that 'it remains for scientific observers and moralists to enlighten their fellow countrymen and women to subjects so momentous to their health'.[47] Although a medic, he denounced tobacco not only on health grounds but because it retarded human happiness. Henry Gibbons went still further, equating medical with moral and religious truth: 'the laws of health are the laws of God'.[48] The inseparability of science and religion could not have been made more explicit.

By the end of the nineteenth century the focus of anti-tobacco propaganda was aimed almost exclusively at the problem of juvenile smoking. This is not to say, of course, that concerns had not been expressed about children by the anti-tobacco societies for some time. As early as 1856 legislation was first suggested for the suppression of juvenile street smoking,[49] but by the turn of the century appeals were being made directly to children, as well as to parents, teachers, social reformers and others who had an interest in the child's development. The main way in which the movement attempted to appeal to the interests of the boys was to assume that they smoked to be like men, and then to challenge this notion of manliness.[50] Smoking was said to be indulged in only by cowards because they were too scared to admit that it made them ill, and it also contradicted manliness because it prevented boys from being big and strong. Children were told in the pamphlets that famous athletes, footballers, doctors, businessmen and soldiers did not smoke. And, as Baden-Powell was frequently keen to tell the nation's future soldiers, scouts who smoked 'generally turn to rotters' afterwards and 'any man who has done any scouting or big game hunting, etc., knows that . . . the best scouts avoid the use of tobacco because they consider it harms their eyesight and sense of smell, on which they have to rely a good deal when reconnoitring by night.'[51] In assuming that all boys smoked purely to appear as men the anti-tobacconists made the same over-simplification as the turn-of-the-century social reformers who did not address the full range of interests of the urban working-class youth. As will be seen in chapter 7, a variety of influences provoked the boy to choose smoking over other 'leisure' pursuits.

In the calls for legislation, the medical evidence cited to support such an action was never that comprehensive. This was because legislators, moralists and scientists shared a set of assumptions about appropriate adolescent behaviour. Consequently, only a few medical investigations were made into juvenile smoking,[52] showing how the child smoker suffered from a variety of illnesses, although some medics pointed out that these problems could be just as much to do with under-nourishment.[53] Anti-tobacconists and the medical profession generally shared the assumption that 'if the adult constitution is unable to resist many of the worst effects of tobacco, the unformed frames of our youth are certain to suffer from it'.[54] Anti-tobacconists never had to explain in detail to their readers exactly why differences should be made between developing and developed bodies. They shared a set of ideas about youth that many of their readers were increasingly accepting. A concern about the psychological development of children had been growing ever since the developments in public school education had sought to prolong the idealised period of childhood. The result was a feeling, increasingly among the middle classes, that a new period of life termed 'adolescence' existed between childhood and adulthood.[55] Smoking was incompatible with these developing ideas since its very precocity contradicted the idea that adolescence was a period of extended childhood, rather than preparation for the adult world. These new notions of adolescence were gaining ascendancy among both the future Liberal legislators and the middle-class social reformers who began to perceive the problems of the urban male youth around the turn of the century. These reformers problematised juvenile smoking as well as many other areas of urban and child life, and they came to be a major influence on the Liberal welfare reforms of the 1900s, of which the Children's Act was a part.[56]

However, it is also difficult in this turn-of-the-century period to separate the anti-tobacco movement's rhetoric concerning the child from attitudes towards the nation and racial degeneration. It was commonplace for anti-tobacconists to attribute the condition of nations to the use of tobacco, Brodie commenting that both the 'Red Indians' and the 'lazy and lethargic Turks' had suffered racial decline through smoking.[57] If Britain was to avoid such a fate then the nation's youth must flourish:

> If our beloved country, is to escape the dire humiliation which recently surprised the French people [the Franco-Prussian War], and if it is to continue to sustain a fore-most rank among nations, its youth must forswear the indulgences into which too many recklessly plunge – gratifications only becoming age – and omit no opportunity of invigorating body and mind, that they may be ever ready for 'life's duty,' lest one day some hostile nation should hurl confederated legions upon our sacred isle, and find Britain but a name, and her sons degenerate.[58]

By the time of the Boer War, when it was claimed that 'perhaps a third of the "rejects" from the army in Lancashire might be attributed to "smoker's heart"',[59] the idea that youths and children should stop smoking for the sake of the nation was commonplace in anti-tobacco literature.

The moral and religious claims about adolescence therefore perfectly matched the agendas of the new 'sciences' of racial eugenics and child psychology. John Quincey Adams Henry, in *The Deadly Cigarette*, stressed the importance of the child to 'Christian civilisation': 'the child is the guarantee of civilisation. It is the nation's first and most valuable asset. The cause that enlists the children inherits the future.' Adolescence was a 'religious' age when the child must be 'saved' from evil influences, 'for if we fail to save the children, we shall certainly lose the State'. Anti-tobacco thought gave equal weighting to religion and science, as both were united when located within fears about national decline and inappropriate adolescent behaviour:

> The expert testimony of the world demands it; the safety of the state requires it; the salvation of the Child necessitates it; the success of life advocates it; the future of Christian civilisation calls for it – and, above all, God wills it. Then death to the deadly cigarette! Deliverance to its deluded devotee! Let learning, love, and law combine to crush the viper, curb the passion, and cure the sin of Juvenile Smoking.[60]

But precisely because anti-tobacco ideas matched wider social concerns about the nature of childhood, it is possible that even in this situation they had little impact and that the juvenile smoking clauses of the 1908 Children's Act arose from quite independent sources. The anti-tobacconists did not have to persuade any other groups because these were themselves developing their own similar agendas. This is no more clear than in a pamphlet entitled *The Physiologist in the Household* by J. Milner Fothergill, who appears to have had no links with the anti-tobacco movement. Written in 1880, it is an early example of how developments in the psychology of childhood, or adolescence, were related to perceived social problems such as juvenile smoking. Fothergill argued that the innocent child was quick to follow its instincts and impulses so that it erred 'as much from ignorance as from vice'. The 'plastic period of youth' ought to be moulded and trained to avoid early maturity, which was a sign of a 'low standard of development'.[61] Town, and especially London, children were singled out for their precocity, and he suggested that the cigarette was particularly symbolic of this problem. To Fothergill, smoking was held to be wrong not because it was intrinsically harmful, but because it was socially incompatible with idealised notions of adolescent behaviour. Such a belief enabled many pro-smoking adults to oppose juvenile smoking as a specific issue.[62] It would be exactly these latter understandings of tobacco and children which would motivate the legislators of 1908.

When the Children's Act prohibited the sale of tobacco products to youths less than sixteen years of age, it symbolised the assumed inability of children to think independently about their consumption decisions. In this sense, juveniles were denied the full rights of the liberal individual at the same time as the state was allowed to interfere in their lives. Scientific evidence was utilised to legitimate this action, though had this science been scrutinised as rigorously as earlier general claims about the effects of tobacco, then it would not have been seen as credible. But other forms of science had created a sharp distinction between the adult and the child which enabled some government intervention into the free forces of the market economy. The male adult, however, was still regarded (by groups interested in the formulation of legislation) from a liberal individualistic framework, in which each man had the power to decide what he could or could not put in his own body. The bourgeois-liberal's ability to discern the taste and quality of a product also extended to the ability to choose which products were good for him in the first place: knowledge for consumption ultimately resided in the individual rather than in institutions beyond his control. This principle remained a powerful bulwark against any anti-tobacco demands to control adult consumption.

But the anti-tobacco movement rarely suggested that consumption should be controlled by the state. It shared that culture of independence which opposed state intervention in matters of individual choice. This liberal culture was not only based on the rights to independence of the individual but on his or her duties to others, to the self, to the family, to God and to the nation. Just as the pro-smokers were able to speak of the purposeful aspects of their consumption, anti-smokers were able to justify their proclamation against a freely traded commodity through the higher purpose they served. The temperance pamphleteer, J. G. Digges, wrote directly about the individual reformer's responsibility:

> The habitually temperate, also, have their responsibility. No man is free to say, 'This does not concern me.' For, though his steady self-control may have hedged him round with safety, there are, in all probability, among his relatives and close personal friends, some to whom this remedy [to cure inebriety] would be as life from the dead; and this may be the glorious achievement of bringing health and happiness to such.[63]

The anti-tobacconists' notion of the relationship between man and society enabled them to seek to persuade other individuals of the folly of their smoking. It did not matter that their understanding of the meaning of tobacco was at odds with the vast majority of the population, for what is important was that they opposed smoking on similar principles to those held by the people who smoked themselves. While anti-smokers and pro-smokers located their attitude to smoking within a broader conception of the purposeful nature of their actions, where they came to meet was in their attitudes to juvenile smoking. Both respected the freedom of the adult individual, however variously this was interpreted, but both acknowledged the lack of freedom in the still developing child. For this section of the smoking community, many accepted the legitimacy of state intervention in this sphere.

Even though the anti-smokers were a minority movement, on the extreme fringe of temperance thought, the fact that they existed at all is indicative of the general culture in which they existed. The liberal attitudes to the rights and duties of the individual which pervaded all aspects of Victorian culture differ very much from the liberal market economy which has developed in the twentieth century. Here, nonconformist religious beliefs have been seen as increasingly anachronistic when applied to the consumption of tobacco. Significantly, the anti-tobacco movement largely collapsed after the introduction of the Children's Act. Instead, there emerged a National Society of Non-Smokers (NSNS), an organisation which in no way sought to interfere in the individual's right to freedom of choice, but which aimed to promote the non-smoker's right to consume other services – trains, theatres, cinemas, buses – in a smoke-free environment. By the inter-war period, virtually nobody campaigned against the evils of smoking in Britain, and although this might be explained with particular reference to the specificities of the history of tobacco and cigarettes, it might also be due to a much broader cultural shift in which there was a different understanding of the relationship between the product, the market and the individual. It is to this new environment – in this case the rise of the cigarette – that the next section of this books turns.

Notes

1 T. Reynolds, *A Memento of the Cambridge Tobacco Riot* (London, 1855), p. 3.
2 *Anti-Tobacco Journal* (hereafter *ATJ*), 3 (January 1859), 25.
3 T. Reynolds, *Smoke Not! No. 5. The Substance of a Lecture Delivered to the Pupils at Totteridge Park, Herts* (London, Elliot Stock, 1866); *Smoke Not! No. 11. To Smokers! Medical and Non-medical. A Sermon Delivered at Ewen Place Chapel, Glasgow* (London, Elliot Stock, 1860); *The Outline of a Lecture (on Tobacco) Delivered in Oxford* (London, Houlston & Stoneman, 1854); *A Lecture on the Great Tobacco Question, Delivered in the Mechanics Institute, Salford* (Manchester, W. Bremner, 1857); for the lecture to the BAAS see B. W. Richardson, *For and Against Tobacco, or Tobacco in Its Relations to the Health of Individuals and Communities* (London, John Churchill, 1865), p. 42.
4 Reynolds, *Lecture on the Great Tobacco Question*, p. 20.
5 *Ibid.*, p. 17; T. Reynolds, *Globules for Tobacco-Olators* (London, Houlston & Stoneman, 1855), p. 22.
6 Reynolds, *Lecture on the Great Tobacco Question*, p. 6.
7 The Papers of John Fraser, University of Liverpool Special Collections (Fraser), 1105.
8 R. B. Walker, 'Medical aspects of tobacco smoking and the anti-tobacco movement in Britain in the nineteenth century', *Medical History*, 24 (1980), 391–402; M. Hilton and S. Nightingale, ' "A microbe of the devil's own make": religion and science in the British anti-tobacco movement, 1853–1908', in S. Lock, L. A. Reynolds and E. M. Tansey (eds), *Ashes to Ashes: The History of Smoking and Health* (London, Rodopi, 1998), pp. 41–77. I am indebted to Simon Nightingale for the influence he has had on this chapter.
9 See J. Goodman, 'Why tobacco? Europeans, forbidden fruits and the panacea gospel', in *Tobacco in History: The Cultures of Dependence* (London, Routledge, 1993), ch. 3, pp. 37–55; James I, 'A counterblaste to tobacco', in R. S. Rait, *A*

Royal Rhetorician (London, Constable, 1900), pp. 29–59; D. Harley, 'The beginnings of the tobacco controversy: puritanism, James I, and the royal physicians', *Bulletin of the History of Medicine*, 67:1 (1967), 28–50; L. Harrison, 'Tobacco battered and pipes shattered: a note on the first British campaign against tobacco smoking', *British Journal of Addiction*, 81 (1986), 553–8.

10 J. M. Price, 'Tobacco use and tobacco taxation: a battle of interests in early modern Europe', in J. Goodman, P. E. Lovejoy and A. Sherrat (eds), *Consuming Habits: Drugs in History and Anthropology* (London, Routledge, 1995), pp. 165–85.

11 J. Browne, *Tobacco Morally and Physically Considered in Relation to Smoking and Snuff Taking* (Driffield, B. Fawcett, 1842).

12 Thomas Cook's journal ran from only 1841 to 1842: T. Cook, *Anti-Smoker Collections* (London, Elliot Stock, 1875).

13 *ATJ*, 1 (November 1858), 1.

14 For specific case studies of other vices, see B. Harrison, *Drink and the Victorians: The Temperance Question in England, 1815–1872* (London, Faber and Faber, 1971); V. Berridge and G. Edwards, *Opium and the People: Opiate Use in the Nineteenth Century* (London, Allen Lane, 1981); D. Dixon, *From Prohibition to Regulation: Bookmaking, Anti-Gambling, and the Law* (Oxford, Oxford University Press, 1991). For a similar analysis of America, see J. C. Burnham, *Bad Habits: Drinking, Smoking, Taking Drugs, Gambling, Sexual Misbehaviour and Swearing in American History* (London, New York University Press, 1993).

15 J. Lizars, *Practical Observations on the Use and Abuse of Tobacco* (Edinburgh, George Phillip, 1854); S. Solly, 'Clinical lectures on paralysis', *Lancet*, ii (1856), 641.

16 Letter from D. Johnson, *Lancet*, i (1857), 22.

17 Letter from J. B. Neil, *Lancet*, i (1857), 179.

18 Letter from S. Solly, *Lancet*, i (1857), 154.

19 Letter from 'Sedentary Suicide', *Lancet*, i (1857), 78.

20 Letter from S. Solly, *Lancet*, i (1857), 153.

21 Letter from H. G. W., *Lancet*, i (1857), 101.

22 Such figures included Joseph Pease, the Darlington Quaker MP Peter and Frank Spence of Pendleton Alum Works; Titus Salt, the famous industrial paternalist; Benjamin Whitworth, the local Liberal MP; A. E. Eccles, cotton manufacturer and Congregationalist Liberal; and Hugh Mason, JP, Chairman of the Manchester Board of Commerce.

23 *Fourth Annual Report of the English Anti-Tobacco Society, 1871* (Manchester, Anti-Tobacco Society, 1872), p. 2.

24 *Eleventh Annual Report of the English Anti-Tobacco Society, 1878* (Manchester, Anti-Tobacco Society, 1879); H. Noel-Thatcher, *The Fascinator; or, the Knight's Legacy. A Prize Essay on the Moral, Social, and Economical Results of the Use of Tobacco* (London, W. Tweedie, 1871).

25 *Beacon Light* (August 1896), 5.

26 *Beacon Light*, 501 (December 1928), p. 1.

27 *The Times*, 'Is smoking injurious to health?' (6 February 1857), p. 10; *The Times*, 'Excessive smoking' (8 April 1857), p. 12; Anon., 'Cigars and tobacco', *New Quarterly Review*, 10 (1861), 22–38; Anon., 'To smoke or not to smoke', *All the Year Round*, 13 (1865), 413–18; [Anon], 'Are our pipes to be put out?', *Once a Week*, 8:187 (27 July 1871), 89–93; F. H. Daly, 'Tobacco-smoking', *Gentleman's Magazine*, 23 (1879), 350–62; Anon., 'Is smoking injurious to health?', *Chambers' Journal*, 61 (1884), 78–80; J. Rochard, 'Tobacco and the tobacco habit', *Popular Science Monthly*, 41 (1892), 670–82; H. P. Dunn, 'Is our race degenerating?', *Nineteenth Century*, 36:210 (August 1894), 301–4.

28 *British Medical Journal* (hereafter *BMJ*), i (1857), 175.

29 *BMJ*, i (1857), 133.

30 *Punch* (14 January 1865), p. 15.

31 *Cope's Tobacco Plant*, 1:7 (October 1870), 75.

32 *Cope's Tobacco Plant*, 1:18 (September 1871), 212; 1:19 (October 1871), 217; 1:29 (August 1872), 350.

33 *The Times* (30 May 1872), p. 7b.

34 See Solly in *Lancet*, i (1857), 153–4. The *Lancet* actually published this letter once more the following week (alongside his second letter) because there had been too many demands for a copy of the past issue and 'the importance of the subject cannot be over-rated' (i (1857), 176).

35 *Ibid.*, p. 176.

36 S. Henn, *The Tobacco Curse: With Weighty Reasons why Christians Should Abstain from It* (Dudley, the author, 1880[?]); J. Driver, *The Nature of Tobacco: Showing Its Destructive Effects on Mind and Body, Especially on Juveniles* (London, Nichols & Co., 1881); J. Stock, *Confessions of an Old Smoker Respectfully Addressed to all Smoking Disciples* (London, Elliot Stock, 1872).

37 *Beacon Light* (September 1900), p. 105.

38 *Lancet*, i (1857), 324.

39 *Ibid.*, 354.

40 *Fourth Annual Report of the English Anti-Tobacco Society, 1871*, p. 4. C. Fothergill, *May Young England Smoke? A Modern Question, Medically and Socially Considered* (London, S. W. Partridge, 1876), p. 13.

41 'Scrutator', *Smoking, or No Smoking? That's the Question: Hear Sir Benjamin C. Brodie, Bart., with Critical Observations,* (London, Pitman, 1860), pp. 3–4, my italics. This pamphlet was based on Brodie's two earlier publications: 'The use and abuse of tobacco', a letter to *The Times* (31 August 1860), p. 9, reprinted in *Littell's Living Age*, 67 (1860), 221–3, and B. C. Brodie, *The Use and Abuse of Tobacco* (London, Partridge, 1860).

42 Richardson, *For and Against Tobacco*.

43 'Medicus', *Smoking and Drinking: The Argument Stated For and Against* (London, Sampson, 1871). See also F. S. S., *Tobacco and Disease, the Substance of Three Letters, Reproduced, with Additional Matter, from the 'English Mechanic'* (London, Trubner, 1872); W. E. A. Axon, *Smoking and Thinking, from the 'English Mechanic'* (Dunfermline, 1872).

44 F. Close, *Tobacco: Its Influences, Physical, Moral, and Religious* (London, Hatchard, 1859), pp. 1–2.

45 F. M. Turner, 'The Victorian conflict between science and religion: a professional dimension', *Isis*, 69 (1978), 356–76; J. H. Brooke, *Science and Religion: Some Historical Perspectives* (Cambridge, Cambridge University Press, 1991).

46 Secretary of the South-street Wesleyan Methodist Sunday School, *Smoking and Chewing Tobacco: The Evils Resulting Therefrom* (London, George Atkinson, between 1876 and 1879); C. Fothergill, *May Young England Smoke?*; H. Jackson, *Is the Use of Tobacco Injurious?* (Barnstaple, H. A. Foyster, 1882); R. L. Carpenter, *A Lecture on Tobacco* (London, National Temperance Publication Depot, 1882); G. B., *Reasons For and Against Smoking* (London, James Nisbett, 1858); J. B. Budgett, *The Tobacco Question: Morally, Socially and Physically Considered* (London, George Philip, 1857).

47 C. R. Drysdale, *Tobacco and the Diseases it Produces* (London, Balliere, Tindall & Cox, 1875).

48 H. Gibbons, *Tobacco and its Effects: A Prize Essay Showing that the Use of Tobacco is a Physical, Mental, Moral and Social Evil* (London, Partridge, 1868), p. 9.

49 T. Reynolds, *Juvenile Street Smoking: Reasons for Seeking its Legislative Prohibition* (London, British Anti-Tobacco Society, 1856).

50 See, for example, W. Finnemore, *The Addison Temperance Reader. With Chapters on Thrift and Juvenile Smoking* (London, Addison Publishing Co., 1906); Rev. Kirk, *A Manly Habit* (Manchester, Anti-Tobacco and Anti-Narcotic League, 1880s); Various, *Juvenile Smoking: Papers . . . on the Evil Influences of Smoking when Indulged in by the Young* (London, Sunday School Union, 1883); R. Stephens, *When a Boy Smokes, Reprinted from 'Young England'* (London, Sunday School Union, 1898); Various, *Juvenile Smoking: Papers Submitted in Competition for Prizes Offered for the Best Essays on the Evil Influences of Juvenile Smoking* (London, Sunday School Union, 1882); C. W., *Juvenile Smoking: An Essay Setting Forth to the Young the Evil Effects of Tobacco Smoking* (Bodmin, Liddell & Son, 1883); J. Forbes Moncrieff, *Our Boys and Why they Should Not Smoke* (Manchester, Anti-Narcotic League, n. d.); H. Reid, *The Question of Manliness: A Chat with Boys on Smoking* (London, International Anti-Cigarette League, 1904); R. Holmes, *The Use of Tobacco by Young People, Considered in Relation to its Effects, Delusions and Prevention* (Manchester, Tubbs & Brook, 1878).

51 J. Q. A. Henry, *The Deadly Cigarette; or the Perils of Juvenile Smoking* (London, Richard J. James, 1907), p. 150; R. Baden-Powell, *Scouting for Boys* (1908; London, Pearson, 1928).

52 The most quoted case was that of Bertillon, who tested 160 students at the Polytechnic school in Paris in 1855 and concluded that smokers tended to be shorter and 'much less likely to obtain certificates for proficiency than the non-smokers': *ATJ*, 29 (1898), p. 59; *The Times* (25 September 1878), p. 4. Perhaps reflecting a lack of follow-up research, this evidence continued to be frequently cited in anti-tobacco literature even in the twentieth century.

53 *Lancet*, i (1883), 1011.

54 W. E. A. Axon, *The Tobacco Question: Physiologically, Chemically, Botanically, and Statistically Considered* (Manchester, John Heywood, 1878), p. 14; *Lancet*, i (1892), 1097.

55 H. Cunningham, *The Children of the Poor: Representations of Childhood since the Seventeenth Century* (Oxford, Blackwell, 1991); J. Springhall, *Coming of Age: Adolescence in Britain, 1860–1960* (Dublin, Gill & Macmillan, 1986).

56 See chapter 7.

57 Brodie, *Use and Abuse*, p. 6. Other early references to the decline of the Turks can be found in the works of Lizars and Richardson.

58 J. C. Murray, *Smoking, when Injurious, when Innocuous, when Beneficial* (London, Simpkin, Marshall & Co., 1871), p. 8.

59 Parliamentary Papers, XXXII, Inter-Departmental Committee on Physical Deterioration, *Minutes of Evidence*, Cd. 2210, 1904, p. 278.

60 Henry, *The Deadly Cigarette*, pp. 13, 15, 178.

61 J. Milner Fothergill, *The Physiologist in the Household. Part 1: Adolescence* (London, Balliere, Tindall & Cox, 1880), p. 14.

62 C. W. McCarthy, *Tobacco and its Effects: A Pamphlet Addressed to Non-Medical Readers* (Dublin, McGlashaw & Gill, 1874); A. E. Hamilton, *This Smoking World* (London, Methuen, 1928), ch. 11, 'A word about juvenile smoking'; *TTR*, 18:205 (January 1885), 3.

63 J. G. Digges, *The Cure of Inebriety, Alcoholism, the Drug and the Tobacco Habit, etc.* (London, A. W. Jamieson, 1904), pp. 5–6.

Part II

Economy:
the cigarette and the mass market in the early twentieth century

4

'Player's please': the cigarette and the mass market

At the Paris Exhibition of 1883, James T. Bonsack demonstrated a fully working model of his new cigarette-making machine which he had first patented in the United States in 1881. Present at the exhibition were George and Harry Wills of the Bristol tobacco manufacturer, W. D. & H. O. Wills, who were immediately intrigued by the mechanical device. In Britain, cigarettes were still hand rolled by large teams of girls and young women, the most skilled of whom could make several a minute. Consequently, they were expensive and only purchased by an elite clientele, a niche market which the manufacturers believed did not hold much potential for expansion. It was out of curiosity, therefore, rather than through any realisation of the future demand for cheap cigarettes, that the Wills brothers decided to purchase the Bonsack machine and, as a matter of business formality, secure sole rights for its use in the United Kingdom.

The impact of the Bonsack machine was to exceed all their expectations. They cautiously began production in the summer of 1883 and by early 1884 Wills had launched the Three Castles, Gold Flake and Louisville brands of cigarette on the market. With 300 cigarettes being manufactured each minute, the Bonsack machine enabled the cigarette to be brought within the price range affordable to the working class. After the Chancellor lowered the tobacco duty by 4*d* in 1887, prices were reduced still further so that, in 1888, the Woodbine and Cinderella brands were launched, retailing at five cigarettes for one penny. Wills then realised the potential of the machine-made cigarette and great efforts were made to ensure that none of its rivals could use a similar device. In 1892 the Company secured the rights to the Bohl cigarette machine, which manufactured at the rate of 300 cigarettes a minute, though less reliably and efficiently: it paid £5,000 merely to prevent a rival from using it and to maintain its monopoly over the cigarette trade. John

Table 4.1 Cigarette sales (by number) of W. D. & H. O. Wills, 1884–93

	Woodbine	Cinderella	Three Castles	Gold Flake	Hearts-ease	Louisville	Total (incl. others)
1884	–	–	778,000	350,000	687,000	2,271,000	6,500,000
1885	–	–	1,325,000	601,000	1,592,000	3,384,000	9,400,000
1886	–	–	2,455,000	822,000	3,391,000	4,793,000	13,961,000
1891	53,425,250	32,045,500	12,657,400	2,691,350	18,579,400	4,407,900	124,230,050
1892	97,593,500	52,398,500	14,882,400	2,128,450	27,706,100	4,165,200	200,337,350
1893	159,350,750	83,430,750	18,103,200	3,907,850	37,238,600	4,586,600	312,992,790

Sources: Wills Archive, Bristol Record Office, 38169/M/1/(a), *Board Meetings*, 6 April 1887; B. W. E. Alford, *W. D. & H. O. Wills and the Development of the UK Tobacco Industry* (London, Methuen, 1973), p. 171.

Player & Sons of Nottingham did begin to use the Elliot machine in 1893, but it was not until its purchase of the Baron cigarette machine in 1896 that it could compete successfully with Wills. The firm of Lambert & Butler used the American Luddington from 1895, as did W. & F. Faulkner from 1897, but its production rate was advertised at only 3,600 cigarettes per hour. By 1899, the Elliot could run at 230 per minute, and although Player's had 18 of these in operation and Stephen Mitchell & Sons had 16, Wills still remained the most competitive, with the Bonsack being improved to 350–500 cigarettes per minute.[1]

Any history of the cigarette's role in British society must begin with this technological explanation of its early popularity. None of the manufacturers predicted the future dominance of the cigarette in tobacco consumption and the Wills Board was actually rather taken aback by the initial success of its brands (see table 4.1). Flue-curing techniques for the preparation of the tobacco leaf had also been recently perfected and this produced a Virginian crop particularly suited to smokers' tastes in cigarettes. From having only a tiny share of the tobacco market in 1890, then, by the end of the First World War, the majority of tobacco consumed in the United Kingdom was in the form of cigarettes (figure 4.1).

Such rationalisation of the processes of manufacture created a world very different from that in which the bourgeois-liberal culture of smoking prevailed. In the nineteenth century, the cultural vision of smoking had directed the activities of the tobacco manufacturers. While this culture of smoking would continue throughout the twentieth century, what becomes most remarkable in the new mass market is the extent to which the relationship between culture and economy was inverted so that the latter came to direct

Figure 4.1 Percentage share of sales: cigarette and pipe tobacco, 1887–1919

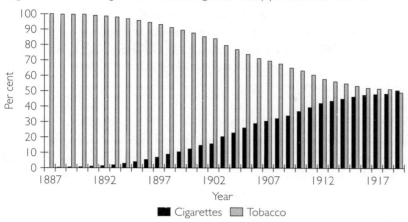

Source: G. F. Todd (ed.), *Statistics of Smoking in the United Kingdom* (London, Tobacco Research Council, 1966).

the former. In order for the economies of scale realisable through the use of the Bonsack to be made profitable, a mass demand had to be created for the new cigarettes. The economic and business factors which stimulated mass production had to be translated into the market so that consumers purchased goods in numbers similar to that at which technology allowed cigarettes to be manufactured. The rationalisation of production therefore had to be extended to a rationalisation of the market: that is, attempts had to be made to control consumers in a manner similar to the control of the factors of production.

How manufacturers hoped to control the market was through advertising. For firms such as Gallaher, Carreras and Player's (but less so with Wills, which relied on the early market lead of Woodbine to sustain sales), advertising and marketing became means through which they could try to structure and order the desires of consumers according to the needs and interests of the manufacturer. These interests were clearly dictated by motives of profit, thereby positioning advertising as an economic-inspired vision of the cigarette which would predominate over the cultural vision offered from the drawing room and gentleman's club of the nineteenth century. The ways in which manufacturers attempted, without ever fully succeeding, to control the culture of consumption is the subject of this chapter. It begins with an overview of the structural and administrative changes which created large-scale, rationalised business enterprises, before moving on to a detailed examination of advertising and the attempt to control the disparate desires and demands of consumers.

In this attempt to create order out of disorder, to regulate patterns of smoking from among the diverse, ritualised practices of consumption, the tobacco manufacturer acted as a kind of economic modernist, attempting to lead the mass of individual consumers to a standardised, homogeneous, capitalist utopia, far different from the Arcadia which was expressive of the Victorian liberal culture of individuality.

The introduction of the Bonsack machine in the manufacture of a product previously only consumed by a wealthy few was typical of the rationalisation of production and the application of scientific methods associated with the 'Second Industrial Revolution'.[2] This 'epoch-making transformation of society' saw the production of cheap versions of old products as well as the proliferation of new goods, such as telephones, bicycles, electric lamps and mechanised transport, all of which are said to have replaced a producer-oriented society with one that was consumer oriented.[3] As well as the economies of scale brought about by the technological advances in production, storage and distribution, certain legal, financial and administrative changes further encouraged the growth of large firms. An expanding middle class became a source of investment, and changes in the Stock Exchange encouraged mergers and acquisitions so that, by the time of the First World War, many of today's largest businesses had become established, such as Watney, Dunlop, Vickers, GKN and Cadbury's.[4]

What happened in the tobacco trade was typical, if not exemplary, of these more general changes. Most significant were the events of 1901–2, when James Buchanan Duke's American Tobacco Company 'invaded' the British tobacco market with the purchase of Ogden's of Liverpool.[5] Aggressive marketing strategies were adopted in the promotion of cheap cigarettes and many patriotic appeals were made to counter the American threat. The leading British firms reacted by forming the Imperial Tobacco Company, which Wills dominated from its foundation (table 4.2).

Following a series of price cuts, special offers, bonus agreements with retailers and the threat of Imperial invading the American market, a truce was called in 1902. The American Tobacco Company agreed to return to the United States, leaving the British market to Imperial and its domestic rivals. British American Tobacco was formed between the two companies to trade in the rest of the world and Ogden's was purchased by Imperial. Litigation continued over the next few years with the outstanding bonus agreements made with retailers by Ogden's,[6] but the market settled down with the

Table 4.2 Capitalisation of the Imperial Tobacco Company Limited, 1901

Business	Purchase price (£)
W. D. & H. O. Wills Ltd (Bristol)	6,992,221
Lambert & Butler Ltd (London)	754,306
Stephen Mitchell & Son (Glasgow)	701,000
John Player & Sons Ltd (Nottingham)	601,456
F. & J. Smith (Glasgow)	525,803
Hignett, Brothers & Co. Ltd (Liverpool)	477,038
Franklyn, Davey & Co. (Bristol)	473,555
William Clarke & Son Ltd (Liverpool)	403,582
Edwards, Ringer & Bigg Ltd (Bristol)	372,603
The Richmond Cavendish Co. Ltd (Liverpool)	319,805
Adkin & Sons (London)	146,497
D. & J. Macdonald (Glasgow)	134,973
Hignett's Tobacco Company (London)	54,183
Total	11,957,022

Source: Alford, *W. D. & H. O. Wills*, p. 287.

dominance of Imperial. Further acquisitions in the manufacturing, distributive and packaging trades were made over the years and internal mergers gradually took place within Imperial, but the units that had once been separate firms with their own distinctive identities remained semi-autonomous, allowing Imperial to escape charges of profiteering after the First World War.[7] An executive committee was formed which centralised leaf buying and laid down company policy on finance, overall company strategy and gross profits on individual brands.[8] Imperial remained the dominant cigarette and tobacco manufacturer throughout the first half of the twentieth century, as demonstrated by the industry profit figures in table 4.3.

The formation of Imperial symbolically demarcated the fragmented consumer economy of the nineteenth century from the mass market of the twentieth. Nineteenth-century tobacco manufacturing had consisted of a large number of independent producers, but the formation of the multinational 'tobacco combine' saw the industry move to a situation between monopoly and oligopoly. The promotional battles which took place between Imperial and Ogden's – backed by American Tobacco – also symbolically demonstrated the arrival of a new style of marketing, though the actual transition would take much longer to permeate the entire industry. Duke's arrogant announcement to the Player brothers that he had come to buy their company

Table 4.3 Net profits and share capital and reserves in the tobacco
industry, 1925

Name of company and year ended	Net profit (£)	Share capital and reserves (£)
Abdulla & Co. (31/12/24)	56,413	575,000
Ardath Tobacco Co. (31/12/25)	288,042	1,124,700
Albert Baker (31/3/25)	34,106	289,200
British American Tobacco (30/9/25)	5,145,238	22,943,076
Carreras Ltd (31/10/25)	773,156	1,020,000
Cope Brothers (31/3/25)	124,222	620,400
Finlay & Co. (30/9/25)	16,588	191,693
R. & J. Hill (31/3/25)	24,939	339,920
Imperial Tobacco Company (30/9/25)	8,884,990	51,148,100
Godfrey Phillips (31/12/24)	74,684	685,500
United Tobacco (South) (30/9/25)	639,843	2,839,621

Source: Economist (20 February 1926).

both personalised and symbolically demonstrated the differences between the
American and British trading methods.[9] The two styles were juxtaposed on
one page of the *Daily Express* in 1901, when two advertisements appeared.
One was for Sweet Caporal, made by American Tobacco, which claimed it
sold at 'popular prices', thereby appealing to a mass base. The other was from
Taddy & Co. and made typical Victorian individualistic differentiations
between the product and the assumed consumer.[10] Taddy catered for different sectors of the market and used much copy which the informed leisured
smoker could read. Sweet Caporal was promoted to be smoked by everybody
and, while the advertisement was brash and bold, it told the reader little
about the actual product.

Ogden's innovative advertising forced responses from the other tobacco
manufacturers. In 1901 Ogden's ran a series of cartoon advertisements which
showed humorous situations, such as a policeman capturing two burglars
stealing hundreds of Ogden's cigarettes. The copy ran: 'Two's company –
three's none!'[11] Importantly, these black and white pictures stood out from
the mass of print that made up most other turn-of-the-century press advertising. The American advertisements were much superior in quality to those of
the British manufacturers, which concentrated mainly on patriotic claims
against the American trust. A Godfrey Phillips advertisement featured Uncle
Sam plunging a dagger in John Bull's back, while another portrayed 'the

British lion crouched defensively over a display of the firm's Guinea Gold cigarettes, snarling at a top-hatted and star-spangled octopus which had swum up to give battle'.[12] Other strategies adopted by the rival firms included price cutting, bonuses to retailers who pushed one firm's goods over another's, new series in cigarette cards and coupon trading (where vouchers given out in cigarette packets could be redeemed for goods listed in a catalogue).[13] The 'tobacco war' saw the introduction of many marketing methods which would become increasingly common in the twentieth century, and the end, for the large manufacturers at least, of certain forms of trading which were more dominant in the Victorian period.

Rationalised production and innovative marketing had to be combined with efficient distribution to ensure the availability of commodities throughout the regions in which they were advertised. What is surprising, given the nature of corporate development in this period, is that Imperial never made a concerted effort to integrate vertically, securing guaranteed retail outlets for its branded goods. However, the cheap price of the tobacco retail licence (5*s* 3*d*), and the low levels of skill required to deal in pre-packaged commodities, meant that the retail trade was constantly open to competition from multiple traders, local corner-shops, general traders, stalls at entertainment complexes, public houses and automatic machines. Multiple firms such as Salmon & Gluckstein were particularly noted for cutting prices, a form of competition which reduced the profits of specialist traders but which, as Arthur J. Wills wrote in a letter to George Wills in 1896, actually increased the sales of the manufacturer.[14] While Imperial and others did not wish to lose the goodwill of the retail trade too much, when they did meet to discuss preventing cutting they were also concerned not to offend the working-class consumer by appearing to maintain artificially high prices.[15] Further discouragement to vertical integration came from the bonus agreements which secured generous discounts on bulk purchases for the distributor, but which required the heavy promotion of Imperial's bonus-bearing goods in the retailer's shop and window displays. Imperial therefore never needed to own the distributive sector of its trade since, by giving retailers a degree of financial security and economic independence, they secured a cultural dominance over them which was bluntly summarised in 1948: 'although he [the producer] sells his goods to distributors, the distributor is only, so to speak, an intermediary between him and the consumer of his goods'.[16] The bonus agreement helped to secure the financial base of the retailer and it enabled Imperial to influence distribution to such an extent that it never needed to undertake vertical integration.[17]

The final stage in the rationalisation of the industry was the transformation of internal selling and marketing systems. Taking the Wills branch of Imperial as a case study, it maintained an extensive system of marketing committees, commercial travellers' meetings, advertisers' reports and sales analyses at a time when inter-war pioneers of market research pointed to its undeveloped state in Britain.[18] The principal committee at Wills was the Branch Management Committee, which operated beneath the centralised bodies of Imperial. In regard to market research, it dealt with opinions from travellers and advertisers and had beneath it a Selling Committee, which dealt more specifically with new product development and questions of changes in selling policy. Beneath this were the sub-committees dealing with advertising, press and posters.[19] Travellers were paid well and their opinions were frequently sought at branch management level, especially when sales for a particular product began to decline. Both before and after the formation of Imperial, travellers met formally every December and their suggestions were discussed by the Board.[20] Although there were a greater number of meetings, the system of travellers was the basic and unchanging form of market research through to the Second World War.[21] Travellers would be asked their opinions on matters as seemingly trivial as the use of new wrappers for particular brands, price changes on the most unimportant lines, the best means of transforming the loose tobacco trade into the more controllable packet trade, and the targeting of areas for product testing (such as the unsuccessful 'big pennyworth' packets of pipe tobacco). All such minor concerns together represent a clear attempt to alter consumer demand, based on a detailed understanding of the marketplace.[22]

A variety of other means were also adopted to ensure effective communication between the firm and its distant consumers. Company representatives would actually visit retailing outlets for the day and see how customers behaved at the point of sale.[23] Advertising inspectors were employed to examine existing outdoor advertisements and potential new sites, and to suggest towns and areas where advertising might need to be made more visible.[24] They were asked to comment on the most effective advertising materials (e.g. glass ash trays, tin shelf strips, water jugs), and to report on regional differences in demand, gender and social group preferences, and the advertising of rival companies. One such report in 1938 demonstrated a keen awareness of the benefits of corporate identity: 'it is obvious that the repetition of advertisements for one brand, or the use of a single slogan such as "Player's Please" is bound to have a greater cumulative effect than a larger number of signs or advertisements for a group of several brands such as we have to advertise'.[25]

Wills further kept an awareness of developments in the press so that it would know the most effective means of communication by this medium, even noting the opinions of members of the public which were occasionally sent in.[26] All these strategies combined represented a detailed study of the market and how best to communicate to it, though absent from it was much of the modern marketing jargon of today or even of interwar textbooks on market research.[27] Following the rationalisation of the process of manufacture in the 1880s, then, there was a clear attempt to make efficient all other areas of the corporation so it could cater to a market which it would also seek to control.

The branded proprietary article was largely the product of the advances in technology in the late nineteenth century. Although tobacco manufacturers had used trademarks (principally for snuff) since the late eighteenth century, it was not until the 1870s and 1880s that branding really developed in its modern form.[28] The brand acted as a source of information for the nature of the product determined by either advertising, a previous sale, or the connotations provoked by the brand name itself or its image. As long as the manufacturer could standardise production, the brand served to inform the consumer about the product, a form of communication wholly different from the oral recommendation required for loose tobaccos made by the local retailer. In the period outlined in the first three chapters, brand names often reflected the diversity and individuality of smoking cultures. Manufacturers, rather than hoping for one product to appeal to all, had to recognise a variety of consumption patterns. The very names which they chose for pipe tobaccos had to reflect the different tastes which existed throughout society. Brand titles were chosen to stress the sweetness of the smoke (Honeycomb, Sweet as a Rose, Sweet Briar, Sunflower, Wild Geranium), its richness of flavour (Gold Leaf, Golden Iris, Golden Cut, Golden Harvest), or its aristocracy or wealthy urbanism (House of Commons, Mayfair, Piccadilly, Old Nobility).[29] Of crucial importance was the range available. A typical example is found in an 1887 advertisement by John Hunter, a by no means large-scale importer and manufacturer of cigars, which listed the twenty-seven types of Havana cigar he sold, the six Mexican and the nineteen British.[30] The manufacturer had to display all his wares, leaving the customer to select the cigar that met his taste, which clearly he himself knew best.

The market for pipe tobaccos was much larger, and as branding became more common manufacturers made some effort to direct preferences, though they still acknowledged the different customer demands. Most pipe tobacco advertisements would feature several brands, with some indicator following each name pointing to its taste or intended market. For instance, Cope's segmented the pipe tobacco market into Cut Cavendish for 'hardy working men, soldiers and sailors', London Shag for 'metropolitans', Tobacco de Luxe for the upper classes, and for the middle-price range there were a number of different tastes: Golden Magnet ('sweetly soothing'), Faust ('delicately fragrant'), Peerless ('exquisitely mild') and Yankee Pride ('purifies the breath and annihilates the microbe').[31] The differences in design mapped on to the differences in society, arguably to the extent that 'the entire range of manufactured goods constituted a representation of society'.[32] Much copy was also common in the advertising for pipe tobaccos. It was intended to give the commodity certain attributes which a particular personality of smoker could recognise. Even as late as 1901, Taddy's advertised its Myrtle Grove Mixture as 'cool, sweet and fragrant' and, alongside, provided a description of the first time Sir Walter Raleigh smoked his pipe and was doused with water by his servant thinking him aflame. Its Grapnel Mixture was full flavoured with Latakia tobacco added to it, and its Rampart Mixture was 'a very successful blend for a smoker who desires a reasonably mild tobacco'.[33]

To a significant extent, then, advertising of the late nineteenth century largely followed, rather than directed, the smoking cultures identified in chapters 1 and 2. From the 1880s onwards, however, advertising began to be used in new ways, to direct culture, to impose a cultural version of the rationality of the machine on the divergent consumption patterns within the mass market. It is easy to exaggerate the phenomenon, and the developments in Britain should not be seen as so well defined as in the United States in the same period. But a discernible trend does emerge in the style of advertising, which clearly sought to create a mass, standardised pattern of consumption, suited to the profit requirements of the economies of scale generated through mass production.[34] In what follows, there is no assessment of the success of the advertisers' efforts, an issue which can only ever be gauged completely after the actual consumption routines of smokers have been understood.[35] But, more simply, there is an assessment of the attempt by manufacturers to structure the culture of the market according to their economic interests. It has been said that such attempts in the early twentieth century were rather unsophisticated compared with the expertise of modern marketing, with decisions based instead on 'hunch and instinct' and 'without pause for reflection'.[36] Yet behavioural psychology was being introduced and promoted in British firms as a means to determine consumer demand in the inter-war period.[37] And, while the rejection of a Gold Flake advertisement by a Wills sub-committee in 1933 on the grounds that it was too 'defensive' was not based on any scientific data, there was perhaps a more implicit understanding of the mechanisms of advertising taking place which requires as much study as any late twentieth century analysis of the codes of advertising.[38]

Advertisers were helped in their project through the expansion of other forms of mass media, in particular the popular press, which grew rapidly after the abolition of the advertising duty in 1853 and the removal of the Newspaper Stamp Duty in 1855. So-called 'consumer magazines', with a large female readership, proliferated and an increasingly literate public was catered for by three important media figures.[39] Sir George Newnes published *Tit-Bits* from 1881 (with a circulation at one point of 850,000) and *Strand Magazine* from 1890. Alfred Harmsworth (later Lord Northcliffe) established *Answers* in 1888 and, most famously, the *Daily Mail* in 1896, while Sir Arthur Pearson started *Pearson's Weekly* in 1890. All had circulation figures approaching or over one million and all relied heavily on advertising for their revenue, with *Strand Magazine* devoting 100 pages to advertisements when it was at its most popular.[40]

Although there was some initial resistance to advertising by sections of the business community who saw it as 'ungentlemanly' and 'against nature' (the Society for the Checking of Abuses in Public Advertising was formed in 1893), expenditure on press and poster advertising gradually rose.[41] At the turn of the twentieth century the annual sum spent on advertising was estimated to be somewhere between £10 million and 20 million, with companies such as Pears spending around £100,000 each year and Lever, another soap manufacturer, spending £20 million over a twenty year period. In the tobacco trade, Wills was initially reluctant to advertise, spending only £2,400 in 1880, though by 1897 it readily spent £5,000 on Gold Flake cigarettes alone. The more commercially aggressive Player's company was said to spend £20,000 per year and estimates of Ogden's of Liverpool went up to £100,000. Table 4.4 shows the amount spent on advertising by most of the major tobacco manufacturers a few years after they had combined to form the Imperial Tobacco Company. By the interwar period, the national advertising bill for all products and services had reached over £30 million and peaked at just over £60 million in 1937, with over 80 per cent of this amount being spent on the press.[42] For the tobacco trade, it is useful to compare the interwar figures for the Player's branch of Imperial with the earlier pre-First World War figures (see tables 4.4 and 4.5).

Table 4.4 Advertising expenditure of Imperial branches, 1911–14 (£)

Branch	1911	1912	1913	1914
Williams & Co.	130	150	150	170
Fancy Goods	341	880	1,005	3,910
Mardon, Son & Hall	350	350	250	250
W. J. Davies & Sons	777	740	807	757
Adkin & Sons	1,330	1,330	1,360	1,800
Franklyn, Davey & Co.	1,665	1,700	1,700	2,231
W. Clarke & Son	1,765	1,815	1,840	1,815
W. A. & A. C. Churchman	2,700	2,650	2,400	2,800
Edwards, Ringer & Bigg	3,420	3,620	3,930	3,900
W. J. Faulkner	6,700	6,600	6,550	6,935
Hignett Bros. & Co.	9,900	7,800	6,800	6,800
Smith & Macdonald	10,175	12,100	12,431	12,881
S. Mitchell & Son	10,060	11,405	12,691	12,948
Lambert & Butler	18,085	19,250	19,920	21,500
Ogden branch	21,600	21,950	24,750	23,125
John Player & Sons	55,750	59,800	60,000	60,000
W. D. & H. O. Wills	49,650	51,830	53,580	53,230
Allan Ramsey	–	–	–	9,500
Total	194,398	203,970	210,164	224,632

Source: Wills, 38169/M/5/(c), *Suggestions to Executive Committee*, p. 32.

Table 4.5 Player's advertising expenditure, 1926–41

Year	Expenditure (£)
1926	486,499
1927	588,295
1930	689,103
1931	648,299
1932	619,070
1933	625,290
1934	653,434
1935	661,313
1936	681,166
1940	324,638
1941	245,139

Source: Player's Archive, Nottingham Record Office, DD PL/6/1/1–17,
Annual Analysis of Trading.

Examining the style and content of advertising, one can detect a move away from matching a particular type of product with a particular type of smoker. Instead, there was a more general approach which sought to demonstrate the potential appeal of the range of a firm's products to a range of consumers: they could cater for all. Cope's advertisement, 'Rinking', appeared at the relatively early date of 1877 (figure 7). Using the latest developments in lithography and the artistry of George Pipeshank, the advertisement was set to appeal to the Victorian bourgeois male, yet it also portrayed a range of different smoking characters. At the roller-skating rink can be seen top-hatted and bowler-hatted men, young and old, men and women, and even an anti-tobacconist, not skating and causing havoc by forcing someone to fall over. The advertisement serves to amuse and capture the attention but it also shows the full variety of potential smokers. Everybody, including women, are seen to be smoking and enjoying themselves. The message is that Cope's Whiffs, Cigaretos, Bouquet, Fairy, Bouquet No. 2 and Peerless brands can be enjoyed by a whole range of people, and that one brand does not have to suit one particular group or individual.

Far more common than picturing the range of consumers was the attempt to use icons which served as lowest common denominators; that is, images either so uncontroversial that they could not offend any particular segment of the market or which used references so culturally conservative that the advertisements had the potential to appeal to all. In particular, images related to Empire, patriotism, monarchy and the consumer's own body were means by which mass manufacturers attempted to appeal to the largest potential mass of consumers.[43] British national identity was frequently celebrated in late Victorian advertising through the use of the Queen, the aristocracy or a familiar institution. Often figures were depicted in period costume – frequently Georgian or classical – in order to lend a solidity to the product, to root the commodity in a sense of Britain's (and possibly the world's) heritage. Such images were common to pipe tobacco advertising, which relied very much on the iconography of national identity. A survey of 190 tobacco names listed in *Tobacco Trade Review* in 1901 demonstrates the extent to which the past played a significant role, thirteen of the brand names actually using the word 'old' in their title. A further thirteen made specific reference to the military (most companies had a type of 'Navy Cut') and thirty-six referred to a particular aspect of Britain's heritage or to an old institution, such as the aristocracy or a public monument. Typical brand names here, which were frequently advertised with an appropriate accompanying image, included Master of

Foxhounds Mixture, Big Ben, May Fair, Exmoor Hunt, Nation's Pride and Royal Salute. While thirty took their names from the product's origins in America (e.c. Golden Virginia), another thirty-five rooted themselves in the British countryside (Double Daffodil, British Oak, Honey Cut, Sweet as the Rose, Marigold).[44]

Many of these themes would be taken up in the advertising of cigarettes, Woodbine being the most popular brand up until the inter-war period. More often, a successful pipe tobacco brand name would be used to sell a new cigarette, Player's Country Life and Roll Call being prominent examples. Cigarette card series were also regularly based around themes related to Empire, the monarchy and the military.[45] The naval image persisted in cigarette branding and advertising, with most companies issuing a Navy Cut cigarette, though Player's was to become the most famous. The naval image served a dual purpose in that it both denoted a popular cultural smoking tradition and connoted one of national pride. The sailor embodied Britishness and could therefore appeal to the entire population of the country's (at that time male) smokers. The military theme was particularly emphasised during the war, as it brought British traditions up to date. If the references in tobacco advertising to Britain's glorious military and naval past were becoming out of date by 1914, they could be brought right into the present because of the mass nature of the new 'Total War'. In the First World War, although the Woodbine was held to be 'Tommy's favourite fag',[46] Player's Roll Call made use of the Tommy Atkins metaphor to give the cigarette its broadest appeal.[47] The 'Tommy' was the ultimate mass man, his identity and individuality were subsumed under the need for a homogeneous image to which the greatest number of people could attach their affections and patriotism. But the use of Tommy in advertising was indicative of a change in advertising style. For whereas military images rooted in the past enabled the individual consumer to reflect on his own identity and note an affinity with the product, the military Tommy was often portrayed as though his whole existence in the war depended on the supply of a particular brand of cigarette.[48]

This passivity of Tommy, weighed under the might of the commodity (figure 8), is typical of a new type of representation in advertising which occurred around the turn of the twentieth century, and which positioned the product in the present rather than the past. The older Victorian form of advertising attempted to take the product to the consumer by highlighting properties that would suit an individual's taste, but increasingly the product began to feature on its own, detaching itself from any group of consumer.

A lesson in English, Smith's advertisement, *c.* 1914   **8**

Frequently, the product would be given its own distinctive personality so that it now held the individuality towards which the mass of consumers (if the advertisement succeeded) would be attracted. The most vigorously presented image of this kind in tobacco advertising in the first two decades of the twentieth century was Carreras' Black Cat, which promoted cigarettes of that name (figure 9). The style would be copied well into the inter-war period,

9   Black Cat, Carreras' advertisement, c. 1910s

with Wills creating Mr Gold and Mr Flake for its Gold Flake cigarettes and Gallaher introducing Sir Park Drive, C. I. G.[49] The trend was typical for the period: a monkey could be found advertising Monkey Brand Soap; the cleaning agent Vim transmogrified into Vimmy; photography had its Kodak Girl; and, more permanently, tyres were advertised by the Michelin Man.[50] To search for meaning or value in these images is, in a certain sense, to miss the point. They were pure gimmicks, but gimmicks devoid of as much significance as possible. They gave the commodity a character which made it autonomous from the consumer. The cigarette then stood beyond all consumers as the lack of meaning in the image could not attach it to a particular segment of the market. And precisely because the face value of the image was associated with no class of consumer, it therefore had the potential to appeal to as many smokers and non-smokers as possible.

By far the most pervasive style of advertising across all commodities was that which referred to the body. Developments in late nineteenth-century patent medicine advertising arguably created a culture that gave constant attention to the needs of the body and which encouraged anxieties about all aspects of the physical self.[51] The patent medicine style soon pervaded other forms of advertising to lead to a general emphasis on health. Lifebuoy soap was the 'children's friend' because it left them in an 'atmosphere of radiant health'[52] and Oxo threw off 'the ill effects of foggy, chilly weather'.[53] By the 1920s and 1930s health issues dominated advertising. Even cigarettes were included in this trend, despite the continued popular usage of such phrases as 'coffin-nails' and 'smoker's heart'. Most famously, on the inner carton of every packet of Craven 'A' Carreras claimed that its cork-tipped cigarette was 'made specially to prevent sore throats' (which were commonly associated with smoking) and had consequently been 'awarded the certificate of the Institute of Hygiene for quality and purity'. Kensitas made the links with health in a less defensive way. In 1930, and borrowing from the Lucky Strike advertising campaigns in the United States, the company ran a series of advertisements which warned people against over-eating. One pictured a cricketer with a dark shadow in which he has a large stomach and double chin. The copy ran as follows:

> Trim! Fit! Active! KENSITAS will help to avoid that future shadow. Men prize the hard firm lines of the figure of fitness. They realise the harm of over-indulgence – eating between meals which causes excess weight. Active men decline to lose the invigorating glow of energy by undergoing harsh dieting and drastic reducing – methods condemned by the medical profession. They accept the guidance of MODERATION which advocates sensible nourishment and no excess, even in smoking. They eat healthfully but not immoderately. When tempted to over-indulge – to eat between meals, they say, '*No thanks, I'll smoke a Kensitas instead.*'[54]

More generally, advertising began to promote the healthy lifestyle to the extent that it appeared as a general utopian vision; commodity culture could

10   Advertisement for Player's Navy Cut, c. 1930s

lead to a new, active, healthy world. Various cigarettes came to be associated with leisure; Greys with a series of outdoor activities such as ice hockey (with contestants smoking in action) and Turf with the more democratic spectator sports, especially racing and football.[55] But Player's was the tobacco company that most frequently linked smoking to leisure and the healthy outdoors. As the copy for one advert ran, 'Whatever the pleasure, Player's complete it',[56] the images in the others of the same series clearly asserting that a healthy lifestyle was incomplete without a cigarette (figure 10).

If health could symbolise the bright future that lay ahead through commodity consumption, then other symbols made greater use of more explicit symbols of a modern age. Wills' Main Line cigarettes were always featured with a train bursting forward into the modern age, the train representing for one commentator, 'constant movement, change, the ability to transport the individual from one situation to another'.[57] Other symbols of aesthetic modernism, such as cars and aeroplanes, also featured prominently in inter-war advertising, especially with Player's Airman brand. And modernism's standardised plain primary-coloured surfaces found their way into brand packaging, such as with Craven 'A', and in the white backgrounds of large advertisements that served to make more prominent the pictured packet of cigarettes. The emphasis on sharp contrast and oblique perspective was utilised to stress a commodity's progressive newness, its essential 'modernity' (figure 11 contrasts Craven 'A' with the older style represented by Woodbine).[58]

Packets of Craven 'A' and Woodbine, c. 1930s   **11**

The most commonly remembered cigarette advertising image of this period is the Player's sailor, an icon which in many ways encapsulated a variety of the styles just described. One might have expected an increasing tendency in advertising to stress newness and the modern, in order to celebrate the innovatory nature of products, but manufacturers also found it convenient to maintain constant brand labels, reworking them to fit modern representational forms. The Player's sailor was typical of this trend. First used in 1883, the lifebuoy being added in 1888, 'Hero' appeared young and old, bearded and clean-shaven, until his image was standardised in 1927 with a design first used in 1905 (figure 12).[59] His original conception, in referring to the national naval heritage, owed much to that late Victorian practice of drawing on traditional symbols of the British past to solidify the image of a new product. By the inter-war period, however, he increasingly appeared in a

12   *Hero*, standard logo of the Player's branch of Imperial Tobacco

more modernist setting, the image being fixed against a clean white background or positioned alongside other pictures, such as those of young people
enjoying healthy exercise. The old was therefore combined with the new,
opening up the appeal of Hero to new groups of consumers. Indeed, this
seems to have been the case as Player's Medium became something of an
androgynous cigarette, unlike the other two leading brands, Craven 'A' and
Woodbine, which maintained strongly gendered associations. The modernist
elements of Player's advertising opened the product to mass consumption,
while the sailor epitomised a dominant notion of British masculinity but at
the same time had sufficient maturity to represent something of an uncle
figure for potential women smokers.[60] The accompanying slogan, 'Player's
Please' (almost always alongside the picture of Hero), was alliterative, memor-
able and geared for the point-of-sale transaction, and the action it suggested
of the consumer was potentially inclusive of the entire mass market. The image
and the instruction were repeated in the advertising for most of Player's
leading brands to the extent that brands no longer had to be mentioned. The
huge commercial success of Player's in the inter-war years has been largely
attributed to this image and Wills struggled constantly to create a comparable
all-embracing promotional image (figures 10 and 13).[61]

The phrase 'Player's please' is significant because of the inclusive appeal it
makes to the mass market. It was part of a general language of 'the mass'
which pervaded much early twentieth-century advertising. Constant reference
to 'the mass' was developed in the business world, which ranged from the
very titles of the press (*People, News of the World*) to the names of retailing
firms (Universal Provider) and, most frequently, in advertising. The 'world',
the 'universe' and 'everybody' featured regularly in this rhetoric. In 1932,
Wills claimed its Capstan brand 'suit[ed] everyone',[62] while much earlier
Ogden's had boasted that its Guinea Gold cigarettes had the 'largest sale in
the world'.[63] The image of the world was even used in its advertisements to
express the 'universal' nature of its sales. In a 1901 image, the globe is the
home of the mass of consumers, whereas Ogden's, and its products, reside in
the clouds above, paternalistically looking down on the world of consumption
(figure 14). This mass base was not confined to tobacco products. Hudson's
soap was 'for the people',[64] Peter's Milk Chocolate was 'sold everywhere',[65]
'thousands of families' used Beecham's Pills,[66] medicine was 'for the million',[67]
and a variety of baking powders, cocoas, chocolates, patent medicines and
other common household goods claimed to have 'world-wide popularity'.[68]
The language of the many, the world, the universal, the mass, pervades the

13   *Player's Please*, Player's advertisement, *c.* 1930s

advertising that can be found in the popular press and periodicals from the turn of the twentieth century. Coupled to this is the use of the word 'every', so Dunlop made a tyre 'for every purpose and every use'.[69] A development of this was to show the variety of situations in which the consumer could use a

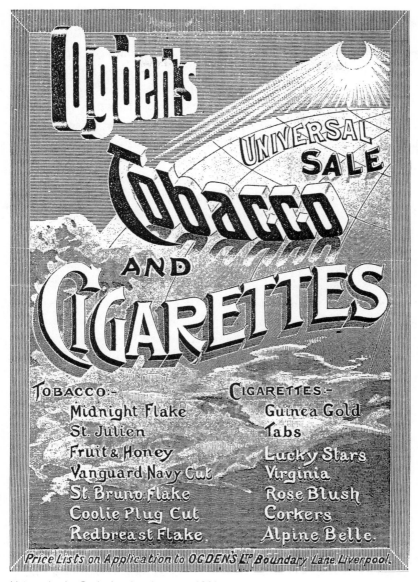

Universal sale, Ogden's advertisement, 1901   **14**

product. Advertisements for Wills' Gold Flake in 1935 asked if 'you' smoke 'in bed', 'when you are busy', 'in your bath', 'to relax', 'to think', 'when you're worried' and in a variety of other moods and situations.[70] A year later, Wills' Star cigarettes were shown, with corresponding pictures, 'between the dances', 'before you turn in', 'between the acts' and 'before supper's served' because, 'There's always time for a Star'.[71] Not only did the manufacturers therefore hope that the cigarette would permeate as much geographical space as possible within the marketplace, but they hoped also to penetrate further into the temporal space of each particular smoker.

At the same time as attempting to create 'the mass', advertisers also identified the individual within it. D. L. LeMahieu refers to the 'paradox of mass communication' in which the most effective strategy adopted by the mass media, cinema and radio in communicating with millions of individuals was to adopt a style that was 'intimate, personal and subjective'.[72] The style was common in advertising as frequent references were made to the personal: 'You smoke a good cigarette for pleasure alone, it satisfies you.'[73] The consumer was both an individual and a part of the mass. In a 1932 advertisement for Gallaher's Park Drive, there is a clear celebration of the mass, a statement that the huge crowd of football fans are all potential Park Drive smokers: 'The crowd in the advertisement, far from symbolizing urban alienation, represents a community of consumers.'[74] But in the bottom left corner of the mass, a spotlight focuses on just a few members of the crowd (figure 15). This seems to highlight the individual in the mass recognising his existence but at the same time demonstrating his relationship with the collectivity of Park Drive smokers. Again, the light shining on the crowd has as its source the manufacturer, Gallaher, looking down as the only true individual upon the mass of consumers below.

The mass nature of the cigarette was also emphasised in the material culture of smoking promotion. Whereas in the nineteenth century the individual collected his own 'paraphernalia of smokiana', it could be said that in the twentieth the manufacturers provided the accompaniments of smoking through coupon trading. Coupon trading was first briefly used by tobacco companies during the tobacco war, but by the 1930s it had transformed the cigarette trade. Smaller producers began placing coupons in cigarette packets in the 1920s to try and break Imperial's dominance of the cigarette market, which stood at 91 per cent in 1921.[75] Carreras introduced coupons on its Black Cat cigarettes in 1925, J. Wix & Sons on its Kensitas brand in 1926; and from 1927 to 1933 eighteen new coupon brands were introduced.[76] In 1927, coupon brands only accounted for 4 per cent of the overall cigarette market, but this had increased to 16 per cent by 1930 and 33 per cent by 1933.[77] Imperial was reluctant to introduce a coupon brand, preferring instead to advertise that 'the value is in the cigarette',[78] but competition, which had

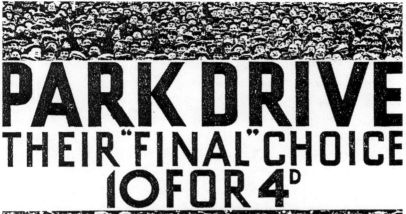

Their 'final' choice, Gallaher's Park Drive advertisement, 1932   **15**

reduced its cigarette market share to less than 70 per cent by 1932, persuaded Wills to launch Four Aces in this year. Another scheme saw 1,200 million miniature playing cards given out with the Capstan and Gold Flake brands from 1932 to 1933. Coupon brands eventually counted for over one-third of cigarette sales, and over £4 million worth of goods were being given away. Other competitions were also introduced, such as predicting the winners of twenty football and rugby league games and handing in the carton hulls representing the purchase of fifty Weights, Woodbines or Robin cigarettes. This competition alone received over 19 million entries.[79]

Eventually, Lt-Col J. T. C. Moore-Brabazon introduced a private member's Bill to ban coupon trading as it was damaging other trades through the mass distribution of jewellery, boots, watches and razors.[80] A Board of Trade committee was set up to investigate the matter and manufacturers complained that they 'found themselves selling gifts rather than cigarettes',[81] but no government action was taken. Manufacturers took matters into their own hands and the Martin Agreement to restrict coupon trading was signed in October 1933 between Imperial and the next six largest manufacturers (Ardath, Carreras, Gallaher, the International Tobacco Company, Godfrey Phillips and J. Wix).[82] The operation was clearly on a massive scale and it involved considerable proportions of the population, with even non-smokers apparently swapping coupons in the *Exchange and Mart*.[83] The strategy worked by encouraging consumers to buy more and more of one product, not for the aesthetic enjoyment of the commodity itself, but to collect vouchers in order to consume ever more products. And these free goods were those that were desired by the mass consumer – watches, bracelets, chains, clothing, teaspoons, braces and, in times of depression, boots and shoes, which were often beyond the reach of the lowest income groups. The objects which came with the cigarette, then, were similarly provided by the manufacturer, on the assumption that the demands of the mass consumer were to some extent homogeneous.

While what has been written above represents the dominant mode of cigarette advertising in the inter-war period, there are a number of important qualifications to be made. Some market segmentation did continue to take place and manufacturers were never able to create a truly 'universal' cigarette. The creation of a mass through advertising was an ideal, the masses as perceived did not always behave as each company's advertising sought to direct them. Consequently, there were numerous points at which manufacturers had to take into account the actual consumption patterns occurring in the marketplace. In particular, and as will be seen in the next chapter, local and traditional markets continued to exist, often based around a form of employment. Wills was therefore still supplying chewing tobaccos to South Wales miners in the 1960s, and its Press and Poster Committee constantly had to discuss regional variations. An analysis of sales in 1930 led the Committee to restrict advertising for Bulwark Cut Plug (a dark solid tobacco) to certain rural and heavy industrial areas.[84] Later, to take just one of many examples, Capstan's provincial press advertising was concentrated on Scotland and the North of England, except for a number of ports in the South.[85] Such examples also raise the question of class differences. This allowed Capstan to be advertised in the most popular press but Three Castles cigarettes, also manufactured by Wills, were pushed in more quality papers such as *The Times* and the *Daily Telegraph*.[86] In 1930, it was further decided by Wills to use little copy in the Gold Flake advertising that was placed in the 'quality' papers, though a more direct message was required for the readers of 'ordinary' papers.[87]

Just as class and region continued to play a role in the mass market, so too did conceptions of femininity and masculinity, with perhaps only Player's Medium being a truly androgynous cigarette. Although chapter 6 will show that women smoked for a variety of reasons beyond the pressures of advertising, there was nevertheless a deliberate attempt to appeal directly to women in the 1920s and 1930s. Craven 'A' became a particularly feminine smoke and Carreras had to make considerable efforts to overcome this stereotype.[88] Many cigarettes also remained essentially masculine in their associations. Despite the advertising to women by Player's Weights, the cheap cigarette range (Wills' Woodbine, Carreras' Clubs, Gallaher's Park Drive, sold at five for one penny before the First World War and at two pence until 1939) was mainly seen as masculine. Indeed, there is a celebration of the male working class in Woodbine's advertising (figure 16), and Carreras mobilised the concept of mass masculinity with a 1932 advertisement for Clubs which featured the following endorsement from Alex Jackson, the Chelsea captain and Scottish football international: 'I fully agree with Alex James that CLUBS is a "he-mans" cigarette – a small smoke with a big kick and certainly no penalties – in fact the best at its price I have ever smoked and I know good cigarettes.'[89]

The mass was also constructed as a given, enabling other cigarettes in the middle price range (10 for 3*d* before the First World War and 10 for 6*d* after: that is, although not the cheapest they were still affordable on a mass basis) to step rhetorically outside it, offering instead a cigarette which allowed ordinary smokers to enter the world of the 'real' smoker, the direct descendant of the Victorian bourgeois male. De Reszke advertisements appealed to the 'educated palate . . . – the cigarette for the few'.[90] Calling itself the 'aristocrat of cigarettes', De Reszke informed its potential customers that:

> The secret of pleasurable smoking lies in the fragrant aroma of pure, properly matured tobacco leaf and the subtleties of skilful blending, which are qualities exclusive to the good cigarette. You smoke a good cigarette for pleasure alone, it

Steel forging, Wills' Woodbine advertisement, c. 1930s

satisfies you, and therefore you smoke in moderation. That is why a good cigarette is more economical than a 'gasper'.[91]

De Reszke cigarettes were not expensive (ten for *6d*) and there was no financial reason why they should not be a part of that mass from which they tried to distinguish themselves. Yet they appealed directly to the emulative tendencies within the market and were mirrored by the similarly priced cigarettes of Sarony ('above the usual standard') and Greys (the 'gentleman in the 10 for 6*d* cigarette world').[92]

These qualifications should not, however, detract from the overall style of inter-war cigarette advertising which was to capture as wide a market as possible for each branded commodity. Even when advertisements did deliberately segment the market, what was often the case was that variations on a theme would be used: the overall intention was for the same product to appeal to as many smokers as possible. The expenditure on tobacco advertising made marketing an industry in itself, one which employed expert systems almost directly comparable with the expertise which went into the technological aspects of production. Advertising attempted to rationalise consumption, to do for the market what the Bonsack had done for the factory. That such an attempt to standardise consumption could never fully succeed is the subject of the next three chapters, as the diversity and particularities of smoking cultures were as prominent in the 1920s and 1930s as they had been in the 1860s and 1870s.

Notes

1 B. W. E. Alford, *W. D. & H. O. Wills and the Development of the UK Tobacco Industry* (London, Methuen, 1973), pp. 143–50, 226, 232; M. Corina, *Trust in Tobacco: The Anglo-American Struggle for Power* (London, Michael Joseph, 1975), p. 6; *Tobacco Trade Review* (hereafter *TTR*), 28:325 (January 1895), 11; M. Dempsey, *Pipe Dreams: Early Advertising Art from the Imperial Tobacco Company* (London, Pavilion Books, 1982); Nottingham Record Office, Player's Archive (hereafter Player's), DD PL 7/5/1, E. G. C. Beckwith, *A History of John Player & Sons*.

2 G. Barraclough, *An Introduction to Contemporary History* (Harmondsworth, Penguin, 1967), pp. 43–64.

3 R. W. Edsforth, *Class Conflict and Cultural Consensus: The Making of a Mass Consumer Society in Flint, Michigan* (New Brunswick, Rutgers University Press, 1987), p.5.

4 P. L. Payne, 'The emergence of the large-scale company in Great Britain, 1870–1914', *Economic History Review*, 20 (1967), 519–42; L. Hannah, *The Rise of the Corporate Economy* (London, Methuen, 1983); P. Wardley, 'The anatomy of big business: aspects of corporate development in the twentieth century', *Business History*, 33 (1991), 268–96.

5 The story has been told in far greater detail and with much greater accuracy than is presented here. See Alford, *W. D. & H. O. Wills*; Corina, *Trust in Tobacco*. The pages of the trade press, *Tobacco Trade Review*, *Tobacco Weekly Journal* and *Tobacco*, are dominated by the news throughout the two years.

6 The case ended in 1906: Corina, *Trust in Tobacco*, p. 104; *TTR*, 38:445 (January 1905), 2–3; *TTR*, 39:457 (January 1906), 2.

7 Alford, *W. D. & H. O. Wills*; Imperial Tobacco, *The Imperial Tobacco Company (of Great Britain and Ireland), Limited, 1901–1951* (London, Imperial Tobacco, 1951); Imperial Tobacco, *The Story of the Imperial Group Limited*, Imperial Group Information Brochure (London, Imperial Tobacco, 1976); Parliamentary Papers (hereafter P. P.), The Monopolies Commission, *Report on the Supply of Cigarettes and Tobacco and of Cigarette and Tobacco Machinery*, Cmnd. 218, 1961; P.P., *Profiteering Act, 1919, Findings by a Committee Appointed to Enquire into the Existence of a Trade Combination in the Tobacco Industry and into the Effects which its Operation has on Prices and on the Trade Generally*, Cmd. 558, xxiii, 1920.

8 Alford, *W. D. & H. O. Wills*, pp. 309–11.

9 *Ibid.*, p. 258.

10 *Daily Express* (8 November 1901), p. 7.

11 John Johnson Collection (hereafter J. J.), Bodleian Library, Oxford, *Tobacco Box*, No. 1.

12 E. S. Turner, *The Shocking History of Advertising* (1952; Harmondsworth, Penguin, 1965), p. 136.

13 J. J., *Publicity Box*, No. 13.

14 Bristol Record Office, Wills Archive (hereafter Wills), 38169/Pr/9/(c), *Pricing Records, 1895–1900*, letter dated 2 March 1896; *TTR*, 22:258 (June 1889), 155.

15 Wills, 38169/Pr/9/(b), *Pricing Records, 1896–1897*, notes of proceedings of meeting of manufacturers, 5 January 1897.

16 Public Record Office, BT 64/533, *Committee on Resale Price Maintenance. The Imperial Tobacco Company. Oral Evidence*, p. 22.

17 The points in this section are outlined at greater length in M. Hilton, 'Retailing history as economic and cultural history: strategies of survival by specialist tobacconists in the mass market', *Business History*, 40 (1998), 115–37.

18 See the Foreword by G. Harrison in P. Redmayne and H. Weeks, *Market Research* (London, Butterworth, 1931); T. A. B. Corley, 'Consumer marketing in Britain, 1914–1960', *Business History*, 29 (1987), 65–83.

19 Wills, 38169/M/6, *Wills Branch Management Committee*.

20 Alford, *W. D. & H. O. Wills*, pp. 159, 214–15; Wills, 38169/M/1/(b), *Board Meetings*, 22 December 1892.

21 Wills, 38169/M/9(b), *Selling Committee Minutes*, 29 January 1940.

22 Wills, 38169/M/1/(b), *Board Meetings*, 22 December 1899; 38169/M/6/(a), *Branch Management Committee*, 23 October 1907.

23 Wills, 38169/M/9/(c), *Selling Committee Minutes*, 29 October 1936.

24 Wills, 38169/M/10, *Advertising Sub-Committee Reports*.

25 *Ibid.*, 38169/M/10/(h) 9–11 February 1938.

26 Wills, 38169/M/8/(j), *Press and Poster Committee Reports*, 24 November 1930; 38169/M/8/(g), *Selling Committee Minutes*, 6 May 1929.

27 M. J. Baker, *Marketing: An Introductory Text* (Basingstoke, Macmillan, 1991); Redmayne and Weeks, *Market Research*.

28 Alford, *W. D. & H. O. Wills*, pp. 27–8.

29 Wills, 38169/Pr/i/a, *Pricing Records*.

30 *TTR*, 20:233 (May 1887), v.

31 A. V. Seaton, 'Cope's and the promotion of tobacco in Victorian England', *Journal of Advertising History*, 9:2 (1986), 5–26.

32 A. Forty, *Objects of Desire: Design and Society 1750–1980* (London, Thames & Hudson, 1986), pp. 62–3.

33 *Daily Express* (8 November 1901), p. 7.

34 An extensive American literature has now emerged on this topic. See, for instance, R. Batchelor, *Henry Ford: Mass Production, Modernism and Design* (Manchester, Manchester University Press, 1994); S. Strasser, *Satisfaction Guaranteed: The Making of the American Mass Market* (New York, Pantheon, 1984); S. Bronner (ed.), *Consuming Visions: Accumulation and the Display of Goods in America, 1880–1920* (New York, W. W. Norton, 1989); T. Smith, *Making the Modern: Industry, Art and Design in America* (Chicago, University of Chicago Press, 1993); J. Meikle, *Twentieth Century Limited: Industrial Design in America, 1925–1939* (Philadelphia, Temple University Press, 1979); R. Marchand, *Advertising the American Dream: Making Way for Modernity, 1920–1940* (Berkeley, University of California Press, 1985).

35 For some of the classic accounts on the effectiveness of advertising see V. Packard, *The Hidden Persuaders* (Harmondsworth, Penguin, 1960); S. Ewen, *Captains of Consciousness: Advertising and the Social Roots of the Consumer Culture* (New York, McGraw-Hill, 1976); M. Schudson, *Advertising: The Uneasy Persuasion* (New York, Basic Books, 1985). For a study of the contemporary tobacco industry claim that advertising does not work, see M. J. Waterson, *Advertising and Cigarette Consumption* (London, Advertising Association, 1982).

36 T. R. Nevett, *Advertising in Britain: A History* (London, Heinemann, 1982), p. 150; E. Field, *Advertising: The Forgotten Years* (London, Ernest Benn, 1959).

37 A. P. Braddock, *Applied Psychology for Advertisers* (London, Butterworth, 1933); F. B. Lane, *Advertising Administration (Principles and Practice)* (London, Butterworth, 1931); H. W. Eley, *Advertising Media* (London, Butterworth, 1932); Redmayne and Weeks, *Market Research.*

38 Wills, 38169/M/8/(p), *Press and Poster Committee Reports, 1933–1934*, no. 16.

39 Nevett, *Advertising in Britain*, pp. 25–31, 67; G. Dyer, *Advertising as Communication* (London, Routledge, 1982).

40 Turner, *Shocking History*, pp. 138–40.

41 *Ibid.*, pp. 78, 105–15.

42 *Ibid.*, pp. 72–4, 146.

43 T. Richards, *The Commodity Culture of Victorian England: Advertising and Spectacle, 1851–1914* (London, Verso, 1991); L. A. Loeb, *Consuming Angels: Advertising and Victorian Women* (Oxford, Oxford University Press, 1994).

44 *TTR*, 34:408 (December 1901), 41–2.

45 Cartophilic Society, *The Tobacco War Booklet* (London, Cartophilic Society, 1951). See also J. J., *B. R. Lillington* and *M. L. Horn* cigarette card collections.

46 *People* (19 December 1915), p. 2.

47 Player's, DD PL 6/22/1, Storekeeper's file containing details of advertising archive.

48 Richards, *Commodity Culture,* p. 158.

49 *TTR,* 57:680 (August 1924), 25; Wills, 38169/M/8/(o), *Press and Poster Committee Reports,* 16 October 1933.

50 Turner, *Shocking History,* p. 170.

51 Richards, *Commodity Culture,* especially ch. 4; Loeb, *Consuming Angels.*

52 *Tit-Bits* (28 January 1922), p. iv.

53 *Daily Express* (21 November 1901), p. 6.

54 *Daily Express* (28 January 1930), p. 2.

55 *TTR,* 53:625 (January 1920), 45.

56 *Sunday Express* (23 February 1935), p. 3.

57 Loeb, *Consuming Angels,* pp. 54–5.

58 P. Johnston, *Real Fantasies: Edward Steichen's Advertising Photography* (Berkeley, University of California Press, 1997), pp. 105–31.

59 Dempsey, *Pipe Dreams,* p. 32.

60 Mass-Observation, File Report 3192, *Man and His Cigarette,* 1949, p. 163, in *The Tom Harrisson Mass-Observation Archives* (Brighton, Harvester Press Microform Publications, 1983).

61 Alford, *W. D. & H. O. Wills,* p. 362.

62 *Tit-Bits* (12 March 1932), p. i.

63 Dempsey, *Pipe Dreams,* p. 34.

64 *Tit-Bits* (27 February 1892), p. i.

65 *Daily Express* (23 November 1901), p. 9.

66 *Tit-Bits* (22 February 1902), p. i.

67 *Tit-Bits* (2 March 1912), p. ii.

68 Loeb, *Consuming Angels,* p. 143.

69 *Daily Express* (3 January 1920), p. 6.

70 Wills, 38169/M/8/(r), *Press and Poster Committee Reports,* 15 January 1935.

71 Wills, 38169/M/8/(t), *Press and Poster Committee Reports,* 25 March 1936.

72 D. L. LeMahieu, *A Culture for Democracy: Mass Communication and the Cultivated Mind in Britain Between the Wars* (Oxford, Clarendon, 1988).

73 Wills, 38169/P/1/(b), *Press Cuttings, 1921–1927.*

74 Loeb, *Consuming Angels,* p. 143. Loeb is referring to an advertisement for Bovril, displayed in 1907, which adopted a similar format.

75 C. L. Pass, 'Coupon trading: an aspect of non-price competition in the UK cigarette industry', *Yorkshire Bulletin of Economic and Social Research,* 19:2 (1967), 124–35.

76 *Ibid.,* p. 126; Alford, *W. D. & H. O. Wills,* p. 335.

77 Pass, 'Coupon trading', p. 126; Monopolies Commission, *Report on the Supply,* p. 20.

78 Wills, 38169/M/8/(h), *Press and Poster Committee Reports,* 4 April 1930.

79 Pass, 'Coupon trading', p. 126; Alford, *W. D. & H. O. Wills,* pp. 349–51.

80 Turner, *Shocking History,* p. 184.

81 Pass, 'Coupon trading', p. 126.

82 Monopolies Commission, *Report on the Supply*, p. 20. See also Pass, 'Coupon trading', p. 127; Alford, *W. D. & H. O. Wills*, pp. 352–3; Corina, *Trust in Tobacco*, pp. 168–71.

83 Turner, *Shocking History*, p. 184.

84 Wills, 38169/M/8/(j), *Press and Poster Committee Reports,* 6 November 1930.

85 Wills, 38169/M/8/(l), *Press and Poster Committee Reports,* 16 April 1932.

86 Wills, 38169/M/8/(h), *Press and Poster Committee Reports,* 19 April 1930; 38169/M/8/(i), 28 April 1930; 38169/M/8/(l), 6 January 1931.

87 Wills, 38169/M/8/(i), *Press and Poster Committee Reports,* 22 April 1930.

88 In 1926 the Company pictured a middle-class man in a suit with the caption, 'Most men like them': *Tobacco*, 546 (June 1926), 55.

89 *Tit-Bits* (27 February 1932), p. 735.

90 *Tobacco*, 547 (July 1926), 37.

91 Wills, 38169/P/1/(b), *Press Cuttings, 1921–1927*.

92 *Daily Express* (31 January 1930), p. 13, (30 January 1930), p. 11.

5

Man and His Cigarette:
masculinity and the
mass market

In 1937, the Mass-Observation team of anthropologists entered the town of Bolton (which they save the pseudonym 'Worktown') to study in detail the leisure habits and daily lives of the British working class. Within a few months they had built up an enormous database of everyday life, compiled largely by ordinary men and women recruited to record the minutiae of their friends' and colleagues' social mannerisms. Mass-Observation focused its attention on such institutions of working-class leisure as the pub, the cinema and the seaside holiday in Blackpool, but it also conducted a survey of smoking, the results of which have never been published.[1] In 1949, using information collected from the Worktown survey of 1937 and from various interviews and questionnaires conducted throughout the Second World War, the organisation compiled a short but incisive monograph on the smoking habits of the nation, entitled *Man and His Cigarette*.[2]

The questions asked by Mass-Observation covered every aspect of what the team saw as the smoking 'ritual'. Respondents were required to give information about what they smoked; when they started; how much they spent; why they had continued to smoke; why they smoked a particular brand; how they lit their cigarette (or pipe); whether they tapped the cigarette before placing it in their mouth; whether they talked with their cigarette in their mouth; where they deposited the ash; whether they inhaled or otherwise; and whether they believed advertisements to have influenced their smoking decisions.[3] Often, the information collected by Tom Harrisson, Charles Madge and their assistants seemingly defied analysis: 'Roughly every second middle-class smoker taps his cigarette before taking it into his mouth. About half of these put the tapped end in their mouth, rather fewer light the tapped end, and the remainder do sometimes the one end, sometimes the other.'[4] Other statistics had a more obvious relation to Mass-Observation's attempt to re-create the social world of the smoker. The team found, for instance, that smokers were more likely than non-smokers to be pub-goers or members of clubs which sold alcohol; that they spent more money on drink than non-smokers; and that they were more likely to play the pools and gamble on horse and dog races.[5]

The reason Mass-Observation analysed smoking in such depth was because, along with the pub, the cinema, the dance hall, the pools and the annual trip to the seaside, the cigarette had become a staple of working-class culture. Tom Harrisson and Charles Madge delved into that culture of the 'mass man' to discover individual motivations behind each drinker's, each smoker's and each cinema-goer's personal pleasure. In doing so, they let working-class men and women 'speak for themselves', enabling them to talk and write about their smoking habits and other everyday activities. This in turn revealed both the extent to which the idealised smoking culture of the nineteenth century influenced the language of smoking in the twentieth century, and the multitude of individual, social and communal factors involved in each smoker's description of his or her pleasure. Decades before the arrival of the new men's studies and the more formalised anthropological accounts of the world of goods, Mass-Observation commented on a range of masculinities played out through the everyday use of commercial objects. It noted how masculine identities could be constructed through the communal use, or shared experience, of the cigarette. It saw how men toyed with the meanings of the cigarette to transform it from its effete, dandified origins into an object which lay at the centre of an often brutal, aggressive and rigorously masculine ritualised language; and, how, in the differences articulated between the pipe and the cigarette, these associations could be further subverted as older men regarded the briar pipe as the true symbol of solid, sober, reliable and steady British masculinity.

Mass-Observation's work forms the basis of this chapter, as men's relationships with tobacco and the cigarette are explored in the period when critics have suggested the homogeneous mass market economy first began to predominate over the segmentation and diversity of the Victorian economy. It begins with an exploration of the survival of that cult of the pipe and the cigar before suggesting that the mass market, while seeing a large decline in the sale of pipe tobacco, enabled a 'middle-brow' culture of pipe smoking to emerge. Within this culture, figures such as J. B. Priestley continued to write their rather pompous eulogies to 'the weed' but in a style which was more egalitarian and which placed less emphasis on hierarchies of connoisseurship and sheer commodity snobbery. In the longer section which follows this, attention will be given to the role of the cigarette within popular culture, focusing on the uses of this form of consumption to assert various masculine identities. Two figures in particular will be used to illustrate changing developments in smoking ideas: how Bulldog Drummond and James Bond brought the smoking culture of their literary precursor, Sherlock Holmes, out of 221b Baker Street and into the mass society of the twentieth century.

The hierarchies of taste created by the Victorian gentleman survived well into the twentieth century, Mass-Observation even believing that the First World War created a huge class divide in smoking, 'with the cigar, the Turkish cigarette, and the gentleman's pipe on one side, and the clay pipe and the cheap pub-sold cigar on the other'.[6] Presumably, the mass manufactured cigarette was so obviously excluded from the 'class' of elite tobacco culture that it was not even worth mentioning. Such a polarisation maps on to the distinctions set up in chapters 1 and 2 between the cultures of the cigar and the clay, but which survived throughout the first half of the twentieth century.

On the one hand, there was a continued celebration of the 'divine weed'. Articles appeared in *Chambers' Journal* which made explicit reference to the art of cigar connoisseurship, a 1935 essay specifically addressing itself to 'smokers of discernment', 'experts' and 'careful observers' who smoked to escape the modern age, while those who enjoyed motor cars, aviation and 'sport generally' lived life at a pace which 'restrict[ed] consumption in favour of the cigarette'.[7] Cigar smokers belonged 'to the few' and demanded 'that touch of art which mass production never knows'.[8] Other articles also fitted well with the Victorian model of smoking, providing detailed knowledge on the collection of tobacco books and paraphernalia, the histories of pipes, tobacco and snuff, anecdotal information on famous smokers past and present, and the more recent childhood hobby of collecting cigarette cards.[9] Most famously, Count Corti's *A History of Smoking* was translated into English by Paul England in 1931, providing the most comprehensive, if largely anecdotal, history of tobacco from its role in the religious rituals of the Mayas and the Aztecs to the 'coming of the cigarette'.[10] The eulogy also found its place, in reminiscences of perfect old-style tobacconists and in the reprinting of famous 'tributes to tobacco' which had formed the backbone of Cope's *Smoke Room Booklets*.[11] Alfred Dunhill, a retailer of fine tobacco products himself, published a number of works which promoted both his company and the 'gentle art of smoking' itself.[12] Some writers even spoke of the jealousy non-smokers had for the comradeship of smoking soldiers, and others wittily, yet boorishly, spoke of the difficulties of depositing one's ash, whether on the carpet ('so what of it'), in a flower pot or in an empty glass, when there was so much 'bigotry' among non-smokers who opposed such a disposal of tobacco refuse.[13]

On the other hand, there was also a continuation of diverse smoking habits and tastes among working-class smokers. A complete listing of the products and brands of the Gallaher tobacco company of Belfast in 1910 provides clues as to the range of preferences within the market. Gallaher sold 23 brands of packet tobacco (reasonably expensive mixtures, approximately 4*d* per ounce and upwards) and a further 15 types of Navy Cut and 43 flakes, all for the pipe. But it also catered for older regional tastes with the sale in bulk of many loose tobaccos signified purely by a description of the type of tobacco ('Brown Cut Cavendish', 'Red Shag', 'Loose Bird's Eye') rather than any brand name. Many of these, however, came to be pre-packaged and Gallaher manufactured 23 brands of plug and cake and 23 types of Irish roll, the cheapest type of tobacco (3*d* per ounce before Lloyd George's budget). By 1935, although branding dominated the company's output, it still produced black rolls, negroheads, bogies, nailrods, pigtails, twists, coils, bars, navy cuts, flakes and plugs, the cheapest of which retailed at 4*d* per ounce in the inter-war period. A similar story can be told of other manufacturers, the sales figures of which tended to consist largely of a few dominant brands but which always had a declining proportion of sales which demonstrated that they were never able to stop catering for local smoking traditions.[14] An analysis of the regional sales figures of Player's in 1937, which had by this time achieved a national market for the sale of its cigarettes, shows that its roll and hard tobaccos still sold well in the North of England and Scotland, whereas its loose tobaccos sold better in the Midlands and the South, as did its branded tobaccos.[15]

But what is more significant in this period is the coming together of an elite and a popular pipe-smoking culture, thanks largely to the steady quality and cheapness of the briar pipe, making it the symbol of 'solid, worthy and respectable' masculinity. As its use declined, the pipe smoker became a more distinctive being in society, and the celebration of its use combined elements of both the snobbery found in the periodical culture's disdain for the cigarette and a championing of the reliable common sense and moderation upon which the nation and Empire were supposedly founded. The *Morning Post*, hardly a middle-class journal, expressed this seemingly dual, but now unified, rhetoric:

Were it not for its soothing influence, it is possible to believe that nervous strain to which our town-dwellers are submitted in this mechanically-driven age would be unendurable. And upon the pipe of tobacco and the glass of ale the sturdy common-sense of the English working-man has been reared . . . In some ways it [the decline of the pipe] must cause regrets. When a thing is made easy it must inevitably lose some of its character. The cigarette, which is always at hand, if it has been called the perfect type of a perfect pleasure, has none of the meditative virtues of the pipe, or the infinite solace of the cigar. It inspires no personal affection, has no individuality of its own. We cannot lovingly rub its grain, or watch maturing through the years in its case. A few puffs and it is thrown away to make way for another of its fellows. It insidiousness leads us to the excess which no pipe smoker knows.[16]

D. L. LeMahieu has spoken more generally of this divide between elite and popular culture in British society in the early twentieth century. For LeMahieu, several figures worked to bring the two cultures together, culminating in a 'middle-brow' culture best epitomised by J. B. Priestley and his radio broadcasts during the Second World War.[17] Priestley was a great lover of his pipe and wrote often of a life's journey in search of the perfect smoke. In this sense he was similar to J. M. Barrie, who happened to find his Arcadia mixture, though Priestley's holy grail was the non-existent but even more personalised 'Boynton's Benediction', Boynton being his middle name. His smoking project was a clear escape from the modernity of the mass age, celebrating instead the 'community of palates' that had existed in the '1910 spirit of smoking' before the arrival of the 'robot' smokers, 'born to raise the dividends of tobacco combines and cartels'.[18] But despite Priestley's borrowing of the language of the by now traditional smoking culture, he did not make his celebration of tobacco exclusionary. Priestley's smoking culture is more egalitarian: he does not place the cigar at the pinnacle of tobacco connoisseurship as he knows his readers could never afford such an item; he does not list an entire cornucopia of tobacco paraphernalia; and he even buys and experiments with branded articles, demonstrating his at least practical acceptance of the commodified marketplace. Most significantly, just as with Barrie, he searches tirelessly for the ideal tobacco, but he finds it not at an expensive specialist off Regent Street, but in a shop 'rather small and in no way to be distinguished from the ordinary' just off the Great North Road in Doncaster.[19]

Priestley's version of solid, dependable, common-sense masculinity therefore unites pipe-smokers from all over the nation, from Mayfair to Bruddersford, and has become an image consciously worked up by politicians as ideologically diverse as Stanley Baldwin and Harold Wilson. It is a point

Table 5.1 Proportions and numbers of pipe smokers in each class and age group in 1948

(a) Among married men

Age group	Class AB		Class C		Class DE		All classes	
	%	000	%	000	%	000	%	000
16–24	*		*		11	30	10	30
25–34	29	20	31	110	19	380	21	510
35–44	35	130	33	190	21	450	25	770
45–64	39	290	33	270	30	810	32	1,360
65 and over	44	60	53	150	48	390	48	610
All age groups	38	510	36	710	26	2,060	29	3,280

Note:
* The number of people in these groups form too insignificant a proportion of the sample (and the total population) for the figures to be meaningful.

(b) Among unmarried men

Age group	Class AB		Class C		Class DE		All classes	
	%	000	%	000	%	000	%	000
16–24	21	50	14	50	9	130	11	230
25–34	36	40	39	70	12	90	18	200
35–44	41	20	25	20	14	70	18	100
45–64	33	30	28	40	30	200	30	270
65 and over	33	10	58	50	55	320	54	380
All age groups	29	140	27	230	20	810	22	1,180

Source: J. W. Hobson and H. Henry, *The Pattern of Smoking Habits: A Study Based on Information Collected During the Course of the Hulton Readership Survey, 1948* (London, Hulton Research Studies, 1948), p. 4.[20]

borne out by the statistics of smoking compiled through the Hulton Readership Survey of 1948, table 5.1 showing that the differences in pipe-smoking rates across the social classes were minimal, though younger working-class bachelors notably preferred cigarettes.

Whatever the reality of the image, tobacco manufacturers and retailers certainly saw an opportunity to capitalise on it. Believing that a return to the pipe away from the cigarette would bring customers back to the specialist rather than the general trader, tobacconists were particularly keen to promote the pipe. In 1928, retailers banded together to form the 'Smoke-a-Pipe Association', a movement designed to benefit the trade as a whole through a national media campaign which depicted pictures of famous men all smoking pipes. Retailers called on their customers to 'Join the Healthier Smoking Movement', deliberately using the 'coffin-nails' connotation of the cheap cigarette to persuade smokers to change their habits.[21] And from 1930, the International Pipe Week was organised by the Briar Pipe Association, its extensive publicity featuring an attractive woman smoking a cigarette saying, 'THIS IS PIPE WEEK – and I like to see a man SMOKE A PIPE. Won't you?' Other cards featured pipes and the slogan, 'The Everyday Sign of Manhood'.[22]

Manufacturers, too, played upon this image, advertisements for navy cut tobaccos usually depicting a strong-jawed, clean-cut, solidly mature naval officer or a country gentleman with 'experience'. Player's Empire brand, Digger, was marketed with images of men further down the social scale, but with an emphasis on hard work, single-mindedness, vision and purpose (figure 17). The very names given to the pipe-tobacco brands further continued the by now traditional marketing ploy of referring to a national institution, which cigarette promotion had significantly shifted away from. *The Smoker's Handbook* for 1936, a comprehensive list of 5,000 retail prices from all the main manufacturers, reveals the extent to which tobacco brands referred to the Empire, the rural aspect of British national identity, the nation's glorious past, its literary heritage or a well-known monument. Wills' popular brand names included Honey Cut, Black Jack, Viceroy, Three Castles, Westward Ho!, Capstan, Bishop Blaze, Empire Tobacco and Pirate. Player's, the second largest branch of Imperial, used names such as Navy Cut, Country Life, Bulwark, Hearts of Oak, Digger, Tawny and Clipper. Imperial's two main rivals, Gallaher and Carreras, marketed on a similar basis: War Horse, Army and Navy, Three Crowns, Hook of Holland and Harlequin for the former, and Turf, Cromwell, Sir Phillips, Guard's and Baron (as well as the Craven and Black Cat blends) for the latter.[23]

No such democratisation or coming together of two smoking cultures took place with the cigar. Hierarchies of connoisseurship were maintained and supported by restrictions of price so that working men would only ever be able to smoke the cheap cigars so frowned upon since the penny Pickwicks of the nineteenth century. Indeed, the distinctions between elite and popular cigar consumption seem to have widened, Mass-Observation's study of the

Advertisement for Player's Digger tobaccos, 1939   **17**

representation of smoking in the cartoons of *Punch* demonstrating that there had been an increasing tendency to make the cigar 'ugly', placing it in the mouth of the bookie, the theatre magnate and the newly rich: 'But its character remains now what it has always been, essentially aristocratic, autocratic, expensive and flamboyant – the character of the rebel who first broke through

Table 5.2 Monthly sales of cigars by Player's, 1937

Month	Sales
January	745
February	1,418
March	2,262
April	3,919
May	2,931
June	4,744
July	4,888
August	4,341
September	9,622
October	17,086
November	100,198
December	95,191

Source: Player's, DD PL 6/3/7, *Monthly Summary of Sales.*

the barricades against smoking and is still congratulating itself on its temerity'.[24] A fine line was thus made in the popular imagination which prevented working-class people from smoking cigars more regularly (though price was an obvious factor here) and which the rich had to tread carefully for fear of risking condemnation if it was felt that they smoked for ostentation rather than pleasure. The cigar was popular at times when display and flamboyancy were sanctioned, the figures in table 5.2 clearly showing its popularity in the festive season. Otherwise, public cigar smoking was only indulged in by the self-consciously and genuinely 'aristocratic', such as by Winston Churchill, the most famous cigar smoker of the century, and by those who engaged in Veblenesque emulative consumption and were presumably unaware of the ridicule served out to them in their literary representations.

By 1949, there were estimated to be 21 million cigarette smokers in the United Kingdom, 13.5 million men and 7.5 million women. That is, of every hundred men in 1949, 81 were smokers, as were 39 out of every 100 women. Cigarettes had become a 'part of life', no longer a luxury, no longer an occasional pleasure; 'without them, life would not be life'.[25] With 11 per cent of average household expenditure being spent on tobacco, smoking was a habit indulged in at all waking hours, the average male smoker consuming fifteen cigarettes a day.[26] Mass-Observation's explanation for this phenomenon centred around reasons of convenience. Many smokers found the pipe too awkward and clumsy compared with the cigarette and enjoyed the fact that less effort was needed in smoking the latter. It could be smoked quickly, between jobs or at a break in work, and represented a pace of life arguably increasingly dominating the lives of many twentieth-century smokers.[27] The three main pipe-smoking occasions were summarised as indoor leisure, outdoor leisure and evenings at home ('all point to relaxation and ease'), but the four main cigarette-smoking occasions were after meals, at social events, before breakfast and as a stimulant, indicating 'nervous habit, alertness plus some tension'.[28]

Of smokers' own explanations for the initial introduction to the habit, social factors predominated, yet individual and psychological factors were more prominent when accounting for the subsequent maintenance of consumption (as well as recognising that cigarettes had a certain hold over them which would later be more scientifically expressed as addiction). Common psychological explanations included the claim that cigarettes soothed the nerves, calmed the spirit, and acted as an antidote to boredom, depression, anxiety and loneliness: 'a solitary indulgence making good the inadequacies of life'.[29] More positively, smoking was held to add to other pleasures, particularly after meals, though in a way that made the smoker 'live perpetually "on the brink of some great delight" that never quite materialises'.[30] Oral gratification was frequently referred to as a factor, as was the need to compensate for other cravings such as eating, kissing or sex. The aesthetics and tactility of the cigarette and its accompanying matches, cases and lighters gave many smokers a great visual and physical pleasure, so much so that some found no gratification from smoking in the dark when these objects could not be observed.[31] But the importance of the social environment was crucial. One smoker admitted to persisting with the habit for eight years in order to maintain an air of sociability, even though he had never actually enjoyed the taste of a cigarette.[32] He also kept cigarettes to give out liberally to colleagues and new acquaintances in order to put everybody 'at their ease'. Another proffered cigarettes at 'that awkward moment when you have met a friend and enquiries to his welfare seem to have exhausted the conversational repertoire'.[33]

What is crucial to understanding the role of the cigarette is the nature of the 'social' in the new mass economy. For many the social had become quintessentially urban, a public, city-based culture in which strangers increasingly assessed one another not through verbal introductions, but through an anonymous interpretation of the material possessions that they carried about themselves. Whereas the pipe and the cigar had often been consumed privately, at home or in the club, alone or among a circle of friends and acquaintances from the same smoking culture, the ease of consumption of the cigarette meant that many more people were now using a standardised product in an increasing number of public places. And because of the anonymity of this public urban culture, commercial and material objects were useful in communicating one's individuality or identity to the countless faceless strangers that one came across every day.[34] It is a point of which Mass-Observation respondents were acutely aware: 'In public places when you feel conscious of people watching you a cigarette helps to promote self-possession and gives you something to do with your hands.'[35]

It was this near ubiquity of the cigarette within public popular culture that gave smoking such an iconic status in the first half of the twentieth century. And it was the First World War which democratised the cigarette more than any other event to produce a commodity so central to that process of cultural 'Blackpooling' that J. B. Priestley claimed typified the new egalitarian spirit of the mass society.[36] The British Tommy Atkins was the ultimate mass man, a standardised version of the nation's soldiery that all could recognise and feel sympathy for. He was not simply the product of the advertising campaigns outlined in chapter 4, but was a cultural reference point which focused people's attention on the front line. Above all, Tommy was a smoker of cigarettes, the 'soldier's friend'; cigarettes having proved necessary in many modern wars for their role as a monetary unit; their ability to create fraternal bonds through the process of gift giving; their ability to steady nerves and enable the soldier to regain self composure, relieve boredom, escape depression and loss; and their ability to prepare both mind and body for battle.[37] During the First World War the threat of constant shelling in the trenches made many men start smoking to steady the nerves, an observation not lost on military and state officials. Benedict Crowell, Assistant Secretary of War, noted that 'tobacco has established its claim to a recognised place in the soldier's life. To men enduring physical hardships, tobacco fills a need nothing else can satisfy.'[38] Newspapers and traders ran campaigns to ensure that soldiers received cigarettes and tobacco in addition to the two ounce weekly ration they received from the War Office.[39] For instance, the *People* called on its readers to send Woodbines – 'Tommy's favourite fag' – in bulk at prices as low as ten for 1*d*, or else to contribute to its massively subscribed 'Tobacco Fund'.[40] Such social pressures created an image of the 'Tommy' as a constant smoker of 'fags' which psychological and physical pressures encouraged him to live up to and which efficient distributive systems ensured he could. In 1918, Tommy returned to Britain knowing that his smoking would be sanctioned in a far greater variety of public places and institutions.

Boredom and comfort again played a role in inducing soldiers to smoke in the Second World War and the civilian population was as equally concerned to ensure that supplies reached the troops.[41] But workers in England also began to smoke increasing amounts, despite the difficulties in procuring favourite brands.[42] Mass-Observation found a 'definite connection between proximity to bombing and active war work, and increased smoking'.[43] Some sections of the population claimed to smoke less during the war but this was usually because of difficulties in obtaining supplies. Mass-Observation felt that people were craving more social contacts during the war and that smoking was a social activity. Cigarettes were at times a substitute for sociability for those who were working nights and long hours.[44]

Two world wars therefore lent a certain universality to the phenomenon of smoking that Mass-Observation would use as the assumption behind its intensive investigations into the use of the commodity in the 1940s. But Mass-Observation was eager to demonstrate that within this apparently homogeneous mass, each smoker held as diverse a range of identities as any number of smoking biographies offered by the individualist accounts of the nineteenth-century periodical literature. It argued that custom, community and convention decided the 'when as well as the how' of the smoker's 'first taste of nicotine', but that the practices of smoking were eventually shaped 'to suit the pattern of his own individuality'.[45] One means by which Mass-Observation broke down this mass culture of smoking was through an analysis of brand preferences. Despite the fact that smokers then (as now) claimed that advertisements did not really affect their own consumption decisions (though it was generally accepted that they could well determine other people's), Mass-Observation was able to make generalisations about brand associations towards which smokers must have been attracted. Perhaps the fact that many smokers consistently failed to recognise their 'favourite' brand under conditions of a blind trial convinced Mass-Observation of the importance of image over substance in determining brand preference.[46] Class was a crucial means of categorisation at the time, with the cheaper brands being labelled as working class and the middle-priced cigarettes (Craven 'A', Gold Flake and Player's Medium) being labelled as mass based, since their price of 6d for ten during the 1920s and 1930s meant that they carried few of the connotations of the 'gasper' held by brands such as Woodbine, Weights, Tenners and Minors (which retailed at 2d for five).

During the inter-war period, one in four cigarettes smoked was of the cheapest variety, leaving the major part of tobacco consumption to consist of the mid-priced range. The expensive cigarettes tended to be longer and wider, as well as consisting of the more expensive Virginian, Turkish and Egyptian blends which could only be afforded by those with a substantial income. The smokers of these cigarettes were the direct descendants of Oscar Wilde and the officers of the Royal Horse Guards, though a certain androgyneity had been given to their consumption, thanks to the antics of the Turkish-smoking 'Bright Young People' of Evelyn Waugh's *Vile Bodies* and the shocking, flippant, arrogant, youthful, and ever-so-trivial behaviour of the self-consciously 'gay and witty and handsome' characters of Noel Coward's *The Vortex* and *Design for Living*.[47]

Because of Player's advertising in the inter-war years which led the way in promoting a company name over and above individual brands, the Player's logo became very much a mass reference point and Players Medium the nearest there was to a truly mass cigarette. By the 1920s Player's Medium accounted for over two-thirds of the company's total cigarette sales and almost all of its Navy Cut range (which also included Mild and Gold Leaf).[48] From just before the Second World War until 1943, it was estimated that every second smoker bought Player's. As Mass-Observation put it, Player's 'pre-eminence' was due to the widespread view that Player's cigarettes were 'safe'. The Player's sailor obtained a central place within the iconography of British popular culture which apparently inspired feelings of affection and antipathy, depending upon the brand preferences of the smoker, and which even re-sulted in a rather tiresome fantasy to provide an insight into Ian Fleming's understanding of female desire.[49] The uncle-figure aspect mentioned in the previous chapter allegedly made him popular among women, a friendly face which gave an assurance of protection; while other smokers were driven to using Hero's head as a target for their ash, one smoker commenting, 'I hate the sight of the bloody man.'[50] No explanation was offered for such feelings, but perhaps the strength of them is a recognition of the pervasiveness of the Player's image. However, Mass-Observation may well have overestimated the mass nature of the cigarette due to the over-representation of the Southern-based middle classes among its respondents. While the sheer volume of Player's Sales statistics (table 5.3) suggests that its cigarettes appealed to all social groups, their popularity in the North was not as spectacular.

The cigarette of the industrial male working class was often the Woodbine. The price of Tenners, Weights, Minors and others at 4*d* for ten meant that this category of cigarette would appeal to those of the lowest incomes, but these other brands were smoked by both genders and were never excluded

Table 5.3 Sales of Player's cigarettes (by number), January 1937

Distribution	Sales
London	1,348,019
East Anglia	260,978
Southern East	179,885
Southern England	188,977
South West	108,206
Wales	204,010
Midlands	371,631
Lancashire/Cheshire	349,134
Yorkshire	201,511
Northern England	74,161
Scotland	118,176
Northern Ireland	57,489
Total UK	3,462,197

Source: Player's, DD PL/6/5/1-10, *Monthly Analysis of Sales and Distribution.*[51]

from other social groups to quite the same extent. Woodbines, however, were essentially working class and male, an association accepted by Wills in its advertisements for the product, the image of the furnace worker, stripped to the waist, signifying the type of masculinity for which the cigarette was known (figure 16). The identity of the product became so fixed that in the film *I'm Alright Jack*, the camera pans in on trade unionist Peter Sellers' packet of Woodbines, marking it as a badge of his class affiliation.

The attention to class differences is perhaps overdone in Mass-Observation's work and there is often little attempt to analyse what the team saw. For instance, they observed that working-class smokers were more likely to hold the cigarette between the thumb and finger, 'with the burning end pointing inwards to the palm',[52] while middle-class smokers held it between the first and second finger. They also noted an 'irrational' habit, common among middle-class smokers, of tapping the cigarette before lighting it, though the sample was roughly equally split between those who put the tapped end in their mouth and those the other.[53] One can speculate that the working-class method of smoking the cigarette owed much to the looseness of the tobacco in cheap cigarettes, the pointing of the burning end inwards towards the palm suggesting the outdoor nature of much of their smoking. The outward projection of the cigarette among middle-class smokers is far more evocative of a more debonair style of masculinity, in which the cigarette is waved nonchalantly in the air during conversation. That the middle classes also tapped the cigarette when there was no longer any need to pack down the tobacco in their well-manufactured expensive brands demonstrates the importance of tactility and performance in the ritualised pleasure of smoking.

The ritualised nature of smoking was observed in great detail by Mass-Observation in its study of pub-based culture. The cigarette became important in public displays of masculinity, either through bodily gesture or verbal communication. The proffering of cigarettes to friends and colleagues in the public house helped define the group, it enclosed a community to the exclusion of non-smokers and continued that public, communal mode of consumption associated with pre-industrial cultures but which survived through and be-yond the nineteenth century. Such group identity, then, provided the arena in which various masculinities could be defined. Mass-Observation noted in particular an aggressively masculine culture among working-class smokers where the very vocabulary built up around the ritual of smoking suggested a particular gender-based smoking identity:

> Smokers tend to talk of *pitching* and *throwing* the stub, rather than, more tamely, of *dropping* it; and quite often it is sent flying to some distance. Their actions, moreover, even more than their language, are frequently clothed in aggressive-ness. Some speak of 'grinding', 'crushing', even 'killing' a stub, and a favourite trick is to burn it to death in the fire or to drown it in the nearest available liquid. One man said: 'I cannot let a stub smoulder. I *must* crush it out.'[54]

Similar results were found in the putting out of matches, one man showing off about his 'dangerous trick' of flicking a match 20 to 30 feet after lighting his cigarette with it. Such aggressive forms of smoking clearly promoted a sense of masculinity which excluded both the middle-class smoker and most women from the male-based working-class public house.

Again, though, and just as with the briar pipe, what is significant about the early to mid twentieth-century culture of the cigarette is the collapse of the boundaries between the elite and the popular. The mass- or working-class-based smoking culture of the public house became frequently enjoined with the smoking culture of Oscar Wilde, Noel Coward and their literary and aristocratic associates. In the ways in which both Bulldog Drummond and James Bond smoked and talked about their tobacco consumption, they were illustrative of wider developments in dominant projections of masculine iden-tity which owed much to the liberal emphasis on individuality but which accepted culturally many of the products of the mass market.

'Sapper' (H. C. McNeile) first introduced the hugely popular Hugh 'Bulldog' Drummond, D.S.O., M.C., in 1920. As a bored ex-captain of the Royal Loamshires searching for excitement, Drummond inadvertently found himself confronting the international criminal and master of disguise, Carl Peterson, in the 'four rounds' which constituted the first four novels (*Bulldog Drummond, The Black Gang, The Third Round* and *The Final Count*). Drummond was a hero very much shaped by the experience of the First World War. A physically powerful man ('slightly under six feet' and over fifteen stone in weight), he was described as having that 'cheerful type of ugliness' which inspired confidence, yet was also always immaculately turned out, knew his way around the clubs of London, and inspired tremendous loyalty from all those who came to know him. A square-jawed patriot, anti-intellectual and anti-communist to the point of advocating black-shirted proto-fascism, Drummond got to the root of a problem through common sense and straightforward tackling of the matter in hand. Like Sherlock Holmes, he had a devoted stooge in his servant James Denny, but he played a minor role as compared with the 'team' of like-minded ex-officers which Drummond led and built up around him, who had followed him through the mud of Flanders but were unfulfilled with the trivialities of civilian life: Algy Longworth, Ted Jerningham, Peter Darrell and Toby Sinclair; men who talked 'a strange jargon of their own – idle, perfectly groomed, bored'.[55]

In both his blunt and direct approach to life and his willingness to be part (though clearly the leader) of a team playing the game of adventure, Drummond differed very much from the singularly and intellectually brilliant Sherlock Holmes. But if Drummond could offer no great individuality of thought and reason, he mirrored Holmes for the idiosyncrasies in his smoking habit. Drummond, in fact, as a cigarette smoker was the direct descendant of Colonel Fred Burnaby in the languid approach he took to life, unless called into action when he would single-mindedly devote his entire effort to the job at hand. His smoking seemed to express that boredom with everyday life which Drummond chose to exaggerate with a flippant, almost flirtatious, use of his silver cigarette case: 'He waved vaguely at the lady in question and then held out his cigarette-case to the girl. "Turkish on this side – Virginia on that," he remarked.'[56] The constant offer of two types of cigarette, with the Virginians often referred to as 'gaspers', belies a refusal to take himself seriously, as though life, in the essentially aristocratic manner, was just a game. However, Sapper always has his hero extracting a cigarette 'carefully', hinting at an appreciation of tobacco which the Woodbine-smoking clerks that appear in *The Black Gang* can never hope to achieve ('the type that Woodbines its fingers to a brilliant orange; the type that screams insults at a football referee on a Saturday afternoon'[57]).

Drummond is thus a sophisticated, aristocratic, rather dandified and hier-archical consumer of the cigarette. Yet he is also very much a part of the mass. The reader is never told of the particular brand which he smokes, and Drummond does not just smoke cigarettes to reflect a certain mood, as does Holmes. He has just come out of the war, is communally bonded to his friends and smokes at all times, when contemplative, when under stress, before the attack and immediately afterwards. Drummond smokes huge quantities in all his adventures and, besides the more explicit references to his habit in the first novel, Sapper largely ignores the qualitative aspects of his hero's consumption. His smoking is therefore unappreciative at times – he smokes when he needs, not wants, to – and the fact that this is simply accepted suggests a different understanding of the qualities of the cigarette which had emerged through observing its use in war. Furthermore, Drummond's cigarette smoking makes him something of the embodiment of straightforward Englishness. His cigarette stands in contrast to, and in defi-ance of, the ostentatious cigar of Carl Peterson which signifies the lack of trust the reader is expected to place in him. Drummond's smoking is there-fore a symbol to contrast with the criminal's cosmopolitan flamboyancy, as is his use of the down-to-earth pipe when in the comfortable domestic setting of his own home. Drummond's pipe is used in the Holmesian manner to stimulate thought, but the reader is told nothing of the paraphernalia that comes with the habit, thus opening up the appeal to all pipe smokers, rather than those who could simply afford the time to cultivate the earlier detective's smoking peculiarities. In smoking both pipe and cigarette, then, and in com-bining effete dandyism with solid, plain-speaking patriotism, Drummond stands somewhere in between the nineteenth-century culture of individuality and the twentieth-century egalitarianism of J. B. Priestley.

Ian Fleming's James Bond, by contrast, first appeared in book form in 1953 in *Casino Royale* (the first Bond film, *Dr No*, was not made until 1962), a time in which the consumer society was said to be in its heyday, popular culture across Europe was supposedly being Americanised, and values of democratic individualism were consequently coming to dominate. Bond, however, was 'the last of the clubland buccaneers' and, as with Drummond, represents a fascinating mixture of British traditions and modernising influences.[58] Following Conan Doyle, smoking and tobacco permeate the Fleming canon, defining both the central character and the host of villains which come his way, as well as acting as a recurring narrative plot device, such as in *Moonraker* when Sir Hugo Drax cheats at cards by examining their reflection in his cigarette box. Bond smokes only cigarettes, but any thought that this could subsume him within the homogeneous mass is quickly eradicated when it is realised that his consumption is imbued with almost the same degree of individuality as that of Holmes. Bond smokes cigarettes called Morland Specials, made of a Balkan and Turkish mixture (referred to as Macedonian in *Moonraker*), specially prepared for him by a tobacconists of the same name on Grosvenor Street and easily identifiable by their three gold bands. These he keeps in his flat, light gun-metal cigarette case which holds fifty at a time and which he lights with his 'black-oxidised Ronson lighter' or his 'well-used gold Dunhill'. When he couldn't smoke Morlands he would move on to Turkish or else 'good old' Senior Service, king size Chesterfields in the United States, Laurens jaune in France and Royal Blend in Jamaica.

Fleming helps mould the personality of Bond through his rather snobbish consumption, and also through a juxtaposition of other characters, none of whom smoke with quite the same distinctive air as Bond. Mathis is a big smoker of Caporals in *Casino Royale*; Bond's friend in the CIA, Felix Leiter, shares the preference for Chesterfields; Sir Hugo Drax, nervously disposed, chooses the less masculine cork-tipped Virginians; Bond girls usually plump for Parliament cigarettes; and British civil servants smoke Player's. M, of course, is constantly with his pipe, symbolising the old England of oak-panelled offices and long lunches at the club. In contrast, Goldfinger and *Live and Let Die*'s Mr Big do not smoke, emphasising their clinical obsession with their criminal activities and their disdain for all pleasures which do not contribute to their master plan. Just as in the Holmes adventures, each character's consumption style says something about the individuality of the smoker. Yet Bond seems to move away from his associations with the detective and, instead, shares much in common with the supposed attributes of the masses. In *Casino Royale*, Bond could hardly be labelled a discriminating consumer, smoking as he does seventy cigarettes in one day, while in later novels his habit takes control of his individuality, unconsciously filling an ash tray on his own in *Live and Let Die* and smoking incessantly throughout a tense game of golf with Goldfinger. If this was masculine behaviour, it had more in common with the culture of the public house than the gentleman's club. When Fleming describes Bond's smoking he uses the same language that Mass-Observation uncovered. Bond usually 'killed' the 'dead' butt of his cigarette, 'trod' on it, 'crushed' it or flicked it on the carpet without a moment's hesitation, and each drag he took was a 'deep' one, taken right down 'sharp' on to the lungs.

Bond's position within the history of British masculinity seems to follow neatly on from Bulldog Drummond. The pipe has now been discarded entirely, emphasising the essential modernity of Bond. Yet this modernity is dependent on Bond's belief in duty and patriotism, of loyalty to the club and in maintaining an air of sophisticated individuality so that one even makes distinctive one's consumption of a standardised product. What is also significant is that Fleming discarded a sidekick or team of friends to help Bond, replacing them with a boss (and thus tying Bond to a profession rather than an amateur 'game') who acts not as a stooge but as the embodiment of Establishment England. From such a position, Bond strides out on his own to right the world's wrongs. When Bond was transferred to the cinema screen, the attention to detail which Fleming gave to his hero's relationship with elite commodities could not be sufficiently transferred, thereby enabling the films to skirt over the more traditional elements of Bond's Britishness, or rather Englishness. Bond was therefore left with a sophisticated smoking veneer but which rather than being hierarchical became all the more accessible and egalitarian, especially through the more democratic persona and Scots accent of Sean Connery, a far cry from the stilted English of David Niven whom Fleming saw as the ideal representation of his literary Bond.[59]

In Bond's interpretation on film there was much borrowing from an established American film genre which featured the urbane, sophisticated smoker as the heightened individualist, going his own way in life, not compromising his ideals in pursuit of what he did or did not believe. An interpretation of films has been missing from this chapter, but in some ways it is not necessary given the ubiquity of the glamorous image of smoking in 1930s, 40s and 50s cinema. Humphrey Bogart towers over all others in this sense, the ultimate smoking idol of the screen, powerfully celebrating the stylish chic of smoking in classics such as *Casablanca*, *The Treasure of the Sierra Madre*, *The African Queen* and *To Have and Have Not*, as well as briefly celebrating hand rolling in *The Maltese Falcon*. To Bogart's name could be added literally hundreds of others, from Edward G. Robinson to James Cagney to Paul Henreid, Clark Gable, Spencer Tracy, Robert Donat, James Stewart and Gary Cooper, all of whom brought the cigarette far closer to the centre of any dominant notion of masculinity than Basil Rathbone's portrayal of a meerschaum-smoking

Holmes ever did. What all of these actors did was to make smoking increasingly important to individual identity, providing working-class cinema-goers with the images with which to construct and articulate their smoking identities in a manner similar to that outlined in the periodical literature of several decades previously. That film and the iconography of the cigarette became so important to men's own sense of identity is evidenced by the unwillingness that many had in giving up smoking once the dangers of lung cancer and heart disease became known. Despite all that is now known about the nature of addiction and the inability of smokers to quit, it is this masculine culture of tobacco that forms the backdrop for the reception of the 1950s smoking–health controversy which will be examined in the final chapters of this book.

Notes

1 Mass-Observation (hereafter M.-O.), *The Pub and the People: A Worktown Study* (London, Cresset, 1987); G. Cross (ed.), *Worktowners at Blackpool: Mass-Observation and Popular Leisure in the 1930s* (London, Routledge, 1990); J. Richards and D. Sheridan (eds), *Mass-Observation at the Movies* (London, Routledge, 1987).

2 M.-O., File Report 3192, *Man and His Cigarette*, 1949.

3 M.-O. Topic Collections, *Smoking Habits 1937–1965*. Box No. 1: *Smoking Habits: Smoking Enquiry 1937*, File A: Questions.

4 M.-O., *Man and His Cigarette*, p. 120.

5 *Ibid.*, pp. 98–9.

6 *Ibid.*, p. 74.

7 Anon., 'The perfect cigar', *Chambers' Journal* (December 1935), 915–16.

8 H. Warner Allen, 'After dinner', *Saturday Review*, 155 (28 January 1933), 91.

9 Anon., 'Cigarette pictures', *New Statesman*, 20 (7 April 1923), 769–71; R. Lynd, 'Smoking in the House', *New Statesman and Nation*, 30 (11 February 1928), 556–7; J. T. Johnston, 'Snuff', *Chambers' Journal*, 20 (29 November 1930), 825–6; J. D. Rolleston, 'On snuff taking', *British Journal of Inebriety*, 34 (July 1936), 1–16; L. Spencer, 'Celebrities as smokers', *Chambers' Journal* (December 1936), 922–4; Sir D. Hunter-Blair, 'Evolution of smoking', *Empire Review*, 69 (February 1939), 83–9; P. E. Thomas, 'Delectable dust: the story of snuff', *Chambers' Journal* (November 1939), 866–7; R. Hargreaves, 'Noxious weed', *Chambers' Journal* (February 1941), 93–6; Anon., 'Books on smoking', *Notes and Queries*, 185 (31 July 1943), 84–5; A. Cruse, 'The charm of cigarette cards', *Strand Magazine* (March 1947), 70–8.

10 Count Corti, *A History of Smoking* (1931; London, Random House, 1996).

11 C. C. Pickering, 'The fragrant weed', *Chambers' Journal*, 18 (17 November 1928), 813–14; W. M. Parker, 'Pipe and pen: some authors' tributes to tobacco', *Chambers' Journal* (January 1948), 51–2.

12 A. H. Dunhill, *The Pipe Book* (London, A and C Black, 1924); A. H. Dunhill, *The Gentle Art of Smoking* (London, Max Reinhardt, 1954).

13 Y. Y., 'Cigarette ends', *New Statesman and Nation*, 5 (21 January 1933), 68–9; R. Lynd, 'Of human pleasures', *Littell's Living Age*, 354 (July 1938), 446–8; A. Hino, 'Of cigarettes and soldiers', *Littell's Living Age*, 356 (July 1939), 443–6.

14 Bristol Record Office, Wills Archive (hereafter Wills), 38169/Pr/6, *Pricing Records*.

15 Nottingham Record Office, Player's Archive (hereafter Player's), DD PL 6/5/1-10, *Monthly Analysis of Sales and Distribution 1936–1957*.

16 *Morning Post* (4 November 1924), in Wills, 38169/P/1/b, *Press Cuttings, 1921–1927*.

17 D. L. LeMahieu, *A Culture for Democracy: Mass Communication and the Cultivated Mind in Britain Between the Wars* (Oxford, Clarendon Press, 1988).

18 J. B. Priestley, *Delight* (London, Heinemann, 1949), pp. 26–7.

19 J. B. Priestley, 'A new tobacco', *Saturday Review*, 144 (13 August 1927), 216–17.

20 The classification of the three groups was as follows: AB – 'the well-to-do and middle classes'; C – 'the lower middle classes'; DE – 'the working classes'. Class AB made up 11 per cent of the sample, class C 17 per cent and class DE 72 per cent.

21 *Tobacco Trade Review* (hereafter *TTR*), 61:727 (July 1928), 17.

22 *TTR*, 64:758 (February 1931), 19; *TTR*, 54:762 (June 1931), 19.

23 *The Smoker's Handbook* (published by *Tobacco*), 1936, in Wills, 38169/(Pr)/7(b), *Pricing Records*.

24 M.-O., *Man and His Cigarette*, p. 60.

25 R. Hoggart, *The Uses of Literacy* (1957; Harmondsworth, Penguin, 1973), p. 56.

26 M.-O., *Man and His Cigarette*, p. 95; J. W. Hobson and H. Henry, *The Pattern of Smoking Habits: A Study Based on Information Collected During the Course of the Hulton Readership Survey, 1948* (London, Hulton Research Studies, 1948), pp. 7–8; G. Harrison and F. C. Mitchell, *The Home Market: A Handbook of Statistics* (London, Allen and Unwin, 1940), p. 91.

27 M.-O. File Report 776, *Smoking Trends: Survey of Male Smoking Habits, 1941*, pp. 8–9.

28 M.-O. File Report 979, *Smoking: Comparisons Between 1937 and 1941 in Smoking Habits*, p. 16.

29 M.-O., *Man and His Cigarette*, p. 136.

30 *Ibid.*, p. 131.

31 *Ibid.*, p. 133.

32 M.-O. Topic Collections, *Smoking Habits, 1937–1965*. Box No. 2, File B, J. G. Chope (248).

33 *Ibid.*, Box 3, File A, P. Moore (416).

34 The literature is now enormous, though the phrase used by Rudi Laermans nicely summarises this type of analysis: 'looking and being looked at are the predominant forms of social contact within large cities'. R. Laermans, 'Learning to consume: early department stores and the shaping of modern consumer culture, 1860–1914', *Theory, Culture, Society*, 10 (1993), 99.

35 M.-O. Topic Collections, *Smoking Habits, 1937–1965*. Box No. 3, File A, P. Moore (416).

36 J. B. Priestley, *English Journey* (1934; Harmondsworth, Penguin, 1987).

37 R. Klein, *Cigarettes are Sublime* (London, Picador, 1995), p. 137.

38 Quoted in A. E. Hamilton, *This Smoking World* (London, Methuen, 1928), p. 7. Hamilton further describes tobacco's place in the trenches as 'akin to that of morphine in the hospital' (p. 7).

39 *TTR*, 47:562 (October 1914), 379–80, 386; *TTR*, 48:571 (July 1915), 259.

40 *People* (19 December 1915), p. 2.

41 M.-O., *Man and His Cigarette*, p. 79. See also the letters to *The Times* in A. Livesey (ed.), *Are We At War? Letters to The Times, 1939–1945* (London, Times Books, 1989), pp. 79–80, 176–7.

42 M.-O. File Report 784, *Supplementary Report on Smoking Habits: Age, Job and Regional Differences in Smoking Habits*, 1941.

43 M.-O. File Report 776, *Smoking Trends: Survey of Male Smoking Habits*, 1941, p. 2.

44 *Ibid.*, pp. 5–6; M.-O., *Broadcast for North American Service*, 19 June 1941, by Tom Harrisson (contained with File Report 784).

45 M.-O., *Man and His Cigarette*, pp. 116–18.

46 Few of Mass-Observation's respondents were willing to admit to being influenced by advertising, though some claimed that repetitive slogans such as 'Player's Please' and 'Better Buy Capstan' influenced other smokers: M.-O. Topic Collections, *Smoking Habits, 1937–1965*. Box No. 2, File A, Grimshaw; Box 3, File A, H. Newman (428); Box 3, File B, D. K. Pitt (446); M.-O., *Man and His Cigarette*, p. 157.

47 E. Waugh, *Vile Bodies* (1930; New York, Dell, 1958), p. 106; N. Coward, 'The Vortex' and 'Design for Living' in *Play Parade* (London, Heinemann, 1934).

48 Player's, DD PL 6/4/1-7, *Monthly Figures for Each Type of Cigarette, 1912–1933*.

49 I. Fleming, *Thunderball* (1961; London, Triad/Granada, 1978), pp. 152–6.

50 M.-O., *Man and His Cigarette*, pp. 160–3.

51 Such figures do not, of course, take into account population sizes per region or the efficiency of the distributive systems. The aim is simply to show that the cigarettes were not equally distributed around the country.

52 M.-O. Topic Collections, *Smoking Habits, 1937–1965*. Box No. 2, File D, G. Lovekin (391).

53 M.-O., *Man and His Cigarette*, pp. 121–2.

54 *Ibid.*, pp. 126–7.

55 H. C. McNeile ('Sapper'), *The Black Gang*, in *Bulldog Drummond: His Four Rounds with Carl Peterson* (London, Hodder and Stoughton, 1930), p. 343.

56 H. C. McNeile ('Sapper'), *Bulldog Drummond* (1920; London, Hodder and Stoughton, 1929), p. 22.

57 *Ibid.*, p. 70.

58 For the best and most recent discussion of Bond's position within film culture and the literary tradition of the spy-detective thriller, see J. Chapman, *Licence to Thrill: A Cultural History of the James Bond Films* (London, I. B. Tauris, 1999).

59 *Ibid.*

6

Consuming the unrespectable: smoking and femininity

By the end of the 1940s, when male smoking rates had reached 80 per cent, approximately 40 per cent of women were regularly consuming cigarettes. If tobacco was not smoked universally, its use was at a level sufficient to label it a truly mass item of commodity consumption. The earlier restrictions against women's smoking had been largely lifted and for many women smoking had become one of the routine procedures of life. In this everyday aspect of consumption, many of the issues discussed in the previous chapter explaining why smoking was important to men have as much applicability to women. There were few gender differences in the alleged ability of the cigarette to relieve stress, to ease social tension, to provide comfort, to alleviate nervous irritability. But, given the Victorian social conventions about the gendered nature of smoking, the means by which these were overcome by generations of women smokers warrants separate treatment. The history of the female smoker is one of changing attitudes to respectable femininity and the use of commercial products to break down once dominant notions.

Perhaps the classic story of women's smoking appears in Dorothy Richardson's autobiographical novels, collected together in *Pilgrimage*. She recounts the experiences of many 'new women' of the 1890s as Miriam, a school governess, begins to yearn for a more liberated lifestyle. She had often rolled cigarettes for her father, but one day decides to smoke herself to confirm that she is capable of more than the role society has assigned to her. Her first cigarette, secretly puffed in the confines of her own bedroom, becomes an explicit rite of passage, the smoke actually stimulating all her senses so that she views her familiar surroundings in a new light: the 'little clouds brought her a sense of power. She had chosen to smoke and she was smoking, and the morning world gleamed back at her.'[1] It is some time before Miriam dares to smoke in public, even among the society of bohemian literary intellectuals with whom she comes to associate. Eventually, while playing billiards with a Mr Corrie, she accepts her first public cigarette, which serves to complete the equality of communication taking place between the two of them. The significance of the moment is not lost on Miriam:

> Contemplating the little screwed-up smile on the features of her partner, bunched to the lighting of his own cigarette, Miriam discharged a double stream of smoke violently through her nostrils - breaking out at last a public defiance of the freemasonry of women. 'I suppose I'm a new woman – I've said I am now, anyhow,' she reflected, wondering in the background of her determination how she would reconcile the role with her work as a children's governess.[2]

Her misgivings about her respectable position remain and she is left to admire fiercely independent women such as Meg and Jan, and the 'powerful' German, Frederika von Bohlen, who declares, 'Tonight I must smoke or die'.[3] When she first meets Mr Wilson (based on H. G. Wells) at a literary gathering she initially refuses his offer of a cigarette, only to realise a few moments later that she should not miss this opportunity to announce her arrival into the world of 'special people, emancipated people'. She summons up the confidence to ask for a cigarette and boldly smokes it before them:

> She sat back in her corner, happy and forgetful. She had not had so much tea as she wanted. She had refused the cigarette against her will. Now she was alive. These weak things would not happen again, and the next time she would bring her own cigarettes. To take out a cigarette and light it here, at home amongst her own people. These were her people.[4]

Richardson's narrative exemplifies the significance of smoking for many turn-of-the-century women and perhaps suggests why little is known about female consumption rates at this time: furtive, private and secret experiments with the cigarette simply do not have a place in the historical record. Yet Miriam's direct confrontation with respectability's behavioural codes might not describe the experience of other women's smoking from different social and economic backgrounds. For them, there is unlikely to have been such a keen awareness of their own individual emancipation and women's smoking may have become acceptable through more general inroads into notions of respectability, a concept which could vary greatly among diverse local communities. Certainly, smoking by women was largely seen as unrespectable across most social classes of the late nineteenth century and consequently very few women smoked at this time, yet how this situation changed cannot solely be explained through the direct confrontation interpretation suggested by

Richardson's life. This chapter, therefore, will pay much attention to women's relationship to the constantly reworked definitions of respectable femininity and will also draw out the divergent reasons for women's smoking and the range of feminine identities symbolised through the use of the cigarette. What will be apparent is the importance of the cigarette in either breaking down accepted patterns of behaviour or in reflecting more general changes in women's lives which allowed new outward projections of femininity to be displayed in particular social contexts. Crucial to the explanation is the social and economic context of women's lives. Were it not for the expansion of employment opportunities which gave young women working in public environments independent incomes, then these challenges to older versions of femininity could not have taken place.[5]

Little evidence has been provided in previous histories of tobacco which could amount to a genuine social history of women's smoking. Most have resorted to the literary and historical anecdotes presented in the Victorian periodical literature to write of the prevalence of aristocratic female snuff taking in the eighteenth century and its subsequent decline in the nineteenth. Many writers also mention how clay pipes were used by both men and women in pre-industrial Britain and the examination of dental remains by archaeologists would appear to confirm this.[6] But a general lack of evidence on consumption practices before the nineteenth century has prevented a test of the assumed prevalence of women's smoking and, if this was the case, how it came to be not only frowned upon but outrightly condemned by mid nineteenth-century respectable society.

There is much to suggest that women's use of the cigarette might not have been originally forbidden, given the frequently observed femininity of the word itself and the attack made upon it by the overtly masculine cigar and pipe smokers. However, the cultural and literary accounts of women's relationship to tobacco and the cigarette immediately gave rise to associations of deviant sexuality and wanton morality. Even before the popularisation of cigarettes among elite circles in the 1850s, Dickens and Thackeray had shocked their readers with cigar-smoking women, the beautifully manipulative Becky Sharp tasting Rawdon Crawley's cigar 'in the prettiest way possible', ensuring his eternal fascination and devotion.[7] Of greater international fame is Mérimée's story of the gypsy girl, Carmen, celebrated in Bizet's opera of the same name. Carmen ensured that women's smoking would always be associated with erotic illicit sexuality, and performances of the opera made great play on the scantily clad women workers of Seville's tobacco factory.[8] In British popular culture, Carmen's literary equivalent would be Cigarette, the wild, 'insolent', 'coquettish', 'mischievous' and boyish, desert-army soldier-girl of Ouida's *Under Two Flags*. A smoker of both cigars and her namesake, Cigarette titillated through her subversion of appropriate femininity, drinking, fighting, swearing, laughing and dancing with the soldiers of what would later be recognised in Frank Lloyd's 1936 film adaptation as the French Foreign Legion. Cigarette's masculine activities did not leave her entirely 'unsexed'; she still carried the 'delicious fragrance of youth' and it was this 'blending of the two that made her piquante, made her a notoriety in her own way'.[9]

'Cigarette' set the tone for the representation of women and smoking in turn-of-the-century art, literature and photography. Ouida's Zu-Zu (a disreputable woman associated with London cavalry officers) was followed by paintings of beautiful women made more alluring through their cigarettes; by E. M. Forster's signification of Jacky's former modelling background in *Howard's End*; by the frequency of the appearance of the cigarette in photographs of the female nude; and by the placing of famous actresses on the very first cigarette cards in the 1890s.[10] It is no wonder that a later oral history interviewee claimed of this period that women 'could smoke if they had no objection to being considered immoral, but to smoke and be also respectable was a contradiction in terms'.[11] How such social censure could manifest itself is expressed in extreme form in the following letter to the *Daily Mail* in 1906, which shows clearly how respectable femininity was defined through the above images of deviance: 'Women who do this [smoke] are slack and casual about everything. They neglect their homes and their families: they neglect their social duties; their God they have ceased to pay any heed to; their husband's authority they reject with ridicule.'[12] Such attitudes were reinforced by medical arguments which claimed that smoking hindered a woman's reproductive abilities. According to Dr Zollner in 1898, smoking deadened a woman's amatory properties since 'love and tobacco' could not live in the same atmosphere.[13]

It is precisely these opinions which the new women of the late nineteenth century were seeking to challenge, though the new woman herself ranged from the unmarried 'blue stocking', the bohemian artist, the 'girl of the period' and even the rising number of middle-class women who took up paid clerical work at the end of the century.[14] As well as Richardson's Miriam, the liberated smoker would make her appearance in novels such as H. G. Wells' *Ann Veronica* (1909) and Grant Allen's *The Woman Who Did* (1895) and, less sympathetically, in the pages of *Punch*, which took much pleasure in

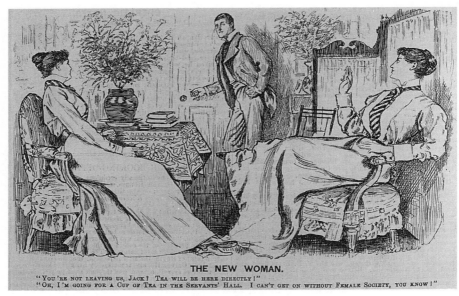

THE NEW WOMAN.
"You 're not leaving us, Jack ! Tea will be here directly !"
"Oh, I 'm going for a Cup of Tea in the Servants' Hall. I can't get on without Female Society, you know !"

18   *The New Woman, Punch* cartoon, 1895

portraying the new woman's supposedly masculine attributes (figure 18). As early as 1893, the trade press was noting how 'considerable business' was being done among 'lady smokers', and much mention was made of how women were symbolically demonstrating their independence by smoking in expensive clubs such as the Pioneer, the Empress, the Grosvenor and the New Somerville, or after dinner in 'society' circles.[15] Early efforts were made to make small, dainty, expensive cigarettes which were frequently scented and gold tipped. Names included Two Roses, Dames, Miranda's Dream, Boudoir, Pour la Dame, Virginia, Gay Grissette and Young Ladies.[16] In 1892, one Manchester entrepreneur even formed a 'Cigar for Ladies Society' to try and sell his Milly brand, which, again, was small and 'delicately perfumed'.[17] Also available were tobacco accessories such as expensive cigarette cases, with jewelled patterns and gold- or silver-tipped corners, popular as wedding and Christmas gifts.[18] Throughout the 1890s, *Tobacco Trade Review* urged retailers to 'work up' the trade while its contemporaries, *Tobacco Weekly Journal*, *Tobacco* and the *Smoker*, invited comment and offered prizes for the best cigarette designed for women.[19] In support, Mark Twain was even inspired to write a favourable letter to the *Daily Mail* and Lady Colin Campbell argued that women had, in fact, the greater right to smoke since smoking calmed the troubled nerves that were generally attributed to them.[20]

More frequent, however, were the attacks made on women's smoking. Along with bicycles, short hair and new fashions in dress, the cigarette was criticised for what it represented. Mrs Lynn Linton followed her earlier attacks on the 'girl of the period' with an 1890s assault on the 'Wild Women' who sought to 'offend' nature and society by going against woman's *raison d'être*: maternity.[21] The only women who did smoke were the old 'withered and unsightly', worn-out country dames with clay pipes and the 'blasphemous' girls of coal-mining districts, neither of whom had anything to do with Linton's definition of respectable femininity: 'they are simply assimilating themselves to this old Sally and that ancient Betty down in the dales and mountain hamlets, or to the stalwart cohort of pit-brow women for whom sex has no aesthetic distinctions.'[22] Linton's fear that society was encouraging this 'blurring of the sexes' was matched by other writers who warned women against adopting masculine habits which might eventually lead to the decline of the race and, according to the Religious Tract Society in 1898, to the growth of female moustaches provoked by the 'constant movement of the lips' while smoking.[23]

At least among the respectable middle classes, such attitudes prevailed into the twentieth century and the social impact of the new woman was only slight. Students were not allowed to smoke at Girton College until the end of the First World War and, in London, although the sight of women smoking in restaurants was a common occurrence in the Edwardian years, this tended to be only in the more bohemian areas of Soho and Chelsea. Of course, the majority of women were not in a position to be so assertive and many, wishing to experiment with smoking, must have done so in private, away from the gaze of the judging public. One can only speculate as to how representative the following quotation must be: 'I remember before the 1914–18 war, mother drawing the curtains and locking the door to smoke a gold-tipped cigarette, then flinging the windows and door wide open to get rid of the smell. She used to wear a green silk kimono so that the smell shouldn't linger in her clothes.'[24]

Beyond the smoking of pioneering new women and by those operating outside conventional respectability (prostitutes and actresses, old women in rural communities), there is little evidence of more widespread female tobacco consumption (for *Tobacco Tade Review*'s representation of the different female smoking types, see figure 19). It is likely that smoking occurred among some working-class communities where the codes of respectable femininity were either applied less stringently or interpreted rather subjectively, but it is not

19   *The sights of London: the Lady Smoker*, Tobacco Trade Review cartoon, 1898

mentioned in those histories of women who were 'untrammelled by conventional notions of decorum'.[25] Further, smoking does not appear in those investigations into working-class women's lives conducted by respectable, middle-class ladies who often found their subjects preferring 'to remain uncertain as to the amount they spend on what others may regard as mere vanities'.[26] However, the trade press did report on Northern factory towns where young women often bought packets of three small cigarettes, known as

Brownies, made specially for 'humbler feminine wants'. Supposedly, it was not uncommon to observe them looking through their change during their midday break to see if they could afford 'a "a" penny [halfpenny] smoke'.[27] It might even have been the case that manufacturers targeted women from an early date. A 1900 advertisement for Ogden's Guinea Gold (selling at ten for $2^{1}/_{2}d$) featured an intimate couple with their heads and bodies hidden behind an umbrella. It is not clear who is lighting the cigarette or who says, 'Give me a little puff – are they OGDEN'S?' or who replies, 'RATHER'.[28] The domestic servant, Louise Jermy, also recalled in her autobiography the arguments she had with her parents over her right to smoke and, given that the Hulton Survey of 1948 found that 17 per cent of women from all social classes aged 65 and over smoked, then it suggests there might have been a rather higher number of young smokers before the First World War, assuming they had been smoking all their adult life.[29] The key to the difficulty of uncovering evidence about working-class women smoking before 1914 might be found in the reactions of one oral history respondent speaking of the inter-war period, when the complicated notion of respectability still greatly influenced everyday life. Asked what she thought of young women who smoked, a former Liverpool factory worker replied that they were 'fast hussies'. Here her words demonstrate a keen awareness of the dominant notions of respectability, but her actions suggest a more intricate understanding of her femininity. When the previous question was immediately followed up with one concerning the extent of smoking by women workers, she replied: 'Oh yes, I'll say they did. They'd think you were a lunatic if you didn't smoke. They'd think you were barmy.' She even admitted that she smoked herself, and that she usually bought Woodbines, that cigarette which chapter 5 showed to have such masculine connotations.[30] These disparities between attitudes and practice, even within the individual smoker, certainly suggest why social investigators found it so difficult to uncover the real nature of working-class expenditure.

Much more evidence begins to appear for the First World War and after, though it remains difficult to offer a comprehensively quantitative or qualitative account of women's smoking. Women's lives have not been studied to quite the same extent as men's, and the significance of the very title of Mass-Observation's ethnography should not be lost: *Man and His Cigarette*. However, it is recognised that the First World War brought unprecedented social changes in women's lives and new representations of femininity. Certain forms of behaviour, such as smoking, were able to enter the public arena as shifts in employment patterns saw hundreds of thousands of women move away from the private world of domestic service and into munitions factories, clerical and commercial positions, and transport work.[31] The munitions workers became 'a distinctive and recognisable group, in streets, cafés and public places, they were undeniably often boisterous and noisy'.[32] And even if the effects did not last, the war did produce many changes of a visible nature as 'young women enjoyed a new financial independence and control over their own lives'.[33] The interpretation is confirmed by oral evidence, many respondents dating the First World War as the time 'the smoking angle quickly came onto the scene' and when the attitude of 'she's common, she smokes' began to disappear.[34] The behaviour of these women provoked something of a moral panic, with organisations such as the National Union of Women Workers, the Young Women's Christian Association, the Mother's Union, the Church Army, the Girl's Friendly Society and the Women Police Volunteers patrolling munitions towns, 'primarily in order to supervise the behaviour of young women'.[35] But the consumption of cigarettes represented an assertion of the heightened public role women had come to have which, if only temporarily, resulted from the experience of individual economic independence and a collective sense of enhanced social freedom.

By the 1920s, women's smoking had obtained a degree of social acceptance, poignantly illustrated by the comments of two former university students interviewed by Mass-Observation. They expressed how they had been disappointed when their deliberately public rituals of smoking failed to provoke any comment from their fellow café customers.[36] There was some criticism, however, of the new symbol of the age, the flapper, who smoked, drank cocktails, danced to jazz and, with Eton crops and androgynous clothing, playfully toyed with alternative constructions of femininity.[37] Best epitomised in Evelyn Waugh's *Vile Bodies*, Agatha Runcible of the 'Bright Young People' notoriously wore trousers, smoked Turkish cigarettes and, though it led to her eventual insanity and subsequent death, even drove that ultimate symbol of the fast new age, the motor car.[38] Cigarettes were attacked by medics writing in the popular press, one in particular attaching the smoking 'problem' to that of night-clubs, 'neither of them good for girls'.[39] They raised similar fears to those which Marek Kohn describes in *Dope Girls*, as wider cultural anxieties came to be attached to consumption decisions: 'the detection of a drug underground provided a way of speaking simultaneously about women, race, sex and the nation's place in the world. It was a symbolic issue in which a larger national crisis was reworked in microcosm.' This discourse on drugs increasingly focused on women: 'actresses, chorus girls, "night club girls", "bachelor girls", "flappers", "women of the unfortunate class"; whether they played the part of victim or harpy, the women of the drug underworld were of the uncontainable class'.[40] The parallel with the cigarette in the 1890s is startling and it may have been that the shift from tobacco to opium enabled some aspects of the prejudice attached to the female smoker to decline. That would seem to be the case in the literary culture of the period, one summary of Galsworthy's fiction commenting that the references to women's smoking in the novels set in the 1920s are so frequent that they do not warrant extensive analysis.[41] And in Bulldog Drummond's adventures, although Peterson's dangerous assistant Irma smokes, thereby suggesting the more underhand connotations of a woman's cigarette, Drummond's wife Phyllis also smokes, suggesting instead a certain ubiquity of the cigarette in the cultural representations of alternative femininities.

What becomes apparent is a gradual yet fairly rapid rise in women's smoking rates in the inter-war years, largely attributable to the changing social and economic context of young women's lives. The employment changes of the First World War continued as only 125,000 of the 400,000 domestic servants who entered the munitions factories returned to their old profession.[42] Although there was no great increase in female employment rates, there was a trend for more young women to work in the public sphere and to continue doing so after marriage until the first child was born. They found work in the new light industries that demanded semi-skilled and unskilled labour, in the service sector and in commercial and financial offices.[43] They consequently had more money to spend, were exposed to ideas and opinions not heard in the private homes of domestic service, and were less subject to conventional constraints on their behaviour.[44] How they spent this money was on forms of leisure and entertainment conducive to smoking. Around 11,000 dance halls were opened in the six years after 1918 and these created romantic environments where the proffering of cigarettes became a common ritual of courtship.[45] Holiday trips, for a week or a day, to resorts such as Blackpool, Morecambe, Brighton, Scarborough and others became massively popular in the inter-war period, creating spaces where young people could behave in ways that might not have been sanctioned at home.[46] Young women also began to frequent public houses (if they were accompanied by a man), especially those found in the new residential suburbs and in the 'roadhouse'-style pubs of the arterial roads leading to the countryside.[47]

This context is important for understanding women's tobacco consumption, as many have emphasised social reasons to explain why they started smoking.

Table 6.1 Average number of cigarettes smoked daily by cigarette smokers, 1948

Age	Men	Women
16–24	12.2	5.4
25–34	15.0	6.8
35–44	15.7	6.9
45–64	15.5	6.0
65 and over	10.6	3.3
All ages	14.6	6.1

Source: J. W. Hobson and H. Henry, *The Pattern of Smoking Habits: A Study Based on Information Collected During the Course of the Hulton Readership Survey, 1948* (London, Hulton Research Studies, 1948), p. 4.

Table 6.2 Proportions of cigarette smokers smoking in varying degrees of intensity, 1948

Smoking intensity (per day)	Men (%)	Women (%)
Heavy or very heavy (over 22)	13.3	1.5
Average (8 to 22)	65.3	30.1
Light (less than 8)	21.4	68.4

Source: Hobson and Henry, *Pattern of Smoking*, pp. 12–13.

Indeed, many male Mass-Observation respondents, writing during the Second World War when the demand for cigarettes frequently outstripped supply, criticised 'girls who really do not smoke although they think they do, and get through a number of their boy-friend's fags. They suck in a little smoke, keep it in their mouths for a few seconds and then puff it out with an accompanying gasp.'[48] Such masculine emphasis on the 'real' nature of smoking misses the importance of the sociability of the cigarette and the desire to give 'the impression of sophistication' attested to by many women respondents.[49] Certainly, the statistics bear this out, tables 6.1 and 6.2 demonstrating that, on average, male smokers smoked fourteen to fifteen cigarettes a day, whereas women smoked only six, and that there were far more confirmed heavy smokers among men than among women. Women also remained light smokers throughout their lives, though the impact of the Second World War appears to have increased both per capita consumption and the proportion smoking among younger women.[50]

By far the greatest influence on women's smoking in the inter-war period was the cinema. As well as providing the social environment favourable to smoking, the cinema presented images which came to influence greatly women's consumption decisions, not just in regard to tobacco. With annual admissions reaching 1,000 million by 1940, and with nearly 5,000 picture houses in 1938, the cinema became the most popular form of working-class commercial entertainment in the inter-war period.[51] Of the images provided to this huge audience, the flapper appeared frequently in the 1920s, most notably in the form of Clara Bow's *It* girl of 1927, but deviant images of women were also provided by Louise Brooks' fallen woman in *Pandora's Box* (1929), the murderous Tallulah Bankhead in *My Sin* (1931), Mae West's carnival dancer in *I'm No Angel* (1933) and Marlene Dietrich's night-club singer in *The Blue Angel* (1930). Dietrich's association with smoking was further established through her sharing of a cigarette with Gary Cooper in *Morocco* (1930) and in her role as the notorious Lily in *Shanghai Express* (1932).[52] The film industry constantly challenged prevailing notions of morality, though for Molly Haskell this was simply 'a vicarious splurge for women who wanted to look and feel daring without actually doing anything', who wished to posture in satin and inhale a cigarette, 'rather than by turning a phrase – or a trick'.[53]

These films, with titles such as *The Careless Woman, Hail the Woman, A Woman of the World, The Lure of the Night Club* and *Speed Crazed*, heralded new forms of behaviour for women which would later be made safe through the glamorisation of smoking in the 1930s and 1940s through stars such as Mary Astor, Ingrid Bergman (though neither she nor any other woman smokes in the most famous smoking film of all, *Casablanca*, 1942) and Rita Hayworth (the publicity material for *Gilda* in 1946 emphasising the centrality of the cigarette to Gilda's image). Of a sample of forty Hollywood films of the 1930s, 30 per cent of heroines were depicted smoking, though only 3 per cent of villainesses.[54] Lauren Bacall famously marked her screen debut in *To Have and Have Not* (1945) standing in the doorway of Humphrey Bogart's hotel room. She asks, 'Anybody got a light?', to which he responds by tossing a matchbox to her across the room which she catches without shifting position. An immediate intimacy was established between the two through smoking, an image which would be consciously exploited in *The Big Sleep* (1946) as the film starts with silhouettes of the pair, he lighting her cigarette, then his own, before two cigarettes are placed in an ash tray, one by one. The cinematic device of using the cigarette as a ritual of courtship was taken to extreme form in *Now Voyager* (1942), as Paul Henreid, in much imitated style, lit two cigarettes in his own mouth before passing one to Bette Davis. This film also serves as an updated, psychoanalytically inspired reworking of Dorothy Richardson's story of Miriam, as Davis' oppressed spinster, Charlotte Vale, originally smokes in secret away from her overbearing mother. She begins to smoke in public to mark her recovery from her low self esteem and she goes on to accept Henreid's numerous cigarettes to mark the various stages of their affair. By the end of the film, she is able to use her knowledge of cork-tipped cigarettes to signify to her sisters her new status as a fully developed woman of the world. This assertive role was a familiar one for Davis, best captured in *All About Eve* (1950) when she contemptuously blew smoke towards a youthful Marilyn Monroe. These sophisticated representations of smoking were a significant influence on many female smokers, as many Mass-Observation panellists were prepared to admit.[55]

It appears that the images of smoking in cinemas were of far greater importance in stimulating demand than the images provided in advertising. The history of cigarette advertising aimed at women is generally one of the manufacturers following trends within society, rather than actually creating them. Indeed, Wills of Bristol was initially reluctant to advertise to women at all, and women's roles in the mass advertising of Victorian and Edwardian Britain were confined to scantily clad, sexually alluring provocations to male demand (figure 20).[56] Women did not regularly feature in advertisements until during the First World War, when they were depicted not actually smoking but in the midst of a scene of seduction. For example, Kenilworth issued an advertisement in 1917 featuring an army officer at a ball. He invites his female companion to 'get away from this mob', to 'find some place where we can be all by ourselves and have a Kenilworth in peace'. In an earlier example from 1916 another army officer relaxes while his female companion punts him along the river. He suggests, 'Let's tie up in the shade for a bit. You must want a rest. And I can see by the way you're looking at my Kenilworth that you'd like one of them too.'[57] The use of the cigarette as a tool of seduction continued: De Reszkes, in the early 1920s, published a series of posters depicting the upper classes smoking in couples in sophisticated environments; and Drapkin's advertisements for Greys featured a futuristic world where both men and women smoked.[58]

In the inter-war period there were still cigarettes such as Jazz aimed especially at women, and throughout the 1920s and 1930s Player's Bachelor (a mid-priced cork-tipped brand) advertising was directed solely at women

Ogden's Tab Album, Ogden's Tabs advertisement, c. 1900   **20**

(figure 21).[59] These advertisements depicted women alone and sophisticated, and emphasised individual, independent pleasure, though the seductive aspect of the cigarette was never too far removed. The more expensive No. 3 brand and the mid-priced Player's Medium also began using women alone in their advertising in the late 1920s, and Player's Weights' first advertisement featuring a female smoker came in 1915. Player's advertising portrayed a range of youthful feminine images, from sailor-girls to sporting tennis players, glamorous socialites, fun-loving clowns and attractive, domesticated women (figure 22). By the early 1930s, Wills' Capstan was being advertised in journals such as *Woman and Home, My Home, Good Housekeeping, Woman and Beauty, Wife and Home* and *Modern Women*, though the firm's Press and Poster Committee eventually felt that these journals might be better suited to advertising Gold Flake Cork Tipped.[60] Many advertisements were thus directly targeted at women and it appears that some market segmentation was taking place on the assumption that tipped cigarettes were preferred by women. Undoubtedly, this was the case, but of the largest selling mid-priced brands, Carreras' Craven 'A', Player's Medium, and Wills' Capstan and Gold Flake advertisements were variously aimed at both men and women together, or

21   Player's Bachelor cigarettes advertisement, 1929

Player's Medium Navy Cut advertisement, 1930 **22**

alternatively to men alone or women alone. The earlier attempts at creating specifically 'feminine' brands largely failed and the mass market advertisers found themselves having to recognise that women were smoking the same popular brands as men. Price and the general iconography of smoking, then, appeared to be more important in stimulating initial female demand than market-led promotion.

What women actually smoked is more difficult to discover, but expensive Turkish brands appear to have been popular among middle-class women and more women smoked filtered varieties, both of which held a minimal proportion of cigarette sales in this period. The successful Craven 'A' was the major exception to this rule and some smokers labelled the many men who consumed this largely feminine brand as 'cranks'. Other mid-priced cigarettes, such as De Reszke, also appealed to women, but the massively popular Player's Medium was a truly androgynous cigarette. Of the cheaper brands, Woodbines maintained their masculine image, but this did not entirely preclude their sale – along with Weights, Minors and Tenners – to both sexes, price perhaps playing a greater role at this end of the market than brand image.[61] Table 6.3 shows the relative popularity of brands according to a Mass-Observation survey conducted in 1943.

A variety of factors, then, contributed to the growth of women's smoking in the inter-war period, and it seems that each new generation of young women smokers went on to become life-long smokers. This gradual pattern

Table 6.3 Proportional brand preferences of Mass-Observation respondents, 1943

Brand	Men (%)	Women (%)
Senior Service	2	5
Embassy	0	3
Greys	1	0
Player's	40	32
Gold Flake	6	9
Craven 'A'	6	16
Top Score	2	1
Weights	12	19
Woodbines	9	5
Churchman's No. 1	9	3
Capstan	4	1
De Reszke Minors	1	3
Various brands	9	19
Others – expensive	9	7
Others – cheap	1	4
Roll their own	10	1

Source: Mass-Observation Topic Collections, *Smoking Habits 1937–1965*, Box No. 4, File D: *Smoking Survey 1943*.

resulted in a gap of a few decades before the proportion of all women smokers matched that of young women smokers, and perhaps explains the persistence of prejudice against women's smoking in the late 1930s and early 1940s. Just as it continues to do so today, there existed a body of medical literature on women and smoking which focused on women's reproductive system, the care of which was elevated into a 'moral and social duty'.[62] Although this criticism was never as strong as in America or Nazi Germany, smoking was held to destroy a woman's body, along with alcohol, 'dangerous dietary regimens', 'education', the 'progress of feminism' and the 'growth of short-sighted selfishness'.[63] The reproductive aspect was emphasised by the NSNS as it singled out women's smoking as a particular social problem, making a concerted effort to campaign against it.[64] T. F. Taylor argued that nicotine contaminated the mother's milk and, more generally, that the habit reduced a girl's chances of marrying since most men 'of moral refinement' would avoid her.[65] Cigarettes damaged the looks of girls and that which made women less desirable to men would eventually lead to a lowering of the birth rate.[66] A specific 'Women's Anti-Smoking and Protective Society' was even set up in Barry in 1931, as the cigarette was placed alongside a number of 'modern' problems ranging from drugs to cosmetics, late hours, cocktails and the whole lifestyle of the young woman.[67] How such attitudes manifested themselves in the popular culture of the time was in the continued prejudice against women smoking in the street (because of the older association with street-walking prostitutes), in the presence of infants (though little medical research had been conducted into this potential problem) and during the performance of any domestic duties.[68]

The massive increase in women's smoking in the Second World War reduced many of its lingering unrespectable connotations, the war acting as a catalyst for many of the changes already outlined for the First World War and the 1920s and 1930s. Again, there is evidence to suggest that the war reinforced the unequal position of women in society, with a similar backlash occurring in the late 1940s, as was said to have happened in the 1920s; but it also made public aspects of daily life which were formerly maintained as private.[69] Mass mobilisation again brought many women into collective spaces and enabled them to take up smoking, oral history testimonies frequently pointing to the war as the time when, working in the factories, women started smoking. However, Mass-Observation also noted how the increase in overall female tobacco consumption might not have been due only to a great increase in the number of smokers but because 43 per cent of women who smoked before the war were now smoking more, thanks to the greater stresses and strains suffered by the civilian population. It found that the general tensions created by war made many women increase their consumption and, in particular, occasions such as air raids created such a psychological break with normality that women in the shelters were incapable of engaging in any activity save either by doing nothing or by simply smoking.[70]

Just as with working-class men's consumption of tobacco, then, sociable environments and communal spaces proved to be crucial factors in encouraging many women to begin smoking, points which women smokers were more prepared to admit than their male counterparts.[71] In contrast, personal and individual factors have been particularly important in explaining why women have continued to smoke, a variety of stresses and strains providing the cultural influences into what is understood as physical addiction. As one Mass-Observation respondent claimed, 'it seems to help when I have something on my mind, either emotional or intellectual – it seems to help me work out a problem.'[72] Other articulate smokers wrote of how smoking helped when tired, how it alleviated boredom and how it reduced nervousness when waiting for something to happen. For many working-class women smokers, such situations too frequently arose, and their continued smoking might best be understood as a means of a break from the daily monotony of housework and child care. As several feminist theorists of leisure and a number of social investigators at the time acknowledged, leisure for many women might constitute just a few moments' rest and the chance to enjoy a cigarette and a brief escape from the realities of daily life.[73]

These explanations of continued smoking have become increasingly important in studies of the post-1945 period. Women's social and economic position has played a central role in making smoking a 'feminist issue', it being frequently argued that while men's continued smoking might be regarded as habitual (or due to sheer physical addiction), women tended to smoke much more to reduce their negative feelings: 'women smoked more when they felt "uncomfortable or upset about something" or when they were "angry, ashamed or embarrassed" or when they wanted to "take their mind off cares and worries".'[74] There has thus been much continuity in the reasons for women's everyday smoking rates. Likewise, recent social policy studies have begun to examine the cultural factors which provoke the first stages of women's cigarette habits, and most of the issues that they have raised have been those discovered to be relevant to the inter-war period. Much recent comment has therefore been made on the prevalence of smoking images in recent Hollywood blockbusters and in women's magazines more generally, but these should be seen as part of a much longer continuous trend which has never really disappeared. Films and advertising have persistently promoted glamorous images of women smoking and the cigarette has never lost its elusive sexual overtones. Young women's, and increasingly girls', leisure activities have continued to be based around social environments conducive to the use of cigarettes. In all of these matters, there are many crossovers with the stimulants to men's smoking, but gender differences in smoking practices have remained. These differences will become more apparent in the final chapters of this book, which move on to describe the reactions to the post-war smoking and health controversy.

Notes

1 D. Richardson, *Backwater* (1916), in *Pilgrimage* (London, Dent, 1967), pp. 37–9.
2 *Honeycombe* (1917), in *ibid.*, p. 436.
3 *The Tunnel* (1919), in *ibid.*, vol. II, p. 84.
4 *Ibid.*, p. 117.
5 However, this chapter is far from a definitive history of women's smoking, hindered as it is by the lack of primary resources commenting on the prevalence of women's smoking. Only a specifically directed oral history project could provide anything like a comprehensive account of the issue through the twentieth century.
6 M. Brickley, A. Miles and H. Stainer, *The Cross Bones Burial Ground: Redcross Way, Southwark, London* (London, Museum of London, 1999), p. 66.
7 W. M. Thackeray, *Vanity Fair* (1847–48; Oxford, Oxford University Press, 1983), p. 130.
8 P. Mérimée, *Carmen* (London, Paul Elek, 1960); R. Klein, 'The Devil in Carmen', *Differences: A Journal of Feminist Cultural Studies*, 5:1 (1993), 51–72.
9 Ouida, *Under Two Flags* (1867; Oxford, Oxford University Press, 1995), pp. 175–6.
10 D. Mitchell, 'The so called "new woman" as Prometheus: women artists depict women smoking', *Women's Art Journal*, 12:1 (1991), 3–9; D. Mitchell, 'Images of exotic women in turn-of-the-century tobacco art', *Feminist Studies*, 18:2 (1992), 327–30; E. M. Forster, *Howard's End* (1910; Harmondsworth, Penguin, 1941); M. Koetzle and U. Scheid, *Feu d'Amour [Seductive Smoke]* (Cologne, Taschen, 1994); John Johnson Collection (hereafter J. J.), The Bodleian Library, Oxford, *M. L. Horn and B. R. Lillington Cigarette Card Collections.*
11 The Tom Harrisson Mass-Observation Archive (hereafter M.-O.), File Report 2192, *Man and His Cigarette*, 1949, p. 71.
12 *Ibid.*, p. 65.
13 E. S. Gonberg, 'Historical and political perspective: women and drug use', *Journal of Social Issues*, 38:2 (1982), 9–23; *Tobacco Weekly Journal* (hereafter *TWJ*), 1:7 (October 1898), 110.

14 V. Glendinning, 'Foreword', in J. Gardner (ed.), *The New Woman: Women's Voices, 1880–1914* (London, Collins and Brown, 1993); G. Cunningham, *The New Woman and the Victorian Novel* (Basingstoke, Macmillan, 1978); G. Anderson, *The White Blouse Revolution: Female Office Workers Since 1870* (Manchester, Manchester University Press, 1988).

15 *Tobacco Trade Review* (hereafter *TTR*), 26:301 (January 1893), 2–3; *TTR*, 31:364 (April 1898), 163.

16 *Ibid.*

17 *Tit-Bits*, 568 (3 September 1892), p. ii.

18 *TTR*, 31:364 (April 1898), 164.

19 *TTR*, 30:353 (May 1897), 225; *TTR*, 32:374 (February 1899), 45; *TTR*, 31:363 (March 1898), 139; *TTR*, 31:364 (April 1898), 163–4; *TWJ*, 1:12 (11 November 1898), 177; *Smoker*, 1:14 (9 April 1892), 209.

20 *Daily Mail* (16 April 1899), p. 11; C. Campbell, 'A plea for tobacco', *English Illustrated Magazine*, 11 (1894), 81–4.

21 L. Linton, 'The girl of the period', from *The Girl of the Period and Other Essays, Vol. I* (1883), reprinted in Gardner, *The New Woman*, pp. 55–60; L. Linton, 'The Wild Women (part I): as politicians', *Nineteenth Century*, 30 (July 1891), 80.

22 L. Linton, 'The Wild Women (part II: conclusion): as social insurgents', *Nineteenth Century*, 30 (October 1891), 596–605.

23 Article in *Girl's Own Paper*, reprinted in *TTR*, 31:370 (October 1898), 454; L. Linton, 'The partisans of the Wild Women', *Nineteenth Century*, 31 (March 1892), 460; Mrs Ester, ' "Between ourselves," a friendly chat with the girls', *The Young Woman*, 3 (1895), 106; R. Pember Reeves, *The Ascent of Woman* (London, John Lane, 1896), p. 58 (the book is a collection of six essays first published in the *Saturday Review* in the early 1890s); J. D. Hunting, 'Women and tobacco', *National Review*, 14 (1889), 218–28.

24 M.-O., *Man and His Cigarette*, pp. 68, 72–3.

25 The quote is that of Charles Booth, taken from C. Chinn, *They Worked All Their Lives: Women of the Urban Poor in England, 1880–1939* (Manchester, Manchester University Press, 1988), p. 93. The social investigator, Arthur J. Munby, does not appear to have made mention of smoking in his study of women in Wigan: see A. V. John, *By the Sweat of their Brow: Women Workers at the Victorian Coal Mine* (London, Croom Helm, 1980) does not mention smoking, despite Munby's observations of a number of what he thought to be masculine traits.

26 C. E. Collett, *Educated Working Women: Essays on the Economic Position of Women Workers in the Middle Classes* (London, P. S. King, 1902), pp. 66–7.

27 *TTR*, 31:364 (April 1898), 163.

28 J. J., *Tobacco*, Box No. 3.

29 L. Jermy, *The Memoirs of a Working Woman* (Norwich, Goose and Son, 1934); J. W. Hobson and H. Henry, *The Pattern of Smoking Habits: A Study Based on Information Collected During the Course of the Hulton Readership Survey, 1948* (London, Hulton Research Studies, 1948), p. 3.

30 Comparative interview conducted by S. Messenger for PhD thesis, 'The lifestyles of young middle-class women in Liverpool in the 1920s and 1930s', School of History, University of Liverpool, 1999.

31 J. Bourke, *Working-Class Cultures in Britain 1890–1960: Gender, Class and Ethnicity* (London, Routledge, 1994).

32 G. Braybon, *Women Workers in the First World War* (London, Routledge, 1981), p. 167.

33 D. Beddoe, *Discovering Women's History* (London, Pandora, 1993), p. 32; D. Beddoe, *Back to Home and Duty: Women Between the Wars 1918–1939* (London, Pandora, 1989).

34 E. Roberts, *Social Life in Barrow, Lancaster and Preston, 1870–1930* (oral transcripts held at Lancaster University Library), Mr. B.1 B, p. 76; Mr. H.1.L., p. 18; Mr. J.1.L., p. 162.

35 J. Lewis, *Women in England, 1870–1950: Sexual Divisions and Social Change* (Brighton, Wheatsheaf, 1984), p. 185.

36 M.-O., *Man and His Cigarette*, pp. 68, 72.

37 R. Graves and A. Hodge, *The Long Weekend: A Social History of Great Britain, 1918–1939* (London, Hutchinson, 1985), pp. 32–59; B. Melman, *Women and the Popular Imagination in the Twenties: Flappers and Nymphs* (Basingstoke, Macmillan, 1988); Beddoe, *Back to Home and Duty*, p. 10.

38 E. Waugh, *Vile Bodies* (1930; New York, Dell, 1958).

39 Dr C. Webb-Johnson, 'Women's clubs: a medical man's opinion on their contribution to health and well-being' (1927), in B. Braithwaite, N. Walsh and G. Davies, *Ragtime to Wartime: The Best of Good Housekeeping* (London, Ebury, 1986), pp. 90–1.

40 M. Kohn, *Dope Girls: The Birth of the British Drug Underground* (London, Lawrence and Wishart, 1992), pp. 4–5.

41 A. Charlton, 'Galsworthy's images of smoking in the Forsyte chronicles', *Social Science and Medicine*, 15 (1981), 636.

42 J. Lewis, 'In search of a real equality: women between the wars', in F. Gloversmith (ed.), *Class, Culture and Social Change: A New View of the 1930s* (Brighton, Harvester Press, 1980), p. 211.

43 Lewis, *Women in England*, pp. 147–56; D. Gittins, *Fair Sex: Family Size and Structure, 1900–1939* (London, Hutchinson, 1982); M. Glucksman, *Women Assemble: Women Workers and the New Industries in Inter-War Britain* (London, Routledge, 1990).

44 I. Waldron, 'Patterns and causes of gender differences in smoking', *Social Science and Medicine*, 32 (1991), 1995.

45 S. Jones, *Workers at Play: A Social and Economic History of Leisure 1918–1939* (London, Routledge and Kegan Paul, 1986), pp. 44–5.

46 G. Cross (ed.), *Worktowners at Blackpool: Mass-Observation and Popular Leisure in the 1930s* (London, Routledge, 1990); J. K. Walton, 'The world's first working-class seaside resort? Blackpool revisited, 1840–1974', *Lancashire and Cheshire Antiquarian Society*, 88 (1992), 1–30.

47 M.-O., *The Pub and the People: A Worktown Study* (London, Cresset, 1987); V. Hey, *Patriarchy and Pub Culture* (London, Tavistock, 1986).

48 M.-O. Topics Collections: *Smoking Habits, 1937–1965*, Box No. 2, File B, G. W. Clark (249).

49 *Ibid.*, Box No. 1.

50 Hobson and Henry, *Pattern of Smoking*, p. 13.

51 J. Richards, *The Age of the Dream Palace: Cinema and Society in Britain 1930– 1939* (London, Routledge and Kegan Paul, 1984), pp. 11–15; P. Stead, *Film and the Working Class: The Feature Film in British and American Society* (London, Routledge, 1989).

52 Beddoe, *Back to Home and Duty*, p. 24.

53 M. Haskell, *From Reverence to Rape: The Treatment of Women in the Movies* (Chicago, University of Chicago Press, 1987), p. 76.

54 H. Graham, *When Life's a Drag: Women, Smoking and Disadvantage* (London, HMSO, 1993), pp. 4–5.

55 M.-O. Topic Collections, *Smoking Habits, 1937–1965*, Box No. 1, File B, R. Bridgens.

56 E. S. Turner, *The Shocking History of Advertising* (1952; Harmondsworth, Penguin, 1965), p. 88; B. W. E. Alford, *W. D. & H. O. Wills and the Development of the UK Tobacco Industry* (London, Methuen, 1973), p. 340.

57 J. J., *Tobacco*, Box No. 4.

58 C. Hall, *The Twenties in Vogue* (London, Octopus, 1983), pp. 150–1; *TTR*, 54:641 (May 1921), 41.

59 *TTR*, 54:643 (July 1921), 49; Nottingham Record Office, Player's Archive, DD PL 6/22/1, *Storekeeper's file containing details of advertising archive.*

60 Bristol Record Office, Wills Archive (Wills), 38169/M/8/(l), *Press and Poster Committee Reports*, 11 January 1932; 38169/M/8/(n), 23 March 1933; 38169/M/8/(p), 20 February 1934.

61 M.-O., *Man and His Cigarette*, pp. 152–4, 164.

62 Lewis, *Women in England*, p. 84.

63 A. Carrell, *Man the Unknown* (London, Hamilton, 1935).

64 *Tobacco*, 533 (January 1927), xxi; A. Cardew, *Women and Smoking* (London, NSNS, n. d.).

65 T. F. Taylor, *Don't Smoke! An Address Given to the Members of the TOC H Unit Wetherby* (London, NSNS, 1944), p. 22; *TTR*, 60:720 (December 1927), 19.

66 *Clean Air*, 6 (December 1930), 13; *Clean Air*, 12 (August 1937), 1; G. Somerville, 'Beauty and health', in W. Lane, *The Modern Woman's Home Doctor* (London, Odham's, 1939), p. 345.

67 *Clean Air*, 6 (December 1930), 13; *Clean Air*, 7 (August 1931), 23.

68 M.-O., *Man and His Cigarette*, pp. 31–7.

69 P. Summerfield, *Women Workers in the Second World War* (London, Routledge, 1989).

70 M.-O. File Report 520, *Women and Morale*, 1940.

71 M.-O., *First Year's Work, 1937–1938* (London, Lindsay Drummond, 1938), pp. 8–23.

72 M.-O., *Man and His Cigarette*, p. 174.

73 M. Spring Rice, *Working-Class Wives: Their Health and Conditions* (1939; London, Virago, 1981), p. 99; E. Green, S. Hebron and D. Woodward, *Women's Leisure, What Leisure?* (Basingstoke, Macmillan, 1990); E. Wimbush and M. Talbot (eds), *Relative Freedoms: Women and Leisure* (Milton Keynes, Open University Press, 1988).

74 B. Jacobson, *The Ladykillers: Why Smoking is a Feminist Issue* (London, Pluto Press, 1981), p. 28.

7

Juvenile smoking and 'the feverish anxiety to become a man'

Many of the late nineteenth-century celebrations of smoking began with a reminiscence of the author's introduction to smoking as a child, a ritual usually promoting either initial disgust overcome by later persistence or an immediate and unswerving admiration for the pleasures of tobacco. If caught in the act by an assiduous parent or schoolmaster, punishment often followed, though invariably it was underlain with a condescending approbation as the new smoker was gently accepted into the world of the harmless luxury. It seems that, for many, smoking by boys was neither a social, medical or moral problem. Instances of its occurrence were formulated into anecdotes of entertainment rather than condemnation, such as when *Tobacco Trade Review* amused its readers with a story of an eccentric family of three sons, aged nine, twelve and fourteen, who all sat down after dinner and smoked cigars with their proud father.[1] However, when social investigators entered the darker streets of the Victorian city and observed children of other social classes smoking, the act no longer seemed so innocent, associated as it was with a whole host of 'bad habits'. As Henry Mayhew complained in 1867: 'The precocity of youth of both sexes in London is perfectly astounding. The drinking, the smoking, the blasphemy, indecency, and immorality that does not ever call a blush is incredible, and charity schools and the spread of education do not seem to have done much to abate this scourge.'[2]

When Mayhew commented on the 'street urchins' of London, their experiments with tobacco must have been conducted through a pipe, an implement difficult to fill, light and maintain, and which seemingly limited the extent of juvenile smoking in the mid nineteenth century. Certainly, references to smoking by youths did not become a commonplace until after the introduction of the cheap, machine-made cigarette in the 1880s. Articles then began to appear regularly in the trade press on the predilection of the young boy for

the cigarette and when, from the 1890s, a second wave of reforming investigators examined the social and economic conditions of the urban poor, the
phenomenon became well documented. *Tobacco Trade Review* commented
on the growing precocity of city-based youth and complained that youngs-
ters invariably smoked the low-profit-yielding penny packets.[3] Evidence also
appeared in the 1904 Committee on Physical Deterioration, with one witness
claiming that half of the boys attending day schools in Scotland smoked. In
an essay in *Studies of Boy Life in Our Cities*, R. A. Bray further added that,
'No one who observes at all closely the habits of the boys of the town can
possibly have failed to notice the very marked increase in the habit of smoking on the part of quite small boys.'[4] By 1907 a member of the Sheffield
Anti-Tobacco League was able to claim, no doubt with some degree of exag-
geration and without quoting his sources, that of the hundred million cigarettes imported into the country every week, fifteen million were smoked by
boys.[5]

Taking into account the problems of such evidence, there does appear to
have been a very real increase in the rates of juvenile smoking in the final two
decades of the nineteenth century. While the convenience and price of the
cigarette itself accounted for much of this growth, the culture of the urban
youth provides the ultimate explanation for the development of a social
activity which has remained a common sight throughout the twentieth century. The first half of this chapter therefore examines the leisure activities,
opportunities and economic situation of young boys in late Victorian and
Edwardian Britain, before turning to the condemnation of this culture by
numerous social investigators and the singling out of the cigarette as a particular symbol of the 'boy labour problem'. In 1908 the Children's Act was
passed, which attempted, in part, to deal with the rise in juvenile smoking by
prohibiting the sale of tobacco and cigarettes to youths less than sixteen years
of age. Although the justifications for such an Act mirrored the arguments of
the anti-tobacco movement, it was a series of other fears surrounding urban
youth culture which explain the origins of the legislation. These specific anti-
juvenile smoking arguments have already been outlined in chapter 3, so this
chapter will merely complete the story by demonstrating how concerns about
national racial degeneration resulted in the attempt to regulate children's
consumption. However, the fears of the social investigators did not correspond at all with the more general pro-smoking culture, and the consumption
of cigarettes by children and youths continued as a normal, unproblematic
social activity for decades after 1908.[6]

In late Victorian and Edwardian Britain, the culture of the urban working-class youth was very much the culture of the street. In what social reformers perceived as the monotony of day-to-day life, school was often disliked, work offered little need for mental application and the crowded home offered little escape. Investigators argued that only the house of the respectable artisan, with its small garden and larger rooms, provided a suitable home in which children could enjoy 'improving' hobbies and interests. Of the majority of the population, the unskilled and the casual workers, overburdened parents showed little interest in their offsprings' activities, thereby forcing children to be 'squeezed into the street'.[7] Once outside, the boy was open to a variety of influences which all formed part of the culture of the street. At one extreme were the violent gangs of 'scuttlers', so feared by respectable society, and at the other the less disruptive rituals of 'larking about'. These activities were 'motivated by a desire to make things happen, to create some form of immediate excitement that would breathe life and spontaneity into the drab daily routine'.[8] The street became an arena for boys to assert the codes of masculinity which they had picked up in the new adult work environments they had entered at the age of fourteen or even earlier. For the investigators, this created 'a species of man-child', 'overwhelmed by the feverish anxiety to become a man'.[9] Alexander Paterson claimed that, with sixpence to a shilling a week spending money to dispose of as he saw fit, the child was able to pass out of parental authority and assume an air of economic and moral independence. Youths were aware of a sense of difference from both childhood and adulthood, and this was expressed in a distinctive street subculture in which they participated until courting and marriage.[10] The cigarette, according to commentators at the time, became a ritualistic communicator of the boy's new social and economic position: 'The choice [of work] once made, . . . the boy very soon falls into the routine of work and in the first fortnight ages rapidly. Hitherto the smoking of cigarettes was a furtive prank, only delightful because forbidden; now it becomes a public exhibition, denoting manhood, independence, and wealth.'[11] Economic considerations meant that cigarettes could not be used as symbols all the time and strategies were adopted to prolong the period of smoking. The following describes in detail the forms of gesture used both to express a form of masculinity (outlined in chapter 5) and to counter certain economic restraints:

> The great joy of the cigarette lies in the lighting of it, and in the first two whiffs. So much is this the case that each one commonly lights his 'fag', draws in the smoke twice, inhaling deeply, breathes it out, spits, and says something, and

then, holding his cigarette in his right hand, extinguishes it with the thumb and first finger of his left, and replaces it in the bottom right-hand pocket of his waistcoat. Ten minutes later the process will be repeated, and by this means, though the boy will seem always to be smoking, he will only consume a penny packet in a day.[12]

This initiation into adulthood was frequently unopposed by a parent population unaware of any medical reasons why boys should not smoke. Oral interviews with smokers who took to the cigarette in the first decade of the twentieth century often produce stories of little or no punishment being meted out, even when the respondent was discovered smoking as young as the age of ten.[13] Many of the social reformers did not oppose tobacco altogether, sharing as they did that culture of the periodical literature which attacked the cigarette while praising the pipe. Their prejudices pointed to the supposedly adulterated and cheap Virginian blends found in penny packets as the root of all health problems and suggested that boys would be better off taking to the briar pipe instead.[14] But such attitudes only reflected adults' own associations between tobacco and mature masculinity which children would need to be unaware of if smoking was not to appear so attractive.

The culture of the street was all the more pervasive in Edwardian Britain since few alternative leisure activities were available to the urban boy. The expansion in leisure and entertainment that characterised this period did not extend to the limited incomes of children and teenagers to form a distinctive youth culture as it did after the Second World War. The cash they did have was enough to buy cigarettes and sweets, but beyond these items their spending horizons were limited, not only by the relative lack of money but also by the lack of products and services on which to spend it. The music hall was frequented by young people, but other forms of activity were restricted as lack of municipal funding limited the number of parks, swimming baths and libraries. Organised youth movements took off at the turn of the century, but these were only able to 'reform' the boy for one or two nights a week. Money was also spent on cheap literature, either comics, journals or 'penny dreadfuls', and on gambling, but what is significant about all these activities is that they were not always alternatives to smoking, the consumption of a cigarette often completing the pleasure obtained from the entertainment.[15]

Children and youths obtained the money with which to purchase cigarettes from a variety of means. Even the youngest, before starting formal work, were said to beg for pennies around stations and tramways, and coppers could be earned through 'running errands, washing steps and window-sills, minding babies, catching vermin, delivering milk or meat, selling papers or matches in the street, cab ducking or carrying bags for strangers'.[16] Older children, while still at school, started part-time work at the ages of eleven and twelve, an experience variously said to have been normal for between 10 and 30 per cent of the urban population, but later estimated to have been the universal practice as every child would have undertaken some paid work outside school, for however brief a period.[17] The usual system was that the earnings from such employment were handed over to the mother, who would then hand back a few pennies for pocket money.[18] Boys who had left school, employed as van boys, messengers, errand boys and in other unskilled 'blind alley' work, still 'tipped up' their wages to their mother, receiving back up to a shilling a week.[19] By the time they were sixteen, many simply paid over what they would have paid as 'board' had they been in private accommodation, retaining an ever more substantial sum for their own entertainment.[20]

Such incomes, however minimal, were still sufficient to purchase the penny packets of Wills' Woodbines and Ogden's Tabs that made up the bulk of the cheap cigarette trade. The respectable tobacco traders always claimed that they did not serve children in their stores, the main outlets being automatic machines and corner-shops. They cited the example of a typical working-class district of Manchester in 1906 in which thirty-three stores were licensed to sell tobacco. Only two were specialist tobacconists, the rest being made up of sweet shops, newsagents, grocers, greengrocers, chemists and even a temperance café. Despite the tobacconists' interests in blaming these stores (they wished to justify an increase in the tobacco licence to drive the non-specialist out of business), it is likely that local stores did stock cheap 'fags' for 'the sake of their juvenile clientele'.[21] Corner-shop traders, not sharing the opposition to juvenile smoking of the social reformers, often broke up packets of cigarettes to sell singles to penniless children or to give out free as tips to children on errands. Back on the street, temporarily more affluent children were known to break up a packet of five among friends and, in the factory, young workers were given the 'jockey' off a large piece of 'twist' fetched for their older work mates.[22]

Given this culture, it is unlikely that the increase in juvenile smoking could be attributed to the marketing campaigns of the tobacco manufacturers, though Player's, Wills and Ogden's must have been aware that their cigarettes were popular among youths and children. At the time, social reformers were quick to blame the tobacco companies. By the end of the 1890s, initially as a means to strengthen soft paper packets, most manufacturers had introduced collections of cards placed individually in packets designed to command loyalties of purchase. It was not long before complaints were vented about the practice, both because of the corrupting influence of the indecent pictures of actresses and models which featured heavily in the early series and because of the alleged encouragement it gave young boys to smoke.[23]

Cigarette cards certainly entered the iconography of early twentieth-century popular culture, becoming a leading promoter of Britain's imperial strength. The smoker could collect pictures of Wills' 'Kings and Queens of England', Ogden's 'Statues and Monuments', famous sportsmen, ships, trains, birds and countless other snippets of information, so that 'no field of popular human knowledge seems to have been left unexplored'. The collection of cards became a major hobby of a substantial proportion of Britain's youth: 'before 1914 it would have been hard indeed to have found a boy in the working class without at least a few dog-eared cards about his person, dreaming of making up, by swap and gambling games, that complete set of fifty.'[24] Robert Roberts believed the cards were of immense educational value, but others were less kind, seeing them as a cynical attempt by the manufacturers to tap into a new market. For social investigators such as C. E. B. Russell, Charles Masterman, R. A. Bray and E. J. Urwick, the problem was that the cigarette had come to represent a number of social and economic evils, which must all be attacked or avoided through the discouragement of juvenile smoking. Manufacturers, retailers and parents might all be criticised for their indifference to the health of the nation's youth, but the problem had become so acute that, by the Edwardian period, legislation and the intervention of the state were required to stamp out the degenerating vice.

The government response to juvenile smoking was part III of the Children's Act of 1908. Sponsored by Herbert Samuel, Parliamentary Under-Secretary of the Home Department, clauses 39–43 of the wide-ranging Act made it illegal to sell tobacco to any person 'apparently under the age of sixteen' and empowered policemen and park-keepers to confiscate cigarettes from children they caught smoking in public.[25] The measure followed the recommendations of the earlier Royal Commission on Physical Training (1903), the Select Committee of the House of Lords on the Juvenile Smoking Bill (1906) and, most importantly, the Inter-Departmental Committee on Physical Deterioration (1904), which proved to be a major influence on the reforms of the Edwardian Liberal government. Calls for government intervention to ban the sale of tobacco and cigarettes had first been made by Thomas Reynolds' anti-tobacco movement in the 1850s, but it was not until the twentieth century that MPs began to take the issue seriously.[26] Private member's Bills to legislate specifically against juvenile smoking were introduced by Sir Ralph Littler in 1903, by Richard Rigg in 1904, and by Thomas Macnamara in 1905 and 1906, but only when the issue was attached to a wider set of child welfare reforms could it pass through Parliament.[27]

Support for the legislative suppression of juvenile smoking came not so much from the long-established anti-tobacco bodies, but from new organisations and active individuals concerned only with juvenile smoking. By 1907, there were fourteen organisations around the country in addition to the British Anti-Tobacco and Anti-Narcotic League and the Anti-Tobacco Legion (the youth section of Reynolds' Anti-Tobacco Society). Based in Edinburgh were the Scottish Anti-Tobacco Society, the Hope Trust and the Boys' Purity League; in Bristol, the Young People's Anti-Smoking League; in Birmingham, the Boy's Anti-Cigarette League and the Juvenile Templars; in Penzance, the R. E. D. Brotherhood; and in London, the British Lads' Anti-Smoking Union, the Band of Love, the League of Six, the Hygienic League and Union for the Suppression of Juvenile Smoking, and the Band of Hope Union.[28] By far the most important was the International Anti-Cigarette League (IACL), founded by the Rev. Frank Johnson, which claimed the support of Robert Baden-Powell and Winston Churchill. Organised through Sunday Schools, the League had 57,000 members by 1904 and 80,000 by 1908, all 'pledged to abstain from smoking at least until the age of 21'.[29] Although it is unlikely that such numbers actually attended their monthly meetings, the prominence of its leaders made it an influential body. Renowned smokers themselves, the likes of Churchill and Baden-Powell saw no inherent dangers in tobacco itself, but clearly constructed juvenile smoking as a physical and moral problem. Their colleagues in the IACL and the Hygienic League would prove to be enthusiastic witnesses to the government's committees on juvenile smoking.[30]

Opposition to the Bills came from the tobacco trade and the proponents of an older, non-interventionist, Liberalism. Retailers disliked the terms which made it illegal to sell tobacco to anyone less than sixteen years of age, thereby placing the onus of responsibility on the seller and not the purchaser.[31] The Tobacco Dealers' Licence Reform Association suggested instead increasing the retail licence to drive out the small traders, who they claimed sold the cheap cigarettes to children.[32] Despite some influence of the Wholesale Tobacconists' Protection Association in reducing the penalties on retailers recommended by the House of Lords, without the support of the manufacturers, which aimed to maximise their distributive outlets, the retail trade's interests were limited in their reception at government level.[33] Opposition in Parliament came from figures such as Lord Cecil, who thought the Bill 'a steam hammer to crack a nut' that would only make smoking seem more manly and exciting.[34] Their attitude was part of a general hostility to the Children's Act and other welfare reforms based upon a concept of the free individual whose rights should not be interfered with by the state. Helen Bosanquet of the Charity Organisation Society supported the institution of the family above all other social bodies for protecting the interests of the child: 'it is the mother's instinct alone which can secure to the child its birthright of tenderness, the State is powerless to provide it at any cost.'[35] And, in specifically opposing the juvenile smoking clauses of the Children's Act, one Conservative MP claimed that it was against the treasured freedom of the Englishman 'to regulate the affairs of private life, not by example or precept, but by the policeman'.[36]

These older values promoting the independent responsibility of the individual to himself and his family were giving way to a more interventionist and reforming spirit within the Liberal Party, itself influenced by the reports of the countless turn-of-the-century social investigators and the widespread anxiety about racial degeneration and decline.[37] Fears were especially prominent in Britain after the Boer War when 'two out of three men willing to bear arms in the Manchester district [were] virtually invalids' and 'perhaps a third of the "rejects" from the army in Lancashire might be attributed to "smoker's heart"'.[38] The recruitment figures seemed to confirm the predictions of national decline prophesied by the eugenicist Karl Pearson only a few years earlier and, together with the social and economic problems highlighted by Booth and Rowntree, the 'British way of life' itself was seen to be under threat. The practical result of the panic was the investigation of almost every aspect of popular culture. Depravity and immorality were observed in the music hall, on the football field and terrace, at the seaside resort and during the courtions rituals of the 'monkey parade': 'even the poor old bicycle was dragged into the act, amidst a blizzard of respectable fears'.[39] Every aspect of urban, working-class life proved worthy of comment. The differences in height and weight of boys from different social classes were measured, and criticism was made of the insufficient, ill-chosen and unnutritious food, poor air quality, low quality schooling, bad mothering and lack of physical recreation facilities with which the boy might help himself out of the problems of an unhealthy environment.[40] For many optimistic social reformers the state was felt to provide a solution to the 'condition of England' question in that 'improvements among the young, particularly the poor, might break that vicious circle of destitution, crime and further destitution'.[41] More collectivist ideals influenced the Liberal legislators of 1908 and the political party began to move away from its Radical, laissez-faire traditions.[42] Ideologically, it was aided by developments in social-Darwinist thought that did not necessarily accept an individualist interpretation of evolution and which legitimated the state's 'right to secure better racial stocks and discourage the bad ones'.[43]

The focus of much of this re-interpretation of the role of the state was the urban child. The Children's Act was therefore very much a part of a more general movement which also included other legislative measures such as the Education (Provision of Meals) Act of 1906 and the Education (Administrative Provisions) Act of 1907.[44] These were all responses to the perceived failure of parental obligation to raise the child according to notions increasingly orthodox among the reforming and legislating classes. Figures such as John Gorst had been influenced by the changes in the concepts of childhood and adolescence which had led to a process of 'sacrilisation' whereby children, transformed from workers into scholars, lost their economic utility but became emotionally priceless to both parents and society.[45] Such beliefs were held by the investigators into the 'boy labour problem', who felt that the messenger boy, van boy and half-timer appeared as a precocious 'man-child' who became independent of parental authority at too early an age.[46] When in work boys were said to have too much money to spend, but when out of work the urban landscape was said to lead to criminality and delinquency. Smoking was a symbol of these fears since it was an act or gesture that demonstrated the boys, attachment to the adult world and an eagerness to escape from childhood. Retrospectively, one might suggest that the juvenile smoking 'problem' in the Edwardian period was a consequence, rather than a determinant, of national physical degeneration. However, to Liberal reformers and legislators, smoking by children and youths became a very real issue, understood as it was by a range of medical and moral arguments that were outlined in chapter 3.

The events of 1908 were therefore the product of an extremely specific historical context, a reaction to a phenomenon which society normally condoned. Indeed, the concerns of the social reformers seem to have existed almost independently of a working-class popular culture which continued to encourage juvenile smoking throughout the inter-war period. After the Children's Act was passed by Parliament, the anti-smoking groups disbanded and the movement as a whole eventually collapsed, to be replaced by the one NSNS, a group far less aggressive in its anti-tobacco agenda (see chapter 9). Anti-smoking arguments continued to appear in publications of Baden-Powell's Scout movement, but commentary on the issue largely disappeared after 1908.[47] Some traders were prosecuted for selling cigarettes to juveniles less than sixteen years of age, but judges appear to have been extremely lenient in their sentencing and the cases brought to the attention of the trade press soon amounted to none. It would, in any case, be difficult to estimate whether the Act was successful in its own aims. As Herbert Samuel commented in 1910, 'Of course, one could not tell whether the children puffed at a cigarette round the corner, or in the secret of their own homes.'[48] After the First World War there was some suggestion that smoking was on the increase among juveniles because of the particular conditions which existed from 1914 to 1918:

> There is no doubt that during the last four years there has been a great increase in the extent of juvenile smoking, due no doubt to the fact that quite young boys have, under the abnormal conditions brought about by the war, been earning comparatively high wages, and that supervision by parents and police has in many cases been less thorough than in the years immediately following the passing of the Children Act.[49]

It is unfortunate that little is known about youth culture in the inter-war period.[50] The late Victorian and Edwardian age represented a peak of youth's visibility, other peaks occurring with the emergence of the 'teenager' in the 1950s and the anxieties over the juvenile crowd in the 1780s that sparked off the Sunday School movement.[51] Mass-Observation's interviews with smokers who would have begun smoking in the 1910s and 1920s suggest, however, that the culture of juvenile cigarette consumption remained largely unaltered from the 1890s. It found that most men had begun smoking by experimenting with cigarettes before they were sixteen. Half of the respondents claimed that they began smoking for social reasons, to impress, imitate, gain confidence or because of fear of being left out. Many told stories of how they tried smoking at very early ages, eager to indulge in that which was forbidden. The desire to be a man was particularly important ('a cigarette adds more than three inches to half-grown statures'), with the pressure here often coming from girls.[52] For the period after the Second World War, Mark Abrams' social survey gives some indication of the high smoking rates among children and youths. In 1959 he estimated that teenagers spent £88 million on tobacco and cigarettes, 10.6 per cent of their total expenditure and equivalent to 6*s* 10*d* per week. Boys spent more money on cigarettes than girls and the working class spent more than the middle class.[53] Taking all this evidence together, the smoking youth, frequently urban, male and working class, seems to have been a common sight from the late nineteenth century onwards.

After smoking became linked with lung cancer and other diseases from the 1950s onwards, government departments and statistical bodies began to investigate more thoroughly the extent of juvenile smoking. What is remarkable is that throughout the 1960s and 1970s, the proportion of male smokers who claimed to have started smoking at less than sixteen years of age remained remarkably consistent at about 30 per cent. For women, the figure also remained stable at 15 per cent.[54] Even in 1996, after years of public health education programmes, just over 10 per cent of children were regular smokers, with girls now more likely than boys to adopt the habit.[55] There has therefore been remarkable consistency in the culture of juvenile smoking which has persisted through a period in which the dangers of cigarettes have become increasingly apparent. Why this has proved to be the case, and why it is that girls are now smoking more than boys, will be covered in the following final section.

Notes

1 *Tobacco Trade Review (hereafter TTR)*, 9:104 (August 1876), 85.
2 P. Quennell, *London's Underworld: Being Selections from 'Those That Will Not Work', the Fourth Volume of 'London Labour and the London Poor' by Henry Mayhew* (London, Spring Books, 1950), p. 50.
3 *TTR*, 30:358 (October 1897), 491.
4 Parliamentary Papers (hereafter P.P.), XXXII, Inter-Departmental Committee on Physical Deterioration, *Minutes of Evidence*, Cd. 2210, 1904, p. 255; R. A. Bray, 'The boy and the family', in E. J. Urwick (ed.), *Studies of Boy Life in Our Cities* (New York, Garland, 1980), p. 98.
5 *TTR*, 40:479 (November 1907), 355.
6 This chapter is based on an earlier article, M. Hilton, ' "Tabs", "fags" and the "boy labour problem" in late Victorian and Edwardian Britain', *Journal of Social History*, 28:3 (1995), 587–607. A similar interpretation based on different evidence can also be found in J. Welshman, 'Images of youth: the issue of juvenile smoking, 1880–1914', *Addiction*, 91:9 (1996), 1379–86.
7 Bray in Urwick, *Studies of Boy Life*, pp. 23–33.
8 S. Humphries, *Hooligans or Rebels? An Oral History of Working-Class Childhood and Youth, 1889–1939* (Oxford, Blackwell, 1981), p. 146.

9 Urwick, *Studies of Boy Life*, p. xii.

10 M. Childs, *Labour's Apprentices: Working-Class Lads in Late Victorian and Edwardian England* (London, Hambledon, 1992).

11 A. Paterson, *Across the Bridges, or Life by the South London Riverside* (London, Edward Arnold, 1911), p. 125.

12 *Ibid.*, p. 142.

13 E. Roberts, *Social Life in Barrow, Lancaster and Preston, 1870–1930* (oral history transcripts held at the Library, University of Lancaster), Mr. A.2.B., p. 96.

14 B. Baron, *The Growing Generation: A Study of Working Boys and Girls in Our Cities* (London, Student Christian Movement, 1911), p. 16.

15 D. Hôher, 'The composition of music hall audiences, 1850–1900', in P. Bailey (ed.), *Music Hall: The Business of Pleasure* (Buckingham, Open University Press, 1986), pp. 73–92; C. E. B. Russell, *Manchester Boys: Sketches of Manchester Lads at Work and Play* (Manchester, Manchester University Press, 1905), p. 65; R. Roberts, *The Classic Slum: Salford Life in the First Quarter of the Century* (Manchester, Manchester University Press, 1971), p. 132; A. Freeman, *Boy Life and Labour: The Manufacture of Inefficiency* (London, P. S. King & Son, 1914), p. 129; J. Gillis, 'The evolution of juvenile delinquency in England, 1890–1914', *Past and Present*, 67 (1975), 96–126; P. Wilkinson, 'English youth movements, 1908–1930', *Journal of Contemporary History*, 4 (1969), 3–23; P. Dunae, 'Penny dreadfuls: late 19th century boys' literature and crime', *Victorian Studies*, 22 (1979), 133–50; M. Clapson, *A Bit of a Flutter: Popular Gambling and English Society, c. 1823–1961* (Manchester, Manchester University Press, 1992).

16 P. Thompson, *The Edwardians: The Remaking of British Society* (London, Routledge, 1992).

17 J. G. Cloette, 'The boy and his work', in Urwick, *Studies of Boy Life*, p. 134; E. Roberts, 'The family', in J. Benson (ed.), *The Working Class in England, 1875–1914* (Beckenham, Croom Helm, 1985); Childs, *Labour's Apprentices*, p. 73.

18 B. S. Rowntree, *Poverty: A Study of Town Life* (Basingstoke, Macmillan, 1901), p. 30.

19 A. Davies, *Leisure, Gender and Poverty: Working-Class Culture in Salford and Manchester, 1900–1939* (Buckingham, Open University Press, 1992), p. 83; Russell, *Manchester Boys*, p. 15.

20 E. Roberts, *A Woman's Place: An Oral History of Working-Class Women* (Oxford, Blackwell, 1984), p. 43.

21 *Tobacco Weekly Journal*, 390 (8 February 1906), p. 105.

22 *TTR*, 31:364 (April 1898), 183; Roberts, *Social Life*, Mr. C.6.P., pp. 19–20; Mr. G.1.P., pp. 56–7; Mr. G.1.P., p. 30.

23 *TTR*, 30:357 (September 1897), 434; Russell, *Manchester Boys*, p. 99.

24 Roberts, *Classic Slum*, p. 134; S. Meacham, *A Life Apart: The English Working Class, 1890–1914* (Massachusetts, Harvard University Press, 1977), p. 162.

25 The Children's Act, 1908. Clauses 39–43 reprinted as a supplement to *TTR*, 42:494 (February 1909).

26 T. Reynolds, *Juvenile Street Smoking: Reasons for Seeking its Legislative Prohibition* (London, British Anti-Tobacco Society, 1856); 'Scrutator', *Smoking or No Smoking? That's the Question: Hear Sir Benjamin C. Brodie, Bart., with Critical Observations* (London, Pitman, 1860); English Anti-Tobacco Society and Anti-Narcotic League, *Monthly Letter*, 177 (January 1891).

27 *TTR*, 36:424 (April 1903), 163; *TTR*, 39:457 (January 1906), 22; Welshman, 'Images of youth', p. 1383.

28 J. Q. A. Henry, *The Deadly Cigarette; or the Perils of Juvenile Smoking* (London, Richard J. James, 1907), pp. 169–71.

29 *The Times* (28 April 1904), p. 8; Welshman, 'Images of youth', p. 1382.

30 P. P., Physical Deterioration, *Minutes of Evidence*, i P.P., IX, Juvenile Smoking Bill, *Report of the Select Committee of the House of Lords*, 1906.

31 *TTR*, 25:297 (September 1892), 260–1.

32 *TTR*, 41:483 (March 1908), 72; *TTR*, 41:483 (March 1908), 83.

33 *TTR*, 40:469 (January 1907), 2.

34 *The Times* (13 October 1908), p. 9; Lord Cecil, *Parliamentary Debates*, 194 (12 October 1908), 43.

35 H. Bosanquet, *The Strength of the People* (1902; New York, Garland, 1980), p. 187.

36 F. Banbury, *Parliamentary Debates*, 194 (13 October 1908), 173–4.

37 D. Pick, *Faces of Degeneration: A European Disorder, c. 1848–c. 1918* (Cambridge, Cambridge University Press, 1989).

38 Arnold White, *Efficiency and Empire* (1911), quoted in E. Evans, *Social Policy, 1830–1914* (London, Routledge & Kegan Paul, 1978), p. 224; P.P., Physical Deterioration, *Minutes of Evidence*, p. 278.

39 G. Pearson, *Hooligan: A History of Respectable Fears* (Basingstoke, Macmillan, 1983), p. 63.

40 Urwick, *Studies of Boy Life*, pp. 259–60, 263.

41 J. Walvin, *A Child's World: A Social History of English Childhood, 1800–1914* (Harmondsworth, Penguin, 1982), p. 166.

42 J. R. Hay, *The Origins of the Liberal Welfare Reforms, 1906–1914* (Basingstoke, Macmillan, 1975); B. Semmel, *Imperialism and Social Reform: English Social-Imperial Thought, 1895–1914* (London, Allen & Unwin, 1960).

43 G. Jones, *Social Darwinism and English Thought: The Interaction Between Biological and Social Theory* (Brighton, Harvester Press, 1980).

44 Welshman, 'Images of youth', p. 1381.

45 J. Gorst, *The Children of the Nation: How Their Health and Vigour Should be Promoted by the State* (London, Methuen, 1906). On 'sacrilisation' see V. Zelizer, *Pricing the Priceless Child: The Changing Social Value of Children* (New York, Basic Books, 1985), an American study but of relevance to the British context found in R. Cooter (ed.), *In the Name of the Child: Health and Welfare, 1880–1940* (London, Routledge, 1992).

46 Childs, *Labour's Apprentices*; H. Hendrick, *Images of Youth: Age, Class and the Male Youth Problem, 1880–1920* (Oxford, Clarendon Press, 1990).

47 R. Baden-Powell, *Scouting for Boys* (1908; London, Pearson, 1928). His advice was repeated in his later *Rovering to Success* (London, Herbert Jenkins, 1930), pp. 74–7.

48 *TTR*, 43:512 (August 1910), 252.

49 *TTR*, 52:614 (February 1919), 17–18.

50 Two exceptions are B. Osgerby, 'From the Roaring Twenties to the Swinging Sixties: continuity and change in British youth culture', in B. Brivati and H. Jones (eds), *What Difference Did the War Make?* (Leicester, Leicester University Press, 1993), pp. 80–95, and D. Fowler, *The First Teenagers: The Lifestyle of Young Wage-earners in Interwar Britain* (London, Woburn, 1995).

51 M. Blanch, 'Imperialism, nationalism and organised youth', in J. Clarke, C. Critcher and R. Johnson (eds), *Working Class Cultures: Studies in History and Theory* (London, Hutchinson, 1979).

52 M.-O., File Report 3192, 1949, *Man and His Cigarette*, pp. 103–4, 107; M.-O. Topic Collections, *Smoking Habits, 1937–1965. Box No. 2: Smoking Habits: Smoking Enquiry 1937*, File B: Reports from male members of M.-O. panel, Fishbein (286).

53 M. Abrams, *Teenage Consumer Spending in 1959 (Part II): Middle Class and Working Class Boys and Girls* (London, Press Exchange, 1961).

54 N. Wald *et al.*, *UK Smoking Statistics* (Oxford, Oxford University Press, 1971), p. 91.

55 L. Jarvis, *Teenage Smoking Attitudes in 1996* (London, HMSO, 1997).

Part III

Science:

cancer and the politics of smoking since 1950

8

Smoking and health: the medical understanding of tobacco

In 1950, in the *British Medical Journal*, Richard Doll and A. Bradford Hill published their preliminary report on the association between smoking and cancer of the lung, concluding famously that 'smoking is a factor, and an important factor, in the production of carcinoma of the lung'.[1] As members of the Medical Research Council's (MRC's) Statistical Research Unit, their investigations had begun in 1947.[2] They interviewed 2,475 patients from 20 London hospitals to test whether the incidence of lung cancer was related to either cigarette consumption or exposure to atmospheric pollution, the other widely held cause of cancer at this time. Their findings demonstrated a clear statistical link between lung cancer and smoking, an association strengthened the more the smoker consumed. What their statistical research could not demonstrate was a causal connection that would satisfy the standards of proof required by laboratory-based science: statistics could not identify the particular carcinogen in tobacco which lay at the root of the problem. It is this difficulty over interpreting the results within the larger area of epidemiological research that has enabled various scientists and tobacco manufacturers to reject or cast doubt on the work of Doll and Hill. They have instead demanded a clinical demonstration of the smoking–cancer link before they will accept a causal connection.

However, statistical science obtained a much greater validity in the pages of the mainstream medical press, the *British Medical Journal* cautiously accepting Doll and Hill's findings as well as the results of similar investigations by Wynder and Graham in the United States.[3] The *Lancet* proved more sceptical at first, emphasising the lack of causality put forward in the research, but the follow-up study by Doll and Hill, published in December 1952, placated many of its anxieties. The *British Medical Journal* went further, accepting that because 'the probability of a causal connexion' was so great it could not be denied.[4] The 1952 article extended the scope of the interviews conducted for the first article, providing greater detail on the smoking habits of the cancer patients and the histories of their consumption and general state of health. It discounted other potential causes of lung cancer/such as petrol lighters, diesel fumes and cigarette holders, which had been suggested in response to the first paper and, although they did not argue that smoking was the only cause of lung cancer, Doll and Hill confirmed that the association was 'real'.[5]

At the same time, several other medics were beginning to turn their attention to the problem and various articles and letters appeared regularly in the medical press in the early 1950s, though the debates only received a minimal airing in the daily newspapers.[6] While many scientists sought to find the causal agent in tobacco smoke by experimenting with mice in the laboratory, Doll and Hill proceeded with their statistical investigations. In 1951, they wrote to every one of the 60,000 doctors on the *Medical Register* asking them to complete a simple questionnaire about their smoking habits, a form reprinted in the *British Medical Journal* to encourage as near to a 100 per cent completion rate as possible.[7] The research into these life histories has continued into the 1990s,[8] but by 1957 the initial results were deemed to be so conclusive that the MRC declared the link between smoking and lung cancer as one of 'direct cause and effect'.[9] Despite the constant refutations and challenges of the tobacco manufacturers, Doll and Hill's findings had become the orthodoxy within most medical circles by the late 1950s, confirmed as they were by a rising flood of supporting scientific papers.[10]

The damage done to health through smoking has increasingly come to dominate the meaning of tobacco. The medical and scientific understanding of the cigarette has had the most significant impact on the role of smoking in British popular culture in the late twentieth century. Medicine has therefore replaced the economic understanding which dominated the history of smoking in the early twentieth century which likewise had eclipsed the cultural ideal of tobacco in the late nineteenth century. This chapter serves as the scientific equivalent of chapters 1 and 4, which outlined earlier ascendant cultural and economic understandings of tobacco. It covers the emergence of the smoking and health controversy in the 1950s in medical bodies such as the MRC, the Royal College of Physicians (RCP), the Socialist Medical Association (SMA), the British Medical Association (BMA) and even the NSNS, all of which had varying degrees of institutional and personnel links with central and local government. Acknowledging important differences of interpretation between such bodies, if together they can be taken as the 'establishment' view, this chapter traces the promotion of the smoking and cancer link through various official and semi-official channels.

The focus of the chapter is on the 1950s and 1960s, the period in which public health campaigns about the risks of smoking were first launched. Initially, the efforts of the government were rather piecemeal, but after being centralised following the publication of the RCP report *Smoking and Health* in 1962,[11] they became increasingly comprehensive throughout the decade, culminating in a voluntary agreement in 1971 in which the tobacco industry agreed to the printing of health warnings on all cigarette packets. By such a time, it can be assumed that everybody had heard of the association between smoking and lung cancer, as well as other illnesses such as heart disease and bronchitis. The interesting period is therefore the first two decades of the smoking and health campaign, when scientific rationality competed with the surviving cultural rationality of the bourgeois male and the economic rationality of the mass manufacturer. Indeed, it has been suggested that the difficulty with which the 'rational advice' of the medic was accepted in British popular culture at this time was due to both the pervasiveness of the manufacturers' advertising imagery and to the older liberal ideals of independence and individuality which opposed state-sponsored campaigns to direct personal consumption.[12] This chapter, however, will present the 'official' view of smoking as presented by successive governments and medical establishments, before such forms of knowledge were interpreted and located in wider smoking cultures (see chapters 9 and 10).

Doll and Hill were not the first to have made the link between smoking and lung cancer. Scientists in Nazi Germany had directed much research into the harmful properties of tobacco, although the results of their work were not generally known to British and American scientists in the 1950s.[13] In Britain, in the early twentieth century, there was something of a lull in the discussion of the medical effects of smoking compared with what there had been in the nineteenth century when the anti-tobacco movement had had some impact. Occasional articles did, however, appear linking smoking with 'soldier's heart', that umbrella term for the poor physical condition of British troops in the Boer and Great Wars.[14] However, in the *Lancet* at least, any medical discussion was firmly couched within the persistent culture of the Victorian periodical literature; thus the harmful effects of smoking would be seen as minimal in comparison to the beneficial relief it gave to stress and anxiety.[15] Likewise, cigarettes might be condemned, but pipes and cigars were applauded and books of verse in praise of 'the leaf' were considered worthy of review in medical journals.[16] There was some debate about tobacco amblyopia (tobacco blindness) and the danger of nicotine and its addictive qualities,[17] but it was common to disassociate the 'craving' for tobacco from the more uncontrollable urges developed for other drugs.[18] The fanatical anti-smoker, Dr Lennox Johnston, did manage to publish an article in 1942 labelling tobacco smoking as an addiction, but his work was on the fringes of the medical profession, a fact best confirmed through his rabid plans for an arson attack on the offices of the BMA, which refused to publish his work in its journal.[19]

The initial reticence of the *Lancet* to accept wholeheartedly the findings of Doll and Hill meant that younger medical journals took the initiative.[20] The outpouring of clinical and epidemiological research spread rapidly to other publications, to the extent that as early as 1954 *Medical World* devoted an entire issue to smoking and lung cancer, various writers summarising debates from their own particular field's approach to the subject.[21] Although a symposium revealed many dissenting voices as to the nature of proof and causality, much of the most informed discussants were not debating whether there was a link but that, given that there was one, what the government ought to do about it. The further publication of Doll and Hill's research on the smoking habits of doctors in the mid 1950s won over many other sceptics, and a leader article in the *Lancet* finally removed any doubts as to that journal's attitude when it spoke of the impossibility of ignoring the evidence that smoking causes lung cancer.[22] The MRC's statement of 1957 best summarised the extent of medical knowledge at this stage in that it did not discount the potential influence of atmospheric pollution on lung cancer but, given the conclusions of so much research from all around the world, argued that cigarette smoking must be blamed in particular, and that the discovery of a number of carcinogens in the smoke provided a 'rational basis for a causal relationship'.[23]

The sheer weight of medical, or specifically epidemiological, evidence pointing to the dangerous effects of smoking produced subsequently is too monumental to be dealt with adequately here, although the most authoritative summaries of the current state of medical knowledge have been provided intermittently by the RCP. The 1962 report, *Smoking and Health*, clarified the arguments by stating that heavy smokers were thirty times more likely to contract lung cancer than non-smokers. The report considered other evidence, taking account of such anomalies as the inability to induce lung cancer in animals through exposure to cigarette smoke and that lung cancer only occurs in a minority of smokers, but failed to see how these findings could detract from the principal fact that 'cigarette smoking is a cause of lung cancer'. The report also confirmed the link with chronic bronchitis, gastric and duodenal ulcers, and coronary heart disease as well as other arterial diseases. What the report did not do was label tobacco as addictive and it only tentatively commented on the lower weight of babies of smoking mothers and the impaired performance of smoking athletes.[24] The 1964 US Surgeon-General's report confirmed the statements of the MRC and RCP in the UK, again emphasising the importance of smoking over air pollution in causing lung cancer and bronchial disorders. Taking into account coronary-artery problems and other cardiovascular diseases, the US report estimated that the overall age-specific death rate among cigarette smokers was about 70 per cent above that for non-smokers. Significantly, while pipes and cigars were generally exempted from such conclusions, filter cigarettes were not, the report concluding that they seemed to offer no protection against disease.[25]

Between the publication of the first and the second RCP report, *Smoking and Health Now*, in 1971, at least another 5,000 scientific papers were produced on the dangerous effects of smoking.[26] The 1971 report was far more aggressive and confident in tone, estimating that 20,000 deaths a year in men aged between 35 and 64 were caused by smoking, and that there was no doubt that smoking caused lung cancer, chronic bronchitis, emphysema, coronary heart disease and coronary thrombosis. Objections to such findings were said to be 'without substance' and a number of debatable issues were clarified (at least in the minds of the report's committee members): lung cancer had been produced in mice exposed to smoke; inhaling did lead to increased risk; filters reduced but did not remove the danger; the risk of death declined rapidly ten years after giving up smoking; and women who smoked during pregnancy did tend to have smaller babies than non-smokers, as well as being more likely to lose their babies from abortion, still-birth and death in the first days of life.[27] At this point, little debate existed within the medical profession on the general conclusions regarding smoking and health, and the above findings have remained the mainstays of scientific opinion against tobacco, the 1977 RCP report in many ways merely providing further detail and confirmation of what was already believed.[28] However, two main further additions to the body of official medical knowledge have arisen since the 1970s. In 1981, a *British Medical Journal* article on lung cancer among non-smoking wives of heavy smokers made passive smoking a major issue.[29] It was hesitatingly accepted by the 1983 RCP report, and although the evidence presented has by no means been as conclusive as that for first-hand smoking, the eighty articles produced by 1988 pointing to the dangers of environmental tobacco smoke convinced the Independent Scientific Committee on Smoking and Health to endorse a link between lung cancer and passive smoking.[30] A second major development, perhaps more publicly discernible in the United States than in Britain thanks to the 1988 Surgeon-General's report, has been in the field of addiction. Tobacco is now usually categorised as an addictive substance along with other psychoactive drugs, nicotine being identified as the cause of physical dependence over and above the social and cultural reasons for the continuation of cigarette consumption.[31] Besides these latter two points, however, what is clear is that by the 1960s the major illnesses which the medical profession now associates with cigarette smoking had been identified and accepted by those experts with an interest in public health.

How such knowledge was accepted by successive governments and presented to the population through public health policies was never straightforward, the often blurred relationship between the politics and science of tobacco having provoked much academic and journalistic debate.[32] From the very beginning of the discovery of the link between smoking and cancer, there has been a gap between what many medics were calling for and what the government actually did in regard to public health education. Richard Doll's immediate impact was on his colleagues at the Central Middlesex Hospital, including Sir Francis Avery Jones and Horace Joules, where Doll had been working part-time at the Gastroenterology Unit.[33] Joules had been vociferously opposed to his own former chain-smoking habit for some years and, as early as February 1951, he used his membership of the Central Health Services Council's Standing Committee on Cancer and Radiotherapy to push for a Ministry of Health campaign on the dangers of tobacco. The Committee was initially against advising the Minister to take such a course, given the perceived paucity of the evidence, but after Joules pushed the issue in 1952 and following the publication of Doll and Hill's follow-up study, Bradford Hill was invited to reiterate his views to the Committee. Further evidence was then considered, prompting the Tobacco Manufacturers' Standing Committee and the Imperial Tobacco Company to put forward their case by distributing forty copies of a rejoinder to Doll and Hill by their own statistician, G. F. Todd. Eventually, after setting up a specific panel to look into the matter in 1953, the Committee had to accept the evidence of a link, and advised the Minister that this link had to be presumed causal until proven otherwise. MacLeod, the Health Minister, had so far refused to answer the repeated questions in Parliament for a government statement on the issue, but he eventually gave way following the recommendations of his Advisory Committee. However, whereas the Committee had presumed causality, in the Commons MacLeod added that he must 'draw attention to the fact that there is so far no firm evidence of the way in which smoking may cause lung cancer or of the extent to which it does so'. After also mentioning in an accompanying press release that the tobacco companies had offered £250,000 to the MRC to examine the smoking and lung cancer link, MacLeod argued that it was 'not possible to come to a final and definite conclusion'. It appears likely that the potential impact of the message was considerably less than what many members of the Advisory Committee had initially intended.[34]

Those convinced of the causal link between smoking and lung cancer were understandably disappointed with such a statement, backed up as it was with no public health education programme. Joules continued to make his presence felt in government committees and in the medical and national press, while the NSNS and the SMA, of which he was a Vice-President, called on the Ministry of Health to launch a 'country-wide educational campaign to warn people of this peril'.[35] Questions continued to be asked in Parliament by the committed Labour activists Edith Summerskill, W. D. Chapman and Marcus Lipton, but the new Health Minister from 1956, Robert Turton, was never likely to provide much of a response given his willingness to be photographed by the press smoking before entering the Commons to answer questions on the issue.[36] The Ministry was aware of the problem, its Public Relation's Officer, S. A. Heald, commenting that the lack of a 'clear categorical statement' enabled the 'man in the street' to 'comfort himself with the thought that we need not make up his mind just yet'. However, in June 1957, the MRC published its first report which spoke of a causal relationship between smoking and cancer and the government was forced, if not to state that it accepted its findings, at least to 'feel' that it was 'right to ensure that this latest authoritative opinion [was] brought effectively to public notice'. Such rhetorical distancing, however slight, reflected a certain unwillingness by the government to be attached wholly to the report, and this was confirmed by its subsequent lack of action.[37]

The Minister's statement and the MRC's report were distributed to every local authority in the country, with instructions reflecting the government's policy that it was up to the individual to make up his or her own mind about the evidence, based on a rational assessment of the known risks. As such, central government did not launch a campaign itself and instead left it to local authorities to decide whether or not to publicise the risks of smoking in their area.[38] This essentially liberal notion of the individual held by the government explains its lack of further action even though the public health researcher Ann Cartwright and her colleagues at Edinburgh University had found that the majority of smokers were in favour of smoking bans on buses and trains and in theatres and cinemas.[39] One hundred and eighteen out of 129 English local authorities did soon launch publicity campaigns through the use of posters, pamphlets, advertisements in the local press, lectures to schools and parent–teacher associations, and even home visits, but they desired more direction from central government.[40] Pressure for further action was maintained in Parliament and from the letters of influential medics such as Charles Fletcher, but the government stuck to the same policy from 1957 to 1962, despite the evidence of Cartwright's Edinburgh survey, which demonstrated that smokers were extremely unlikely to change their habits even when they had heard of the dangers involved.[41]

Following the publication of the first RCP report, however, central government was galvanised into action. The Ministry of Health's Central Council for Health Education (CCHE) set up a Co-ordinating Committee on Smoking and Health (CCSH), which first met in August 1962 and brought together officials from the main government departments concerned with smoking and health, plus representatives from the RCP, the CCHE, the BMA, the Society of Medical Officers of Health and other concerned bodies.[42] In addition, an Advisory Group on Publicity was set up in April 1962, comprising officials from the Ministries of Health and Education and independent teaching and medical representatives.[43] Within fifteen months of the RCP report, over one million posters had been issued, with activities further extending to the production of films; assessments of the media presentation of public health; the observance of smoking and health campaigns in the rest of the world; the effectiveness of local authority campaigns; and smoking policies on public transport and in hospitals, as well as a statutory increase in the penalties awarded to those caught selling cigarettes illegally to children.[44] The Central Office of Information even commissioned a private research firm, Armstrong-Warden Ltd, to analyse various types of publicity campaign.[45] However, the CCSH began to meet infrequently, as it transpired that only Charles Fletcher and the Ministry of Health officials could provide constructive ideas (it last met in March 1966.)[46] It also faced opposition from the poster advertising industry, which refused at first to display anti-smoking propaganda, for fear of offending its more lucrative clients within the tobacco industry.[47] The poster industry had good reason for such anxieties, the RCP pointing out in 1971 how little the £100,000 spent annually on the anti-smoking campaign appeared compared with the £1,300,000 spent on road safety awareness or even the £52 million spent by the tobacco industry on sales promotion in 1968.[48]

For those concerned with expanding the anti-smoking campaign, there were some successes, particularly when Kenneth Robinson, a persistent Labour critic of the tobacco industry, became Minister of Health from 1964 to 1968. In 1962, the Postmaster General banned television advertisements which presented cigarettes in ways which over-emphasised pleasure, manliness, fashion and romance or which featured heroes of the young that might inspire emulative behaviour. This was extended in 1965 to a blanket ban on TV cigarette advertising, despite the protestations of the Tobacco Advisory Council that such sales promotion had never actually served to increase total demand. Subsequently, government and industry engaged in negotiations for piecemeal extensions to the limitations on advertising, such as ceilings on expenditure and the cessation of cinema and radio advertising, but these efforts still fell far short of the bans on all tobacco advertising called for in perennial Labour and sometimes Conservative private member's Bills (there would be thirty-five of these between 1964 and 1995, only one of which received Royal Assent).[49] The CCHE struggled to extend its campaigns throughout the 1960s, holding a conference to demonstrate the seriousness of the issue.[50] In short, then, although governments accepted a causal relationship between smoking and cancer, little was done to interfere with the smooth running of the cigarette industry.

It was not until the end of the decade that a noticeable shift took place in government policy. In 1968, the Health Education Council (HEC) was set up and its modern anti-smoking campaigns were based on research into actual smokers' attitudes. Also, in 1971 the ambivalence which had marked government attitudes to smoking and health was to some extent resolved when the second RCP report demanded further action. In that year, a voluntary agreement was introduced to place government health warnings on cigarette packets, the negotiations for which helped lead to the collapse of the Conservative backbencher's, Sir Gerald Nabarro, equivalent private member's Bill which would have created a legal precedent.[51] Following the recommendations of the RCP, the lobbying and campaigning organisation, Action on Smoking and Health (ASH), was set up with funding from the Department of Health and Social Security. Although this only amounted to an annual grant of £115,000 by 1982, ASH became an effective countervailing force to the power of the tobacco industry in the 1970s and 1980s It had some influence in raising the tax on tobacco, particularly in 1981, when two tax rises brought the price of a packet of twenty cigarettes past the psychological £1 barrier and reduced sales by 10 billion cigarettes. Further voluntary arrangements were also put in place to limit sponsorship in the late 1970s, but the tobacco-friendly Health Minister, Kenneth Clarke, was the more typical face presented in the government's dealings with the industry in the 1980s than the short-lived anti-smoking Ministry of Sir George Young. At the same time, however, the activities of the HEC ensured that government health campaigns remained up to date with developments in the medical understanding of smoking, and by 1983 it had an annual budget of £2 million to spend on campaigns against the cigarette.

The activities of ASH also marked a new relationship between science and the state, whereby the medical profession (and especially that section concerned with public health) saw its official and cultural authority expand still further. The promotion of medical knowledge came to be instigated by ostensibly independent bodies but which had close institutional and personnel links with the central bureaucracy. During the 1980s and 1990s, the anti-smoking message has come from organisations such as the British Heart Foundation, the Cancer Research Campaign, the Chest, Heart and Stroke Association, and the Imperial Cancer Research Fund. Most significantly, those close links between bodies such as ASH, the RCP and the HEC were confirmed in 1984 when David Simpson of ASH approached the BMA, asking it to launch a campaign against smoking which it had previously avoided. The BMA, infuriated at the lack of impact that the voluntary agreements had had on the 100,000 smoking-related premature deaths it estimated occurred each year, began both an education campaign and a concerted lobbying effort to support Laurie Pavitt's parliamentary activities to ban the sponsorship of sporting events by tobacco companies (the Labour MP had first introduced a private member's Bill in 1966). The campaign obtained much media attention with its central messages that 'tobacco is a killer' and that the activities of the industry ought to be restricted. The efforts of these semi-official institutions of the state succeeded in further making public the developments in medical knowledge. At the same time, central government activity continued to amount to secretly arranged voluntary agreements with the tobacco industry. For instance, in 1985 tar and nicotine levels were published on cigarette packets, an act which promised much impact given the furore that had surrounded *Which?* magazine's initial publication of these figures in 1971.[52]

Most anti-smoking campaigners would therefore hold that governments have been slow to respond to the advice of professional medics who have promoted preventive medicine. The explanations for the level of government activity appear to be twofold. First, there are clear economic considerations, which include the ability of the tobacco industries to lobby and collude with government officials, and the financial or fiscal implications for the government of any attempt to restrict tobacco consumption. As early as 1952, Horace Joules was talking of a conspiracy of interests between tobacco companies, the government (which received at the time £610 million from the tobacco tax) and the national press, which relied on advertising revenues for its existence.[53] Such an obvious but crucial explanation has subsequently been expounded at greater length in *Smoke Ring* by the campaigning journalist, Peter Taylor, and in Mervyn Read's more recent *Politics of Tobacco*. Both writers have provided illuminating detail on the financial importance of the tobacco industry and how it has been able to exploit this over the last fifty years to influence government policy. The case is still relevant at every budget, when Chancellors juggle the interests of the Treasury, the tobacco industry and the health of the nation in setting the tax on tobacco.

A second factor is more ideological in that the culture of the independent, liberal individual continued, particularly in regard to smoking. In the political sphere, this has often been translated into an aggressive libertarianism which has opposed all forms of government intervention perceived to smack of the so-called 'nanny state', and politicians have feared offending voters who have been frequently unwilling to have the state regulate their entrenched personal habits.[54] Related to this are the liberal attitudes to medicine which have questioned the authority of epidemiological research. From a long history beginning with the sanitary improvement reforms in the 1840s in response to the cholera epidemic, statistics-based methods have transformed medicine from its traditional curative role in treating the individual to a preventive one which places the onus on the abstract de-personalised mass of individuals to change its behaviour. Even when the medical profession became generally convinced of the value of statistical methods (and the work on smoking and health played a major role in this), translating this into policy was another matter. For, while statistical evidence was able to obtain a dominant position in modern preventive medicine, it was far more problematic to use statistics as the basis for government policy when what was required was a change in individual smoking patterns. Certainly, the *Lancet* troubled itself over the implications of the research throughout the 1950s and 1960s, and although the RCP reports made quite specific recommendations for government policy it was not until the 1984 BMA campaign that the medical profession logically translated epidemiology into policy. Here, it spoke not of the rights of the individual to consume whatever he or she pleased, but of the rights of the individual to life. The BMA deliberately aimed its campaign not against the smoker, but against the tobacco industry, whose advertising and economic power it perceived to be restricting freedom of choice. The smoker was, therefore, constructed as an innocent victim of the exploitative manufacturers.[55] To the BMA at least, such arguments resolved the dilemma of liberal citizenship and legitimated a more pro-active smoking and health policy.

This notion of the rational individual acting with independence and freedom in the marketplace came to influence much of the early anti-smoking health campaigns. Until 1957, the government believed that the statement made in the House of Commons in 1954 was sufficient to enable the smoker to assess the evidence for him- or herself. When it became obvious that further action was necessary following the MRC report in 1957, the government stuck to the policy of letting people 'make up their own minds on the subject'.[56] The posters initially produced by the government, to be made available to local authorities to distribute at their own discretion, reflected this policy or broader liberal attitude to public health. The early posters featured no persuasive rhetoric and were entirely devoid of any visual imagery. Their copy ran as follows:

> SMOKING AND HEALTH: It is my duty to warn all cigarette smokers that there is now conclusive evidence that they are running a greater risk of contracting cancer than non-smokers. The risk mounts with the number of cigarettes smoked. Giving up smoking reduces the risk.
>
> Medical Officer of Health

> TO ALL SMOKERS: There are now the strongest reasons to believe that smokers – particularly of cigarettes – run a greater risk of lung cancer than non-smokers. The more cigarettes smoked the greater the risk.[57]

Given the content of the MRC statement, it would have been entirely reasonable to have offered more quantitative information about the nature of this 'risk', while remaining within the policy of presenting the bare facts for smokers to decide for themselves what action to take.

The guidance provided for children did elaborate on the dangers of smoking, a lecture to be given at schools explaining how smoking led to cancer of the lung. But the pamphlets for children to read themselves assumed the same rational workings of the mind that were perhaps more common among middle-class professional males. In *What Do You Really Think About Smoking?*, written in December 1957, a short story featured a young boy named Peter, caught smoking at school. Along with his 'old friend' Pam, 'who had a logical mind', they sought advice on smoking from a number of thoughtful members of their families: from Peter's older brother, a pipe-smoking student at Technical College; from his medical student cousin; from the design student Stella who smokes to be fashionable; and from Pam's mother, who wished she had never started smoking because of the expense involved. In classic utilitarian imagery, there is even a representation of a set of scales at the end, measuring the relative weight of the arguments for and against. Peter assesses each argument and concludes: 'I may smoke a pipe later, but cigarettes – no. Fashion isn't really important, while money is if it helps you to do the things you really like. I expect we'll get over our shyness later on. As for cancer – well, who wants to risk that?' The style was replicated in a short cartoon of *The Adventures of the Wisdom Family*, episode 'What – no smoking?'. In this, young Jim sees the 'silly chump' and 'ass' Jones smoking, provoking him to ask his father why he started smoking. The father then reflects on his rebellious school days, when his straw-boated public schoolboy friends laughed at his unhealthy performance in a sports race. Jim goes on to calculate the money his father wastes before asking about the risks of lung cancer. Both pamphlets represent boys who rationally decide things for themselves and who have access to well-informed middle-class cousins and parents, aspects of life not perhaps that typical for the average smoking youth. And, with a somewhat diluted and non-prescriptive effect, the doctor at the end of the *Wisdom Family* strip informs the father that, although there is a seven times greater risk of smokers contracting lung cancer, 'it still does not sound as if the risk is very great, so there's no need to panic, whatever you decide to do.'[58]

With the publication of the RCP report in 1962, the aims of the anti-smoking campaign remained essentially the same in that the Ministry of Health sought to persuade young people not to start smoking and to convince adult smokers to reduce consumption, having accepted that it would be difficult to get them to quit entirely.[59] However, there was a move towards a more visually arresting and aggressive type of message, with posters simply featuring a cigarette, the smoke from which spelt the word 'cancer'. One pictured the letter 'C' of cancer smoking a cigarette and another a pound note rolled as a cigarette. Both proclaimed boldly that 'Cigarettes cause lung cancer', though the latter carried the message, 'Smoking is an expensive way of damaging your health'. Posters targeted at the young also became more egalitarian, or at least devoid of the class specificity which was characteristic of the pamphlets of 1957; one poster featured four sheep smoking with the copy, 'Why be another sheep? Before you smoke -THINK.'[60] Although pamphlets using the 'hip' language of the day were specifically ruled out, the CCHE did begin to research the culture of the juveniles at whom the publicity material was targeted.[61] A report by A. C. McKennell in 1963 found that posters with straightforward messages, such as the sheep image and the burning pound note, were more effective with the young as they liked the challenge of the message ('before you smoke – think') and could easily understand the reference to wasted expenditure.[62] In a further report in 1964, the film *Smoking and You* was found to be effective in getting over the medical message, but largely unsuccessful in encouraging children to associate their own lives with the potential dangers of smoking.[63] In addition, the importance attached to preventing juvenile smoking was supported by letters outlining this policy to local authorities, and a circular to all tobacco retailers reminded them of the legislation on the sale of cigarettes and tobacco goods to children less than sixteen years of age.[64]

For adult smokers, there was a recognition that the policy of letting individuals make up their own minds was clearly not working as too few smokers were giving up their habit.[65] This did not lead to a change in policy direction, though there was something of a move to ensure that the same message was repeated more frequently. One means of maximising the impact of a public health campaign was to focus on just one town. In Scotland, the 1959 campaign in Edinburgh was followed up by similar campaigns in Dunfermline in 1964 and in Clydebank in 1965. Prior to the launch of publicity materials in these areas, leading officials, doctors and schoolteachers were told of the campaign before press conferences were held to ensure massive coverage in the local media. Tactics during the short period included the distribution of pamphlets to every household; the placement of posters in prominent positions around the town; the use of advertisements in the local newspapers and on local radio; loudspeakers; sandwich-boards; banners; lectures; meetings and film shows, as well as the use of publicity centres in caravans in the city centre where interested passers-by could receive more detailed information and advice on how to quit. In Dunfermline, an eighteen-feet-high domed 'Smokarama' was introduced which ran a seven minute film on the health hazards facing the smoker. However, as with Edinburgh, and in spite of the use of ever more modern techniques of persuasion, both the Dunfermline and Clydebank campaigns could not be counted as successes in the impact they had on smoking rates.[66]

More generally, similar localised educational programmes designed to let the smoker decide for him- or herself were delivered by means of two mobile anti-smoking units (later extended to three). Costing only £13,000 for their two years' service, the units were launched in October 1962 with much aplomb by Enoch Powell, the Health Minister, in front of BMA House in London. With each van manned by two male university graduates, by July 1964 the three units had covered 125,000 miles, worked 910 operational days, visited 207 local authorities in England, Scotland and Wales, visited 1,700 schools, gained the participation of 375,000 children and provided 4,000 film showings. A typical programme would consist of a three day trip to a town, with primary and secondary schools visited during the day, youth clubs at night and a final presentation at the town hall, where a display would be set up accompanied by a public lecture. When the visits were co-ordinated with local authorities' own efforts the mobile units achieved much local publicity. No measurement took place of their impact on smoking rates, but given that the propaganda material differed in no way from that used in other campaigns, the reactions of both juvenile and adult smokers to the lectures and posters might also have followed a similar pattern.[67]

All of these efforts were minimal compared with what health campaigners now argue is necessary to change public attitudes in the long term. Yet the posters, pamphlets, lecture tours and mobile units were in line with both the liberal notions of the individual and the attitudes towards the financial costs of smoking and health campaigns held by the majority of government officials. One alternative, though, was available from the 1950s which engaged with the smoker's own feelings, desires and attitudes towards his or her habit, but which involved considerably greater costs. Anti-smoking clinics first appeared in 1957 at the London School of Hygiene and Tropical Medicine and were later run by a range of private, official and semi-official bodies.[68] The first non-official clinic was set up in Liverpool by Lennox Johnston, the Chairman of the NSNS, who claimed to be motivated by both a belief that smoking was physically addictive and in response to requests for help from smokers who wished to quit.[69] The NSNS had originally been created in

1926 to protect the rights of non-smokers to travel in trains, visit the theatre or go to the cinema in a smoke-free environment, although there had been some crossover with the older anti-tobacco movement of the nineteenth century, whose offices it inherited. Through its intermittent journal, *Clean Air*, and the writings of its first Secretary, F. J. Phillips, the NSNS fought for greater consideration from smokers during the inter-war period, though the survival of the older moralising tone of nineteenth-century anti-tobaccoism saw its members often labelled as cranks by a mainly pro-smoking society. After the Second World War, and still operating on a tiny budget of around £500 a year, the second Secretary, the Rev. Hubert Little, continued Phillips' tone. The more scientific interpretations of smoking and addiction offered by the medic Johnston (though he himself was not lacking in missionary zeal) encouraged the NSNS to begin helping smokers break away from their habit, a development which eventually culminated in 1987 when Quit was formed as an offshoot of the NSNS.[70]

The Liverpool clinic was run intermittently and was based on the group therapy technique prominent in Alcoholics Anonymous. Johnston followed up the sessions with breaks to the seaside and a special week-long anti-smoking course held on the Isle of Wight which attracted considerable media attention, not least because *The Times* sent a journalist to report in a light-hearted manner on the proceedings.[71] At the end of the year there was talk of creating an official Smokers Anonymous, given the favourable response to the clinics by the public.[72] The Liverpool experiment proved short-lived, but in 1959 the Salford Medical Officer of Health and member of the NSNS, Dr J. L. Burn, set up a further clinic and, at Middlesex Hospital, where Horace Joules had stimulated an anti-smoking environment, a successful clinic was organised from 1962. After the RCP report was published with its recommendation that more clinics should be created, local hospitals and health authorities began to take the lead. By 1963, there were two proposals for private clinics in Newbury and Oxford, five clinics already set up in NHS hospitals, and another thirty either in existence or under consideration in local health authorities throughout England. Following requests from its own staff, the Ministry of Health even held its own clinics in the lunch hour at Alexander Fleming House.[73] Although there was much variety in the practices adopted, typical sessions included an initial interview to determine the type of smoker, his or her smoking history, habits and general state of health, the smoking habits of close associates, the reasons for wishing to stop, and domestic and work-related problems which might be regarded as relevant.

The medical officer, psychologist or counsellor would then decide on what kind of treatment was most appropriate, ranging from group therapy to hypnotherapy, a gradual withdrawal or complete cessation, and the number of follow-up sessions required. Artificial aids to help people stop smoking were also commonly used; these ranged from special menthol or dummy cigarettes, holders and filters to sweets, chewing gum and worry beads, as well as silver nitrate mouth washes, prescribed iron, nicobrevin and the more popular lobeline tablets, and even injections of small amounts of nicotine. Subsequent sessions would be arranged and the smoker's progress would be logged, while help would be provided for the common feelings of listlessness and irritability.[74]

The Ministry of Health investigated this anti-smoking policy to a considerable extent, visiting and reporting on the methods and experiences of the various clinics around the country. Success differed from town to town, the clinic in Huddersfield being overwhelmed with patients who continued to come in subsequent weeks, while the experiment in Rotherham prompted only a few 'cranks' to turn up for the initial session. A common occurrence was for the clinic to see an initial flood of applicants, an enthusiastic first night, then a rapid falling off in numbers as smokers realised there was no 'magic formula' to cure their habit, 'craving', dependency or, as it was increasingly understood, addiction. The success of the enterprise often depended on the enthusiasm and persistence of the medical officer organising the sessions. J. L. Burn in Salford estimated that one-third of his patients stopped altogether, another third cut down, but a final third were persistent or confirmed smokers who could not, or did not really wish to, stop. The numbers of ex-smokers produced by the clinics only ever ran into the hundreds as such a hands-on approach could never reach that many patients. Indeed, the Ministry of Health was reluctant to pursue them as a realistic policy beyond the mid 1960s because of the impracticality of organising the sessions, finding and training the personnel necessary to take over from the referrals by general practitioners, and because of the financial constraints of its budget.[75]

The clinics did, however, represent an attempt at smoking cessation based on the experience of the smokers themselves rather than through the presentation of a particular type of rational cost–benefit analysis which characterised the early years of the public education programme. The clinics stood in contrast to the general policy of presenting a limited number of facts which smokers were supposed to assess for themselves, coming to a reasoned decision about the continuation of their habit. This dominant policy persisted in the anti-smoking campaign right through until the 1980s, when the BMA decided to take a more pro-active line against the tobacco industry. At the same time, health policy workers had come to appreciate the differences in experience of the smoker, depending on region, age, gender, class and ethnicity, differences which would eventually translate into practical health programmes. That they have had a still limited impact on smoking rates is due to the continuation of cultural influences which have encouraged new generations to take up smoking. Furthermore, other more influential government departments have proved unwilling to follow the anti-smoking policies of the Ministry of Health, a fact demonstrated most recently in concessions made to Formula One motor racing in the restrictions placed on sports sponsorship.

While governments and health workers have sought to provide the dominant image of tobacco and cigarettes in the post-1945 period, the limitations placed on their message has meant that a particular type of rationality has been put forward in the anti-smoking educational material. Epidemiology has gained an authoritative position within medical science and preventive medicine now permeates all aspects of public health policy, but because the smoking and health issue rests essentially on the activities of individual consumers, the options available to governments have been limited, outright prohibition never being a possibility for a drug so widespread in modern society. Public health policy has therefore been left in the realms of appeals to smokers as rational individuals. Such appeals in the early years of anti-smoking propaganda reflected the social and economic background of policy workers themselves and therefore resonated most clearly with those bourgeois-liberal smokers who had always stressed the importance of independent and individual assessments of the smoking habit. That this has been the case is evidenced in the figures for smoking rates among different social classes. Whereas in 1945 smoking rates had been similar across different income groups, by 1994 it was found that among unskilled and manual workers, 42 per cent of men and 35 per cent of women smoked, but that these figures were as low as 15 per cent of men and 13 per cent of women of the professional classes.[76] Just as bourgeois smokers had the time and cultural capital to read about and cultivate their smoking habit, so too did their late twentieth-century counterparts have the time and intellectual resources to weigh up the medical evidence against smoking. How this knowledge was presented to these different groups through various media is the subject of the next chapter, while chapter 10 examines the culture of various types of smoker throughout the smoking and health controversy.

Notes

1 R. Doll and A. B. Hill, 'Smoking and carcinoma of the lung: preliminary report', *British Medical Journal* (hereafter *BMJ*), ii (1950), 746.

2 E. L. Kennaway and N. M. Kennaway, 'A further study of the incidence of cancer of the lung and larynx', *British Journal of Cancer*, i (1947), 260–98.

3 *BMJ*, i (1950), 1477; *BMJ*, ii (1950), 767–8; E. L. Wynder and E. A. Graham, 'Tobacco smoking as a possible etiological factor in bronchiogenic carcinoma: a study of 648 proved cases', *Journal of the American Medical Association*, 143 (1950), 329–36.

4 *Lancet*, ii (1950), 257; *BMJ*, ii (1952), 1299–1301.

5 R. Doll and A. B. Hill, 'A study of the aetiology of carcinoma of the lung', *BMJ*, ii (1952), 1271–86.

6 See chapter 9 for the coverage of the scientific debates about smoking and health in the national daily newspapers.

7 *BMJ*, ii (1951), 1157, 1460.

8 R. Doll, R. Peto, K. Wheatley, R. Gray and I. Sutherland 'Mortality in relation to smoking: forty years' observation on male British doctors', *BMJ*, i (1994), 901–11.

9 R. Doll and A. B. Hill, 'The mortality of doctors in relation to their smoking habits: a preliminary report', *BMJ*, i (1954), 1451–2; R. Doll and A. B. Hill, 'Lung cancer and other causes of death in relation to smoking: a second report on the mortality of British doctors', *BMJ*, ii (1956), 1071–81; MRC, *Tobacco Smoking and Cancer of the Lung* (London, HMSO, 1957).

10 For the best bibliography on the scientific investigations of the relationship between smoking and health in this period, see P. S. Larson, H. B. Haag and H. Silvette, *Tobacco: Experimental and Clinical Studies. A Review of the World Literature* (Baltimore, Williams and Wilkins, 1961). It contains well over 5,000 references.

11 RCP, *Smoking and Health* (London, Pitman Medical, 1962).

12 R. B. Scott, 'Some medical aspects of tobacco-smoking', *BMJ*, i (1952), 671–5.

13 G. D. Smith, S. A. Ströbele and M. Egger, 'Smoking and health promotion in Nazi Germany', *Journal of Epidemiology and Community Health*, 48 (1994), 220–3; B. Charlton, 'How Hitler tried to stub out smoking', *The Times* (7 July 1994), p. 17; J. C. Burnham, 'American physicians and tobacco use: two Surgeons General, 1929 and 1964', *Bulletin of the History of Medicine*, 63 (1989), 1–31; D. Cuthbertson, 'Historical note on the origins of the association between lung cancer and smoking', *Journal of the Royal College of Physicians*, 2 (1968), 191–6.

14 *Lancet*, 'Is the soldier smoking too much?', ii (1915), 584; J. Parkinson, 'The immediate effect of cigarette smoking on healthy men and on cases of "soldier's heart"', *Lancet*, ii (1917), 232–6.

15 *Lancet*, ii (1910), 1431; *Lancet*, 'Smoking in the theatre', i (1913), 1181; *Lancet*, 'The role of tobacco in the war', ii (1914), 857–8; *Lancet*, 'The soldier and the cigarette', ii (1917), 248–9. For an overview of both the *Lancet's* and the *BMJ's* attitude to smoking in this period, see P. Bartrip, 'Pushing the weed: the editorialising and advertising of tobacco in the *Lancet* and the *British Medical*

Journal, 1880–1958', in S. Lock, L. Reynolds and E. M. Tansey (eds), *Ashes to Ashes: The History of Smoking and Health* (Amsterdam, Rodopi, 1998), pp. 100–29.

16 *Lancet*, 'The seasoned tobacco pipe', i (1911), 1523; *Lancet*, 'Pipe, cigar or cigarette', i (1912), 1019; review of *Smoke Rings and Roundelays* in the *Lancet*, i (1925), 611–12; *Lancet*, 'Nicot and the discovery of tobacco', ii (1931), 275.

17 *Lancet*, 'De-nicotinised tobacco', ii (1925), 32; *Lancet*, 'Acute nicotine poisoning', i (1936), 555.

18 The most authoritative statements came from the Rolleston Committee of 1926 and W. E. Dixon: *Lancet*, ii (1921), 1071; H. Rolleston, 'An address on the medical aspects of tobacco', *Lancet*, i (1926), 961–5; W. E. Dixon, 'The tobacco habit', *British Journal of Inebriety*, 25 (1927–28), 99–121; *Lancet*, 'The cigarette habit', i (1932), 864.

19 L. M. Johnston, 'Tobacco smoking and nicotine', *Lancet*, ii (1942), 742. He later recounted (with classic missionary fervour) the difficulties he faced in getting his work accepted in his book, *The Disease of Tobacco Smoking and its Cure* (London, Christopher Johnson, 1957).

20 V. Berridge, 'Science and policy: the case of post-war British smoking policy', in Lock *et al.*, *Ashes to Ashes*, pp. 143–63, footnote 27. See also various letters in correspondence columns of the *Lancet*, 1950–54.

21 *Medical World*, 80 (1954).

22 *Lancet*, i (1957), 1337–8.

23 MRC, *Tobacco Smoking*, p. 4.

24 RCP, *Smoking and Health*, pp. 38–9.

25 United States Department of Health, Education and Welfare, *Smoking and Health. Report of the Advisory Committee to the Surgeon General of the Public Health Service* (Washington, DC, GPO, 1964).

26 P. S. Larson and H. Silvette, *Tobacco: Experimental and Clinical Studies. A Review of the World Literature. Supplement I* (Baltimore, Williams and Wilkins, 1968); P. S. Larson and H. Silvette, *Tobacco: Experimental and Clinical Studies. A Review of the World Literature. Supplement II* (Baltimore, Williams and Wilkins, 1971).

27 RCP, *Smoking and Health Now* (London, Pitman Medical, 1971).

28 RCP, *Smoking or Health* (London, Pitman Medical, 1977).

29 T. Hirayama, 'Non-smoking wives of heavy smokers have a higher risk of lung cancer: a study from Japan', *BMJ*, 282 (1981), 183–5.

30 RCP, *Health or Smoking*? (London, Pitman Medical, 1983); Department of Health and Social Security, *Fourth Report of the Independent Scientific Committee on Smoking and Health* (London, HMSO, 1988); P. Jackson, 'The development of a scientific fact: the case of passive smoking', in R. Bunton, S. Nettleton and R. Burrows (eds), *The Sociology of Health Promotion: Critical Analyses of Consumption, Lifestyle and Risk* (London, Routledge, 1995), pp. 103–15.

31 United States Department of Health and Human Services, *The Health Consequences of Smoking: Nicotine Addiction. A Report of the Surgeon General* (Washington, DC, GPO, 1988); Berridge, 'Science and policy', pp. 154–5.

32 See especially P. Taylor, *Smoke Ring: The Politics of Tobacco* (London, Bodley Head, 1984); M. D. Read, *The Politics of Tobacco: Policy Networks and the Cigarette Industry* (Aldershot, Avebury, 1996).

33 C. C. Booth, 'Smoking and the Royal College of Physicians', in Lock *et al.*, *Ashes to Ashes*, pp. 192–7; F. A. Jones, 'Ashes to ashes: witness on smoking', in *ibid.*, pp. 198–201; K. Ball, 'Horace Joules' role in the control of cigarette smoking', in *ibid.*, pp. 214–15.

34 *The Times*, various issues, 1951–54, questions in Parliament; Public Record Office, Kew (hereafter PRO), MH 55 1011, *1946–1954: Cancer of the Lung: Investigation.*

35 *The Times* (1 March 1954), p. 2g, (9 February 1956), p. 5d, (9 May 1956), p. 6b; PRO, MH 55 2221, *1954–1957: Cancer of the Lung and Tobacco Smoking: Minister's Statement: Correspondence Arising*; MH 55 2224, *1957–1958: Smoking and Lung Cancer: Health Education Policy: Correspondence.*

36 *The Times* (3 May 1955), p. 3e, (20 March 1956), p. 10c, (27 March 1956), p. 4c, (17 April 1956), p. 5a, (8 May 1956), p. 6c, (29 January 1957), p. 6c; *Daily Mail* (27 March 1956).

37 PRO, MH 55 2203, *1957–1960: Public Health: Propaganda – Smoking and Cancer of the Lung: Publicity Policy.*

38 PRO, MH 55 2224, *1957–1958: Smoking and Lung Cancer: Health Education Policy: Correspondence.*

39 A. Cartwright, F. M. Martin and J. G. Thomson, *Health Hazards of Smoking: Current Popular Beliefs* (1959), pp. 9–10, manuscript in PRO, MH 55 2225, *1958–1959: Smoking and Lung Cancer: Health Education Policy: Correspondence.*

40 PRO, MH 55 2203; MH 55 2227, *1960–1962: Smoking and Lung Cancer: Health Education Policy.*

41 PRO, MH 55 2203; MH 55 2204, *1961–1962: Public Health: Propaganda – Smoking and Cancer of the Lung: Publicity Policy*; MH 55 2225, *1958–1959: Smoking and Lung Cancer: Health Education Policy: Correspondence*; MH 55 2226, *Jan.–Nov. 1960: Smoking and Lung Cancer: Health Education Policy: Correspondence.*

42 PRO, MH 151 18, *1962–1965: Smoking and Health: Campaign Policy*; MH 154 178, *1962–1965: Smoking and Health: Health Education Co-ordinating Committee: Minutes and Papers.*

43 PRO, MH 154 180, *1962–1965: Smoking and Health: Health Education Sub-committee on Publicity Materials: Copies of Minutes and Tables*; MH 55 2204, *1961–1962: Public Health: Propaganda – Smoking and Cancer of the Lung: Publicity Policy*; MH 55 2237, *1962: Smoking and Health: Advisory Group on Publicity.*

44 PRO, MH 55 2236, *1962: Smoking and Health: Anti-Smoking Clinics*; MH 151 18, *1962–1965: Smoking and Health: Campaign Policy.*

45 *The Role of Publicity in the Smoking and Health Campaign: A Report for the Central Office of Information by Armstrong-Warden Ltd.*, in PRO, MH 55 2237, *1962: Smoking and Health: Advisory Group on Publicity.*

46 PRO, MH 151 20, *1966–1969: Smoking and Health: Campaign Policy.*

47 PRO, MH 151 13, *1962–1968: Smoking and Lung Cancer Posters: Censorship by Outside Bodies.*

48 RCP, *Smoking and Health Now*, p. 2.

49 PRO, MH 151 21, *1962–1966: Smoking and Health: Tobacco Advertising*; MH 154 183, *1964–1966: Smoking and Health: Tobacco Advertising – Policy*; Read, *Politics of Tobacco*, p. 151.

50 *Joint Medical Research Council, Ministry of Health and Social Sciences Research Council Conference on Smoking* (1966) and *The Extension of the Smoking and Health Campaign: Report and Recommendations* (1967), in PRO, MH 151 20.

51 *The Times*, various issues, January–June 1971.

52 *Which?* (14 September 1971), 280–5; BMA, *Smoking Out the Barons: The Campaign Against the Tobacco Industry. A Report of the British Medical Association Public Affairs Division* (Chichester, Wiley Medical, 1986). The above two paragraphs are largely taken from Read, *Politics of Tobacco*, and Taylor, *Smoke Ring*.

53 *Lancet*, ii (1952), 781.

54 Read, *Politics of Tobacco*; J. Culver, *Government Health Warning: A Study of the Development and Implementation of Anti-Smoking Policies in the UK* (Sheffield, Sheffield City Polytechnic, Department of Policy Studies Dissertation, 1982).

55 BMA, *Smoking Out the Barons*, p. 12; Berridge, 'Science and policy'; J. Lewis, *What Price Community Medicine? The Philosophy, Practice and Politics of Public Health since 1919* (Brighton, Wheatsheaf, 1986); *Lancet*, 'Smoking or health?', i (1962), 519–20.

56 PRO, MH 55 2204.

57 PRO, MH 55 960: *1953–1960: Public Health Propaganda – Cancer: Smoking and Lung Cancer – General Correspondence*.

58 PRO, MH 55 960.

59 PRO, MH 55 2204.

60 PRO, MH 82 209, *27/9/1962–22/4/1962: Smoking and Health Mobile Unit Project: Itineraries, Description of Equipment, etc., and Other Materials*.

61 *Daily Mail* (22 February 1963).

62 A. C. McKennell, *Results of a Copy Test on Five Posters* (1963), in PRO, MH 151 26, *1962–1962: Smoking and Health: Social Surveys*.

63 A. C. McKennell, *Report on the Audience Reaction Test of the Film 'Smoking and You'* (1964), in *ibid*.

64 PRO, MH 55 2233, *1960–1962: Smoking and Lung Cancer: Correspondence*; MH 55 2234, *1957–1958: Smoking and Lung Cancer: Health Education Policy: Correspondence*.

65 PRO, MH 151 19, *1965–1966: Smoking and Health: Campaign Policy*.

66 A. Cartwright, F. M. Martin and J. G. Thomson, *Consequences of a Health Education Campaign* (Edinburgh, University of Edinburgh, Department of Public Health and Social Medicine, 1959); F. M. Martin and G. R. Stanley, *The Dunfermline Anti-Smoking Campaign* (Edinburgh, University of Edinburgh, Department of Public Health and Social Medicine, 1964); F. M. Martin and G. R. Stanley, *Report on the Clydebank Anti-Smoking Campaign* (Edinburgh, University of Edinburgh, Department of Social Medicine, 1965).

67 PRO, MH 82 205, *March 15, 1962–Sept 11, 1962: Organisation of Two Mobile Units: Programme and Financial Estimates*; MH 82 206, *12/7/1962–6/12/1962: Correspondence Regarding the Inaugural Ceremony of the Mobile Units*; MH 82 207, *19/7/1962–10/2/1965: Smoking and Health – Mobile Units: Miscellaneous Papers, Memoranda, Progress Reports, etc.*; MH 82 208, *13/10/1962–23/6/1964: Smoking and Health Mobile Units Progress Reports*; MH 154 177, *1963–1965: Smoking and Health: Health Education Co-ordinating Committee. Preparations for Meetings and Subsequent Action.*

68 PRO, MH 55 2236, *1962: Smoking and Health: Anti-Smoking Clinics.*

69 *Guardian* (27 February 1958), p. 7; *The Times* (27 February 1958), p. 5b; *The Times* (24 March 1958), p. 5a.

70 *Clean Air* (and its quarterly supplement *The Non-Smoker*), various issues, 1928 to 1950. Because of its small size little remains of the NSNS'activities. Tom Hirst, the leading figure in the organisation in the 1960s and 1970s, held a large archive of material relating to the early history of the NSNS, but almost all of this was destroyed (leaving only a couple of small boxes) in 1995 after his death. I am grateful to David McCabe, Chief Executive of Quit, for his help in accessing what remained of this material.

71 *Guardian* (16 June 1958), p. 12, (5 July 1958), p. 6; *The Times* (4 August 1958), p. 4a, (29 September 1958), p. 5d, (1 October 1958), p. 5g.

72 *The Times* (8 December 1958), p. 6e.

73 PRO, MH 55 2236; MH 151 18, *1962–1965: Smoking and Health: Campaign Policy*; MH 154 178, *1962–1965: Smoking and Health: Health Education Co-ordinating Committee: Minutes and Papers*; MH 154 187, *1964: Smoking and Health: Anti-Smoking Clinics.*

74 PRO, MH 55 2236; MH 151 18; MH 154 189, *1964–1966: Smoking and Health: Medical Research Council.*

75 PRO, MH 55 2236; MH 154 186, *1962–1963: Smoking and Health: Anti-Smoking Clinics*; MH 154 187, *1964: Smoking and Health: Anti-Smoking Clinics*; A. Cruickshank, 'Smokers' Advisory Clinic – Ministry of Health: a preliminary report on an experimental project', *Monthly Bulletin of the Ministry of Health and the Public Health Laboratory Service*, 22 (1963), 110–16; E. G. W. Hoffstaedt, 'Anti-smoking campaign: some general observations on the smoking problem and the place of "smokers' clinics"', *Medical Officer* (31 January 1964), 59–60; G. Edwards, 'Hypnosis and lobeline in an anti-smoking clinic', *Medical Officer* (24 April 1964), 239–43.

76 P. Hooper, *Smoking Issues: A Quick Guide* (Cambridge, Daniels Publishing, 1995), p. 3.

9

The presentation of medical knowledge in the media

The first report of the RCP in 1962 is universally recognised as a landmark in the history of the public understanding of the medical dangers of smoking. It attracted tremendous discussion, selling out its initial print run within the first few days of its launch on 7 March, plus a further 20,000 copies after just six weeks.[1] The national newspapers reported in detail on its findings and recommendations, many devoting their entire front page to the headline news. Depending on which newspaper was bought, however, readers could face very different presentations of what the RCP was attempting to convey about 'smoking and health'. Journalists and editors could be highly selective in the facts they chose to report, and the other news items that often appeared on the same page could either reinforce or contradict the RCP's evidence.

For instance, the *Guardian* summarised in detail the medical evidence and proposals of the RCP to demonstrate 'the overwhelming case against tobacco'. It accepted entirely the findings of the report, called on the government to intervene with a major national campaign and devoted countless column inches to assess the impact on individual smokers, the tobacco industry and the medical profession. For two months after the report's publication, an article on smoking and health appeared in virtually every edition of the newspaper. The RCP could not have asked for a more faithful presentation of its views. Similarly, *The Times* provided an accurate and detailed synopsis, though here the counter-arguments of the manufacturers and other medics received a greater prominence than they had in the *Guardian*. *The Times* also chose to offer its own qualification after accepting the evidence associating smoking with lung cancer: 'like all scientific hypotheses this one has only probability. It both awaits confirmation and is open to the possibility of disproof.'[2] The 'rational man' was free to make his own decision so government intervention was unnecessary, especially if it was to impose advertising restrictions. *The Times* later justified this opinion by asserting that for the 'moderate smoker' the 'hazard is not of an order that seems to call for official intervention', though it offered no medical evidence of its own for this diluted agreement with the RCP findings.[3] The *Daily Mirror* followed the *Guardian* in accepting the report, but it almost hysterically demanded a further statement from the government to clarify the situation since the manufacturers disputed the evidence. For the rest of March, the *Mirror* continued to sensationalise the 'cigarette peril', even bringing Marge Proops in to offer advice on quitting, though all mention of smoking and health had disappeared from the pages of the tabloid by the second half of 1962, whereas the broadsheets continued to report on developments in medical knowledge.[4] In contrast to the *Guardian*'s comprehensiveness, *The Times*' 'rational' qualifications and the *Mirror*'s short-lived melodramatics, was the almost oblivious attitude of the *Daily Express*. The story was consigned to page six and, although there was a powerful diagrammatic representation of the relative risks of smoking, there was only a cursory summary of the RCP report. Further, this was positioned next to an analysis of the smoking habits of the nine-man RCP panel of experts and equal weighting was given to the manufacturers' refutations. Follow-up reporting was minimal, nothing detracting from the general attitude of the *Express*, which seemed to be more concerned with the impact on share prices. Indeed, its leader of 8 March took this implication as its starting point, arguing that there was nothing to fear because 'shrewd observers in the City think that people who want to smoke will continue to do so. And the vast majority of them, being reasonable in their use of cigarettes, will live long and healthy lives.'[5]

A similar diversity existed in the reporting in the Sunday newspapers three days later. Broadsheets such as the *Observer* and the *Sunday Times* accepted and discussed the RCP's evidence at length, the former even going so far as to propose increasing the tobacco duty, a suggestion with which, judging from the evidence of the correspondence columns, not all its readers were in agreement. Within this short period of time, the popular press had moved away from the so-called 'cancer scare'. Although the *Sunday Pictorial* summarised the RCP findings, the *News of the World* reported only on the more upbeat news that the Russians were developing a cancer-free cigarette and the *People* simply noted the increased demand for anti-smoking pills. Such optimistic attention to potential solutions to the problem were not necessary in the *Sunday Express*, which chose instead to print a cartoon of an old woman smoking in the street with the caption, 'Grandma, forty cigarettes a day for the last sixty-odd years haven't done you any harm – why change now?' If this did not convince the *Sunday Express'* readers that no action was required on their behalf, the columnist and arch-sceptic Colm Brogan launched a savage attack on Enoch Powell for converting his Health Ministry into a 'Ministry of Fear' through his anti-smoking campaign.[6]

From such a range of journalistic reactions, the findings and recommendations of the RCP must only rarely have reached members of the public in a form which would have satisfied the original authors. Yet this spectrum of attitudes to the report, ranging from informed acceptance to belligerent opposition, is particularly illustrative of the complicated manner in which the scientific developments outlined in chapter 8 were presented to the public throughout the 1950s, 1960s and 1970s. After the second RCP report of 1971, even the *Express* was forced to confirm a link, but before this time the central conclusions of medical research into smoking and health were hardly ever presented to the public in a manner in which the scientists of the RCP or the leading anti-smoking campaigners of government circles would have been satisfied. If a smoker, whether physically addicted or otherwise, sought to justify his or her continued consumption, there were plentiful resources available to dispute the 'official' versions of medical knowledge presented in Ministry of Health propaganda and RCP reports (see chapter 8). It does not matter that a full analysis of the facts available would have made it extremely difficult for a lay person to deny a link between smoking and lung cancer, or that much of the media's assessment of the evidence presented was ignorant of recent medical research; that disputes and alternative understandings of science were created and offered in print is crucial if the ordinary smoker's attitude to the smoking and health controversy is to be explained.

This chapter therefore begins with a case study of how four newspapers, *The Times,* the *Guardian,* the *Daily Express* and the *Daily Mirror,* reported developments in smoking and health in the 1950s and 1960s, before going on to discuss the presentation of the same issues on BBC radio and television. It finishes with a brief overview of the books and pamphlets published by practising medics which sought to explain 'the facts' of smoking and health to a wider public. Some of these were important channels in which tobacco manufacturers and sympathetic scientists were able to dispute the interpretations of the BMA, MRC, RCP and Ministry of Health, question the whole legitimacy of epidemiological research and offer alternatives to account for the rise in deaths from lung cancer. The sheer weight of the evidence against smoking would have made it difficult for any lay person to reject it entirely, but no smoker could ever be in a position in which he or she could rely on an independent, rational or supposedly objective analysis of the evidence. Science never appeared to the smoker as an ideologically free body of knowledge since, as the summary of responses to the RCP report in 1962 has already suggested, popular printed, aural and visual forms of communication interpreted, accepted, rejected and constructed their own views of the smoking and health controversy in often fundamentally different ways from one medium to another.

Prior to the publication of the results of Doll and Hill's first study, the main tobacco issue of interest to the British press was the shortage of dollars with which to purchase American leaf.[7] The consequent threat of a tobacco shortage in the late 1940s provoked Hugh Dalton to urge restraint in consumption, calling on the 'patriotic duty' of individuals to change their personal smoking habits in the 'national interest'. Such appeals to a collective spirit might be thought typical of post-war austerity measures, but most newspapers instead championed the 'rights' of the working man to smoke onwards, the *Express* believing the issue of tobacco supplies to pensioners warranted front-page headline news in 1947.[8] That tobacco was held to exist beyond the restrictions of rationing marked it out as a special commodity within popular culture. The discussion of the economic and social aspects of smoking was significant as it set the agenda for how newspapers would regard the association between cigarettes and lung cancer. When restrictions on smoking (rationing, bans in public places to limit consumption) were discussed in Parliament, politicians treated the issue in a light-hearted manner, but when shortages reached such a level that the issue became more serious, *The Times* warned that the pipe was perceived to be 'the symbol of a staunch common-sense, of a phlegmatic determination not to be stampeded into political or intellectual excess'. For its readers, this excess meant 'distasteful' state 'paternalism' which contravened the rights of the individual who 'should be allowed to smoke where [he or she] likes'.[9] Although the *Guardian*'s readers provided many novel ideas to limit consumption, the attitude of the paper paralleled *The Times* when it agreed with Clement Attlee that state proscriptions were likely to backfire and that it was 'desirable' 'to preserve the same freedom for ordinary men and women' that Winston Churchill enjoyed with his cigar.[10]

This unity of attitudes demonstrates the triumph of the older bourgeois smoking ideal within the media culture of the immediate post-war period. It leant itself to a certain complacency, or at least a haughty disdain, for any medical developments taking place which sanctioned against cigarettes. When letters did appear linking smoking to dyspepsia, duodenal ulcers, heart disease and 'perhaps lung cancer' as early as 1948, they provoked no further comment. The suggestion by the seasoned anti-tobacco campaigner, Lennox Johnston, that tobacco was a luxury and should be taxed accordingly was met with derision in the *Guardian*.[11] There was something of a general acceptance that smoking might induce minor ailments such as the occasional cough, and that the nation would, on the whole, be healthier if it stopped smoking since 'no one has ever yet proved that tobacco is *good* for your health'.[12] But such comments ought to be seen as indicative of the confidence with which smokers regarded their pleasure and 'minor vice'. When Doll and Hill's work first appeared in 1950, only a cursory mention was made in the *Mirror* and nothing at all in the *Express*, a policy which persisted throughout the early 1950s.[13] *The Times* only devoted small articles to each development in the medical journals, though the correspondence columns often featured letters from Horace Joules warning that the issue needed to be taken more seriously.[14] Even at this early date the *Guardian* provided the most coverage, and an article in January 1953 gave Joules' views an extensive airing in which he argued that the link between smoking and cancer had been confirmed and that it was up to the government and 'the consuming public' to 'face their responsibilities'.[15]

From the very beginning of the post-war smoking and health controversy, then, the styles of the national press were already beginning to develop into those summarised in the reactions to the 1962 RCP report. The statement by the Health Minister, Iain MacLeod, in 1954 was reported extensively in the *Guardian* and *The Times*, though the doubts over causality caused the *Guardian* to limit its own response to suggesting that individuals should be free to make up their own minds about the 'incontrovertible' association.[16] By 1957, however, the intelligent and informed debates on medical knowledge had committed the *Guardian* to a campaign for government action, and writers and readers of *The Times* engaged in a sustained and educated debate of both the evidence and its implications for government policy. MacLeod's statement and the MRC report were also given front-page prominence in the *Mirror* and the *Express*, the latter typically downplaying the findings and the former not yet committing itself to one side of the 'great smoking controversy'.[17] The reporting styles would continue into the 1960s, the 1964 report of the US Surgeon-General being consigned to the back page of the *Mirror* and almost entirely ignored by the *Express*. By the RCP's second report in 1971, however, the medical evidence was deemed of such importance that all the newspapers provided exhaustive coverage of the implications of the research, the *Express* however maintaining its now idiosyncratic position in the doubt it cast on causal and statistical 'proof'.[18]

The belligerence of the *Express* towards the medical establishment appears surprising in comparison with other newspapers. The answer to its scepticism might be found through an examination of the private interests of its proprietor, Lord Beaverbrook. From the very beginning of the controversy, the *Express'* independent path was highlighted through its concentration on the impact on share prices of MacLeod's 1954 statement.[19] Similarly, it was quick to report that the British Empire Cancer Campaign (BECC) found the smoking 'theory . . . poorly founded and unlikely to explain the great increase in lung cancer during the last ten years', an interpretation stretching Alexander Haddow's original doubts about causal proof.[20] The item stands out because the *Express* did not usually regard the BECC's annual reports as newsworthy, suggesting a degree of selectivity mirrored by the omission of any references to lung cancer in the speech of Sir Robert Sinclair at his Imperial Tobacco Company's annual general meeting, a speech in which other newspapers noted that he at least acknowledged the existence of a 'controversy' in his attempts to dismiss it.[21] Instead, the *Express* actively encouraged a smoking culture, launching a 'Cut that Tax' campaign in 1953 in response to the increase in duty imposed by R. A. Butler that year. It planned to obtain 10 million signatures in a nation-wide petition to be presented to Churchill to defend the interests of the ordinary smoker, represented in the paper by Mr Butt, that part of the cigarette which belonged to the smoker; 'the rest is Mr Butler's'.[22]

Throughout the 1950s, the *Express* willingly mentioned alternative theories on the cause of lung cancer, such as exhaust and coal fumes, and the science correspondent, Chapman Pincher, gently argued against a national education campaign while doubts still remained about the 'association' between smoking and health.[23] Pincher continually attacked the medical establishment, mocking the attempts to induce cancer in mice and inventing ridiculous lies that doctors were turning their attention to smoked kippers as a possible cause of lung cancer.[24] His opposition to what he saw as interfering paternalism was the one constant from 1957 to 1962, when the *Express* published only five articles on smoking and health. His response to the RCP report proved equally sceptical, telling 'civilised' moderate smokers to continue their enjoyable habit.[25] He was ready to support alternative theories of the causes of lung cancer and was later quick to point out how one of the ten members of the US Surgeon-General's panel in 1964 intended to continue smoking. And, in 1965, while again no mention was made of the actual scientific understandings of tobacco, he condemned the great 'blow to freedom' and 'outrageous interference' that was the TV advertising ban, instigated by the 'usual muddle-headed' 'socialists' in the Labour Party with all their 'huffing and puffing'.[26]

Without any direct evidence of Beaverbrook's personal influence, the *Express*' celebration of individual liberty over state intervention has to be taken as the motivation behind its unwillingness to accept the medical establishment's arguments supporting a causal relationship between smoking and cancer. In its opposition to the Labour government, the *Express* condemned Kenneth Robinson's proposal to end coupon trading in cigarettes in 1967, arguing that, because 'all the resources of modern science have been unable to identify the causative agent of lung cancer', the Health Minister's only reason for curbing smoking must have been to interfere with people's enjoyment of life.[27] Even in 1971, when all other newspapers had come to agree with the RCP after the publication of its second report, Chapman Pincher insisted on insinuating that the whole thing was a conspiracy to legitimate increased taxes. The *Express* stuck to its by now traditional line that smoking was an individual matter and that smokers should be allowed to decide for themselves without the influence of government propaganda, especially since there was still much confusion over the evidence. Elsewhere there was a vague acceptance that smoking was likely to cause ill health, but this point was hardly emphasised, the initial comments on the RCP report being couched in terms of its implications for fiscal policy.[28] What is clear is that if, say, the *Express* had been the only source of information on public health for a smoker prior to 1971, then there was little in it to persuade him or her to give up the habit.

In stark contrast to the aggressive pro-smoking populism of the *Express* was the sober discussion and early acceptance of an association between smoking and ill health found in the less popular broadsheet, the *Guardian*. Despite a tendency to share in that culture which celebrated the freedom to smoke wherever one wanted, the *Guardian* did not use this individualist ethic to dismiss the value of preventive medicine, the conclusion of which demanded changes in personal behaviour encouraged through state-sponsored public health campaigns. Instead, it provided thorough and serious reports of developments in science from the very beginning of Doll and Hill's findings in

1950, it dismissed manufacturers' counter-arguments, it reported with eagerness the campaign in Parliament and it regularly mentioned scientific developments in Britain and the United States.[29] In 1954, the *Guardian* readily accepted a causal relationship as 'incontrovertible' and its commitment to an interventionist welfare state did not predispose it to oppose a government-backed public health programme.[30] Indeed, although articles still blamed other factors such as atmospheric pollution and diesel fumes, and writers such as Alistair Cooke claimed that the causal link between cigarettes and cancer was not 'positively answered beyond dispute', this was from within an editorial policy that accepted the statistical association as sufficient to warrant calls for greater public awareness of the dangers of smoking.[31]

By the early 1960s, not only had the *Guardian* been calling for a publicity campaign for some years, but there was an acknowledgement that smokers had to 'act responsibly towards themselves' in order to resolve the ideological tension between individual behaviour and government intervention.[32] Readers reflected this intelligent discussion, with one letter published a month before the RCP report complaining of the rather 'chummy way' in which the smoking and health issue had been dealt with in the national press, the *Guardian* itself not escaping this particular criticism.[33] After 1962, the health hazards of smoking were accepted almost beyond debate, the arguments of the sceptics being referred to as 'logical acrobatics'.[34] During the late 1960s the dangers of smoking were taken as a given and discussion in the *Guardian* focused on methods of quitting and on local and national health campaigns to curb smoking. In 1971, the second RCP report was given minimal coverage, presumably because its findings were no longer news, or at least there was no requirement for further discussion since it contained no controversial evidence or recommendations for which the paper had not been campaigning for almost the last decade. In polarised contrast to the readers of the *Express*, then, *Guardian* readers had been given every encouragement to quit smoking throughout the 1960s.

The comprehensive account of smoking and health issues in the *Guardian* was more than matched by *The Times*, yet the cultural and political commitments of the two papers were very different. While the *Guardian* quickly overcame its objections to state interference in personal consumption in the interests of public health, *The Times* maintained a principled opposition to government action up until the second report of the RCP. *The Times* was the leading medium through which the smoking culture of bourgeois-liberal individualism was maintained. Any discussion of the scientific properties of tobacco throughout the 1950s and 1960s was always located within the smoky atmosphere of the gentleman's club. Lengthy feature and leader articles regularly appeared on topics such as the superiority of the 'manly' pipe over the 'nervous' cigarette; the history of the cigar; the problems of smoking in private and public rooms; women and cigars; cigarette card collecting; smoking in church; the problems of getting good tobacco at Spanish fishing ports; tobacco's reception in the seventeenth century; the decline of formality in smoking rituals; reprints from the 'Great Tobacco Controversy' of 1857; the history of small, specialised firms and retailers; plus a lengthy correspondence on the best form of pipe cleaner.[35] In short, these articles celebrated the broader culture of smoking in almost exactly the same style as nineteenth-century periodical literature, Sherlock Holmes even making the occasional appearance to typify the 'greatest' ever smoker.[36] His shadow loomed over every discussion of smoking and health within *The Times*, and the pervasiveness of this culture within elite circles is no better demonstrated than in the perennial guffaws and reminiscences provoked by any discussion of tobacco in Parliament.

More significant still was the degree to which pro-smoking attitudes shaped the discussion of the medical evidence. From the very first reports of Doll and Hill's investigations, a light-hearted tone was adopted best exemplified in a 1955 leader article which championed the travails of the underdog hamsters at Leeds University which had been subjected to cigarette smoke for eight months without contracting lung cancer.[37] While *The Times* did offer the most extensive coverage of the medical findings, as well as some of the most informed discussion, it also presented alternative explanations and promoted a general scepticism throughout the 1950s.[38] Major scientific investigations would thus be accepted but leader articles would then offer other suggestions such as 'the ageing of the population, more reliable methods of diagnosis, atmospheric pollution, and occupational hazards', which all prevented any 'final judgement'.[39] *The Times* therefore proved to be an engaged participant in the construction and understanding of scientific knowledge.

Between the publication of the significant medical reports, *The Times* drifted away from its objective discussion of events towards what Horace Joules described as a 'conspiracy of silence' in 1958 and what Christopher Wood would later claim was a product of the newspaper's reliance on tobacco advertising revenues.[40] Certainly, there was a degree of complacency, a leader in 1961 which condemned juvenile smoking being followed two months later by another columnist's glorious and romantic reminiscence of his own smoking youth.[41] The crucial debate for *The Times* was the degree of government intervention in advertising restrictions, smoking bans and education campaigns. In defence of the individual who, it was claimed, was free to make up his or her own mind about smoking and health, the newspaper opposed all forms of government intervention. A rationale for such a position could be provided if it was demonstrated that the case against the cigarette was by no means conclusive. Perhaps in consequence, then, articles continued to appear that cast doubt on the dominant medical opinion, and leader articles discussing the TV advertising ban were prone to comment that causative 'proof' was still lacking.[42] Those figures and organisations who called for more intervention were likely to be criticised – the ideas of the NSNS being labelled as 'cranky' – and any developments in the search for a safe cigarette always suggested a solution for which smokers might continue to wait.[43]

The second report of the RCP in 1971, however, significantly altered the policy of *The Times*. It accepted the findings and recommendations of *Smoking and Health Now* (without using the word 'causal' itself), and claimed in a leader article that although it remained opposed to the imposition of a prohibitive duty, it was now in favour of restrictions on smoking in public places, limitations on advertising, warnings on packages and differential taxation levels to encourage safer forms of smoking. It provided a nuanced justification for intervention in claiming that it was not 'unreasonable to have a category of goods or services freely available but not freely promotable by public advertisement'.[44] It was this lack of such a principled distinction which had previously prevented *The Times* from supporting any incursions into its faith in the liberal marketplace. Prior to 1971, its ideological worries and support for an older smoking culture had provoked a highly complicated picture of the meaning of tobacco and the cigarette. Detailed summaries of all the major medical pronouncements were given, but the analysis which invariably followed imagined smoking as a defiant gesture against a perceived expanding welfarism that enabled scientists to interfere with individual consumption decisions.

Politically, then, *The Times* held much in common with the *Express*, the amount of evidence presented to their readers significantly distinguishing the two. A similar relationship might also be said to have existed between the left-wing *Guardian* and its politically allied tabloid, the *Daily Mirror*, were it not for the *Mirror*'s concern for the leisure interests of the ordinary working man. Because smoking continued to play a central role in working-class culture and because the *Mirror* focused on the more entertaining aspects of everyday life, it seemed unwilling to present pessimistic analyses of tobacco. Consequently, before the Minister's first public statement in 1954, virtually no articles appeared on smoking and health. Even the front-page coverage given to the Minister's announcement was interspersed with subheadings such as 'other factors', 'not clear-cut' and 'not conclusive'.[45] This was followed by a complete absence of smoking and health issues until the next sensational event of 1957, when a huge headline, 'Smoking and Cancer and You. It's Every Man for Himself', made the message more straightforward. Here, there was a call for a reinstatement of the government's war-time radio doctor, Charles Hill, and a demand for a national health campaign.[46] Again, after the initial furore, the *Mirror* retreated from its earlier claims, choosing instead to ridicule the efforts of the NSNS and local hospitals in helping smokers quit and being particularly keen to print optimistic features which referred to potential solutions to the problem; solutions which involved no action on the part of the smoker as he or she could sit back and wait for the arrival of the safe filter or synthetic cigarette, electric shock cure or the removal of the carcinogenic agent.[47]

After 1962, the *Mirror* actively campaigned for further government efforts to reduce smoking, fully accepting the findings of the RCP and requiring more information so that individuals could make up their own minds. The momentum was sustained in the campaigns launched by Enoch Powell in 1963 and the US Surgeon-General's report, but always the centrality of smoking to British popular culture was acknowledged on other pages of the *Mirror*: the efforts of the CCHE appeared in articles next to large advertisements for Player's cigarettes; Andy Capp puffed his way through every cartoon strip, even joking that he was giving up 'buyin' fags'; and Harold Wilson was celebrated as Pipeman of the Year in 1966.[48] The empathy which the *Mirror* held for its readers was maintained during the reporting of the second RCP report. The findings were sensationally presented, but no discussion of them subsequently took place, as the *Mirror* preferred to emphasise short-term solutions. An editorial called for the development of reduced-tax safer cigarettes, while Marge Proops recommended cigars, Keith Waterhouse the pipe and William Fletcher herbal cigarettes. Only Woodrow Wyatt campaigned in opposition to the perceived working-class interest in his call to double the tobacco duty.[49] His opinion stands out amid the more general attitude of the *Mirror* to save the smoker the effort of quitting by having the state or the medical establishment provide the cure or the alternative. Such reporting would have made the dangers of smoking apparent to its readers and would probably have provoked further discussion, but the *Mirror*'s lurid presentation of the risks was always interspersed with an almost cheerful hope that the scientists would provide an answer. For the smoker troubling him- or herself over whether to quit, the *Mirror* may have tipped the balance in favour of further succumbing to, or making an excuse of, his or her addiction.

All such dissemination of the increasingly accepted medical risks of smoking within the national newspapers was reinforced by the regular discussion and presentation of the issues on BBC radio and television. Immediately after the Second World War, Charles Hill continued to give his 'Radio Doctor' reports on the Home Service, several of which discussed the health effects of smoking. At this time these were said to range from a slight quickening of the pulse to 'smoker's cough', though any dangerous effects were only induced by excessive smoking.[50] *Woman's Hour* was particularly keen to present programmes on smoking, perhaps reflecting assumptions about the mother's role in looking after the health of the family, although many of the programmes specifically dealt with women's smoking. From 1945 to 1971 there were nearly fifty programmes on various aspects of tobacco and cigarettes, but the significance of *Woman's Hour* lay in the attention it gave to the risks of smoking in the early years of the health controversy. In 1952 a psychologist, a physiologist and a physician were invited to discuss the implications of Doll and Hill's report, concluding that 'the chances of getting cancer of the lung are greater for those people who do smoke a lot'.[51] From then on, *Woman's Hour* held regular interviews with medics and scientists, reflecting a broader coverage of the BBC which saw over 150 national and local radio programmes commenting on smoking and health from the time of the first government statement in 1954 to two months after the publication of the RCP report in 1962.[52]

The statement of the MRC received considerable attention, but what characterised BBC reporting was the equal weight given to the arguments of the medical establishment and the tobacco manufacturers as though both were legitimate positions, however diametrically opposed. Often the two sides of the argument would be simply summarised by the BBC and occasionally only Alexander Maxwell of the tobacco manufacturers would be interviewed.[53] But even when the pro-tobacco lobby was not given an airing, presenters were keen not to scare their listeners, as R. R. Bomford concluded in 1954: 'don't have sleepless nights thinking because you've smoked a few or even a lot of cigarettes in your time, you're bound to get this illness, because that certainly isn't true.'[54] The BBC's other main medical correspondent, C. L. Boltz, finished his programmes in similar style: 'Put it another way. Statistical results of the sort I've mentioned mean that the warning lights are at caution. But it's worth remembering that they are not yet red.'[55] In these admittedly early years of the smoking and health controversy, there were also some direct misinterpretations of the evidence. Patricia Brent, noting the lower death rate from lung cancer among women, ignored the statistics on women's smoking rates and concluded that women were less likely to get cancer, which was good for her as she admitted smoking twenty-five cigarettes a day.[56] Brent is important because she conducted numerous interviews with media-friendly medics, engaging in a sober-minded acknowledgement of the latest findings, yet she was also known to sign off her interviews with a cigarette.[57]

Such contradictory messages to her audience were reinforced by an affability that pervaded BBC programming. Almost as a means of psychologically avoiding the consequences of the various reports, sceptics would resort to the witty quip to dismiss the evidence, such as the comment that it was no coincidence that 'jumpy, nervy people' were most likely to be non-smokers since they were addicted to statistics instead.[58] But humour was also the reserve of a wider smoking culture and what characterises so many discussions of smoking on the radio in the 1950s and early 1960s is the descent into anecdote and personal reminiscence to conclude the discussion. *Any Questions* was particularly illustrative of this trend. In 1956, Arthur Street peddled out the Mark Twain quotation that giving up smoking was the easiest thing in the world to do; he had tried it a thousand times. Later that year, Ralph Whiteman told listeners how he began smoking at the age of eleven, thereby provoking jokes about Winston Churchill's smoking from fellow panellist, Ted Leather. In a discussion of the legitimacy of government-imposed smoking bans in 1957, Stephen McAdden found it relevant to tell of smoking in bed with his wife, an inducement to light-heartedness taken up by his ostensible opponent, Roy Jenkins. And in 1962, while Sir John Wolfenden and John Arlott puffed away at their pipes during a post-RCP report discussion, the pro-interventionist Bernard Braden added that he was now going to light his sixth instead of his forty-sixth cigarette of the day, to much laughter and applause.[59] Even though such debates provided space for some serious discussion of the contents of the medical findings, the resort to humour perhaps encouraged a wider cultural preference to avoid facing the full implications of the alleged risks of smoking. Whether this preference was an actual reflection of existing attitudes in society is questionable given the annoyance which listeners expressed towards a 1957 question-and-answer programme because panellists were said to have evaded the important issues and not appeared entirely interested.[60]

This style of presentation remained the norm until 1962, when a *Panorama* programme of 12 March memorably opened with Richard Dimbleby positioned in front of a mountain of cigarettes said to be consumed by the average smoker in one year. Later in the programme, John Partridge, Chairman of the Tobacco Manufacturers Standing Committee (TMSC), was able to discuss the RCP report with Sir Robert Platt, President of the College, but the first fifteen minutes were devoted to outlining its main points and what its impact had been on the general public.[61] From then on, smoking and lung cancer was no longer presented as a controversy but as an accepted medical relationship. Taking just one example from 1966, *Focus on Smoking*, the radio programme began with a summary of the dangers of smoking by the Chief Medical Officer, Sir George Godber, who stressed that he had given such warnings since the publication of his first annual report in 1960. Charles Fletcher was then interviewed about Doll and Hill's work and the subsequent investigations by other medics, before Dr Patrick Lawther dispelled the common belief that air pollution was the cause of cancer. H. J. Eysenck was given some time to talk of his theory of genetic disposition to cancer, but the overall emphasis of the programme was reiterated by Godber, who again spoke of the dangers of smoking in the concluding minutes.[62] Fletcher had become a regular and erudite populariser of the medical establishment's understanding of the dangers of smoking by the 1960s, the BBC feeling that he was the best person to present their smoking policy.[63] But *Woman's Hour* was the series which most frequently spoke of tobacco and smoking, discussing both the medical and policy implications of any new item of research and interviewing veteran anti-smoking campaigners such as Christopher Wood and Tom Hurst, Chairman of the NSNS.[64] By 1971, BBC radio programmes had become extremely direct, with titles such as 'On the Habit that Kills'. A special edition of *Panorama* was broadcast on television to coincide with the publication of the RCP report to ensure it obtained maximum publicity, especially the contention that smoking was estimated to contribute to 100,000 deaths a year from various diseases, including 30,000 from lung cancer.[65]

Certainly, the BBC felt that it was sufficiently covering the developments in smoking and health. During the 1960s, it corresponded regularly with the Ministry of Health on the appearance of smoking in its programmes and on the degree of publicity given to the Ministry's education campaigns. In 1967, in a meeting with the Minister and Lord Hill of the Independent Television

Association, Lord Normanbrook, Chairman of the BBC, argued that the BBC gave adequate air time to anti-smoking films, but he did not wish to interfere with portrayals of everyday life – of which smoking was an integral part – provided by entertainment and drama series. However, an informal directive was sent to programme makers to make greater efforts to portray non-smoking as a normal social activity and smoking was banned in TV studios. In 1969, the BBC banned cigarette advertising in its publication, the *Radio Times*, but by 1971 many anti-smoking campaigners might still have been disappointed with the BBC's efforts. For instance, although smoking was discouraged on children's and discussion programmes, if guests insisted, the BBC allowed them to light up to help settle their nerves.[66] The smoking and health issue was clearly presented by the BBC, but again this must be located within a broader culture which often reflected and possibly reinforced the centrality of smoking in everyday life.

The ambiguities surrounding the smoking and health controversy were not only shaped by a culture which had for decades promoted smoking as a normalised activity, but were due also to the conflicting statements made by a not quite unitary medical establishment. Annoyance at the lack of clarity provided on radio and in the popular press led many medics to publish their own summaries of the evidence against tobacco. Most popular was Charles Fletcher's *Common Sense About Smoking*, which obtained some influence on the press, but this 1963 work had been preceded by several other books and pamphlets, the products of both the centre and the fringe of mainstream medical thought. At the same time, the tobacco companies obtained the services of a number of authorities who supported their arguments, and there existed a number of medics sceptical of the validity of epidemiology who were willing to publish their doubts. Such a diversity of opinion, whether inspired by the grants of the TMSC or otherwise, clearly served to sustain a 'controversy' in the popular media that the scientists of the RCP and MRC no longer thought existed.

A number of these popular science pamphlets were written by moralists who wished to condemn tobacco from both a medical and religious point of view, arguing that to induce voluntarily disease in the body that was divinely given was a 'violation of stewardship'. Such arguments had their precursors in the nineteenth-century self-denying anti-tobacco tradition and it is not surprising that many criticised smoking as a symbol of a secular age – 'the physical, mental and moral Cancer of the nations' – along with fast women, motor cars and juvenile delinquency. Some were easy for the dominant smoking culture to dismiss as the privately published work of cranks, but other less obviously evangelical tracts obtained a wider currency as the medical evidence against tobacco accumulated.[67] Lennox Johnston had suffered numerous set-backs to his call for smoking to be regarded as an addiction in the 1940s and consequently for its effects on the body to be categorised as a disease. Few accepted his research and the difficulties he faced in getting his work pub-lished were recounted in his autobiographical *The Disease of Tobacco Smoking and its Cure*. His bitterness at the early setbacks he suffered from a sceptical medical establishment developed into an almost enraged jealousy as he criti-cised Doll and Hill for acting too late on findings which he claimed to have discovered years previously. The trips he made to London to study how to plan an arson attack on the unbelievers at BMA House signified the evangel-ical nature of his lone crusade, but his work eventually became more ortho-dox as the momentum against tobacco built up. His use of the word 'disease', a term used only by the most convinced anti-smokers of the time, even demonstrated a coincidental foretaste of how dominant medical opinion would understand the properties of tobacco in later decades.[68]

Autobiographical sketches in stop-smoking guides were not the rhetorical flourishes which gained wider acceptance for one's arguments amid a post-war medical culture which stressed a sober-minded independent assessment of observed facts. More typical, then, were presentations of the evidence which attempted gradually to convince the smoker of the dangers based on simple summaries of the major research findings in Britain and the United States, before offering advice on different ways to quit smoking or at least to reduce the risks to damaged health. Koskowski published a thorough and almost academic exposition of the history and pharmacology of tobacco, while the veteran US tobacco researcher, Alton Ochsner, who had first sus-pected an association between smoking and lung cancer in the 1930s, had his summary of his US work published in Britain as well.[69] By the late 1950s the general consensus emerging among the medical profession was highlighted by a range of similar works which presented the findings on the dangers of smoking in extremely straightforward terms. These tended to be sanctioned by the medical establishments for which the authors worked, so that J. L. Burn and Robert McCurdy wrote in their capacities as Medical Officers of Health, Norman Macdonald was published through the SMA and Harvey Flack through the BMA.[70] Eventually, Charles Fletcher of the RCP simplified the findings of the 1962 report in a Penguin Special, clearly presenting the links between smoking and lung cancer, chronic bronchitis, pulmonary thrombosis, heart disease, and the contribution to gastric and duodenal ulcers.[71] By the end of the 1960s, government departments were contributing to the publication of popular pamphlets, especially those designed for children to use in schools.[72]

All of these pamphlets were styled on the assumption that there were an existing number of incontrovertible facts. Once presented to the individual reader, in a logical and ordered manner, the smoker would take time on his or her own to consider these dangers before deciding to quit, since the facts 'spoke for themselves'. Not all medics accepted these 'facts', however, and many harked back to an older medical culture which thought the best guide to health was determined through the personal relationship between the individual and the doctor.[73] These medics were reluctant to assume causality from statistical association.[74] Their attitude would persist in the correspondence columns of the *Lancet* and in works such as that of Michael Schroeder which partially accepted the statistical conclusions but which continued to emphasise the ability of smokers to work out their own physical condition and adapt their smoking habits accordingly.[75]

Statistical interpretation came under a more direct attack from Ronald Fisher, the renowned geneticist. Closely associated with the tobacco manufacturers, Fisher wrote a deliberate rejoinder to Doll and Hill's findings, suggesting that the authority they had come to obtain was the result of a repetition of their experiment rather than a thorough test of it. He questioned the sampling techniques of the epidemiologists, as well as their apparent failure to examine other factors such as poisons in cigarette paper and the various pollutants common to urban life. Instead, he posited the notion that one's 'individual genotype' predisposed one to both lung cancer and the habit of smoking, therefore admitting an association but denying any mutual causality.[76] His ideas were taken up by other industry-funded scientists. H. J. Eysenck's *Smoking, Health and Personality*, published in 1965, argued that 'lung cancer and smoking are related, not because smoking causes lung cancer, but because the same people predisposed genetically to develop lung cancer were also predisposed genetically to take up smoking'.[77]

Eysenck provided both academic authority and a positive alternative theory to the defensive arguments employed by the tobacco industry from the 1950s. The views of the manufacturers were essentially that statistical research did not determine causality, especially since lung cancer was observed in non-smokers; that the problem of atmospheric pollution and other alternatives had been insufficiently explored; and that the carcinogenic agent had not been identified. While Eysenck's work could be quoted as an appealing theory for the more fatalistic type of smoker, these three objections to the epidemiological research were always presented to the press in response to, and sometimes in anticipation of, major smoking and health reports. The manufacturers ensured that their denials were known within popular culture, such as when the TMSC distributed 100,000 copies of its pamphlet rejecting the report of the MRC in 1957, and G. F. Todd's problems with the RCP report were made readily available to the press in 1962.[78] At this time, the comments of the manufacturers on medical issues had much greater authority than a more cynical public would now have it. Their gift of £250,000 to the MRC in 1954 to further research into smoking and health was said to have 'inspired the public's trust in their policy and judgement'.[79]

What characterised the dissemination and production of medical knowledge of the relationship between smoking and lung cancer in the 1950s and 1960s was the incredible diversity of its presentation across the popular media. It is not simply a matter of examining which medical facts appeared on the radio and in daily newspapers because, contrary to what 'common sense' doctors expected in early health campaigns, the 'facts' never did 'speak for themselves'. Every one of the main findings of the MRC, the RCP and the US Surgeon-General received some degree of popularisation on the radio and in the four newspapers examined in this chapter, except perhaps in the *Daily Express*, whose coverage was minimal to the point of deliberate avoidance. But how those facts were read or heard by the public depended very much on the style and ideology of the medium concerned. Each report which confirmed a link between smoking and ill health might have appeared alongside a complete denial of the relationship or, if it was accepted as established or even proven, it might have been contradicted once the initial furore over the medical evidence had subsided. Popular forms of media shared in the broader pro-smoking culture to the extent that the tabloids were reluctant to depress their readers with bad news about a central pillar of working-class life. Similarly, the liberal concerns about independence and individuality shaped the presentation of science through more elite media, manifesting themselves particularly in a jocular light-hearted treatment of the issues or in an aggressive scepticism triggered from a belief that preventive medicine offered a threat to British 'freedom'. Furthermore, the same cultural influences which influenced the presentation of science in the popular media might also have shaped the general public's attitude to the dangers of smoking. How medical knowledge of tobacco came to be understood within the minds of smokers themselves, however, is the subject of the next chapter.

Notes

1 Another 30,000 copies were sold in the United States in the same period: *Guardian* (25 April 1962), p. 16.

2 *The Times* (8 March 1962), p. 13b.

3 *Ibid.* (24 March 1962), p. 13c.

4 *Daily Mirror* (8 March 1962), pp. 1, 2, 16–17, (9 March 1962), p. 15, (15 March 1962), p. 8, (4 April 1962), p. 25.

5 *Daily Express* (8 March 1962), pp. 6, 8.

6 *Observer* (11 March 1962), p. 1, (18 March 1962), p. 1; *Sunday Times* (11 March 1962), p. 1, (18 March 1962), p. 1; *News of the World* (18 March 1962), p. 3; *Sunday Pictorial* (11 March 1962), p. 13; *People* (11 March 1962), p. 11; *Sunday Express* (11 March 1962), p. 5, (18 March 1962), p. 16.

7 Anon., 'Britain's tobacco crisis', *Illustrated London News*, 213 (1948), 232–3; Anon., 'Tobacco standard; cigarette currency', *Economist*, 152 (1947), 526–7. What follows is taken from a comprehensive survey of *The Times*, the *Guardian*, the *Daily Express* and the *Daily Mirror*.

8 *Daily Express* (16 April 1947), pp. 1–2.

9 *The Times* (22 March 1947), p. 5d, (25 April 1947), p. 5f, (28 April 1947), p. 7g.

10 *Guardian* (30 April 1947), p. 4.

11 *The Times* (20 August 1948), p. 5e; *Guardian* (21 August 1948), p. 4, (25 August 1948), p. 4.

12 *Daily Express* (21 August 1948), p. 2.

13 *Daily Mirror* (29 September 1950), p. 6.

14 *The Times* (28 August 1951), p. 5f.

15 *Guardian* (16 January 1953), p. 12.

16 *Ibid.* (13 February 1954), p. 4.

17 *Daily Express* (13 February 1957), p. 1; *Daily Mirror* (13 February 1957), p. 1.

18 *Daily Express* (6 January 1971), p. 8.

19 *Ibid.* (13 February 1954), p. 1.

20 *Ibid.* (8 July 1953), p. 5; Haddow's speech is quoted in greater length in the *Guardian* (8 July 1953), p. 5 and *The Times* (8 July 1953), p. 3a.

21 *Daily Express* (19 February, 1953), p. 7; *Guardian* (19 February 1953), p. 10; *The Times* (19 February 1953), pp. 4a, 112a, 13a.

22 *Daily Express* (29 October 1953), pp. 1, 4, (30 October 1953), pp. 1, 4.

23 *Ibid.* (8 May 1956), p. 1.

24 *Ibid.* (12 July 1957), p. 6.

25 *Ibid.* (17 March 1962), p. 6, (29 March 1962), p. 14.

26 *Ibid.* (9 February 1965), pp. 1, 8, (10 February 1965), pp. 5, 8.

27 *Ibid.* (24 October 1967), pp. 1, 8.

28 *Ibid.* (6 January 1971), pp. 1, 8, 15, (7 January 1971), p. 6, (15 January 1971), p. 8.

29 *Guardian* (5 February 1952), p. 3.

30 *Ibid.* (13 February 1954), p. 4.

31 *Ibid.* (23 June 1955), p. 15, (13 July 1955), p. 5, (9 September 1955), p. 3.

32 *Ibid.* (2 July 1957), p. 6.

33 *Ibid.* (2 February 1962), p. 6.

34 *Ibid.* (13 January 1964), pp. 8–9.

35 *The Times* (28 July 1949), p. 5d, (18 November 1953), p. 9d, (21 July 1954), p. 7d, (25 June 1955), p. 6g, (13 July 1955), p. 9g, (3 April 1956), p. 12f, (27 October 1956), p. 7c, (9 April 1957), p. 2g, (30 December 1957), p. 7d.

36 *Ibid.* (24 August 1948), p. 5d, (3 May 1955), p. 11d.

37 *Ibid.* (20 July 1955), p. 9d.

38 *Ibid.* (28 August 1951), p. 5f, (31 August 1951), p. 5e.

39 *Ibid.* (13 February 1954), pp. 6g, 7c, 12.

40 *Ibid.* (15 October 1958), p. 7g; C. Wood, 'How to stop', in C. M. Fletcher, H. Cole, L. Jeger and C. Wood, *Common Sense About Smoking* (Harmondsworth, Penguin, 1963), pp. 107–28. *The Times* sued for libel, eventually causing Wood to withdraw the allegations in subsequent editions: *The Times* (24 July 1963), p. 5e.

41 *Ibid.* (16 January 1961), pp. 11c, 15a, (24 March 1961), p. 7a.

42 *Ibid.* (9 February 1965), p. 13d.

43 *Ibid.* (26 July 1968), p. 8h, (5 August 1968), p. 6h, (15 April 1969), p. 26e.

44 *Ibid.* (6 January 1971), p. 13a.

45 *Daily Mirror* (13 February 1954), pp. 1, 16.

46 *Ibid.* (28 June 1957), pp. 1–2, 10–11.

47 *Ibid.* (4 January 1957), p. 7, (29 October 1958), p. 8, (22 April 1960), p. 3, (29 March 1962), p. 23.

48 *Ibid.* (9 January 1964), p. 8, (23 January 1964), p. 19, (7 July 1965), p. 8, (15 October 1966), p. 1.

49 *Ibid.* (6 January 1971), pp. 1, 11, 24, (8 January 1971), pp. 2, 8, (11 January 1971), p. 6, (15 January 1971), p. 15, (26 January 1971), p. 7.

50 BBC Written Archives, Caversham (hereafter BBC), Radio Scripts, Charles Hill (The Radio Doctor), *Good Health*, 25 April 1947.

51 BBC, Radio Scripts, *Woman's Hour*, *Women Smoking*, 11 June 1952.

52 BBC, Smoking Policy Files, R78/2695/1: *Smoking and Health*.

53 BBC, Radio Scripts, Patricia Brent, *Topic for Tonight*, 27 June 1957; Professor Alexander Haddow, *Commentary on the Report of Smoking and Lung Cancer*, 28 June 1957; *At Home and Abroad*, 28 June 1957; BBC, TV Programmes, *Panorama*, 1 July 1957.

54 *Ibid.*, R. R. Bomford, *Good Health*, 29 January 1954. He made several other statements of this nature throughout the 1950s.

55 *Ibid.*, C. L. Boltz, *Statistics and Cancer (European Service)*, 13 January 1956. He made similar comments on the Home Service.

56 *Ibid.*, Patricia Brent, *Topic for Tonight*, 8 May 1956.

57 *Ibid.*, *Woman's Hour*, *Out of the News: Report on the MRC by Patricia Brent and Ritchie Calder*, 8 July 1957.

58 *Ibid.*, *Behind the News*, 17 February 1954.

59 *Ibid.*, *Any Questions,* 30 March 1956, 11 May 1956, 7 November 1957, 9 March 1962.

60 BBC, Radio Script Files, *An Audience Research Report on 'Smoking and Cancer'*, 18 July 1957.

61 BBC, TV programmes, *Panorama*, 12 March 1962. Copy of script obtained from PRO, MH 55 2204: *1961–1962: Public Health. Propaganda – Smoking and Cancer of the Lung: Publicity Policy.*

62 BBC, Radio Scripts, *Focus On Smoking*, 1 November 1966.

63 BBC, Smoking Policy Files, *Talks: Charles M. Fletcher, File 1, 1943–1962*; *File 2, 1952–1970.*

64 BBC, Radio Scripts, *Woman's Hour*, 11 February 1963 and 12 January 1968.

65 *Ibid.*, R. Cutforth – Radio Four Reports, *On the Habit that Kills*; *Guardian*, 5 January 1971, p. 1.

66 BBC, Smoking Policy Files, R78/2695/1: *Smoking and Health*; R73/403, *Cigarette Advertising in BBC Publications, 1968–1971.*

67 G. Robinson and S. Winward, *Smoking* (London, Crusade, 1958); p. 3; G. Shepherd, *Facts About Smoking* (Rugby, G. Shepherd, 1956); H. R. Hardcastle, *The Ethics of Smoking at the Wheel* (Lyndhurst, the author, 1949); W. Hawkins, *'My Dear Old Pipe'* (Peterborough, the author, 1947); H. King, *Cigarette Smoking and Lung Cancer: The Remedy* (Southport, Holsum, 1962).

68 L. M. Johnston, *The Disease of Tobacco Smoking and its Cure* (London, Christopher Johnson, 1957). See also J. Theed, *Smoking and Cancer* (London, Television Times, 1954); M. Clement, *Smoking and Cancer: Facts that Every Smoker Ought to Know!* (Bognor Regis, Health Science Press, 1953).

69 W. Koskowski, *The Habit of Tobacco Smoking* (London, Staples Press, 1955); A. Ochsner, *Smoking and Cancer: A Doctor's Report* (London, Frederick Muller, 1955).

70 J. L. Burn, *Smoking and Lung Cancer* (London, Chest & Heart Association, 1961); R. N. C. McCurdy, *Smoking, Lung Cancer and You* (London, Linden Press, 1958); N. Macdonald, *Your Chest Could be Healthy: Smoking and Lung Diseases* (London, Socialist Medical Association, 1958); H. Flack, *Smoking: The Dangers* (London, British Medical Association, 1961).

71 C. Fletcher *et al.*, *Common Sense.*

72 V. M. Hawthorne, *Facts About Smoking* (Edinburgh, Scottish Home & Health Department, 1967); N. Imlah, *The Choice is Yours: Finding Out the Facts* (London, Geoffrey Chapman, 1971); R. Kind and J. Leedham, *Don't Smoke!* (London, Longmans, 1966).

73 A. Abrahams, *The Human Machine* (Harmondsworth, Penguin, 1956), p. 121.

74 S. Russ, *Smoking and its Effects, with Special Reference to Lung Cancer* (London, Hutchinson, 1955).

75 M. Schroeder, *Better Smoking* (London, Allen & Unwin, 1964).
76 R. A. Fisher, *Smoking, the Cancer Controversy: Some Attempts to Assess the Evidence* (London, Oliver & Boyd, 1959).
77 H. J. Eysenck, *Smoking, Health and Personality* (London, Weidenfeld & Nicolson, 1965), p. 15.
78 PRO, MH 55 1011, *1946–1954: Cancer of the Lung: Investigation*; *Daily Mirror* (5 July 1957), p. 5; G. F. Todd, *Comments on the Report on Smoking and Health by a Committee of the Royal College of Physicians*, in MH 55 2232, *1954–1962: Smoking and Lung Cancer: Reports and Memoranda*.
79 *Lancet*, i (1956), 748.

10

'It never did me any harm': science in culture

Ian Fleming's James Bond was a great smoker. Chapter 5 outlined the spy's prolific consumption of his blended Balkan and Turkish Morland specials with their 'higher nicotine content'. But, ever up-to-date, Bond became health conscious in *Thunderball*, published in 1961 one year before the RCP report. Realising that smoking doubled the effects of a hangover and following the warnings from his medical officer, Miss Moneypenny and his Scottish house-keeper, May, Bond checked into a health clinic where he reduced his daily habit from sixty Morlands to ten Duke of Durhams. The latter were an American filter brand selected by Bond because the authoritative Consumers' Union rated them with the lowest tar and nicotine content. Health restored, Bond was thus ready to face once more his non-smoking adversary, Ernst Blofeld.[1]

For a writer so dependent on smoking as a signifier of his hero's masculinity, it was remarkable that Fleming showed so much concern and awareness of the dangers of smoking, though his own smoking-induced deterioration in health provides an obvious explanation for this interest. Bond's difficulty in breaking the habit in *Thunderball* is perhaps reflective of wider cultural responses to health awareness campaigns. Throughout the book, Bond struggles against his 'sinful' indulgence, to the disapproval of M, the pipe-smoking, sceptical traditionalist, until he becomes the self-confessed 'world's authority on giving up smoking' (he adds unoriginally that this is because he is always giving up). He even gives out advice, recommending his switch to the Dukes brand as the best first step to quitting. He himself never succeeds, occasion-ally 'drawing the smoke deep down into his lungs and letting it out with a long, reflective hiss'.[2] His weakness stands in contrast to the criminal profes-sionals he is up against, thirty to forty of whom do not smoke, though one is in such control of his vices that he can quite happily break a cigarette in two and smoke only one half at a time. It is a theme repeated in film as the non-smoking Mr Osaka warns Bond in *You Only Live Twice* (1967) that he is taking a risk as cigarettes are 'bad for the chest'. This time Sean Connery nonchalantly acknowledges the advice before proceeding to light up.

Whereas Bond's addiction to tobacco might once have been seen as a feminised loss of independence, his weakness in the face of the known health risks adds a human touch to his almost mechanical efficiency. Ironically, it also re-instils certain masculine attributes, the hard-smoking Fleming deliberately giving Bond an independence from MI6's medical officers, who appear at the beginning of the book with their formulaic dictates to good health. They do not consider Bond's individual needs as a smoker, nor the satisfaction or relief from stress that the cigarette contributes to Fleming's broader definition of physical and mental health. They fail to recognise the importance of a deep lungful of smoke to Bond's physical, psychological and essentially masculine identity as a smoker. And they do not realise that their homogenising rational advice cannot account for the individual and idiosyncratic rationality demanded of men in the deadly spy profession. Fleming's Bond never quits smoking as it is too central to both his private and public self.

The triumph of the culture of smoking over its known physical dangers within the Bond novel is given romantic elaboration by Fleming. For the masses of smokers amid the general public, the term 'cognitive dissonance' would be applied instead. Medical workers noted from an early stage the ability of smokers to be aware of the publicised dangers of tobacco, yet also an ability to refute this evidence either by their continued consumption and disbelief or a vague optimism that it would not happen to themselves. This chapter articulates that so-called dissonance, providing a brief cultural history of smoking in the post-war period which explains beyond any physical addiction why smoking cessation rates have not been as high as health campaigners would have liked. It examines why different groups have rejected the medical evidence which connects smoking causally with lung cancer, why they have sometimes acknowledged such a relationship but not acted in the manner demanded by the health professionals, and why young adults who have been brought up in an environment at school which was keen to publicise the risks of smoking have begun to smoke.

Bond's experiences in *Thunderball* are particularly illustrative of this story. He demonstrates a general awareness that smoking is harmful and in response he intends to quit. Yet he does not succeed because he cannot disassociate smoking from his sense of self, both in the aid it is perceived to give to his profession and in his private identity which posits his individuality against a supposedly interfering medical establishment. As such, his attempts to stop smoking become just as much a routine as his smoking was originally, and the constant interplay of his acceptance of the medical evidence and his obstinate negation of it serves to instil a quixotic struggle in his day-to-day existence. All these features can be seen in the post-war history of smoking; from the bourgeois-gentlemanly backlash against the medical findings of the 1950s, to the aggressive masculinity which asserted itself in a defiant popular culture, and on to the practice of quitting which has become so regular and routine a feature of the smoker's career that, just as in Italo Svevo's *Confessions of Zeno*, it has become almost a life-long activity in itself.[3] The experience of Bond is in many ways illustrative of both male and female smokers, though there are many other factors which have determined a dependence on cigarettes, particularly for the socially and economically disadvantaged. But even these factors have been strengthened by the 'dissonance' of culture which has seen the transmission of positive images of smoking in films and advertising alongside the negative campaigns of the HEC. It is this survival of the economy and cultures of smoking outlined in the first two sections of this book which explains the reception of the scientific studies into smoking and health.

From the very earliest investigations into the effectiveness of smoking and health campaigns, there was an awareness of the smokers' differing responses to what they had read or heard. In 1959, £4,350 was spent on an intensive campaign in Edinburgh which involved press advertisements, meetings, 3,000 posters in public places, the distribution of 150,000 campaign leaflets and 30,000 copies of the BMA's *Smoking: The Facts*. A follow-up survey estimated that 81 per cent of the population in Edinburgh knew of the campaign and that 73 per cent saw, heard or read something about smoking and lung cancer during the campaign period. Before the arrival of the publicity material 30 per cent of smokers accepted (with varying degrees of qualification) that smoking was linked to lung cancer, a figure which increased to 53 per cent afterwards. While roughly a quarter of smokers remained undecided, the number of smokers doubting or disagreeing with the evidence fell from 28 per cent to 23 per cent. Smokers were more willing to accept that smoking affected common illnesses such as bronchitis, catarrh, indigestion and especially breathlessness and coughs, and that these factors were more likely to induce them to give up than the fear of lung cancer. The investigators also found that those in white-collar occupations were much more likely to accept the evidence than semi-skilled or unskilled workers. Significantly, however, and despite an increased awareness of the dangers, there was no change in the proportion of the population who were smokers after the campaign had come to an end.[4]

It was concluded that the style of the campaign was deeply problematic, based as it was 'upon rationalistic assumptions concerning perception and motivation to which the facts of human psychology lend little support'. Such perceptive insights into the rhetoric of health awareness programmes were backed up by equally incisive explanations for smokers' attitudes and behaviour:

> The man in the street is familiar with the commonplace, everyday illnesses and symptoms, and believes that he can understand their causation. Lung cancer is by comparison rare and hedged about by taboos; since it is known to carry a very high fatality rate, theories which impose a major responsibility for its causation upon the individual, as distinct from forces outside his control, are more likely to provide a reaction of denial and rejection . . . The tendency to adjust one's beliefs so as to exonerate one's own behaviour is shown not only in the distribution of attitudes to the cigarette smoking–lung cancer hypothesis, but also in the common view that only heavy smoking is dangerous, with heavy smoking being defined as a level of consumption one step higher than one's own.[5]

The report on the Edinburgh experiment preceded what many other investigations would find throughout the 1960s: that smokers were often aware of the publicised risks; that many disputed the association with lung cancer; that many often thought that others were at risk but not themselves; and that all such beliefs were used to justify a continuation of their habit. Similar results were found in a preliminary survey conducted in 1963 just eighteen months after the publication of the first RCP report. Only 49 per cent of adolescents (aged fifteen to twenty) and 28 per cent of adult smokers accepted that smoking would affect their health in the future (with 24 per cent of adolescents and 11 per cent of adults accepting with some qualification), suggesting a low degree of awareness of the dangers of smoking. Yet when asked whether smoking might affect other people's health, 85 per cent of adolescent and 81 per cent of adult smokers thought it did so. The comparative figures for non-smokers were 91 per cent of adolescents and 86 per cent of adults, but whereas smokers were twice as likely to qualify their acceptance of the dangers by attributing them to heavy smoking, non-smokers were twice as likely to offer an unqualified acceptance of the dangers.[6]

These figures present a complicated story since it is clear that although by the early 1960s the vast majority of the population was aware of the smoking and health controversy, it did not follow that smokers were accepting the official version of the relationship. This was due in part to the range of alternative explanations presented by the media and tobacco manufacturers, and because smokers themselves were extremely inventive in explaining the consequences of their own smoking. Even if alternative explanations had not been given any room in the mass media, it appears likely that smokers might still not have translated official medical knowledge into appropriate action, given their apparent willingness to assume an immunity in themselves from the dangers of smoking, but a susceptibility in other smokers. This is exactly the 'logical acrobatics' that the *Guardian* complained of in 1964 which were held to have led to a continuation of consumption patterns despite it being 'unlikely' that there were 'many adult citizens now unaware of the conclusions'.[7] What follows is a cultural explanation for these 'logical acrobatics', the apparent discrepancies in the statistics of smoking attitudes and behaviour.

Any new understanding of a product must necessarily be interpreted initially from within the existing dominant culture. For tobacco, the scientific investigations published in the 1950s were consequently discussed by a prevailing written culture of smoking which had by then become something of a tradition. In the inter-war period, J. M. Barrie and Sir Arthur Conan Doyle had given way to Count Corti and A. E. Hamilton, but by the post-war period the mantle had been assumed by the novelist Compton Mackenzie, the exclusive retailer and manufacturer, Alfred Dunhill and the perennial champion of the divine weed, J. B. Priestley.[8] Mackenzie's *Sublime Tobacco* was a full-length version of the nineteenth-century periodical article, tracing the history of smoking from its origins to the present day, providing all the required purposeful information which supplemented and made possible a sixty-page idealised reminiscence of his own 'smoking life'.[9] Extracts of his nostalgia found their way into his *Spectator* column, which continued to celebrate the cigar and the pipe in the same style as that found in the articles of his smoking companion, Priestley, writing in the *New Statesman*.[10] Though there was an awareness that only cigarette smoking was linked to lung cancer, their pomposity created an atmosphere that good smokers were somehow beyond the ravages of the disease. Priestley admitted that 'there may be something in this lung cancer idea' but the great and heavy smokers of the halcyon days of his smoking youth had never seemed to 'suffer from lung cancer'. In fact, in 1961, he suspected 'a good deal of disguised puritanism among medical men' and his blunt, Northern, matter-of-fact tone cast doubt on what had been said against smoking, though his motivations were not based on any evidence that he chose to present.[11] Priestley and Mackenzie articulated at much greater length for the pipe and cigar what Fleming wished to convey through Bond's difficulties with the cigarette. This culture was reflected across the popular media, from the reporting on the annual Pipeman of the Year contests in the *Daily Mirror* to special features on the pipe in the *Evening Standard*.[12] Radio broadcasts had earlier meandered their way through the pipe dreams of the presenter's memories, one claiming he learnt to smoke from a foreign beauty named after the Egyptian queen, Nefertiti.[13] The *Guardian*, amid its uncompromising acceptance of the dangers of smoking, still found space to write of the 'blissful tranquillity' of the cigar and the art of the briar pipe, which was said to have become a 'tribal badge' for the utilitarian Englishman.[14]

The articles cannot be dismissed as referring to a gentlemanly smoking culture distinct from that associated with the cigarette, since the emphasis on independence and individuality shaped the responses to the smoking and health controversy more generally, for all tobacco types. In a development of the *Guardian's* link between smoking and national identity, *The Times* claimed that filter cigarettes had proved to be more popular in the United States because the 'British don't scare easily', thus building on its earlier general pro-smoking patriotism.[15] Chapman Pincher in the *Daily Express* took the attitude to the extreme, a 1957 column almost urging smokers to unite in defiance against the 'interfering' medics.[16] Even the *Lancet* claimed, when it was coming to accept a causal link between smoking and lung cancer, that smokers were better people: they were 'restless, energetic, impulsive, independent, interesting men, ardent in the pursuit of enterprises which appealed to them, and seeking service during the war with combat units'. In contrast, non-smokers were 'bland, steady, dependable, hard-working, rather uncommunicative family men who tended during the war to gravitate to specialised non-combat units'.[17] Beyond the natural audience for this rhetoric that one might have found in the readers of these newspapers, the quintessentially working-class Andy Capp in the *Mirror* demonstrated a similar resistance to medical developments. His daily cigarette only left his mouth once a year, to be replaced with a cigar in celebration of his trip to the races to see the handicap named after him.[18]

Taking their cue from this mutinous lead, as well as from the range of alternative explanations offered in the press, readers began to interpret the scientific evidence for themselves. Even children, *The Times* reported in 1957, were able to pick and choose which doctor's opinion they would follow from the newspapers.[19] *Mirror* readers were particularly adept at armchair science. The phrase 'smoking never did me any harm' became a mantra for that type of smoker for whom 'the possibility of lung cancer' presented no 'scare'. They did not intend to give up when they were aged forty-three, 'felt fine' and had 'been smoking since [they were] ten'.[20] Letters were printed throughout the 1960s which encouraged the prevalence of this rather ill-informed defiance, but others at least presented diesel fumes as an alternative explanation.[21] Here, they followed the alternatives previously suggested by *Guardian* readers, in the range of suggestions offered on the BBC's *Any Answers* and in the hundreds of letters sent in to the Ministry of Health by members of the public, all of which served as testaments to both the knowledge and inventiveness of smokers. Their responses included placing the blame purely on excessive smoking; on petrol lighters; on shop-made as opposed to hand-made cigarettes; on saltpetre, ammonia and other additives claimed to be in tobacco; on chemical fertilisers; on the acidity of certain tobacco types; on heredity factors; on air pollution and other problems associated with big city life; and, most intriguingly, on 'the spiritual disease of man' induced by the welfare state which 'crushes the life out of our people'. Convoluted theories emerged such as that of Halliday Sutherland, who claimed that smoking could not be carcinogenic since smokers would develop finger cancer from where they held their cigarettes. Others suggested that the anti-smoking message was simply the latest 'fad' of the medical profession, a fashion guaranteed within a year to be 'as dead as the Flying Saucers'. By far the most frequent deduction made was that because they had elderly relatives who had smoked all their lives they had nothing to fear; therefore they could continue smoking themselves.[22] In short, smokers were, as health campaigners quickly observed, keen to provide solutions which removed any responsibility from themselves. That this desire was not specific to one particular social or economic cohort of the population is demonstrated by the similar diversity of medical opinion which had appeared in the correspondence columns of the *Lancet* in the first half of the 1950s, and in the continued disbelief in smoking's causal relationship with cancer among a minority of doctors and medical students in the late 1960s.[23]

When the official medical evidence was presented to smokers free from the interpretations of the media, smokers proved adept at finding loopholes in the anti-smoking message. Tests of audience reactions to anti-smoking films and posters in the early 1960s found that smokers were particularly sceptical of the statistical presentations and were 'most fertile in finding logical objections to the evidence', such as with the inference of causality. When the act of smoking itself was portrayed as a 'dirty, unromantic' habit, smokers were noted to react in opposition to the overall message and there was a strong tendency for them not to associate the anti-smoking message with themselves, despite an appreciation of the potential impact of a poster on others.[24] A certain fatalism lay behind many of these attitudes, mixed with an optimistic faith in one's own ability to resist disease. Older smokers tended to believe that they were beyond redemption, while younger smokers inverted the statistics to assess the greater likelihood of not contracting lung cancer. And both types, a *Guardian* article observed in 1963, made themselves 'immune to the effects of propaganda' as they awaited 'the emergence of some smoking phoenix from the ashes' in the form of a cancer cure or the introduction of a harmless cigarette.[25]

All of these attitudes to smoking were largely the product of social and economic circumstances which recent research has increasingly shown to have been of considerable importance in provoking low smoking cessation rates in certain groups of the population. Health policy workers have increasingly come to recognise the importance of smoking 'to reduce stress and to demarcate short periods of relaxation from the normal routine'.[26] For men, this has often been in the paid work context, but for women cigarettes have presented a break from domestic work. For both, smoking has become related to income. 'Poor smokers' 'cleave to the anodyne qualities of tobacco and defend their habit on grounds of entitlement in disadvantage and of solidarity with others in the same circumstances'. They are 'in a malign spiral: most likely to take up smoking; least likely to give up smoking; least able to afford smoking; most likely to suffer material hardship; and most likely to suffer increased hardship because of their expenditure on cigarettes'.[27] The alleviation of stress has weighed more heavily on smokers' minds than the long-term health consequences, many of which have been re-interpreted to lower the individual risk for the smoker.

These factors are even more significant for women than for men. Between 1948 and 1990, male smoking rates fell from 82 per cent to 38 per cent but for women from 41 per cent to only 31 per cent. Smoking rates for young women had become higher than those for men, particularly among disadvantaged groups in youth cultures which encouraged the symbolic use of the cigarette 'where other sources of self-esteem, including education and employment, are beyond reach'. As these women became older, they found themselves in low income households in socially deprived and frequently hostile neighbourhoods and facing caring responsibilities in the domestic sphere for which smoking represented a brief moment of escape, a coping strategy for when they found life 'a drag'.[28]

While these social and economic factors played an important role in the continuation of smoking habits, the statistic that three-quarters of all social classes try smoking in their youth suggests a number of wider cultural factors which impact on society as a whole. Certainly, cigarettes have continued to permeate all aspects of popular culture. The headline treatment given to the news that pensioners were to be assured of a tax relief on their weekly ration of tobacco during the supply shortages of the late 1940s and early 1950s demonstrates the extent to which smoking was being officially recognised as a social necessity immediately prior to the smoking and health scare.[29] And as the health scare came to be formulated by the popular press, glamorous images of smoking were constantly featured, pictures of movie stars and 'starlets' often portrayed with a sophisticated cigarette in their mouth. Inevitably, the *Express* went beyond the reflection and reinforcement of the cigarette's role in popular culture and explicitly chose to celebrate its worldwide egalitarian ubiquity. To refer to just two examples, a feature article showed how important the cigarette was to the art of the dance choreographer, Robert Helpmann, as he always smoked taking ballet dancers through their moves. And a 1969 full-page royalty piece headlined with the news that Princess Margrethe of Denmark's 'recipe for taking off the strain' was 'a cigarette and a glass of lager'.[30]

In film the cigarette appeared everywhere, continuing to connote feminine chic and masculine strength. The sexualised overtones of smoking in films of the 1930s and 1940s did not subside. Indeed, in *North by Northwest* (1959), the allure and eroticisation of the cigarette seemed to reach its apotheosis as Hitchcock built on the sexual connotations he had earlier established in *Rear Window* (1954). When Cary Grant meets Eva Marie Saint on the train there is an immediate sexual tension between the two of them. Unable or unwilling to show a scene of intimate physical contact, Grant is instead portrayed awkwardly trying to light her cigarette from his personalised book of matches. Saint reaches for the hand that holds the lighted match, and slowly brings it towards her cigarette, so that she controls his courteous act. After lighting up, she moves his hand back and blows out the match. The scene is a deliberate play on the act of sex, a point reinforced by Saint's almost post-coital exhalation of smoke and the later shot of the train entering a tunnel. But while earlier Hollywood films had glamorised smoking among the rich and the beautiful, post-war films democratised that sophistication and brilliance. For instance, in British realist cinema's *Room at the Top* (1958), Laurence Harvey's Joe Lampton maintains his affinity with his working-class roots through his smoking of Capstans. Yet Harvey's character also believes that he should be denied nothing in an increasingly affluent world and he pursues the rich but unhappy Simone Signoret, their moments of intimacy marked each time by Lampton's lighting of her cigarette. In the sexualised use of the cigarette, *Room at the Top* becomes an almost Northern working-class equivalent of Paul Henreid and Bette Davis' far more cosmopolitan profundity in *Now Voyager*.

The iconic status of the cigarette as used by Lampton provoked contemporary comment, as did the aggressive masculinity of Sean Connery's James Bond.[31] In 1969 health education workers singled out Bond for particular criticism, as his 'toughness' had been identified as a major incitement to adolescent smoking among boys who wished to appear adult.[32] Such a positive portrayal of smoking from the point of view of the manufacturer was not overlooked in later years, and the American firm Philip Morris admitted to paying $350,000 for the placement of its products in *Licence to Kill* (1989). By this time, such a form of promotion was highly attractive to cigarette manufacturers, limited as they were by voluntary agreements on advertising content. Sylvester Stallone was paid $300,000 by another US company, Brown & Williamson, to smoke Kools in *Rhinestone* (1984) and the internationally successful *Rambo: First Blood Part II* (1985) and *Rocky IV* (1985). Somewhat ironically, given the anti-smoking programmes aimed at children at the time, Philip Morris paid $42,000 for product placement in *Superman II* (1980).[33]

During the 1960s, though, television provided another visual representation of the smoker which served, if not to glamorise smoking, at least to present it as a normal social activity. Despite the pressure on the BBC to cut down on the frequency with which smoking appeared in its programmes, a number of TV characters and presenters were noted for their smoking. The Ministry of Health encouraged the BBC to cut out smoking in *Z-Cars*, as it was felt to be of a type which encouraged 'hero worship'. In a typical week of broadcasting in 1967, only two out of forty-two presenters who appeared as themselves smoked on screen (David Nixon and Christopher Chataway), but it was noted that a large number of guests on their shows tended to smoke to 'settle their nerves'. In drama, Soames and Jocelyn Forsyte smoked occasionally and the men frequently smoked cigars in *The Forsyte Saga*. In entertainment, the BBC was worried that smoking in *The Likely Lads* presented a particularly attractive image for the cigarette. It was not worried by *Till Death Us Do Part*, as Alf Garnett's pipe and the cigarette constantly dangling from the mouth of his wife, Else, were not held to be inducements to juvenile smoking. This was possibly true, though such images, along with Hawkins' roll-ups in *Softly, Softly* and the argument between the Rt Hon. Mervyn Pugh and his wife, Janet, over their smoking in bed in *Whitehall Warriors* in the same week, all attested to, and possibly encouraged, the view that smoking was not generally a problematic form of consumption.[34]

This wider culture of smoking was completed by a rapidly expanding expenditure on advertising by the cigarette manufacturers. Many of the themes within this advertising were direct continuations of those found in the inter-war period, the emphasis being to provide images which appealed to as broad a section of the population as possible. Part II of this book has demonstrated the limitations of advertising's impact on overall demand for cigarettes, but this is not to say that manufacturers did not change their policy to counter the impact of the smoking and health controversy. Even before the publication of the RCP report in 1962, the proliferation of advertising images was seen as a counterbalance to the increasingly frequent negative messages of the medical authorities. It matters little that manufacturers have argued that this has only been to stimulate demand for particular brands, for the overall effect has been to make the cigarette advertisement a mainstay of everyday visual culture. In 1957, tobacco companies spent just over £1 million on cigarette, tobacco and cigar advertising on commercial television, a figure which had shot up to £4.5 million by 1960, £1.5 million of this increase being from just 1959. This may have been due to a realisation of the potential of TV advertising, but when press display and television advertising expenditures are put together the figure was as high as £8,323,500 in 1960, £2,662,300 more than in 1959. The Advertising Inquiry Council estimated that the total amount spent on promotion by the industry for this year was approximately £20 million, a figure five times higher than the pre-war peak in 1935.[35] Following the TV advertising ban of 1965, an increasingly competitive industry turned to coupon trading, which saw promotional costs spiral still further, resulting in a trade war in the late 1960s. Various other forms of price and non-price competition were also undertaken, including the eventual introduction of the king-size filter cigarette.[36]

Government restrictions on advertising and voluntary agreements since 1962 have limited the stylistic content of the promotional images, the regulations set down by the Advertising Standards Authority immediately after the

RCP report severely limiting the promotion of the sexual overtones of smoking. The glamorous images of men and women found in film were also curtailed, though there was in any case a long history of limited gendered cigarette promotion in Britain. According to H. J. Eysenck, whose studies of the personalities of smokers influenced tobacco company policy, women were not put off buying a brand because it looked masculine, but the reverse was undoubtedly the case. For this reason, few sustained appeals were made to women. Player's launched a successful series of advertisements in the 1960s building on the 'Player's Please' slogan, but the 'People Love Player's' images featuring young couples in the healthy outdoors were also later prohibited. With such restrictions, cigarette advertising has instead been characterised by its imaginative innovations, the Benson & Hedges 'Pure Gold' campaign from 1962 to 1977 utilising clever photography which always made the packet of cigarettes the 'hero' of the setting. In deliberately making the packet the star, advertisers were only offering an updated, better understood and more sophisticated version of the imagery first used in the early twentieth century. Further restrictions prompted the 1977 launch of the surrealist photographs which made Benson & Hedges advertisements notably eye catching for the surprises they held within the apparently realist picture. Here again, the images succeeded those of the early twentieth century, being so deficient in their cultural or social connotations that they could not have offended any specific group of consumers.[37] What was most important from the manufacturer's point of view was that all these images were viewed regularly, ensuring the continued dominance of the marketing message over that of the health campaigners.

This 'dissonance' of culture that saw advertising images, film representations, social and economic realities, and the survival of a liberal smoking tradition juxtaposed with the promotion of the dangers of smoking by established medical bodies manifested itself in peculiar circumstances. Major news stories would provoke a rush on anti-smoking pills and techniques, but thereafter, while there was a vague acceptance that smoking was bad for you in the popular media, there would be little discussion or reminder of why and how this was exactly the case.[38] In part, this is explained by the general understanding of cancer in popular culture, shared alike by newspapers and the population as a whole. Referred to even as 'the C word' in some working-class communities, cancer was a taboo surrounded by myth, fear and shame, to be avoided in conversation at all times. A survey conducted in 1954 found that while 80 per cent of women could easily recognise the symptoms of breast cancer, over half had delayed a visit to the doctor for three months, inspired by the belief that cancer was incurable. What is significant here is that, while there was no denial of the existence of cancer, the absence of any discussion prevented the actions that medical professionals would have advised. A leader article in the *Guardian* complained of the 'obscurantism' which had surrounded the disease and that more public discussion was required. People clung to the belief that there was 'something shameful in suffering from the disease' and that 'bad living' and 'not keeping clean' were among the causes of cancer: 'in any further efforts which may be made to dissipate this perilous ignorance it may be found that the main problem is to counter deep-seated and irrational emotions rather than plain misunderstanding or lack of knowledge.'[39]

Before the publication of the MRC report in 1957, then, there was a context of a public understanding of cancer which limited a detailed discussion of the dangers of smoking. Throughout the 1960s, the popular press ignored many of the finer points of detail about the relationship between smoking and lung cancer, an unintentional consequence of which was the lack of seriousness attached to the process of giving up. Stop-smoking measures were presented as necessary but it was taken as implicit that everybody knew for what reason. Indeed they did, but the absence of purposeful reminders diluted the magnitude of a failed attempt to quit. Stopping smoking almost became a habit and an activity in itself, a routinised ritual that fitted well with the processes of starting again. If the dangers of smoking had inspired the initial desire to quit, their removal from popular guidelines for quitting made it all the easier to forget why one was trying to quit in the first place.

During the tobacco shortages of the late 1940s and the impact of the budget increases in the tobacco duty, the BBC's *Woman's Hour* had devoted several slots in its schedule to help people give up smoking.[40] The psychology presented in these programmes borrowed heavily from a longer tradition of stop-smoking guides which had appeared from the beginning of the century. Arthur King's 'scientific cure' first appeared in 1913, inspired by his treatment of alcoholics who had been regarded as suffering from a 'disease' much earlier than those who could not give up tobacco.[41] In the 1940s and early 1950s, the NSNS published its own guides, as did firms specialising in self-improvement literature.[42] The pamphlets blended a pop-Freudian analysis with a pop-Nietzschean solution which usually involved a battle to overcome the subconscious before a mastery of one's own ego led to a triumph of the will over one's addiction. While some would add a religious dimension to this science, inventing a 'super-conscious' spiritual level existing beyond the subconscious,[43] the following quotation from Leslie Bell's 1947 *How to Stop Smoking* typifies the genre:

'I am I, the Self, the Ego!' I spoke the words to myself, slowly and distinctly; *thought* each word, *felt it deep down to my innermost being*. And I felt better: deliberately, over and over again, I asserted quietly yet decisively my supremacy. *Insisted* on my complete mastery of all things animate, and animate as I; stressing my mind with the over consciousness of my being . . . AS A POWER, 'I am I' . . . I could say it, *feel it*, and with this self instituted mental strength; with this new and *sure* trust in myself, I returned to the problem, *certain of the outcome . . . The initiative was with me* for I had already assumed my proper supremacy: with vivid suddenness the solution had come to me when – on putting my mind once more to the destruction of the tobacco habit – I found that the craving was no longer acute.[44]

Self mastery gave way to much more explicit advice, with guide books in the 1950s suggesting different methods of quitting. These included immediate cessation, the 'aesthetic method', taking pills such as lobeline, auto-suggestion and the gradual reduction in consumption method.[45] However, when Kurt Salzer suggested the 'health method' as one of his thirteen ways of quitting, he made only passing reference to the dangers of smoking, adding that he did not 'want to cite the terrible consequences which excessive smoking may have on . . . health' or 'dwell too much on these alarming medical statements'.[46] Terrible and alarming they may have been, but by passing over them Salzer avoided the reasons why much of the medical profession desired people to quit in the first place.

Newspapers popularised such methods following the publication of the medical reports against smoking. In 1957, the *Guardian* adopted a light-hearted tone in discussing the difficulties of giving up, stimulating a camaraderie in the activity of quitting which had so marked much of the original social nature of smoking.[47] By 1963 a culture of 'giving up' emerged at the start of each new year,[48] a culture taken to its limits by the *Mirror* in 1971 when several of its journalists tried to quit at the same time. They each tried a different stop-smoking device and reported on their progress every few days, inviting their readers to empathise with this new club of non-smokers. Stopping smoking was an activity to be shared and was presented in the *Mirror* as almost a lifestyle choice in itself, as divorced from the health aspects of tobacco as much as Andy Capp's persistent 'drooper'. When some of the journalists admitted defeat and began smoking again, their failure was reported with humour and high spirits as an understandable weakness that all smokers go through. What was not mentioned were the publicised dangers of smoking to which they had once more presumably made themselves susceptible.[49] A similar story was followed on the radio as Judith Chalmers and Doreen Forsyth both had their semi-successful attempts to quit recorded month by month. Although their efforts were interspersed with more serious reports on the Second World Conference on Smoking and Health in 1971, plus interviews with Richard Dunwoody of ASH, a certain clubbability was emphasised that made stopping almost as much an everyday social activity as smoking itself.[50] That this was the case is illustrated in Ben Petmecky's novel which personalised the plight of the common man's attempts to quit. The hero, Arthur Matthews, does eventually stop to relieve himself of his Freudian, infantile desire to suck at the equivalent of a nipple or a thumb. But the tribulations he experiences throughout the story only serve to demonstrate the difficulty of giving up and the sympathy which ought to be given to those who fail at one attempt but smoke on to quit another day.[51]

As the dissonance embedded within the culture of smoking alleviated the pressures to quit, so too did it readily permit the entry of new smokers into its ranks. Smoking rates are again on the increase for youths and juveniles, but in the 1950s and 1960s children began to smoke for the same reasons they had always begun: to symbolically enter an adult world. This was despite high levels of knowledge of the dangers of smoking about which children had been educated at school. A number of surveys were carried out into children's and adolescents' attitudes to smoking from the late 1950s. In 1959, as little as 6–8 per cent of boys and girls aged eleven to eighteen believed that smoking did not cause any harm, nearly 60 per cent accepting the link with cancer and the rest acknowledging some degree of physical damage caused by smoking.[52] In 1967, 69 per cent of adolescent smokers (aged between sixteen and twenty) and 87 per cent of non-smokers accepted that smoking increased the risk of lung cancer, suggesting that the actual proportion of adolescents who had at least heard of the risks of smoking was heading towards 100 per cent.[53] Young smokers had therefore been told of the dangers by the 1960s and, as with adults, proved adept at accepting or rejecting the evidence presented to them. Whether they believed it or otherwise, it appears to have had little effect on smoking rates. In 1959, by the time boys left school approximately one-third had become regular smokers, another nine out of ten of whom had tried smoking at some earlier stage. The equivalent figures for girls were approximately just less than 10 per cent, with two-thirds having experimented with smoking.[54] Other studies confirmed this trend of younger starting ages for boys, and higher smoking rates were also noted among secondary schools as opposed to grammar schools and among juvenile delinquents and young soldiers.[55] By 1964, only 14 per cent of males and 25 per cent of females had not tried smoking by the time they were adolescents aged sixteen to twenty, and in 1966 50 per cent of boys and 36 per cent of girls aged fourteen to sixteen classified themselves as regular or occasional smokers.[56] Although this figure was high compared with other studies which had the figure at approximately one-third, it was clear that experimenting with smoking was an almost universal ritual of growing up in post-war Britain.[57]

An increasingly affluent teenage market enabled levels of individual consumption to rise and encouraged shop owners not to turn down this source of demand. Interviews with children less than sixteen years of age revealed that they had no difficulty in obtaining cigarettes, the local shop rather than the tobacconist or vending machine being the major source of supply. Here, cigarettes were often obtained in singles from shopkeepers who were willing to break open packets to cater for limited incomes. Their attitudes to juvenile smoking might have been influenced by short-term financial rewards, but wider opinions held by a pro-smoking society suggested that for many the phenomenon was not problematic. Thirty-four per cent of young smokers in 1960 claimed that their parents did not mind their smoking and this figure was still 10 per cent for those with parents who were non-smokers themselves.[58] This was a culture which if it did not actually encourage juvenile smoking did not condemn it either, children for years practising on chocolate cigarettes before, as health campaigners worried, they moved on to the real thing.[59] Anecdotal evidence also suggests a lack of concern among parents, one mother even being seen putting two cigarettes in her nine-year-old child's pockets as he got on the bus for a school trip.[60] In another study in 1963, one-third of children claimed to have received their first cigarette from their mother, father or uncle, though this proportion was later reduced when some children admitted that it had not been with their family's knowledge or consent.[61]

McKennell's findings of 1967 summarise what many other investigations had previously found and would subsequently discover.[62] Whereas most children experimented with their first cigarettes before the age of twelve, it was not until they were sixteen that they became regular smokers, the intervening years forming a very clear intermediate stage between non-smoking and smoking in which 'curiosity', 'the desire to appear big and grown-up' and 'to conform to the behaviour of one's friends' featured prominently.[63] Parental attitudes were observed to have a significant effect on juvenile smoking, and although all claimed to be against their child's smoking many became lax and indifferent in practice. On the impact of the health campaigns, McKennell emphasised the 'boomerang' effect which frequently occurred when the message provided by the publicity material was too divorced from the recipient's standpoint. Apparently, all the adolescents and adults he interviewed had heard of the relationship between smoking and lung cancer but smokers often remained sceptical and failed to apply the knowledge to themselves. Adolescents found 'rationalisations for exempting themselves from risk'[64] and held a number of what he identified as popular misconceptions: that there was much disagreement between the experts; that doctors smoked as much as other people; and that lung cancer caused fewer deaths than road accidents. Children, just as much as adults, then, were actively participating in a pro-smoking culture which often interpreted scientific evidence to its own varied ends.

What is apparent from all the public health investigations of the 1950s, 1960s and 1970s is the extent to which the population was aware of the publicised dangers of smoking. Yet it would be naive to assume that awareness of the official view of the relationship between smoking and lung cancer necessarily resulted in an acceptance of that relationship and a consequent alteration of individual smoking behaviour. Too few smokers behaved as utility maximisers, rationally offsetting long-term damage to health against short-term pleasure. The story of the reception of science in this period is far too complicated for such a form of analysis. For the vast majority of smokers, news of the developments in smoking and health research was filtered through different media, most of which held a similar range of ideological and social preferences about smoking commonly found among the general population, scientists included. Once reaching the eyes or the ears of the smoker, the news was then located within a cultural framework which might range from a rational acceptance of the known facts and result in a giving up of the habit to a fatalistic hope that those who disputed the evidence would turn out to be correct and that one could continue smoking in the meantime. That the authority of epidemiology as a science of 'proof' was still being contested in this period provided much fuel for those smokers who wished to remain sceptical of the evidence. The basis for this criticism was found in the cult of individuality which opposed the homogenising influences of all forms of policy based on perceived standardising statistics. This was an ideology which had dominated the understanding of smoking from the early nineteenth century, and which was becoming accessible to an expanding number of affluent and educated ordinary smokers who recognised the importance of the cigarette to their sense of self.

The centrality of smoking to masculine and feminine identity was developed from an early age in the desire to appear sophisticated and older and was reinforced by a culture which made the cigarette especially polysemous. From its sexual and erotic connotations in the ritual of courtship to the communality of masculine camaraderie at work or in the public house, the cigarette served a variety of purposes in the interactions of everyday life. It thus maintained its position as both at once an ordinary and an extraordinary visible commun- icator of social relations. When smoking was held to be harmful to health, therefore, the medical profession was not competing simply with the defences and protestations of the tobacco manufacturers or the belligerence, scepticism or fatalism of smokers, but the whole wider promotion of smoking which refused to deny the cigarette's crucial role in everyday life. Ironically, in all of the investigations summarised above, researchers always found that the majority of smokers and non-smokers were actually in favour of transforming this cultural climate, supporting bans on smoking in public places which would ultimately make it a much less normal everyday habit. The economic and bureaucratic powers, which included tobacco manufacturers, civic offi- cials and providers of public transport and private communal entertainment, were able to oppose successfully such incursions into 'this smoking world'. In this, they were supported by a cultural framework first formulated by an elite literate group of smokers in the nineteenth century, but which had come to dominate many aspects of the popular culture of smoking during the 1950s and 1960s.

Notes

1 I. Fleming, *Thunderball* (1961; London, Triad/Ganada, 1978).
2 *Ibid.*, p. 71.
3 I. Svevo, *Confessions of Zeno* (1923; Harmondsworth, Penguin, 1964). The point is elaborated at greater length in R. Klein, *Cigarettes are Sublime* (London, Picador, 1995).
4 A. Cartwright, F. M. Martin and J. G. Thomson, *Consequences of a Health Campaign* (1959), in Kew Public Record Office (hereafter PRO), MH 55 2225, *1958–1959: Smoking and Lung Cancer: Health Education Policy: Correspondence.*

5 A. Cartwright, F. M. Martin and J. G. Thomson, 'Health hazards of smoking: current popular beliefs', *British Journal of Preventive and Social Medicine*, 14 (1960), 160–6.

6 A. C. McKennell, *Smoking and Health: A Preliminary Report on a Continuing Study of Public Attitudes to Smoking* (January 1964), in PRO, MH 151 27, *1964–1966: Smoking and Health: Social Surveys*.

7 *Guardian* (13 January 1964), p. 8, (16 January 1964), p. 18.

8 A. H. Dunhill, *The Gentle Art of Smoking* (London, Max Reinhardt, 1954).

9 C. Mackenzie, *Sublime Tobacco* (London, Chatto & Windus, 1957).

10 C. Mackenzie, 'Sidelight', *Spectator* (19 February 1954), 206.

11 J. B. Priestley, 'Fifty years of tobacco', *New Statesman*, 62 (1961), 47–8.

12 *Daily Mirror* (15 October 1966), p. 1; *London Evening Standard* (9 April 1963), pp. 18–20.

13 BBC Written Archives, Caversham (hereafter BBC), Radio Scripts, Sigrid Lockwood, *Tobacco Smoke*, 7 August 1950; Donald Boyd, *In Praise of Tobacco*, 30 August 1956.

14 *Guardian* (23 June 1956), p. 5, (20 December 1956), p. 6, (22 November 1965), p. 7, (23 December 1965), p. 6.

15 *The Times* (7 April 1958), p. 7f.

16 *Daily Express* (12 July 1957), p. 6.

17 *Lancet*, i (1958), 680–1. Perhaps unsurprisingly, as medical journals became more committed to the anti-tobacco cause, smokers were instead found to be the more 'neurotic' type of individual: N. Cherry and K. Kiernan, 'Personality scores and smoking behaviour: a longitudinal study', *British Journal of Preventive and Social Medicine*, 30 (1976), 123–31.

18 *Daily Mirror* (22 June 1968), p. 20.

19 *The Times* (20 July 1957), p. 8f.

20 *Daily Mirror* (28 June 1957), p. 10.

21 *Ibid.* (3 March 1962), p. 8, (2 February 1965), p. 6.

22 *Guardian* (14 May 1956), p. 6, (17 May 1956), p. 8; BBC, Radio Scripts, *Any Answers*, 5 April 1956, 15 March 1962; PRO, MH 55 1012, *1953–1957: Cancer of the Lung: Investigation: Correspondence*; MH 55 2221, *1954–1957: Cancer of the Lung and Tobacco Smoking: Minister's Statement: Correspondence Arising*.

23 G. W. Lynch, 'Smoking habits of medical and non-medical university staff: changes since RCP report', *British Medical Journal*, i (1963), 852–5; J. M. Bynner, *Medical Students' Attitudes Towards Smoking: A Report on a Survey Carried out for the Ministry of Health* (London, HMSO, 1967); C. Fletcher and R. Doll, 'A survey of doctors' attitudes to smoking', *British Journal of Preventive and Social Medicine*, 23 (1969), 145–53.

24 PRO, MH 151 26, *1962–1964: Smoking and Health: Social Surveys*: A. C. McKennell, *Results of a Copy Test on Five Posters* (1963); A. C. McKennell, *Report of the Audience Reaction Test of the Film 'Smoking and You'* (1964); Smith Warden Ltd, *Observations on the Smoking and Health Campaign Being Conducted by H. M. Government* (1962).

25 *Guardian* (6 August 1963), p. 4.
26 K. Mullen, *A Healthy Balance: Glaswegian Men Talking About Health, Tobacco and A lcohol* (Aldershot, Avebury, 1993).
27 A. Marsh and S. McKay, *Poor Smokers* (London, Policy Studies Institute, 1994).
28 H. Graham, *When Life's a Drag: Women, Smoking and Disadvantage* (London, HMSO, 1993); I. Waldron, 'Patterns and causes of gender differences in smoking', *Social Science and Medicine*, 32 (1991), 989–1005. See also the Canadian research, L. Greaves, *Smoke Screen: Women's Smoking and Social Control* (London, Scarlet Press, 1996).
29 *The Times* (19 March 1954), p. 10c, (3 January 1955), p. 7c, (1 March 1955), p. 4e.
30 *Daily Express* (1 March 1963), p. 3, (22 October 1969), p. 7.
31 *Guardian* (1 January 1962), p. 7.
32 *Liverpool Echo* (1 May 1969), p. 1; *The Times* (2 May 1969), p. 4a.
33 G. Parr, 'Smoking', *Sight and Sound* (December 1997), 30–3.
34 BBC, Smoking Policy, T16/583, *Programme Policy: Smoking 1959–1967*; R78/2695/1, *Smoking and Health*.
35 Advertising Inquiry Council, *Advertising Tobacco: A Study of Expenditures and of Trends in Sales Promotion* (1962), in PRO, MH 55 2233: *March 8–28, 1962: Smoking and Lung Cancer: Action Following Report of Royal College of Physicians on Smoking and Health: Policy and Publicity. Correspondence.*
36 *The Times*, various issues, 1965–70.
37 E. S. Atkinson, 'Cigarette advertising: a history', *British Journal of Photography*, 128 (1981), 1190–1.
38 BBC, Radio Scripts, *Roundabout*, 19 March 1962.
39 *Guardian* (22 October 1954), p. 6.
40 BBC, Radio Scripts, *Woman's Hour*, 9 May 1947, 11 June 1952.
41 A. King, *The Cigarette Habit: A Scientific Cure* (Kingswood, The World's Work, 1913); J. H. Wodehouse, *The Smoking Habit: Its Dangers and Cure* (London, Health for All, 1927).
42 W. Hawkins, *'My Dear Old Pipe!'* (Peterborough, the author, 1947); J. C. Romer, *How to Give Up Smoking* (Rushden, Stanley L. Hunt, 1949); H. Brean, *How to Stop Smoking* (Kingswood, The World's Work, 1952).
43 M. H. Noor, *How to Stop Smoking* (Bradford, Norton Wells, 1949).
44 L. Bell, *How to Stop Smoking* (London, Postlib, 1947), p. 9.
45 M. H. Reynard, *How to Stop Smoking Cigarettes* (Bristol, Movana, n. d.); H. A. Clarke, *How to Overcome the Smoking Habit and Conquer Craving* (Dawley, Shropshire, the author, n. d.); E. Chesser, *When and How to Stop Smoking* (London, Jarrolds, 1963).
46 K. Salzer, *Thirteen Ways to Break the Smoking Habit* (London, Duckworth and Co., 1959).
47 *Guardian* (31 May 1957), p. 8, (3 July 1957), p. 3, (12 July 1957), p. 7.
48 *Ibid.* (2 January 1963), p. 6, (8 January 1963), p. 8.
49 *Daily Mirror*, various issues, January 1971.

50 BBC, Radio Scripts, *Woman's Hour*, 27 January 1971, 1 July 1971, 20 September 1971, 31 December 1971.

51 B. Petmecky, *Confessions of a Tobacco Addict* (London, Muller, 1963).

52 A. Cartwright and J. G. Thomson, 'Young smokers: an attitude study among school children, touching also on parental influence', *British Journal of Preventive and Social Medicine*, 14 (1960), 28–34.

53 A. C. McKennell and R. K. Thomas, *Adults' and Adolescents' Smoking Habits and Attitudes* (London, HMSO, 1967), p. 131.

54 A Study Group of the Public Health Department, 'The smoking habits of school children', *British Journal of Preventive and Social Medicine*, 13 (1959), 1–4.

55 PRO, MH 55 2226, *Jan.–Nov. 1960: Smoking and Lung Cancer: Health Education Policy*; J. P. Crowdy, 'Smoking habits of young soldiers', *British Journal of Preventive and Social Medicine*, 15 (1961), 84–8; S. J. Dimond, 'Smoking habits of delinquent boys', *British Journal of Preventive and Social Medicine*, 18 (1964), 52–4; J. W. Palmer, 'Smoking, caning, and delinquency in a secondary modern school', *British Journal of Preventive and Social Medicine*, 19 (1965), 18–23.

56 PRO, MH 154 188, *1964–1967: Smoking and Health: Social Survey – Children*.

57 B. Lemin, 'A study of the smoking habits of 14 year old pupils in six schools in Aberdeen', *Medical Officer* (5 August 1966), 82–5.

58 Cartwright and Thomson, 'Young smokers', p. 31.

59 PRO, MH 154 174, *1962–1964: Smoking and Health: Associated Problems Related to Children*; *Daily Mirror* (5 July 1968), p. 15.

60 Joint Consultative Committee for Primary and Secondary Education, *Smoking and Cancer of the Lung*, in PRO, MH 55 2226.

61 W. Duffy, *An Eighteen Month Study into the Pattern of Smoking Among Ten Thousand Children Attending Thirty Schools in Staffordshire*, in PRO, MH 154 174.

62 J. M. Bynner, *The Young Smoker* (London, HMSO, 1969); A. Marsh and J. Matheson, *Smoking Attitudes and Behaviour* (London, HMSO, 1983).

63 McKennel and Thomas, *Adults' and Adolescents' Smoking*, pp. 2–5.

64 *Ibid.*

Conclusion, or 'why lighting up is cool again'

In Tony Harrison's recent poem/film, *Prometheus*, an 'old cough-wracked ex-miner' visits the abandoned, dilapidated cinema in which he spent his smoking youth. From there he watches on the screen a reworking of the classical Greek myth, a modern Prometheus represented as a golden idol forged from the bodies of several redundant miners. The messenger of the gods, Hermes, takes the statue through Europe on a journey down the Danube to Athens, visiting on the way Dresden, Birkenau, Auschwitz, Ceaucescu's Romania and other scenes of the punishments of the twentieth century metaphorically meted out by Zeus when he discovered that Prometheus had stolen the fire hidden from mortals. The Promethian spirit of daring disobedience is seen too in the continued smoking of the old man watching in the cinema. Mourning the decline of the pits, the trade unions and the socialist ideas he had spent his life fighting for, as well as the working-class popular culture of the cinema, the dance hall, the pub and the bookie that he had so enjoyed, he smokes on in defiance of a society that has wrecked and prohibited all that he had been brought up to appreciate and value. He berates the rules that do not permit him to smoke, before reminiscing about the great smoking days of the silver screen:

> T'whole bloody place full of Nos:
> no bloody smoking, spitting, booze,
> no even lighting up in t'loos.
> [. . .]
> In t'pit and t'flea-pit cigarettes
> were contraband to these tight gets.
> Underground makes sense. But bloody 'ell
> banning fags in t'flicks as well!
> Sometimes I think t'whole bloody land
> 's made bloody baccy contraband.

When Bogey lit up so did I,
smoke curling past one closed eye.
Bogey gets best smoker's prize,
cig-smoke crinkling up his eyes.
[...]
Who smokes now? Them were the days
when women smoked in negligées.
[...]
I learned cig-skills from what I'd seen
sexy smokers do on t'screen.
I were convinced that good cig-suction
were t'secret weapon of seduction.
It seemed that shared cigs allus led
them passionate puffers off to bed.
And when you knew they'd had their shag
first thing both did were light a fag!
And have a fag's what I do here
in memory of yesteryear.
'Cos now this place is derelict
I can't get chucked out, nabbed or nicked
for smoking all them fags their law
wouldn't let me smoke afore.
I come here now to treat missen
to all them fags not dragged on then.

The memories stir his defiance. He raises his fist at Hermes on the screen and turns to his own cinema audience:

Smokers of the world unite!
On t'count o' three, all light up, right?
1–2–3 ...
You've all been cowed.
I've changed the law and it's allowed.
Try again then. 1–2–3:
all light your fags now after me.[1]

His plea, though, is doomed. Hercules does not appear to rescue Prometheus or the old man from the daily damage he is doing to his lungs. At the end of the poem, the old man attempts to destroy Hermes by lighting the petrol at the messenger's feet with his 'half-smoked ciggy'. He believes he has beaten his tormentor, only for the immortal Hermes to reappear and mock the old man's pathetic bravado. Crushed, the old man staggers back to his seat, his smoker's cough crippling his movements until, with one last emphysematic whimper, he collapses and dies.

The old man completes, and in many ways summarises, the array of characters chosen in this book to illustrate or highlight certain features in the history of smoking in British popular culture. He most directly resembles Andy Capp, that comic product of the mass market who is self consciously and belligerently working class. But his paean to the smoking culture of his cinema-going days mirrors much of that language and celebration of 'the weed' found in chapter 1. His personalised memories of the films and stars that he saw individualise his habit in a manner paralleling the idiosyncrasies of Sherlock Holmes. His smoking is likewise not idle or self indulgent. The cigarette clutched between his fingers has become, for him, a symbol of socialism, of an age now past and of his anger at a society which seeks to control and discipline him in the economy, in politics and in popular culture. For a brief moment, smoking cigarettes re-enfranchises him and locates him as a romantic figure with a lineage stretching back to Bertie Cecil and self referentially running through Humphrey Bogart, Edward G. Robinson and James Cagney. And, just as J. B. Priestley, Harold Wilson, Stanley Baldwin and the literary adventurer Richard Hannay held the briar pipe to be quintessentially British, so too does the old man make his cigarette a symbol of his nation. His country, though, is very different from that smoked for in the semi-elitist journal articles of the nineteenth century. It is instead a further extension of that egalitarian 'culture for democracy' of Priestley's *English Journey*. His smoking represents a working-class Britain in which mass-based, urban and communal leisure patterns were there to be celebrated, not mocked or condemned. Yet within his praise for the homogeneous cigarette, the anonymous old man draws heavily on that smoking culture made dominant through its persistence in the printed document. Despite the demands of any physical addiction, he continues to smoke to his death because the cigarette is a crucial signifier of his individuality and his identity. Here, he continues that obstinate refusal to incorporate the advice of the medical profession into his everyday consumption routines. The actions of this dying socialist mirror the fanaticism of such right-wing libertarians as the *Daily Express'* Chapman Pincher who have opposed the perceived attempts of governments and health campaigners to direct individual decisions. With his references to Cagney and Bogart, the old man illustrates a new rebelliousness in the actions of smokers, each directing an individualist crusade against the supposed health-obsessed fitness culture of the late twentieth century. His agonised death is merely a bitter and ironic end to a smoking life dedicated to resisting the attempts to direct popular culture. While he smokes he symbolises an almost subcultural trend to posit the cigarette as a signifier of rebellion against so-called 'health faddism'. And this, in turn, explains why in recent years – as countless contemporary films, magazines, books and individuals attest – 'lighting up is cool again'.[2]

Despite all that is now known by medical experts about the effects of the cigarette on heart disease, lung cancer and other illnesses, as well as the dangers of environmental tobacco smoke, a culture of smoking has persisted which has in 1999 resulted in a rise in the number of adult smokers for the first time in twenty years.[3] This culture is firmly rooted in that liberal notion of smoking which came to dominate in the late nineteenth century. Ideas of independence and individuality were constantly held up to temper the homogenising influences of the mass market and to resist the likewise stand-ardised formulas of health campaigners in the post-Second World War period. But while this culture of celebrated individuality was essentially masculine and largely bourgeois in the nineteenth century because of the nature of the books and journals through which it was promoted, by the late twentieth century it has become a rhetoric or discourse which all can now borrow and utilise. So much is this the case that a great variety of smokers from all social classes and genders have written their eulogies to the 'divine lady nicotine'. While the old man of Harrison's *Prometheus* illustrates one end of the social spectrum, a more traditional hymn in praise of the cigar can be found in the Cuban Gabriel Cabrera Infante's work. The culture persists too in the ash-tray art of Damien Hirst; in the academic and literary 'ode' to the cigarette by the American Richard Klein; in the ironic smoking novels of Richard Beard and Christopher Buckley; and, in sharp contrast to the identities of the original proselytisers of the smoking 'cult', in a recent album by the Canadian singer k.d. lang, *Drag*, which features such smoking classics as 'Smoke Dreams', 'My Old Addiction' and 'Love is Like a Cigarette'.[4] In this sense, we all share in that culture of smoking made dominant in late nineteenth-century periodical literature.

But while notions of independence and individuality have been more demo-cratically applied to the cigarette as well as the pipe and the cigar, what is also significant about these concepts is the way they have come to influence the politics of tobacco and health. In the arguments which have arisen over the health effects of smoking it is the duties, responsibilities and legitimate spheres of influence of government activity which have been pitted against the rights and freedom of choice of the individual. Perhaps unsurprisingly for a debate contested by powerful economic concerns, a certain polarisation has taken place between health campaigners and pro-smoking forces. The former have sought to justify the extension of state activity through the scientific under-standing of addiction, involuntary activity and passive smoking, but the latter's liberalism has often been transformed into an industry-sponsored libertarian-ism far removed from the sophisticated mixture of rights and duties associated with the Victorian creed. What both sides have often done is to obscure the complex social and cultural factors necessary for any understanding of smok-ing in contemporary societies.

The tobacco debate has revolved around the role of the state. Because pre-ventive medicine ultimately relies on some degree of individual responsibility, there is a fine line between legitimate government advice and unjustified gov-ernment control. Pro-smoking bodies have therefore argued in several industry-financed books that beyond all the defences of smoking based on the economic and social importance of tobacco, the validity of the medical evidence and the alternative theses presented in psychology, there is also an ideological aspect. They argue that because individuals are 'free to pursue their own unique goals' they have a responsibility too to respect 'the freedom of other individuals to pursue their own ends simultaneously'. It is assumed that all individuals have the ability to make 'rational and coherent decisions regarding the con-duct of their own lives'. This pre-supposes the implausible scenario in which consumers have perfect access to all information in order to make such deci-sions, yet the argument is extended to call for a general limitation of govern-ment activity in the free market: 'if government is going to be allowed to enact coercive measures that arbitrarily restrict the liberties and trample the rights of smokers, where will employment of this restrictive power end?'[5]

The main organisation through which such arguments are propagated in Britain is FOREST, or the Freedom Organisation for the Right to Enjoy Smoking Tobacco. Launched by Sir Christopher Foxley Norris in 1979 and Chaired by Lord (Ralph) Harris of High Cross, the tobacco industry-funded smokers' rights group set out to 'restore and establish freedom of choice'.[6] Throughout the 1980s and 1990s it has reacted against the 'liberty snatchers' of ASH and persistently called for greater provision for smokers on trains and in restaurants, invoking always the traditional 'British virtue' of 'tolerance'. The tobacco issue is frequently presented as a Pandora's Box to be opened by medical paternalists, the 'mad officials' of Brussels and regulation-obsessed 'socialists', all of whom would prefer we live in a 'climate of fear' whereby medicine becomes 'a mask for the enhancement of state power and the destruction of individual liberty'.[7] In its latest publication, *Murder a Cigarette*, Harris and Judith Hatton accept that smoking is a factor in increasing the risk of disease, but argue, with some effect, that these risks have been grossly exaggerated. Their concluding remarks return, however, to the issue of liberty, suggesting in apocalyptic tones that the 'SS brigade' with its 'perverted puritanical enjoyment of stopping the enjoyment of others' is leading a tyrannical yet supposedly 'democratic' process which aims to 'steamroller' a whole range of 'individual likes and dislikes'.[8]

At the opposite end of the spectrum are the health campaigners who have approached the question of the liberal individual in an entirely different manner. Though a shared cultural belief has been shown in chapters 9 and 10 to have limited the early anti-smoking message throughout the 1960s, organisations such as ASH and the BMA have begun to lead a more pro-active movement. In particular, the 1984 campaign by the BMA turned the liberal individual argument on its head in its positioning of the smoker as a 'victim' of the manipulationist tendencies of the tobacco industry. Such a policy theoretically provided smokers with 'rights against identifiable victimisers' and allowed the 'expert' to speak and act for them.[9] As the BMA Secretary, Dr John Harvard, said at the initial press conference: 'Tobacco companies are responsible for a massive cover-up exercise carried out worldwide by an industry which callously ignores the medical facts . . . Doctors are in a unique position to speak out for the rights of the individual. As doctors, we must all now speak out or be guilty of collusion.'[10] Later policies have spoken instead of the rights of the 'innocent' non-smoker, forced as he or she is to breathe in the dangerous fumes of environmental tobacco smoke. Harris and Hatton argue that science and ideology have been closely linked here, the passive smoking issue becoming a powerful rhetorical tool to extend anti-smoking measures: 'a totally bogus invention designed to stigmatise smokers'.[11] The research into passive smoking has so far been considerably less thorough and by no means as conclusive as that for primary health damage, but it has obtained a dominating cultural authority, with groups such as ASH working hard to ensure the immediate dissemination of any new developments in medical knowledge. The death of the entertainer Roy Castle from what has been understood as passive smoking made awareness of the issue particularly acute and this has enabled the identification of the smoker not as a free individual but as a social deviant actively involved in harming innocent bystanders.[12]

These two ideological standpoints – the smoker as victim of the manufacturer or of his or her own addiction, and the non-smoker as victim of the smoker – have resulted in a much more aggressive campaigning programme. ASH has lobbied the government to limit the promotion of tobacco, it has deliberately attacked the tobacco industry for allegedly withholding facts about its 'lethal product' and, until the collapse of the case in March 1999, it has encouraged 'individuals to come forward and sue the tobacco companies for the damage it has done'.[13] More generally, it has promoted a policy to change cultural attitudes to smoking so that smokers will come to be seen by society as involved in a dirty and immoral addiction which runs counter to the health-conscious 1990s. The trend has become more acute in the United States, blanket bans on smoking in public places serving to position the smoker as 'pariah', cast aside by the wider community.[14] British comment-ators have looked across the Atlantic for signs of cultural change and several have predicted that in Britain, too, 'smoking may soon become, like sex, an activity that can be conducted only in private among consenting adults'.[15]

It is against such a background that a backlash against the health-promoting culture has been held to have occurred. According to this analysis, smokers are rebelling against 'the public control and self-control of individual life through science and reason'. According to Rabin and Sugarman, writing from across the Atlantic: 'This resistance is a facet of the glorification of the uniqueness and expressiveness of the "authentic" person in American culture. It symbolises an individualism that has long been seen as accentuated in the United States as compared with other democratic and modernised societies.'[16] The reaction might be stronger in the United States, where the controls on smoking have been much more stringent, than in Britain, but the effects of the reaction are still noticeable, fought as it has been largely through Holly-wood films. In such international successes as *Pulp Fiction*, *Basic Instinct*, *Smoke*, *Sleepers*, *Die Hard with a Vengeance* and *The English Patient*, smoking has been glamorised through its association with an attractive or rebellious lead actor. A recent study of popular films conducted by the Health Educa-tion Authority found a number of significant differences in the top ten films of 1990 and 1995: films in 1995 featured four times as much smoking as in 1990; twice as many smokers were the stars of the films in 1995; the Marlboro brand was especially promoted as a desirable cigarette in 1995; smoking was increasingly associated with intense and stressful images rather than sexy and romantic ones; smoking served as shorthand for the 'baddies'; there had been an increase in positive verbal references to smoking; and three times as many smoking characters were portrayed as 'rebellious' in 1995 than in 1990.[17]

But if the promotion of smoking in film is the direct consequence of the reaction to the perceived draconianism of US smoking and health measures, there has also been a more general celebration of smoking in many areas of British popular culture. Youth and lifestyle magazines have represented smoking in a fashionable light, images of stars often connoting ideas of power and individuality. Men's, women's and fashion magazines such as *Loaded, GQ, FHM, Vogue, Elle, The Face, I-D, Dazed and Confused* and *Time Out* have been studied and shown to have portrayed smoking as a 'realistic' part of everyday life for the fashionable and glamorous. Often a 'mixed message' is conveyed as anti-smoking articles are placed alongside attractive images of young smokers. In just a three month period, *Loaded* and *The Face* were each seen to have presented over twenty positive smoking images to their readers.[18] The policy has been deliberate. In 1998 *Loaded* magazine ran a special feature on an attractive model smoking cigars in her underwear. The publication date clashed with the month of the National No-Smoking Day, but the *Daily Star* newspaper chose to reprint the images from *Loaded* instead of the anti-smoking message. They appeared under the headline, 'Michelle lights up to celebrate No Smoking Day'.[19] Health policy workers have conducted extensive studies into such magazines and have found them to be important sources for the reinforcement of smoking among young people.[20]

The smoking revival permeates other media too. Newspapers continue to run features on 'the way we smoked' when cigarettes were not known to damage health.[21] The emergence of the modern cigar bar has provoked widest comment as this American phenomenon has reached Britain. While prohibitive costs determine the indulgence in Cuban cigars in pleasant surroundings as a financially elite culture, articles present the new cigar cult in aspirational style. They borrow directly from the language of smoking of the nineteenth century, inviting readers to 'strike a light and savour these ostentatious smokes like fine wines'.[22] This has led to a flood of books and magazines celebrating the cigar and smoking more generally in recent years, collections of 'the cigar in art' firmly rooting the smoking of this type of tobacco alongside the finest aesthetic experiences of life.[23] The cigar also enables the consumer to share and enjoy the identity of 'smoker', to project an individuality of nonconformity, or at least an independence from the pro-health culture, but the attendant risks are minimal compared with the cigarette since cigar smoking does not involve inhalation. For those smokers who can afford it, then, cigars offer an opportunity to experience a traditional smoking culture mixed with a modern urge to demonstrate how one's appreciation sets one apart from the mortality-conscious crowd.

This renewed emphasis on the positive aspects of smoking does not of course override the massive continuities in social and economic circumstances which increase the importance of smoking to groups in deprived or stressful life circumstances.[24] Nor does it deny the continued importance of advertising as at least a significant visual representation of the cigarette, though scholars continue to debate the direct impact such economic images have on actual smoking rates.[25] What the pro-smoking culture does account for, however, is the increased smoking rates among girls in the 1990s and the eventual rise in adult smoking rates noted for the first time in 1999. The positive smoking images have been closely related to the high rates of girls' smoking in that girls are not smoking for compensatory factors to do with low self esteem but to share in a general pro-smoking environment which encourages those who are already self confident and socially skilled to take to cigarettes to complement their self identity. While sport and the desire to be fit have dissuaded some boys from smoking, these factors have not been so prominent among girls wishing to appear slim and attractive.[26] So it is this broader cultural framework which continues to associate smoking with positive attributes which explains why it was, in 1996, that 15 per cent of girls aged between eleven and fifteen were regular smokers compared with just 11 per cent of boys.[27]

Perhaps what is more significant about the above interpretation is that it comes from public health workers. Throughout the post-war period, health campaigns have failed to overturn the culture which encourages juveniles to smoke. The explanation offered in this book is that there was a discrepancy between the culture of smoking and the rationality of health education. It is this culture, a direct descendant from the context of late nineteenth-century liberalism, which has maintained a complex but enduring legacy in the relationship between smoking, identity and individuality. Neither the understandings of tobacco offered in the health literature, in the political debates about government intervention and the sanctity of the individual, or in the law courts which have attempted to understand why people continued to smoke after 1962 have matched the cultural interpretation necessary for any complete analysis of smoking and society. Indeed, it is only within the last few years that the environment of the smoker has been fully embraced in health campaigns. The most recent anti-smoking images have appealed not to the rational sense of the young smoker or suggested didactically that smoking is not good for self image. Instead, they have presented images which recognise that smoking is a central part of youth culture but that visually sophisticated teenagers must trade off cigarettes with other beauty products, since the effects of smoking on the skin and complexion only serve to offset the positive aspects of wearing make-up.[28]

Whether such campaigns will have any success in reducing juvenile smoking rates is difficult to predict. The increase in the number of adult smokers demonstrates that the perceived problem is more widespread. It is summed up in the attitudes of smokers who can be remarkably well informed about the health risks of smoking, yet continue to smoke because lifestyle decisions, the pleasure of the tobacco itself and the cultural connotations of the cigarette are more important than long-term health considerations. To dismiss their justifications as the self deception or self delusion of the inebriate is far too simplistic since for many their smoking is at a rate below that at which pure physical addiction is said to occur. To quote just one example from any number of articles which have appeared in the national press throughout the 1990s:

> And smokers are the people that I want to be – poets and fighters, not lawyers or accountants. More than once I've ended a spate of abstinence because I've been sitting in a café and I've seen a woman looking hip and jaunty sporting a Marlboro Light and I think – that's me, that's me! It might read like the behaviour of a teenager but it feels like a celebration of life.
>
> I know a lot of it's delusion. I know that middle managers smoke and that there's nothing cool about lung cancer. I know I'm addicted and that getting over that isn't about some strangling control thing. And one day I want to have a baby and I know that ultimately I want to CHOOSE LIFE.
>
> Maybe next week.[29]

In the context of chapter 9, such journalism might be labelled flippant and irresponsible, but it also encapsulates a number of trends which have come together in this book. In its reference to the branded commodity it alludes to the crucial influence of multinational and monopoly manufacture in the history of smoking. In its emphasis on the centrality of the cigarette to identity it reflects the pervasive nature of a liberal culture of smoking originally bourgeois but now democratic and universal, shared across classes and genders. And in its reference to the scientific understanding of tobacco it demonstrates just how much medicine was, and continues to be, located within a wider culture of smoking. The cigar, the pipe and the cigarette might be discouraged by an increasingly dominant health-conscious social policy, but the older celebration of the 'perfect pleasures' of the 'divine lady nicotine' continue to underlie the significance of tobacco in British popular culture.

Notes

1 T. Harrison, *Prometheus* (London, Faber & Faber, 1998), pp. 28–30.

2 The particular quotation is from the cover of *Bizarre* magazine, March/April 1998, though a similar reference may have been made from countless other articles over the last few years.

3 *Guardian* (4 March 1999), p. 22.

4 G. Cabrera Infante, *Holy Smoke* (1985; London, Faber & Faber, 1997); R. Klein, *Cigarettes are Sublime* (London, Picador, 1995); R. Beard, *X20* (London, Flamingo, 1997); C. Buckley, *Thank You for Smoking* (London, Andre Deutsch, 1995); k.d. lang, *Drag* (Warner Bros Records Inc., 1997).

5 R. D. Tollison and R. E. Wagner, *Smoking and the State: Social Costs, Rent Seeking and Public Policy* (Lexington, MA, Lexington Books, 1988), pp. 109, 114; R. D. Tollison (ed.), *Smoking and Society: Towards a More Balanced Assessment* (Lexington, MA, Lexington Books, 1986).

6 P. Taylor, *Smoke Ring: The Politics of Tobacco* (London, Bodley Head, 1984), pp. 133–4.

7 C. R. Tame and D. Botsford, *Not Just Tobacco: Health Scares, Medical Paternalism and Individual Liberty* (London, FOREST, 1996); J. Leavey (ed.), *The FOREST Guide to Smoking in London* (London, Quiller, 1996). A full list of FOREST's numerous publications, including its newsletter, *Free Choice*, can be obtained from its offices at 2 Grosvenor Gardens, London SW1W 0DH.

8 R. Harris and J. Hatton, *Murder a Cigarette: The Smoking Debate* (London, Duckworth, 1998), p. 145.

9 R. L. Rabin and S. D. Sugarman (eds), *Smoking Policy: Law, Politics and Culture* (Oxford, Oxford University Press, 1993), p. 9.

10 BMA, *Smoking Out the Barons: The Campaign Against the Tobacco Industry. A Report of the British Medical Association Public Affairs Division* (Chichester, Wiley Medical, 1986), p. 10.

11 Harris and Hatton, *Murder a Cigarette*; *Guardian* (13 October 1998), p. 19.

12 Anon., 'Action on Smoking and Health: a brief description' (London, ASH, 1993) and *ASH Annual Reports*. Other pamphlets and publicity material are available from ASH, 16 Fitzhardinge Street, London W1H 9PL.

13 ASH, publicity folder, 1997; available from ASH.

14 Rabin and Sugarman, *Smoking Policy*, p. 65; R. Troyer and G. Markle, *Cigarettes: The Battle over Smoking* (New Brunswick, NJ, Rutgers University Press, 1983), p. 88; *Guardian* (2 February 1998), p. 14.

15 B. Macintyre, 'The dying of the light', *The Times Magazine* (10 June 1995); H. Lacey, 'The smokers' last gasp', *Independent on Sunday, Real Life* (5 November 1995), p. 3.

16 Rabin and Sugarman, *Smoking Policy*, p. 66.

17 K. MacKinnon and L. Owen, *Smoking in Films – A Review* (London, HEA, 1997).

18 L. Owen, *Smoking, Magazines and Young People* (London, HEA, 1997). See also B. Jacobson and A. Amos, *When Smoke Gets in Your Eyes: Cigarette Advertising*

Policy and Coverage of Smoking and Health in Women's Magazines (London, BMA, 1985).

19 *Loaded* (April 1998); *Daily Star* (12 March 1998), p. 3.

20 D. Gray, A. Amos and C. Currie, 'Exploring young people's perceptions of smoking images in youth magazines', *Health Education Research*, 11:2 (1996), 215–30; A. Amos, C. Currie, D. Gray and R. Elton, 'Perceptions of fashion images from youth magazines: does a cigarette make a difference?', *Health Education Research*, 13:4 (1998), 491–501.

21 *Guardian* (tabloid) (27 July 1997), pp. 4–5.

22 *Independent on Sunday, Real Life* (20 December 1998), p. 8; *Guardian* (15 December 1998), p. 5; *Evening Standard* (12 January 1998), p. 8.

23 T. Conran, *The Cigar in Art* (Woodstock, NY, Overlook Press, 1996).

24 A. Marsh and S. McKay, *Poor Smokers* (London, Policy Studies Institute, 1994); H. Graham, *When Life's a Drag: Women, Smoking and Disadvantage* (London, HMSO, 1993); R. Dorsett and A. Marsh, *The Health Trap: Poverty, Smoking and Lone Parenthood* (London, Policy Studies Institute, 1998).

25 For a good bibliography on the issue, see J. C. Luik, *Do Tobacco Advertising Bans Really Work? A Review of the Evidence* (Ontario, The Niagara Institute, 1994).

26 L. Michell and A. Amos, 'Girls, pecking order and smoking', *Social Science and Medicine*, 44:12 (1997), 1861–9; A. Amos, D. Gray, C. Currie and R. Elton, 'Healthy or druggy? Self-image, ideal image and smoking behaviour among young people', *Social Science and Medicine*, 45:6 (1997), 847–58.

27 Figures quoted from Tobacco Manufacturers' Association documents (available on request).

28 Health Education Authority campaign 1998–99 appearing in female youth magazines such as *MINX* and *More*.

29 E. Heathcote, 'Never gonna give you up', *Independent on Sunday, Real Life* (6 December 1998), p. 3.

Bibliography

Archival collections

BBC Written Archives, Caversham
  Smoking policy files
  TV and radio scripts
Bodleian Library, Oxford
  John Johnson Collection
Brewhouse Yard Museum, Nottingham
  Advertising materials of the Player's branch of the Imperial Tobacco Company
Bristol Record Office, Bristol
  Wills Archive
Colindale National Newspaper Library
Lancaster University
  Roberts, E., *Social Life in Barrow, Lancaster and Preston, 1870–1930* (oral transcripts held at Lancaster University Library)
Nottingham Record Office, Nottingham
  Player's Archive
Public Record Office, Kew
  Board of Trade papers, BT 64, BT 72
  Ministry of Health files, MH 55, MH 82, MH 151, MH 154
Quit offices, London
  Materials on National Society of Non-Smokers
The Tom Harrisson Mass-Observation Archives, Brighton, Harvester Press Microform Publications, 1983
University of Liverpool, Special Collections
  The Papers of John Fraser
University of Sussex, Library
  Mass-Observation Archive, Topic Collections, *Smoking Habits 1937–1965*
Wellcome Institute for the History of Medicine, Library
  Various papers

Newspapers, periodicals, journals and series

Academy
All the Year Round
Annual Reports of the English Anti-Tobacco
    Society
Antiquary
Anti-Tobacco Journal
ASH Annual Reports
Athenaeum
Beacon Light
Bentley's Miscellany
Bizarre
Bookworm
British Journal of Preventive and Social
    Medicine
British Medical Journal
Chambers' Journal
Cigar and Tobacco World
Clean Air
Contemporary Review
Cope's Smoke Room Booklets
Cope's Tobacco Leaves for the Smoking
    Room
Cope's Tobacco Plant
Cornhill Magazine
Country Life
Daily Express
Daily Mail
Daily Mirror
Daily Star
Empire Review
English Illustrated Magazine
Every Saturday
Fraser's Magazine
Free Choice
Gentleman's Magazine
Good Words
Guardian
Harmsworth Magazine
Illustrated London News
Independent on Sunday
International Journal of Psychoanalysis
Lancet

Littell's Living Age
Loaded
London Evening Standard
London Society
Macmillan's Magazine
Medical Officer
Medical World
Monthly Letter of the English Anti-Tobacco
    Society and Anti-Narcotic League
National Review
New Quarterly Review
New Statesman
New Statesman and Nation
News of the World
Nineteenth Century
The Non-Smoker
Notes and Queries
Observer
Once a Week
Parliamentary Debates
Penny Magazine
People
Popular Science Monthly
Practical Magazine
Punch
Saturday Review
Smoker
Spectator
Strand Magazine
Sunday Express
Sunday Mirror
Sunday Pictorial
The Sunday Times
Temple Bar
The Times
The Times Literary Supplement
Tit-Bits
Tobacco
Tobacco Trade Review
Tobacco Weekly Journal
Which?
Young Woman

Primary, literary and medical books and articles

'A Veteran of Smokedom', *The Smoker's Guide, Philosopher and Friend*, London, Hardwicke & Bogue, 1876.

Abrahams, A., *The Human Machine*, Harmondsworth, Penguin, 1956.

Abrams, M., *Teenage Consumer Spending in 1959 (Part II): Middle Class and Working Class Boys and Girls*, London, Press Exchange, 1961.

Alexander, F. W., *Tobacco: Discovery; Origin of Name; Pipes; The Smoking Habit and its Psychotherapy*, London, 1930.

Allen, G., *The Woman Who Did*, London, John Lane, 1895.

Anderson, D. L. and L. McNicoll, *Personal Hygiene for Boys*, London, Cassell, 1915.

Anon., *Cigars and Tobacco, Wine and Women, as they are, by a Modern Epicurean*, London, Kent & Richards, 1849.

Anon., *A Doctor's Fallacy on Smoking and Smokers Examined by One Who Smokes*, London, Wesley, 1857.

Anon., *The Evils of Tobacco Using: An Anti-Tobacco Pamphlet*, London, Kellaway, 187[?].

Anon., *Juvenile Smoking, Reprinted from the 'Dublin University Magazine'*, London, Partridge, 1877.

Anon., *Smoke and Flame*, Manchester, Manchester Anti-Narcotic League, 189[?].

Anon., *Smoking and Tobacco: An Essay*, London, 1880.

Anon., *Tobacco Duty: Memorial Praying for the Abolition of the Extra Duty Imposed in the Budget of 1878*, Liverpool, 1879.

Anon., 'Tobacco standard; cigarette currency', *Economist*, 152 (1947), 526–7.

Anon., *To Smoke or Not To Smoke (for College Students)*, London, NSNS, 193[?].

Anon., *Tobacco Talk and Smokers' Gossip: An Amusing Miscellany of Fact and Anecdote*, London, Redway, 1884.

Apperson, G. L., *The Social History of Smoking*, London, Martin Secker, 1914.

Arnold, A., *A Woman on Tobacco*, Manchester, Anti-Narcotic League, 1885.

Axon, W. E. A., *The Good and Evil of Tobacco*, London, Elliot Stock, 1878.

Axon, W. E. A., *Smoking and Thinking, from the English Mechanic*, Dunfermline, Clark & Son, 1872.

Axon, W. E. A., *The Tobacco Question: Physiologically, Chemically, Botanically, and Statistically Considered*, Manchester, John Heywood, 1878.

Baden-Powell, R., *Rovering to Success*, London, Herbert Jenkins, 1930.

Baden-Powell, R., *Scouting for Boys*, London, Pearson, [1908] 1928.

Barclay, J., *Ale, Wine, Spirits, and Tobacco: A Lecture Delivered Before the Leicester Literary and Philosophical Society*, London, Bosworth & Harrison, 1861.

Baron, B., *The Growing Generation: A Study of Working Boys and Girls in Our Cities*, London, Student Christian Movement, 1911.

Barrie, J. M., *My Lady Nicotine*, London, Hodder & Stoughton, [1890] 1902.

Beard, R., *X20*, London, Flamingo, 1997.

Beatty-Kingston, W., *A Journalist's Jottings*, London, Chapman & Hall, 1890.

Bell, L., *How to Stop Smoking*, London, Postlib, 1947.

Bewlay & Co. Ltd, *Tobacco Leaves*, London, Bewlay, 1888.

Bosanquet, H., *The Strength of the People*, New York, Garland, [1902] 1980.

Braddock, A. P., *Applied Psychology for Advertisers*, London, Butterworth, 1933.

Braithwaite, D. and S. P. Dobbs, *The Distribution of Consumable Durables: An Economic Study*, London, Routledge, 1932.

Bray, R. A., *Boy Labour and Apprenticeship*, New York, Garland edn, 1980.

Bray, R. A., *The Town Child*, London, Fisher Unwin, 1908.

Brean, H., *How to Stop Smoking*, Kingswood, The World's Work, 1952.

British Anti-Tobacco Society, *Smoke Not! No. 10: Report of a Meeting for the Discussion of the Great Tobacco Question*, Manchester, William Bremner, 1857.

British Anti-Tobacco Society, *Smoke Not! No. 18: A Prize Essay on Smoking, by Miss Annie Jones*, London, Pitman, 1862.

British Anti-Tobacco Society, *Smoke Not! No. 23: An Occasional Paper of the British Anti-Tobacco Society, Embracing the Recent Researches of M. Jolly on Tobacco Smoking in France*, London, Elliot Stock, between 1865 and 1869.

British Anti-Tobacco Society, *Young Britons' League Against Smoking*, Manchester, British Anti-Tobacco Society, n. d.

British Medical Association, *Smoking Out the Barons: The Campaign Against the Tobacco Industry. A Report of the British Medical Association Public Affairs Division*, Chichester, Wiley Medical, 1986.

Brodie, B. C., *The Use and Abuse of Tobacco*, London, Partridge, 1860.

Brooks, J. E., *Tobacco: Its History Illustrated by the Books, Manuscripts and Engravings in the Library of George Arents*, 4 vols, New York, Rosenbach, 1943.

Browne, J., *Tobacco Morally and Physically Considered in Relation to Smoking and Snuff Taking*, Driffield, B. Fawcett, 1842.

Buckley, C., *Thank You for Smoking*, London, Andre Deutsch, 1995.

Budgett, J. B., *The Tobacco Question: Morally, Socially and Physically Considered*, London, George Philip, 1857.

Burn, J. L., *Smoking and Lung Cancer*, London, Chest & Heart Association, 1961.

Burton, R., *The Anatomy of Melancholy*, New York, Tudor Publishing, 1948.

Bynner, J. M., *Medical Students' Attitudes Towards Smoking: A Report on a Survey Carried out for the Ministry of Health*, London, HMSO, 1967.

Bynner, J. M., *The Young Smoker*, London, HMSO, 1969.

Byron, Lord, *The Poetical Works of Lord Byron*, London, John Murray, 1857.

Cardew, A., *Women and Smoking*, London, National Society of Non-Smokers, n. d.

Carpenter, R. L., *A Lecture on Tobacco*, London, National Temperance Publication Depot, 1882.

Carrell, A., *Man the Unknown*, London, Hamilton, 1935.

Cartwright, A., F. M. Martin & J. G. Thomson, *Consequences of a Health Education Campaign*, Edinburgh, University of Edinburgh, Department of Public Health and Social Medicine, 1959.

Chesser, E., *When and How to Stop Smoking*, London, Jarrolds, 1963.

Clarke, H. A., *How to Overcome the Smoking Habit and Conquer Craving*, Dawley, Shropshire, the author, n. d.

Clement, M., *Smoking and Cancer: Facts that Every Smoker Ought to Know!* Bognor Regis, Health Science Press, 1953.

Close, F., *Tobacco: Its Influences, Physical, Moral, and Religious*, London, Hatchard, 1859.

Collett, C. E., *Educated Working Women: Essays on the Economic Position of Women Workers in the Middle Classes*, London, P. S. King, 1902.

Collins, W., *The Moonstone*, Ware, Wordsworth, [1868] 1993.

Collins, W., *The Woman in White*, Harmondsworth, Penguin, [1859–60] 1994.

Conran, T., *The Cigar in Art*, Woodstock, NY, Overlook Press, 1996.

Cook, T., *Anti-Smoker Collections*, London, Elliot Stock, 1875.

Cook, T., *Anti-Smoker Selections, First Series, Science v Tobacco, A Selection of Medical Testimonies*, London, Elliot Stock, 1874.

Cook, T., *Anti-Smoker Selections, Second Series, Religion and Common Sense versus Tobacco*, London, Elliot Stock, 1874.

Coward, N., *Play Parade*, London, Heinemann, 1934.

Cruickshank, A., 'Smokers' Advisory Clinic – Ministry of Health: a preliminary report on an experimental project', *Monthly Bulletin of the Ministry of Health and the Public Health Laboratory Service*, 22 (1963), 110–16.

Cundall, J. W., *'Pipes and Tobacco': Being a Discourse on Smoking and Smokers*, London, Greening, 1901.

Department of Health and Social Security, *Fourth Report of the Independent Scientific Committee on Smoking and Health*, London, HMSO, 1988.

Dickens, C., *The Pickwick Papers*, Ware, Wordsworth, [1836–37] 1993.

Digges, J. G., *The Cure of Inebriety, Alcoholism, the Drug and the Tobacco Habit, etc.* London, A. W. Jamieson, 1904.

Dixon, W. E., 'The tobacco habit', *British Journal of Inebriety*, 25 (1927–28), 99–121.

Doll, R. and A. B. Hill, 'Lung cancer and other causes of death in relation to smoking: a second report on the mortality of British doctors', *British Medical Journal*, ii (1956), 1071–81.

Doll, R. and A. B. Hill, 'The mortality of doctors in relation to their smoking habits: a preliminary report', *British Medical Journal*, i (1954), 1451–2.

Doll, R. and A. B. Hill, 'Smoking and carcinoma of the lung: preliminary report', *British Medical Journal*, ii (1950), 739–48.

Doll, R. and A. B. Hill, 'A study of the aetiology of carcinoma of the lung', *British Medical Journal*, ii (1952), 1271–86.

Doll, R., R. Peto, K. Wheatley, R. Gray and I. Sutherland, 'Mortality in relation to smoking: forty years' observation on male British doctors', *British Medical Journal*, i (1994), 901–11.

Doyle, A. Conan, *The Adventures of Sherlock Holmes*, Harmondsworth, Penguin, 1994.

Doyle, A. Conan, *The Case-Book of Sherlock Holmes*, Ware, Wordsworth, 1993.

Doyle, A. Conan, *The Return of Sherlock Holmes*, Ware, Wordsworth, 1993.

Doyle, A. Conan, *The Sign of Four*, Oxford, Oxford University Press, 1993.

Doyle, A. Conan, *A Study in Scarlet*, Oxford, Oxford University Press, 1993.

Driver, J., *The Nature of Tobacco: Showing Its Destructive Effects on Mind and Body, Especially on Juveniles*, London, Nichols & Co., 1881.

Drysdale, C. R., *Tobacco and the Diseases it Produces*, London, Balliere, Tindall & Cox, 1875.

Dugdale, N., *Nicotine and Health or Smoke from a Doctor's Pipe. A Short Discourse on How to Avoid some of the Effects of Smoking*, London, John Bale, 1936.

Dunhill, A. H., *The Gentle Art of Smoking*, London, Max Reinhardt, 1954.

Dunhill, A. H., *The Pipe Book*, London, A and C Black, 1924.

Edwards, G., 'Hypnosis and lobeline in an anti-smoking clinic', *Medical Officer* (24 April 1964), 239–43.

Eley, H. W., *Advertising Media*, London, Butterworth, 1932.

Eysenck, H. J., *Smoking, Health and Personality*, London, Weidenfeld & Nicolson, 1965.

Fairholt, F. W., *Tobacco: Its History and Associations, Including an Account of the Plant and its Manufacture*, London, Beccles (printer), 1876.

Finnemore, W., *The Addison Temperance Reader. With Chapters on Thrift and Juvenile Smoking*, London, Addison Publishing Co., 1906.

Fisher, R. A., *Smoking, the Cancer Controversy: Some Attempts to Assess the Evidence*, London, Oliver & Boyd, 1959.

Flack, H., *Smoking: The Dangers*, London, British Medical Association, 1961.

Fleming, I., *Casino Royale*, *Live and Let Die*; *Moonraker*; *Diamonds are Forever*; *From Russia, With Love*; *Dr. No*; *Goldfinger*; *For Your Eyes Only*; *On her Majesty's Secret Service*; *You Only Live Twice*; *The Man with the Golden Gun*; *The Spy Who Loved Me*, all London, Pan Books.

Fleming, I., *Thunderball*, London, Triad/Granada, [1961] 1978.

Fletcher, C. M., H. Cole, L. Jeger and C. Wood, *Common Sense About Smoking*, Harmondsworth, Penguin, 1963.

Forshaw, C. F., *A Short History of Tobacco with its Effects upon the General Health, and its Influence on the Teeth, or, is Smoking Tobacco Injurious? No*, Stanningley, Yorkshire, Birdsall, 1887.

Forson, R. S., *'X' versus 'YZ'. Is Smoking Tobacco Injurious? Don't Know*, Bradford, M. Field, 1888.

Forster, E. M., *Howard's End*, Harmondsworth, Penguin, [1910] 1941.

Fothergill, C., *May Young England Smoke? A Modern Question, Medically and Socially Considered*, London, S. W. Partridge, 1876.

Fothergill, J. Milner, *The Physiologist in the Household. Part 1: Adolescence*, London, Balliere, Tindall & Cox, 1880.

Freeman, A., *Boy Life and Labour: The Manufacture of Inefficiency*, London, P. S. King & Son, 1914.

G., B., *Reasons For and Against Smoking*, London, James Nisbett, 1858.

Gibbons, H., *Tobacco and its Effects: A Prize Essay Showing that the Use of Tobacco is a Physical, Mental, Moral and Social Evil*, London, Partridge, 1868.

Gissing, G., *New Grub Street*, Ware, Wordsworth, [1891] 1996.

Gorst, J., *The Children of the Nation: How Their Health and Vigour Should be Promoted by the State*, London, Methuen, 1906.

Grahame, K., *Pagan Papers*, London, Elkin Matthews & John Lane, 1893.

Hamilton, A. E., *This Smoking World*, London, Methuen, 1928.

Hamilton, W., *Poems and Parodies in Praise of Tobacco*, London, Reeves & Turner, n. d.

Hardcastle, H. R., *The Ethics of Smoking at the Wheel*, Lyndhurst, the author, 1949.

Harrison, G. and F. C. Mitchell, *The Home Market: A Handbook of Statistics*, London, Allen & Unwin, 1940.

Harrison, T., *Prometheus*, London, Faber & Faber, 1998.

Hawkins, W., 'My Dear Old Pipe', Peterborough, the author, 1947.

Hawthorne, V. M., *Facts About Smoking*, Edinburgh, Scottish Home & Health Department, 1967.

Henn, S., *The Tobacco Curse: With Weighty Reasons why Christians Should Abstain from It*, Dudley, the author, 1880[?].

Henry, J. Q. A., *The Deadly Cigarette; or the Perils of Juvenile Smoking*, London, Richard J. James, 1907.

Hobson, J. W. and H. Henry, *The Pattern of Smoking Habits: A Study Based on Information Collected During the Course of the Hulton Readership Survey, 1948*, London, Hulton Research Studies, 1948.

Hodgkin, T., *Fifty-Four Objections to Tobacco*, London, Partridge, 1862.

Hoffstaedt, E. G. W., 'Anti-smoking campaign: some general observations on the smoking problem and the place of "smokers' clinics"', *Medical Officer* (31 January 1964), 59–60.

Hoggart, R., *The Uses of Literacy*, Harmondsworth, Penguin, [1957] 1973.

Holmes, R., *The Use of Tobacco by Young People, Considered in Relation to its Effects, Delusions and Prevention*, Manchester, Tubbs & Brook, 1878.

Hopkins, J. W., *Alcohol and Tobacco: Their Effect upon the Body*, Birmingham, Templar Works, 1906.

Howie, J. M., *The Effects of Tobacco on the Nutrition of Nerve and Muscle*, Manchester, Anti-Narcotic League, 187[?].

Imlah, N., *The Choice is Yours: Finding Out the Facts*, London, Geoffrey Chapman, 1971.

Infante, G. Cabrera, *Holy Smoke*, London, Faber & Faber, [1985] 1997.

Jackson, H., *Is the Use of Tobacco Injurious?* Barnstaple, H. A. Foyster, 1882.

James I, 'A counterblaste to tobacco', in R. S. Rait, *A Royal Rhetorician*, London, Constable, 1900, pp. 29–59.

Jarvis, L., *Teenage Smoking Attitudes in 1996*, London, HMSO, 1997.

Jermy, L., *The Memoirs of a Working Woman*, Norwich, Goose & Son, 1934.

Johnson, L. M., *The Disease of Tobacco Smoking and its Cure*, London, Christopher Johnson, 1957.

Kennaway, E. L. and N. M. Kennaway, 'A further study of the incidence of cancer of the lung and larynx', *British Journal of Cancer*, i (1947), 260–98.

Kind, R. and J. Leedham, *Don't Smoke!* London, Longmans, 1966.

King, A., *The Cigarette Habit: A Scientific Cure*, Kingswood, The World's Work, 1913.

King, H., *Cigarette Smoking and Lung Cancer: The Remedy*, Southport, Holsum, 1962.

Rev. Kirk, *A Manly Habit*, Manchester, Anti-Tobacco and Anti-Narcotic League, 1880s.

Koskowski, W., *The Habit of Tobacco Smoking*, London, Staples Press, 1955.

Lane, F. B., *Advertising Administration (Principles and Practice)*, London, Butterworth, 1931.

Lane, W., *The Modern Woman's Home Doctor*, London, Odham's, 1939.

lang, k. d., *Drag*, Warner Bros Records Inc., 1997.

Larson, P. S., H. B. Haag and H. Silvette, *Tobacco: Experimental and Clinical Studies. A Review of the World Literature*, Baltimore, Williams & Wilkins, 1961.

Larson, P. S. and H. Silvette, *Tobacco: Experimental and Clinical Studies. A Review of the World Literature. Supplement I*, Baltimore, Williams & Wilkins, 1968.

Larson, P. S. and H. Silvette, *Tobacco: Experimental and Clinical Studies. A Review of the World Literature. Supplement II*, Baltimore, Williams & Wilkins, 1971.

Lewin, L., *Phantastica: Narcotic and Stimulating Drugs*, London, Kegan Paul, 1931.

Livesey, A. (ed.), *Are We At War? Letters to The Times, 1939–1945*, London, Times Books, 1989.

Lizars, J., *Practical Observations on the Use and Abuse of Tobacco*, Edinburgh, George Phillip, 1854.

Lynd, R., *Essays on Life and Literature*, London, Dent, 1951.

Macdonald, N., *Your Chest Could be Healthy: Smoking and Lung Diseases*, London, Socialist Medical Association, 1958.

Machen, A., *The Anatomy of Tobacco*, London, Redway, 1884.

Mackenzie, C., *Sublime Tobacco*, London, Chatto & Windus, 1957.

Marsh, A. and J. Matheson, *Smoking Attitudes and Behaviour*, London, HMSO, 1983.

Martin, F. M. and G. R. Stanley, *The Dunfermline Anti-Smoking Campaign*, Edinburgh, University of Edinburgh, Department of Public Health and Social Medicine, 1964.

Martin, F. M. and G. R. Stanley, *Report on the Clydebank Anti-Smoking Campaign*, Edinburgh, University of Edinburgh, Department of Social Medicine, 1965.

Mass-Observation, *First Year's Work, 1937–1938*, London, Lindsay Drummond, 1938.

Mass-Observation, *The Pub and the People: A Worktown Study*, London, Cresset, 1987.

McCarthy, C. W., *Tobacco and its Effects: A Pamphlet Addressed to Non-Medical Readers*, Dublin, McGlashaw & Hill, 1874.

McCurdy, R. N. C., *Smoking, Lung Cancer and You*, London, Linden Press, 1958.

McKennell, A. C. and R. K. Thomas, *Adults' and Adolescents' Smoking Habits and Attitudes*, London, HMSO, 1967.

McNeile, H. C. 'Sapper', *Bulldog Drummond: His Four Rounds with Carl Peterson*, London, Hodder & Stoughton, [1920] 1929.

Medical Research Council, *Tobacco Smoking and Cancer of the Lung*, London, HMSO, 1957.

'Medicus', *Smoking and Drinking: The Argument Stated For and Against*, London, Sampson, 1871.

Mérimée, P., *Carmen*, London, Paul Elek, 1960.

Moncrieff, J. Forbes, *Our Boys and Why they Should Not Smoke*, Manchester, Anti-Narcotic League, n. d.

Murray, J. C., *Smoking, when Injurious, when Innocuous, when Beneficial*, London, Simpkin, Marshall and Co., 1871.

Noel-Thatcher, H., *The Fascinator; or, the Knight's Legacy. A Prize Essay on the Moral, Social, and Economical Results of the Use of Tobacco*, London, W. Tweedie, 1871.

Noor, M. H., *How to Stop Smoking*, Bradford, Norton Wells, 1949.

Ochsner, A., *Smoking and Cancer: A Doctor's Report*, London, Frederick Muller, 1955.

Ouida, *Under Two Flags*, Oxford, Oxford University Press, [1867] 1995.

Parliamentary Papers, IX, Juvenile Smoking Bill, *Report of the Select Committee of the House of Lords*, 1906.

Parliamentary Papers, XXXII, Inter-Departmental Committee on Physical Deterioration, *Minutes of Evidence*, Cd. 2210, 1904.

Parliamentary Papers, The Monopolies Commission, *Report on the Supply of Cigarettes and Tobacco and of Cigarette and Tobacco Machinery*, Cmnd. 218, 1961.

Parliamentary Papers, Profiteering Act, 1919, *Findings by a Committee Appointed to Enquire into the Existence of a Trade Combination in the Tobacco Industry and into the Effects which its Operation has on Prices and on the Trade Generally*, Cmd. 558, xxiii, 1920.

Partington, W., *Smoke Rings and Roundelays: Blendings from Prose and Verse from Raleigh's Time*, London, John Castle, 1924.

Paterson, A., *Across the Bridges, or Life by the South London Riverside*, London, Edward Arnold, 1911.

Petmecky, B., *Confessions of a Tobacco Addict*, London, Muller, 1963.

Phillips, F. J., *A Pamphlet Addressed to Youth*, London, NSNS, n. d.

Phillips, F. J., *Health Education: A Critical Survey of the Board of Education's Handbook*, London, NSNS, 1942.

Prescott, H. P., *Tobacco and its Adulterations*, London, 1858.

Priestley, J. B., *Delight*, London, Heinemann, 1949.

Priestley, J. B., *English Journey*, Harmondsworth, Penguin, [1934] 1987.

Pritchett, R. T., *Smokiana, Historical and Ethnographical*, London, Quaritch, 1890.

Quennell, P., *London's Underworld: Being Selections from 'Those That Will Not Work', the Fourth Volume of 'London Labour and the London Poor' by Henry Mayhew*, London, Spring Books, 1950.

Reade, A. A., *Study and Stimulants*, Manchester, Heywood, 1883.

Redmayne, P. and H. Weeks, *Market Research*, London, Butterworth, 1931.

Redway, G. [A. Machen?], *Tobacco Talk and Smoker's Gossip*, London, Redway, 1886.

Reeves, R. Pember, *The Ascent of Woman*, London, John Lane, 1896.

Reid, H., *The Question of Manliness: A Chat with Boys on Smoking*, London, International Anti-Cigarette League, 1904.

Reynard, M. H., *How to Stop Smoking Cigarettes*, Bristol, Movana, n. d.

Reynolds, T., *Globules for Tobacco-Olators*, London, Houlston & Stoneman, 1855.

Reynolds, T., *Juvenile Street Smoking: Reasons for Seeking its Legislative Prohibition*, London, British Anti-Tobacco Society, 1856.

Reynolds, T., *A Lecture on the Great Tobacco Question, Delivered in the Mechanics Institute, Salford*, Manchester, W. Bremner, 1857.

Reynolds, T., *A Memento of the Cambridge Tobacco Riot*, London, 1855.

Reynolds, T., *The Outline of a Lecture (on Tobacco) Delivered in Oxford*, London, Houlston & Stoneman, 1854.

Reynolds, T., *Smoke Not! No. 5. The Substance of a Lecture Delivered to the Pupils at Totteridge Park, Herts*, London, Elliot Stock, 1866.

Reynolds, T., *Smoke Not! No. 11. To Smokers! Medical and Non-medical. A Sermon Delivered at Ewen Place Chapel, Glasgow*, London, Elliot Stock, 1860.

Reynolds, T., *Smoke Not! No. 25. Smoking: A Sure Sign of England's Future Decline*, London, Pitman, 1873.

Rice, M. Spring, *Working-Class Wives: Their Health and Conditions*, London, Virago, [1939] 1981.

Richardson, B. W., *For and Against Tobacco, or Tobacco in Its Relations to the Health of Individuals and Communities*, London, John Churchill, 1865.

Richardson, D., *Pilgrimage*, London, Dent, 1967.

Richardson, F. W., *Is Tobacco-Smoking Injurious? Yes*, 2nd edn, Leeds, 1887.

Ritchie, W., *The Workman's Pipe: What it is, and What it does, a Lecture*, London, Partridge, 1871.

Robinson, G. and S. Winward, *Smoking*, London, Crusade, 1958.

Rolleston, J. D., 'On snuff taking', *British Journal of Inebriety*, 34 (July 1936), 1–16.

Romer, J. C., *How to Give Up Smoking*, Rushden, Stanley L. Hunt, 1949.

Rowntree, B. S., *Poverty: A Study of Town Life*, Basingstoke, Macmillan, 1901.

Royal College of Physicians, *Health or Smoking?* London, Pitman Medical, 1983.

Royal College of Physicians, *Smoking and Health*, London, Pitman Medical, 1962.

Royal College of Physicians, *Smoking and Health Now*, London, Pitman Medical, 1971.

Royal College of Physicians, *Smoking or Health*, London, Pitman Medical, 1977.

Russ, S., *Smoking and its Effects, with Special Reference to Lung Cancer*, London, Hutchinson, 1955.

Russell, C. E. B., *Manchester Boys: Sketches of Manchester Lads at Work and Play*, Manchester, Manchester University Press, 1905.

Rylands, T. G., *An Enquiry into the Merits and Demerits of Tobacco Smoking*, 2nd edn, Warrington, Thomas Hurst, 1843.

S., F. S., *Tobacco and Disease, the Substance of Three Letters, Reproduced, with Additional Matter, from the 'English Mechanic'*, London, Trubner, 1872.

Salzer, K., *Thirteen Ways to Break the Smoking Habit*, London, Duckworth & Co., 1959.

Schroeder, M., *Better Smoking*, London, Allen & Unwin, 1964.

'Scrutator', *Smoking, or No Smoking? That's the Question: Hear Sir Benjamin C. Brodie, Bart., with Critical Observations*, London, Pitman, 1860.

Secretary of the South-street Wesleyan Methodist Sunday School, *Smoking and Chewing Tobacco: The Evils Resulting Therefrom*, London, George Atkinson, between 1876 and 1879.

Sexton, G., *The Great Tobacco Controversy: A Battle of Smoke*, London, James Gilbert, 1857.

Shepherd, G., *Facts About Smoking*, Rugby, G. Shepherd, 1956.

Shew, J., *Tobacco: Its History, Nature and Effects on the Body and Mind*, Manchester, 1876.

Silberberg, L., *Tobacco: Its Use and Abuse*, London, Habana Cigar Company, 1863.

Skelton, J., *Is Smoking Injurious? The Arguments Pro and Con Rationally Considered*, London, the author, 186[?].

Stephens, R., *When a Boy Smokes, Reprinted from 'Young England'*, London, Sunday School Union, 1898.

Stock, J., *Confessions of an Old Smoker Respectfully Addressed to all Smoking Disciples*, London, Elliot Stock, 1872.

Svevo, I., *Confessions of Zeno*, Harmondsworth, Penguin, [1923] 1964.

Tanner, A. E., *Tobacco, From the Grower to the Smoker*, 5th edn, London, Pitman, 1950.

Taylor, T. F., *Don't Smoke! An Address Given to the Members of the TOC H Unit Wetherby*, London, National Society of Non-Smokers, 1944.

Thackeray, W. M., *Vanity Fair*, Oxford, Oxford University Press, [1847–48] 1983.

Theed, J., *Smoking and Cancer*, London, Television Times, 1954.

Thompson, J., *Three Fashionable Luxuries: Namely, Smoking, Chewing and Snuffing; or, Facts About Tobacco, Including its History, Nature, and Effects*, Scarborough, the author, n. d.

Trask, G., *To His Highness the Prince of Wales: A Letter*, London, Elliot Stock, 1861[?].

Trollope, A., *The Way We Live Now*, London, The Trollope Society, [1874–5] 1992.

United States Department of Health and Human Services, *The Health Consequences of Smoking: Nicotine Addiction. A Report of the Surgeon General*, Washington, DC, GPO, 1988.

United States Department of Health, Education and Welfare, *Smoking and Health. Report of the Advisory Committee to the Surgeon General of the Public Health Service*, Washington, DC, GPO, 1964.

Urwick, E. J. (ed.), *Studies of Boy Life in Our Cities*, New York, Garland, 1980.

Van Patten, N., 'An unacknowledged work of Arthur Machen?', *Papers of the Bibliographic Society of America*, 20 (1926), 95–7.

[Various], *Juvenile Smoking: Papers . . . on the Evil Influences of Smoking when Indulged in by the Young*, London, Sunday School Union, 1883.

W., C., *Juvenile Smoking: An Essay Setting Forth to the Young the Evil Effects of Tobacco Smoking*, Bodmin, Liddell & Son, 1883.

Waugh, E., *Vile Bodies*, New York, Dell, [1930] 1958.

Wells, H. G., *Ann Veronica*, London, Virago, [1909] 1980.

Wilde, O., *The Works of Oscar Wilde*, London, Collins, n. d.

Williams, C., *Cholera and Tobacco Smoking: Some Thoughts Thereon*, London, Bodmin, Liddell & Son, 1890.

Wodehouse, J. H., *The Smoking Habit: Its Dangers and Cure*, London, Health for All, 1927.

Wyatt, W., *Reading Anti-Tobacco Society: Organised in the Interest of Humanity, and Especially for the Benefit of the Young, Who are the Hope of the Church and the World*, Reading, published by the society, 1887.

Wynder, E. L. and E. A. Graham, 'Tobacco smoking as a possible etiological factor in bronchiogenic carcinoma: a study of 648 proved cases', *Journal of the American Medical Association*, 143 (1950), 329–36.

Young Briton's League Against Smoking, *A1 or C3?*, Manchester, British Anti-Tobacco Society, n. d.

Selected secondary printed books and articles

Alexander, M., *The True Blue: The Life and Adventures of Colonel Fred Burnaby 1842–1885*, London, Rupert Hart-Davis, 1957.

Alford, B. W. E., *W. D. & H. O. Wills and the Development of the UK Tobacco Industry*, London, Methuen, 1973.

Altick, R., '*Cope's Tobacco Plant*: an episode in Victorian journalism', *Papers of the Bibliographic Society of America*, 45 (1951), 333–50.

Altick, R., *The Presence of the Present: Topics of the Day in the Victorian Novel*, Columbus, Ohio State University Press, 1991.

Amos, A., C. Currie, D. Gray and R. Elton, 'Perceptions of fashion images from youth magazines: does a cigarette make a difference?', *Health Education Research*, 13:4 (1998), 491–501.

Amos, A., D. Gray, C. Currie and R. Elton, 'Healthy or druggy? Self-image, ideal image and smoking behaviour among young people', *Social Science and Medicine*, 45:6 (1997), 847–58.

Anderson, G., *The White Blouse Revolution: Female Office Workers Since 1870*, Manchester, Manchester University Press, 1988.

Appadurai, A. (ed.), *The Social Life of Things: Commodities in Cultural Perspective*, Cambridge, Cambridge University Press, 1986.

Atkinson, E. S., 'Cigarette advertising: a history', *British Journal of Photography*, 128 (1981), 1190–1.

Bailey, P. (ed.), *Music Hall: The Business of Pleasure*, Buckingham, Open University Press, 1986.

Baker, M. J., *Marketing: An Introductory Text*, Basingstoke, Macmillan, 1991.

Barraclough, G., *An Introduction to Contemporary History*, Harmondsworth, Penguin, 1967.

Batchelor, R., *Henry Ford: Mass Production, Modernism and Design*, Manchester, Manchester University Press, 1994.

Bechhofer, F. and B. Elliot (eds), *The Petite Bourgeoisie: Comparative Studies of an Uneasy Stratum*, Basingstoke, Macmillan, 1981.

Beddoe, D., *Back to Home and Duty: Women Between the Wars 1918–1939*, London, Pandora, 1989.

Beddoe, D., *Discovering Women's History*, London, Pandora, 1993.

Benson, J. (ed.), *The Working Class in England, 1875–1914*, Beckenham, Croom Helm, 1985.

Berridge. V., 'Morality and medical science: concepts of narcotic addiction in Britain, 1820–1926', *Annals of Science*, 36 (1979), 67–75.

Berridge, V., 'Morbid cravings: the emergence of addiction', *British Journal of Addiction*, 80 (1985), 233–43.

Berridge, V. and G. Edwards, *Opium and the People: Opiate Use in the Nineteenth Century*, London, Allen Lane, 1981.

Biagini, E. F., *Liberty, Retrenchment and Reform: Popular Liberalism in the Age of Gladstone, 1860–80*, Cambridge, Cambridge University Press, 1992.

Bourke, J., *Working-Class Cultures in Britain 1890–1960: Gender, Class and Ethnicity*, London, Routledge, 1994.

Braithwaite, B., N. Walsh and G. Davies, *Ragtime to Wartime: The Best of Good Housekeeping*, London, Ebury, 1986.

Brandt, A., 'The cigarette, risk, and American culture', *Daedalus*, 119 (1990), 155–76.

Braybon, G., *Women Workers in the First World War*, London, Routledge, 1981.

Brickley, M., A. Miles and H. Stainer, *The Cross Bones Burial Ground: Redcross Way, Southwark, London*, London, Museum of London, 1999.

Brivati, B. and H. Jones (eds), *What Difference Did the War Make?* Leicester, Leicester University Press, 1993.

Bronner, S. (ed.), *Consuming Visions: Accumulation and the Display of Goods in America, 1880–1920*, New York, W. W. Norton, 1989.

Brooke, J. H., *Science and Religion: Some Historical Perspectives*, Cambridge, Cambridge University Press, 1991.

Bunton, R., S. Nettleton and R. Burrows (eds), *The Sociology of Health Promotion: Critical Analyses of Consumption, Lifestyle and Risk*, London, Routledge, 1995.

Burnham, J. C., 'American physicians and tobacco use: two Surgeons General, 1929 and 1964', *Bulletin of the History of Medicine*, 63 (1989), 1–31.

Burnham, J. C., *Bad Habits: Drinking, Smoking, Taking Drugs, Gambling, Sexual Misbehaviour and Swearing in American History*, London, New York University Press, 1993.

Cartophilic Society, *The Tobacco War Booklet*, London, Cartophilic Society, 1951.

Chapman, J., *Licence to Thrill: A Cultural History of the James Bond Films*, London, I. B. Tauris, 1999.

Charlton, A., 'Galsworthy's images of smoking in the Forsyte chronicles', *Social Science and Medicine*, 15 (1981), 633–8.

Childs, M., *Labour's Apprentices: Working-Class Lads in Late Victorian and Edwardian England*, London, Hambledon, 1992.

Chinn, C., *They Worked All Their Lives: Women of the Urban Poor in England, 1880–1939*, Manchester, Manchester University Press, 1988.

Clapson, M., *A Bit of a Flutter: Popular Gambling and English Society, c. 1823–1961*, Manchester, Manchester University Press, 1992.

Clarke, J., C. Critcher and R. Johnson (eds), *Working Class Cultures: Studies in History and Theory*, London, Hutchinson, 1979.

Cooter, R. (ed.), *In the Name of the Child: Health and Welfare, 1880–1940*, London, Routledge, 1992.

Corina, M., *Trust in Tobacco: The Anglo-American Struggle for Power*, London, Michael Joseph, 1975.

Corley, T. A. B., 'Consumer marketing in Britain, 1914–1960', *Business History*, 29 (1987), 65–83.

Count Corti, *A History of Smoking*, London, Random House, [1931] 1996.

Cross, G. (ed.), *Worktowners at Blackpool: Mass-Observation and Popular Leisure in the 1930s*, London, Routledge, 1990.

Crossick, G. and H.-G. Haupt (eds), *Shopkeepers and Master Artisans in Nineteenth-Century Europe*, London, Methuen, 1984.

Culver, J., *Government Health Warning: A Study of the Development and Implementation of Anti-Smoking Policies in the UK*, Sheffield, Sheffield City Polytechnic, Department of Policy Studies Dissertation, 1982.

Cunningham, G., *The New Woman and the Victorian Novel*, Basingstoke, Macmillan, 1978.

Cunningham, H., *The Children of the Poor: Representations of Childhood since the Seventeenth Century*, Oxford, Blackwell, 1991.

Cuthbertson, D., 'Historical note on the origins of the association between lung cancer and smoking', *Journal of the Royal College of Physicians*, 2 (1968), 191–6.

Davies, A., *Leisure, Gender and Poverty: Working-Class Culture in Salford and Manchester, 1900–1939*, Buckingham, Open University Press, 1992.

De Grazia, V. and E. Furlough (eds), *The Sex of Things: Gender and Consumption in Historical Perspective*, London, University of California Press, 1996.

Dempsey, M., *Pipe Dreams: Early Advertising Art from the Imperial Tobacco Company*, London, Pavilion Books, 1982.

Department of Health, *Report of the Scientific Committee on Smoking and Health*, London, HMSO, 1998.

Dixon, D., *From Prohibition to Regulation: Bookmaking, Anti-Gambling, and the Law*, Oxford, Oxford University Press, 1991.

Dorsett, R. and A. Marsh, *The Health Trap: Poverty, Smoking and Lone Parenthood*, London, Policy Studies Institute, 1998.

Douglas, M. and B. Isherwood, *The World of Goods: Towards an Anthropology of Consumption*, London, Allen Lane, 1978.

Dunae, P., 'Penny dreadfuls: late 19th century boys' literature and crime', *Victorian Studies*, 22 (1979), 133–50.

Dyer, G., *Advertising as Communication*, London, Routledge, 1982.

Edsforth, R. W., *Class Conflict and Cultural Consensus: The Making of a Mass Consumer Society in Flint, Michigan*, New Brunswick, Rutgers University Press, 1987.

Evans, E., *Social Policy, 1830–1914*, London, Routledge & Kegan Paul, 1978.

Ewen, S., *Captains of Consciousness: Advertising and the Social Roots of the Consumer Culture*, New York, McGraw-Hill, 1976.

Field, E., *Advertising: The Forgotten Years*, London, Ernest Benn, 1959.

Fine, B. and E. Leopold, *The World of Consumption*, London, Routledge, 1993.

Forty, A., *Objects of Desire: Design and Society 1750–1980*, London, Thames & Hudson, 1986.

Fowler, D., *The First Teenagers: The Lifestyle of Young Wage-earners in Interwar Britain*, London, Woburn, 1995.

Gardner, J. (ed.), *The New Woman: Women's Voices, 1880–1914*, London, Collins & Brown, 1993.

Gilbert, D. G., *Smoking: Individual Differences, Psychopathology, and Emotion*, Washington, DC, Taylor & Francis, 1995.

Gillis, J., 'The evolution of juvenile delinquency in England, 1890–1914', *Past and Present*, 67 (1975), 96–126.

Gittins, D., *Fair Sex: Family Size and Structure, 1900–1939*, London, Hutchinson, 1982.

Gloversmith, F. (ed.), *Class, Culture and Social Change: A New View of the 1930s*, Brighton, Harvester Press, 1980.

Glucksman, M., *Women Assemble: Women Workers and the New Industries in Inter-War Britain*, London, Routledge, 1990.

Gonberg, E. S., 'Historical and political perspective: women and drug use', *Journal of Social Issues*, 38:2 (1982), 9–23.

Goodman, J., *Tobacco in History: The Cultures of Dependence*, London, Routledge, 1993.

Goodman, J., P. E. Lovejoy and A. Sherrat (eds), *Consuming Habits: Drugs in History and Anthropology*, London, Routledge, 1995.

Graham, H., *When Life's a Drag: Women, Smoking and Disadvantage*, London, HMSO, 1993.

Graves, R. and A. Hodge, *The Long Weekend: A Social History of Great Britain, 1918–1939*, London, Hutchinson, 1985.

Gray, D., A. Amos and C. Currie, 'Exploring young people's perceptions of smoking images in youth magazines', *Health Education Research*, 11:2 (1996), 215–30.

Greaves, L., *Smoke Screen: Women's Smoking and Social Control*, London, Scarlet Press, 1996.

Green, E., S. Hebron and D. Woodward, *Women's Leisure, What Leisure?*, Basingstoke, Macmillan, 1990.

Hall, C., *The Twenties in Vogue*, London, Octopus, 1983.

Hannah, L., *The Rise of the Corporate Economy*, London, Methuen, 1983.

Harley, D., 'The beginnings of the tobacco controversy: puritanism, James I, and the royal physicians', *Bulletin of the History of Medicine*, 67:1 (1967), 28–50.

Harris, R. and J. Hatton, *Murder a Cigarette: The Smoking Debate*, London, Duckworth, 1998.

Harrison, B., *Drink and the Victorians: The Temperance Question in England, 1815–1872*, London, Faber & Faber, 1971.

Harrison, L., 'Tobacco battered and pipes shattered: a note on the first British campaign against tobacco smoking', *British Journal of Addiction*, 81 (1986), 553–8.

Haskell, M., *From Reverence to Rape: The Treatment of Women in the Movies*, Chicago, University of Chicago Press, 1987.

Hay, J. R., *The Origins of the Liberal Welfare Reforms, 1906–1914*, Basingstoke, Macmillan, 1975.

Hendrick, H., *Images of Youth: Age, Class and the Male Youth Problem, 1880–1920*, Oxford, Clarendon Press, 1990.

Hey, V., *Patriarchy and Pub Culture*, London, Tavistock, 1986.

Hilton, M., 'Retailing history as economic and cultural history: strategies of survival by specialist tobacconists in the mass market', *Business History*, 40 (1998), 115–37.

Hilton, M., '"Tabs", "fags" and the "boy labour problem" in late Victorian and Edwardian Britain', *Journal of Social History*, 28:3 (1995), 587–607.

Hooper, P., *Smoking Issues: A Quick Guide*, Cambridge, Daniels Publishing, 1995.

Humphries, S., *Hooligans or Rebels? An Oral History of Working-Class Childhood and Youth, 1889–1939*, Oxford, Blackwell, 1981.

Imperial Tobacco, *The Imperial Tobacco Company (of Great Britain and Ireland), Limited, 1901–1951*, London, Imperial Tobacco, 1951.

Imperial Tobacco, *The Story of the Imperial Group Limited*, Imperial Group Information Brochure, London, Imperial Tobacco, 1976.

Jacobson, B., *The Ladykillers: Why Smoking is a Feminist Issue*, London, Pluto Press, 1981.

Jacobson, B. and A. Amos, *When Smoke Gets in Your Eyes: Cigarette Advertising Policy and Coverage of Smoking and Health in Women's Magazines*, London, BMA, 1985.

Jervis, J., *Exploring the Modern: Patterns of Western Culture and Civilisation*, Oxford, Blackwell, 1998.

John, A. V., *By the Sweat of their Brow: Women Workers at the Victorian Coal Mine*, London, Croom Helm, 1980.

Johnston, P., *Real Fantasies: Edward Steichen's Advertising Photography*, Berkeley, University of California Press, 1997.

Jones, G., *Social Darwinism and English Thought: The Interaction Between Biological and Social Theory*, Brighton, Harvester Press, 1980.

Jones, S., *Workers at Play: A Social and Economic History of Leisure 1918–1939*, London, Routledge & Kegan Paul, 1986.

Kiernan, V. G., *Tobacco: A History*, London, Hutchinson, 1991.

Klein, R., *Cigarettes are Sublime*, London, Picador, 1995.

Klein, R., 'The Devil in Carmen', *Differences: A Journal of Feminist Cultural Studies*, 5:1 (1993), 51–72.

Koetzle, M. and U. Scheid, *Feu d'Amour [Seductive Smoke]*, Cologne, Taschen, 1994.

Kohn, M., *Dope Girls: The Birth of the British Drug Underground*, London, Lawrence & Wishart, 1992.

Laermans, R., 'Learning to consume: early department stores and the shaping of modern consumer culture, 1860–1914', *Theory, Culture, Society*, 10 (1993), 99.

Leavey, J. (ed.), *The FOREST Guide to Smoking in London*, London, Quiller, 1996.

Lee, P. N., *Statistics of Smoking in the United Kingdom*, 7th edn, London, Tobacco Research Council, 1976.

LeMahieu, D. L., *A Culture for Democracy: Mass Communication and the Cultivated Mind in Britain Between the Wars*, Oxford, Clarendon, 1988.

Lewis, J., *What Price Community Medicine? The Philosophy, Practice and Politics of Public Health since 1919*, Brighton, Wheatsheaf, 1986.

Lewis, J., *Women in England, 1870–1950: Sexual Divisions and Social Change*, Brighton, Wheatsheaf, 1984.

Lock, S., L. Reynolds and E. M. Tansey (eds), *Ashes to Ashes: The History of Smoking and Health*, Amsterdam, Rodopi, 1998.

Loeb, L. A., *Consuming Angels: Advertising and Victorian Women*, Oxford, Oxford University Press, 1994.

Luik, J. C., *Do Tobacco Advertising Bans Really Work? A Review of the Evidence*, Ontario, The Niagara Institute, 1994.

MacKinnon, K. and L. Owen, *Smoking in Films – A Review*, London, HEA, 1997.

Mangan, J. A. and J. Walvin (eds), *Manliness and Morality: Middle-Class Masculinity in Britain and America, 1800–1940*, Manchester, Manchester University Press, 1987.

Marchand, R., *Advertising the American Dream: Making Way for Modernity, 1920–1940*, Berkeley, University of California Press, 1985.

Marsh, A. and S. McKay, *Poor Smokers*, London, Policy Studies Institute, 1994.

McCracken, G., *Culture and Consumption: New Approaches to the Symbolic Character of Consumer Goods and Activities*, Bloomington, Indiana University Press, 1988.

Meacham, S., *A Life Apart: The English Working Class, 1890–1914*, Massachusetts, Harvard University Press, 1977.

Meikle, J., *Twentieth Century Limited: Industrial Design in America, 1925–1939*, Philadelphia, Temple University Press, 1979.

Melman, B., *Women and the Popular Imagination in the Twenties: Flappers and Nymphs*, Basingstoke, Macmillan, 1988.

Mercer, H., *Constructing a Competitive Order: The Hidden History of British Anti-Trust Policy*, Cambridge, Cambridge University Press, 1995.

Michell, L. and A. Amos, 'Girls, pecking order and smoking', *Social Science and Medicine*, 44:12 (1997), 1861–9.

Miller, D., *Material Culture and Mass Consumption*, Oxford, Basil Blackwell, 1987.

Miller, D. (ed.), *Acknowledging Consumption: A Review of New Studies*, London, Routledge, 1995.

Mitchell, B. R. and P. Deane, *Abstract of British Historical Statistics*, Cambridge, Cambridge University Press, 1971.

Mitchell, D., 'Images of exotic women in turn-of-the-century tobacco art', *Feminist Studies*, 18:2 (1992), 327–30.

Mitchell, D., 'The so called "new woman" as Prometheus: women artists depict women smoking', *Women's Art Journal*, 12:1 (1991), 3–9.

Mort, F., *Cultures of Consumption: Masculinities and Social Space in Late Twentieth-Century Britain*, London, Routledge, 1996.

Mullen, K., *A Healthy Balance: Glaswegian Men Talking About Health, Tobacco and Alcohol*, Aldershot, Avebury, 1993.

Naremore, J. and P. Brantlinger (eds), *Modernity and Mass Culture*, Bloomington, Indiana University Press, 1991.

Nevett, T. R., *Advertising in Britain: A History*, London, Heineman, 1982.

Owen, L., *Smoking, Magazines and Young People*, London, HEA, 1997.

Packard, V., *The Hidden Persuaders*, Harmondsworth, Penguin, 1960.

Parr, G., 'Smoking', *Sight and Sound* (December 1997), 30–3.

Pass, C. L., 'Coupon trading: an aspect of non-price competition in the UK cigarette industry', *Yorkshire Bulletin of Economic and Social Research*, 19:2 (1967), 124–35.

Payne, P. L., 'The emergence of the large-scale company in Great Britain, 1870–1914', *Economic History Review*, 20 (1967), 519–42.

Pearson, G., *Hooligan: A History of Respectable Fears*, Basingstoke, Macmillan, 1983.

Pick, D., *Faces of Degeneration: A European Disorder, c. 1848–c. 1918*, Cambridge, Cambridge University Press, 1989.

Pringle, P., *Dirty Business: Big Tobacco at the Bar of Justice*, London, Aurum, 1998.

Rabin, R. L. and S. D. Sugarman (eds), *Smoking Policy: Law, Politics and Culture*, Oxford, Oxford University Press, 1993.

Read, M. D., *The Politics of Tobacco: Policy Networks and the Cigarette Industry*, Aldershot, Avebury, 1996.

Richards, J., *The Age of the Dream Palace: Cinema and Society in Britain 1930–1939*, Routledge & Kegan Paul, 1984.

Richards, J. and D. Sheridan (eds), *Mass-Observation at the Movies*, London, Routledge, 1987.

Richards, T., *The Commodity Culture of Victorian England: Advertising and Spectacle, 1851–1914*, London, Verso, 1991.

Roberts, E., *A Woman's Place: An Oral History of Working-Class Women*, Oxford, Blackwell, 1984.

Roberts, R., *The Classic Slum: Salford Life in the First Quarter of the Century*, Manchester, Manchester University Press, 1971.

Schudson, M., *Advertising: The Uneasy Persuasion*, New York, Basic Books, 1985.

Seaton, A. V., 'Cope's and the promotion of tobacco in Victorian England', *Journal of Advertising History*, 9:2 (1986), 5–26.

Semmel, B., *Imperialism and Social Reform: English Social-Imperial Thought, 1895–1914*, London, Allen & Unwin, 1960.

Shreffler, P. A., *Sherlock Holmes by Gas Lamp: Highlights from the First Four Decades of 'The Baker Street Journal'*, New York, Fordham University Press, 1989.

Smith, G. D., S. A. Ströbele and M. Egger, 'Smoking and health promotion in Nazi Germany', *Journal of Epidemiology and Community Health*, 48 (1994), 220–3.

Smith, T., *Making the Modern: Industry, Art and Design in America*, Chicago, University of Chicago Press, 1993.

Sobel, R., *They Satisfy: The Cigarette in American Life*, New York, Anchor Books, 1978.

Springhall, J., *Coming of Age: Adolescence in Britain, 1860–1960*, Dublin, Gill & Macmillan, 1986.

Stead, P., *Film and the Working Class: The Feature Film in British and American Society*, London, Routledge, 1989.

Strasser, S., *Satisfaction Guaranteed: The Making of the American Mass Market*, New York, Pantheon, 1984.

Summerfield, P., *Women Workers in the Second World War*, London, Routledge, 1989.

Tame, C. R. and D. Botsford, *Not Just Tobacco: Health Scares, Medical Paternalism and Individual Liberty*, London, FOREST, 1996.

Taylor, A. J. P., *English History, 1914–1945*, Harmondsworth, Penguin, 1976.

Taylor, P., *Smoke Ring: The Politics of Tobacco*, London, Bodley Head, 1984.

Thompson, P., *The Edwardians: The Remaking of British Society*, London, Routledge, 1992.

Tollison, R. D. (ed.), *Smoking and Society: Towards a More Balanced Assessment*, Lexington, MA, Lexington Books, 1986.

Tollison, R. D. and R. E. Wagner, *Smoking and the State: Social Costs, Rent Seeking and Public Policy*, Lexington, MA, Lexington Books, 1988.

Trentmann, F., 'The transformation of fiscal reform: reciprocity, modernisation, and the fiscal debate within the business community in early twentieth-century Britain', *Historical Journal*, 39:4 (1996), 1005–48.

Trentmann, F., 'Wealth versus welfare: the British Left between Free Trade and national political economy before the First World War', *Historical Research*, 70:171 (1997), 70–98.

Troyer, R. and G. Markle, *Cigarettes: The Battle over Smoking*, New Brunswick, NJ, Rutgers University Press, 1983.

Turner, E. S., *The Shocking History of Advertising*, Harmondsworth, Penguin, [1952] 1965.

Turner, F. M., 'The Victorian conflict between science and religion: a professional dimension', *Isis*, 69 (1978), 356–76.

Umberger, E., *Tobacco and Its Use*, New York, Rochester, 1996.

Wald, N., *et al.*, *UK Smoking Statistics*, Oxford, Oxford University Press, 1971.

Waldron, I., 'Patterns and causes of gender differences in smoking', *Social Science and Medicine*, 32 (1991), 989–1005.

Walker, R. B., 'Medical aspects of tobacco smoking and the anti-tobacco movement in Britain in the nineteenth century', *Medical History*, 24 (1980), 391–402.

Walker, R. B., *Under Fire: A History of Smoking in Australia*, Melbourne, Melbourne University Press, 1984.

Walsh, U., 'Nicotine in Dickensland', *Dickensian*, 30 (1934), 217–21.

Walton, J. K., 'The world's first working-class seaside resort? Blackpool revisited, 1840–1974', *Lancashire and Cheshire Antiquarian Society*, 88 (1992), 1–30.

Walvin, J., *A Child's World: A Social History of English Childhood, 1800–1914*, Harmondsworth, Penguin, 1982.

Wardley, P., 'The anatomy of big business: aspects of corporate development in the twentieth century', *Business History*, 33 (1991), 268–96.

Waterson, M. J., *Advertising and Cigarette Consumption*, London, Advertising Association, 1982.

Welshman, J., 'Images of youth: the issue of juvenile smoking, 1880–1914', *Addiction*, 91:9 (1996), 1379–86.

White, L., *Merchants of Death: The American Tobacco Industry*, New York, William Morrow, 1988.

Wilkinson, P., 'English youth movements, 1908–1930', *Journal of Contemporary History*, 4 (1969), 3–23.

Wimbush, E. and M. Talbot (eds), *Relative Freedoms: Women and Leisure*, Milton Keynes, Open University Press, 1988.

Winstanley, M., *The Shopkeeper's World, 1830–1914*, Manchester, Manchester University Press, 1983.

Zelizer, V., *Pricing the Priceless Child: The Changing Social Value of Children*, New York, Basic Books, 1985.

Index